The Social Edge

Published by Thornwick 2018

Copyright Anthony Costello 2018

First published in Great Britain by Thornwick in 2018

Address details for Thornwick can be found at www.thornwickpress.com and contact at admin@thornwickpress.com

Thornwick Ltd Reg. No 11063757
A CIP catalogue record for this book
is available from the British Library

ISBN 978-1-912664-00-9

Typeset in Bembo by Palimpsest Book Production Ltd,
Falkirk, Stirlingshire

Printed and bound in Great Britain by Clays Ltd, Elcograf S.p.A.

Anthony Costello

The Social Edge

The Power of Sympathy Groups for our Health, Wealth and Sustainable Future

THORNWICK

Contents

Preface

This book provides evidence on how we might harness the power of sympathy groups, the smallest social gatherings beyond families, to create social trust and benefit at scale. As a doctor and medical scientist I tread with trepidation on the turf of sophisticated social scientists, network theorists and psychologists. But the book offers a new cocktail of four ingredients. First, a focus on a particular and ancient social structure, what Robin Dunbar calls the sympathy group, the gathering of around 15 or so people who share a common interest, and who meet to face a challenge through conversation and shared effort. Coming together in small groups can empower us in more ways than we realise. The book describes key features of sympathy groups at the social edge, along with their allied qualities of relatedness, self-organisation and co-production. To support this argument I examine the neglected role of social trust in history, and of sympathy groups in the sweep of human events.

Second I relate the story of our own 'trials of wicked women', social experiments to assess the role of women's groups in tackling maternal and child survival in south Asia and Africa. These large population studies, working with some of the most marginalised people in the world, taught us that women's sympathy groups coming together to solve their own health problems brought dramatic changes in survival of mothers and their newborn infants, even where access to health care was terrible. As I watched poor women bring creativity and humour to their own solutions,

I realised that modern society has lost its compass, the essence of what made humans so successful in our cultural evolution. What emerges from our studies, and the power of everyday sympathy in business, organisations and citizenship, is that human progress is fundamentally about social trust.

Third, I defend, without shame, the value of rigorous and randomised social experiments. Science can inform governments and policymakers about the power (or impotence) of various sympathy groups for health, wealth, governance and the environment. Just as medicine through repeated experiment overthrew old, ineffective practices and identified treatments that work, so decision makers must examine the evidence for new policies to tackle the wicked problems of our age. For the uninitiated, the landmark studies of great pioneers illustrate the principles of scientific experiments and evidence collected from populations. The beauty and pitfalls of randomised trial designs are weighed up. Stories help us to propose hypotheses, experiments to dispose of or defend them. Both are essential. But this process is not the sole prerogative of medicine and science. Economists and social scientists have dipped their toes in the waters of experimental evaluation but have a long way to go. It's a journey they should make. So I explore experiments in areas beyond health and survival. Using accepted criteria for when to do a large scale social experiment, I propose 22 studies which could use sympathy groups at the social edge to tackle some of the most pressing challenges of our time – for survival, wellbeing, prosperity, climate change and good government. These range from initiatives to tackle loneliness in old age, prisoner recidivism, long term medical conditions, stress in motherhood, hospital service delivery, business performance, whether management consultancy works, strategies to tackle climate resilience, and corruption, and how to release, or at least lubricate, government gridlock.

Finally, I've illustrated how people can feel empowered in their everyday lives and benefit from a return to mutual help. I've also summarised key lessons for policymakers, and for decision makers in every organisation. What relevance do sympathy groups have to everyday life? How can these ancestral structures link with modern organisations and communications? How can small group power and participation be truly effective rather than tokenistic? And how can we create the conditions for citizens' voices and a truly relational state at scale. Individualism and technology alone cannot solve our global problems. We can use the creativity of sympathy groups to find non-linear solutions to non-linear and complex problems. Our groups can go viral if we create the conditions to nurture them, because they touch a deep impulse in the human psyche.

Anthony Costello, September 2018

Part 1

Sympathy Groups

An Ecology for Social Action

CHRONICLES OF DEATHS UNSEEN

In the early noughties I sat in a tropical garden analysing verbal autopsies collected from the families of mothers who had died in childbirth. The women had delivered in two districts, West Singhbhum and Saraikela, of Jharkhand, one of the poorest states in India. My hosts were Prasanta Tripathy and Nirmala Nair, who had set up a small charity called Ekjut. It meant 'coming together'. Their office was in their home town of Chakradharpur. Trained in medicine, Prasanta has spent four decades in community health work and we'd met when Prasanta took his Masters degree in London. His wife Nirmala is herself a brilliant and popular women's health specialist. Together we had planned a women's group study focused on poor tribal communities, to replicate some exciting findings from Nepal about cutting death rates of mothers and infants. Gratefully, we received modest funds from the UK Health Foundation.

Prasanta and Nirmala had sculpted a glorious garden on their tiny half-acre plot to create a sense of the wealth of forests and native plants. They had planted a specimen of every local tree. Labelled were teak, mahogany, coconut, custard apple, varieties of mango, *neem*, avocado, lychee, guava, *sal, gulmohar,* bamboo, lemon, pomegranate, papaya, *sheesham, chikoo* (fruit with an odd potato look), *karanj,* and flame of the forest. An ancient *arjun* tree vibrated from a large nest of mynah birds. The drumstick leaves

7

provided 'poor man's' vitamin C. Below grew curry leaves, mint, chilli, zucchini beans (*kundru*), okra (*bhindi*) and maize. In winter there was coriander and tomato, onion and several varieties of spinach (*sag*). The trees were a haven for parrots, mynahs, drongos, egrets, ibis, cuckoos, owls, tweeters, sunbirds, pheasants, and even vultures. Prasanta told me the vultures were rare now, wiped out by agricultural drugs found in carrion meat.

Their Garden of Eden attracted an arkload of wildlife. Frogs, lizards, snakes, scorpions, mice, mongooses, jackals and every variety of insect. Occasionally the village saw wild elephants and ground bears. Two months earlier, elephants had trampled to death the uncle of their *adivasi* (tribal) cook, Pratima. In some villages they burnt cakes of chilli to act as elephant repellents.

Nirmala handed me copies of the interviews with families after a mother had died. The fieldworkers wrote the stories longhand in Sanskrit, which Nirmala translated into English. They described the heart-breaking dilemmas of poor women in their final hours. One could only imagine their fear during the complications in childbirth – and the impotence of their sisters, husbands and mothers-in-law; the tears of their older children or siblings. Such unnecessary suffering was squalid and banal. Chunni, for example, lived in the village of Bandunasa in West Singhbhum district. Her husband, Laalamani and his sister Budhni, lived with Chunni in a forest shack, without cultivable land of their own. They made baskets and plates from bamboo and leaves. At 32, Chunni had had three daughters. The youngest had died at two years from malaria. Now she was pregnant for a fourth time but didn't visit the health centre because she had had no problems. She had a month's supply of iron tablets from a government camp, and three shots of tetanus toxoid from a village quack. She ate less during pregnancy – a smaller baby would be easier – but still drank *handia*, the local beer, and worked as hard as ever.

Two weeks before her due date she noticed a foul-smelling discharge. She could not get to a clinic because the monsoon-flooded roads were bad, she was too gravid to walk, and the family had no money or transport. She felt weak, dizzy and complained of night blindness. It's a common symptom of vitamin A deficiency from a diet lacking in meat and green leafy vegetables. During the last few days before delivery her fetal movements slowed.

Her sister-in-law, Budhni, assisted Chunni's delivery at home in the rear of their bamboo and wattle hut. Her husband wore his white bandana scarf, cowrie necklace and *lungi*, and boiled tea. He washed the pots outside, keeping an eye on the older children. The labour pains started around 6pm. The first couple of hours went as expected, but soon her sister-in-law had an uneasy feeling. Budhni's friend went to find the *dai* (traditional birth attendant) who lived a mile across the fields but she was away at a relative's wedding. Around midnight the pain intensified. Despite her strong contractions the baby seemed to make little progress. After an exhausting night, a flaccid baby boy was stillborn at dawn. No one knew how to revive him. He lay pale and lifeless on an old white cotton sari with a blood red trim. After the placenta came out, Budhni cut the cord with a local knife. But Chunni continued to bleed, clots and puddles forming on the ochre mud floor. To control the bleeding, Budhni applied hot fomentation to the abdomen. She made a poultice of hibiscus leaves, the crushed stem bark of cassia, egg albumen, calcium, turmeric and pulse seeds. The haemorrhage slowed then stopped.

As the day brightened Chunni could barely move and she refused to eat. She was dizzy and breathless. In the afternoon, she asked for vegetables. Budhni refused because vegetables after childbirth are inauspicious. The next day Chunni's feet and face started to swell, and she stayed on her charpoy. Laalamani wondered about taking her to a health centre but she was weak and bedridden. The rain was heavy, so he decided to wait. The tribal traditional healer came with his treatments of leaves, stem bark, and roots in decoctions, powders and pastes – *tulsi, nalla, vepa,* and *tangedu.* Chunni struggled on for nine days, rarely rising from her bed. On the tenth day, around 6am, Chunni became breathless and died a few minutes later.

A fortnight later, in the interview with Sonu, an Ekjut worker, Laalamani said: "If we'd had money, we could have gone to see a doctor. If she ate more after delivery and hadn't bled so much, she could have survived."

He admitted she had drunk lots of *handia* during pregnancy. Was this why she was frail and weak, he asked?

The diagnosis was that Chunni died from severe anaemia and post-partum haemorrhage. No blood tests, of course, but weakness and breathlessness are symptoms of anaemia. Her poor diet and slow bleeding after birth would have exacerbated the thinning of her blood. The final straw would have been heart failure, exacerbated by infection. A medical diagnosis from this oral autopsy suggests some medical solutions. If Chunni had had antenatal care she could have received nutrition advice and iron and vitamin supplements. If she had had a midwife in attendance the management of labour would have progressed faster. And the midwife might have resuscitated the baby. If she had got to a hospital a haemo-globin test would have shown anaemia. A blood transfusion from a relative was possible. The answers must come from a structured health system that reaches out to poor women like Chunni. All true.

But what if we make a social edge diagnosis? Why was Chunni so isolated and alone? Would involvement in a group of mothers have helped her to seek care during pregnancy? Would a group loan have provided money to travel to hospital and pay for the tests? Would information from other women have lifted taboos about vegetables after birth? Would a neighbour have assisted Budhni during the labour and reduced Chunni's anxiety and stress, to bring smoother contractions? A group of women who visited her after birth would have brought her food and comfort and advice. Their love and solidarity might have relieved the growing sense of despair in Chunni's heart when she had lost a second child. Sharing of food and cash would have brought some respite to Chunni and Laalamani's poverty. She might have reached a health facility. As she lay on her charpoy, their support might have stopped her worrying about basket production to support the family food supply.

Or were there other issues? Why was she drinking during the preg-nancy? Had she reached the end of her tether? Were she and Laalamani happy? Were there infidelities? Did she want the baby? Her symptoms after birth were not always physical. Might the stillbirth have reawakened the grief and despair of her youngest child's death? Did she fall into a postnatal depression, which reached its zenith after the end of the first week? On that fateful morning, when depressive symptoms are most severe, did Chunni take her own life? Did she swallow fertiliser poison or take an overdose of a poisonous plant? We don't know. But with more friendships beyond her family, more comfort and love, would she have died?

The medical verbal autopsy diagnosis can be nothing more than a guess. A white coat is a straitjacket to keep us behind the walls of physiology, not straying into the social space. Of course Chunni needed access to a midwife, referral to a hospital, and treatment for her blood loss. But the margin at the social edge of these *adivasi* women is narrow and precipitous. It doesn't take much to tip over into the ravine. Building even a small social fence at the edge of the cliff might do as much as placing an ambulance at the bottom.

We can test this idea further from the case of Shivangi Majhi from the village of Nilaigoat. Shivangi was 30 years old, the first wife of Lakhan Majhi, from the Santhal tribe. Was Lakhan related to Baba Tilka Majhi, an *adivasi* hero, who held off the British for weeks during a tribal rebellion in 1784? A great famine had stirred the people to take up arms. When Baba was finally arrested in Bhagalpur, East India Company officers tied him to a horse and dragged him over stones to the Collector's house. The British soldiers hung his bruised and battered body from a banyan tree. Today, at the same spot, a statue stands in his memory.

Lakhan Majhi was less heroic. After eight years of marriage Shivangi had not conceived. So he took a second wife, who bore him four girls in quick succession. Exhausted by the demands of his second family he went back to Shivangi, who was now living with her parents. She had never gone to school and helped her parents with the work on the land, the cooking and the forest gathering. They had one bicycle and owned not much more than an acre of land. Shivangi was thrilled to become pregnant for the first time, which removed the stigma and shame of infertility. She had gone for a check-up during her sixth and eighth months of pregnancy, examined by an auxiliary nurse midwife. She received two tetanus injections and took her newspaper-wrapped iron tablets for two months. They tasted horrible and gave her indigestion. She worked as hard as ever, but took less food and *handia* than before she fell pregnant. Twice she had had fever for a few days, but didn't think it necessary to seek care.

In mid-July, after the rains came, she noticed a heavy watery discharge trickling down her thigh. It lasted for two days. Then at two in the morning, when she started having labour pains, they sent for the *dai*. She didn't arrive until 8am. Because Shivangi's pains were irregular, she told them to call the village healer. He was away in the forest but he came in the evening to give two 'hot' injections to speed up contractions. As he left he asked to hear of progress in the morning. The pain increased through the night, and Shivangi became distressed and confused. At dawn, she began to shake uncontrollably and lost consciousness. Lakhan and Shivangi's mother had no idea what to do. A few minutes later she died.

The autopsy diagnosis wasn't difficult: toxaemia of pregnancy, or eclampsia, a precipitous rise in blood pressure, which caused the convulsion. With drugs to lower blood pressure or an immediate caesarean section she would have survived. The exact mechanism is not understood. At Harvard University there is an empty plinth waiting for a statue of the first person to discover the cause of eclampsia.

Care is straightforward: a midwife to monitor blood pressure, magnesium sulphate, oxytocics, and a caesarean section. The treatments are not complex, but they didn't reach Shivangi. The state maternity cash transfer might have helped the family's access to care but it didn't come in time. The scheme had yet to reach the forests of Jharkhand.

The social diagnosis though creates a new and complementary set of solutions. Lakhan neglected Shivangi in pregnancy, preferring his younger second bride. Living with only her parents and husband did not help Shivangi when complications arose. With friends she could have found a local health worker to give advice or make a home visit. A sisterhood network might have shared information about an alternative *dai* or warned her about using a village healer. One of them might have known a nearby midwife, or protected her from the quack's 'hot' injections. With birth support, the family might have refused and sought alternative care. The medical and the social bring complementary benefits.

But a hospital won't always fix the problem. The case of Harina Santhal illustrates this. She lived in a remote village, Karosai, 15 miles from a primary health centre. Harina was the second wife of Nandiya Santhal. His first wife had died along with her baby after a caesarean section. Nandiya returned to live with his mother and four brothers. Although they had more than four bighas of land (about six acres) much was barren. Wild elephants from the forest were a constant threat. Later, when Nirmala interviewed Nandiya, he had bruises on his face from scaring elephants away from their crops.

They had married when Harina was 18 and she fell pregnant within six months. She was careful. She took her haematinics and tetanus injections and stopped drinking *handia*, but ate less than before she was pregnant. Her workload was heavy. At six months of the pregnancy she had fever for one day but soon felt better. After three days her fever returned and she vomited and passed loose stools. In the evening she had pain in her belly, and threw a series of convulsions and lost consciousness. Her family were fraught. Nandiya went to find some men to help carry her to the road-head. He hoped he could find a taxi to go to the private clinic 10 kilometres away. When he returned with a posse of men, Harina had delivered a stillborn girl, the placenta and a small pool of blood. They placed her on a bamboo stretcher, carried her to the road-head and moved her to the private doctor's clinic in a local shopkeeper's pick-up. They arrived close to midnight but the doctor wasn't there. The attendant told them Harina was serious and must go to the large Mercy hospital, another 50 kilometres away. After Nandiya and his mother promised to pay 800 rupees, the shopkeeper agreed to take them.

Harina lay in the pick-up on some blankets, purring but unresponsive. At the Mercy, a sleepy junior doctor examined her, and, without any blood tests, diagnosed brain malaria. She needed a blood transfusion so he referred her to the Tata Main Hospital, another 20 kilometres away. Nandiya and his mother whispered. They couldn't afford the costs at Tata Main. The doctor had given them an antimalarial injection so they decided to take her home. A taxi driver offered them a reduced rate because he was heading back close to Karosai. Harina lay on the back seat, breathing in gulps. As they approached the road-head she let out a long sigh. Soon they realised she was dead.

The diagnosis from the verbal autopsy was evident, severe cerebral malaria in pregnancy. Nandiya, who had lost his first wife, had done all he could. The delays were not his fault. The medics failed to treat her infection, although this was an endemic zone. If they had set up a quinine infusion and put her under observation on a ward she might have survived. On such slender margins are life-and-death decisions made.

In south Asia, illness and hunger are a daily reality. The silent emergency of maternal and child deaths goes unnoticed. A medical analysis points to infection, poor nutrition and lack of medical care as primary causes. An analysis at the social edge unearths different ones, the causes of the causes.

The names of patients and relatives have been changed.

THE LAYER OF FIFTEEN

How can we create an ecology for social trust which harnesses the power of self-organising groups? In our everyday business we choose whether to compete or to co-operate, to seek for ourselves or to share, to do things alone or as part of a group. Living in groups is our human condition. We were born to share and struggle, to care for others, be sensitive to their feelings, divvy up food, and work together on tasks. A balance between the individual and the group drove our evolution as the most successful species on earth. Survival of the fittest individual, and sibling rivalry, drives human success in many ways. But other traits determine success within and between groups: the size and cohesion of the group, the division of labour within it, the ability to communicate and to read the intention of others. Group diversity and our willingness to sacrifice personal for collective benefit create trust.

In our complex modern world we dream of a magical trinity of prosperity, health and a sustainable lifestyle. In reality, poverty and sickness in the bottom third of the global population run side by side with over-consumption by the rest. Forces of power, history and economics have created a chimera of wealth and deprivation. Whether we're rich or poor, we are hectored to change the way we live our lives. The rich should consume less, exercise more, go green. The poor should stay clean and healthy, access credit, work harder, and extract more from their meagre land holding. The challenge to find a balance is formidable. And there are forces beyond our personal control. Population growth, migration and climate change are a toxic mix. As a species will we make it? Some authors see things getting steadily better and promote 'rational optimism'.[1] Others see only rapacious hubris, 'a global catastrophe', a sixth great extinction.[2]

Top-down, intrusive approaches to 'behaviour change' don't work well either. Our methods are technological and professional, even coercive. People who know best send messages. My own medical profession over-simplifies or ignores behaviour change for better health. We're obsessed by disease rather than health. We forget Sidney Webb's question about whether we should be "pulling people out of swamps, or doing swamp drainage?" When we do actually focus on prevention we learn that people don't like to be told what to do. Those of us who are rich enjoy our creature comforts. We don't want to stop consuming and travelling. In reality, austerity isn't much fun. And the poor are already told what to do: villagers by chiefs, workers by bosses, newly-wed wives by husbands, pregnant women by mothers-in-law. Being told what to do by well-meaning outsiders is rarely effective. How can we create conversations between people to build trust and achieve lasting change at scale. Can we be more scientific at exploring the nature of our social edge?

In biology and conservation, the edge is where the action is. Edges are boundaries between ecosystems: at the coastline between land and sea, at the riverbank, the hedgerow. And also microscopically at the epithelium, cell wall, and between the nucleus and cytoplasm. The most dynamic interactions, which attract a rich diversity of species or metabolites or ideas for change, are at the edge. Create an edge and the action will follow. Our social edge is where groups form, from families to local sympathy groups. The ecological principle is habitat protection. Create an environment for sympathy groups and we will generate ideas and action, for good or bad depending upon the social motives. If we help these groups flourish, other good things will happen, things that we don't expect. Groups are unpredictable, non-linear.

Charles Darwin taught us that we come from simpler animals. His tree of life starts with the simplest organisms and evolves to the most complex. Scientists know that the secrets of the complex lie in the simple. The biggest breakthroughs in biology have emerged from studies of bugs and yeasts and fruit flies. In human social behaviour we need to do the same, to understand better the simplest systems of human interaction. In fact, Darwin did recognise the value of mutual aid, as well as competition, for survival. In his 1871 work, The Descent of Man, he wrote: "With respect to the impulse which leads certain animals to associate together, and to aid each other in many ways, we may infer that in most cases they are impelled by the same sense of satisfaction or pleasure which they experience in performing other instinctive actions."

From an evolutionary perspective, human circles of acquaintance are not random. Robin Dunbar and his team of cultural anthropologists at Oxford University describe groups in a series of hierarchical layers.[3] Each layer is three times larger than the layer inside it. The survival clique, our immediate family group, of five or so people, provides us with our most intense emotional support. The next layer of around 15 persons represents the 'sympathy group', the most elemental of our ancestral groups. In monkeys and apes this is the grooming clique, which helps to defuse the stress of living in much larger groups. In human evolution, this was the group of people most likely to help you in a crisis, "the set of individuals who will come to your help when you need it".[4] The third layer of around 50 people represents good friends and neighbours. In Paleolithic times, 50 people provided enough female gatherers and male hunters to sustain a food supply. An overnight band of families came together for protection from predators.

The 150 layer, the so-called critical Dunbar number, represents the limits of our social brain. Our large brains evolved, he argues, to manage increasing social complexity. From archaeological evidence, and cultural clues like funerary relics and the debris of rituals and hunting, human social groups emerged more than 100,000 years ago. A hundred and fifty was the critical number of people with whom we could manage relationships and friendship. The social brain hypothesis proposes that our expanding brain size evolved to cope with variety in social groups. The 150 layer offers further evolutionary advantages: defence of territory and protection against predators. With 150 we can guard reproductive mates and exchange information about critical resources such as food, water and prey. Most hunter-gatherer societies, past and present, cluster close to this number.

Figure 1   Dunbar Human Groups

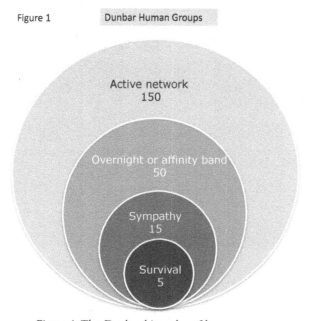

Figure 1. The Dunbar hierarchy of human groups

In modern times, 150 emerged as the average size of eighteenth century English villages and of US rural communities. A hundred and fifty is an approximate average for religious congregations, for factory units, and for our Christmas card list. The Dunbar number also describes the size of functional groups within business, the armed forces and boarding schools. The military understand clearly the value of social divisions and hierarchies but also creative small group relationships within a command and control structure. Military hierarchy follows a tripling pattern. A company, troop or squadron of soldiers of 150-200 subdivides into a platoon or troop of 40-50 men or women, with the smallest military unit, a section, patrol or squad, of around 10-15 members.

Figure 2 Soccer team of British soldiers with gas masks, World War 1

Figure 3. British platoon soldiers at a funeral in France
during World War 1

Groups need to generate loyalty and trust. Throughout history, social rituals and techniques in depersonalisation ensure cohesion and subordination to the group. New recruits must demonstrate their loyalty and courage, face daunting initiation, or undergo what the Americans call 'hazing', the Russians 'dedovshchina', Australians 'bastardisation', and Indian sub-continental schools and colleges, 'ragging'. Severe ordeals of endurance include overnight long distance runs, public humiliation, servitude, grovelling before senior members, sleep deprivation, pledging to complete formidable physical tasks, painting, tattooing or shaving. Occasionally extremes of behaviour lead to fatalities. Where hazing was common in US units in Vietnam and among Russian troops in Chechnya, fragging rates, the killing of commanding officers by their juniors, also increased. So effects can be negative as well as positive.

Figure 4. A fraternity initiation from the yearbook of
Dartmouth College, c. 1896

More recently, Dunbar has proposed two further layers. The 500 layer is the minimum number for an isolated community to protect against in-breeding, and the number of acquaintances we can manage. The torture of email and social media overload, which stretches the emotional limits of modern metropolitan humans, suggests our stressless IT layers might be smaller. Nonetheless acquaintanceship represents a critical source of valuable connections for employment. These are the 'weak ties' described in one of the most cited social science papers ever published. In 1973, sociologist Mark Granovetter showed that in a modern, urban society like New York, where social groups overlap and allow people to have multiple identities and roles, the ability to get a job correlated with the number of 'weak ties' or casual acquaintances we have.[5] In cities, the strong ties of the extended family group can be a hindrance. In a rural, subsistence economy the extended family work together. Finally, Dunbar's 1500 layer is the number of people whose faces we can put names to within our ethnolinguistic tribe or neighbourhood. The 1500 layer was critical in social evolution for trading goods and information exchange. It allowed us to find a mate from outside genetically linked groups. And to manage broader defence when several groups were under attack.

This book focuses on small sympathy groups, that layer of 15 or so people that meet at our social-family edge. These confidants come together to analyse and act on local problems and threats. As neighbours, friends and colleagues, group members are those we are most likely to trust or learn to trust. They can ensure our survival. Many studies have shown the power of social relationships in protecting us against premature death. Psychologist Julianne Holt-Lunstad and colleagues analysed 148 studies where measures of social relationships were made and showed that their absence was as strong a predictor of death as smoking or alcohol intake, and a much better predictor than obesity or lack of exercise.[6] In every society sympathy groups nurture our children and assist parents to protect us in infancy. Sympathy groups can start political movements, assist entrepreneurs, or create plays and films. They join forces as choirs or sports teams, improve our farms, and refine our management of organisations. In everyday life they are the bedrock of consultation, consent and conflict resolution. And our genes and brain chemistry drive their co-operative power.

Sympathy groups are not necessarily an intrinsic force for good. One of the founders of social science, Ibn Khaldun, born in Tunisia in 1332, realised the power of small groups when he wrote the Muqaddimah. He lived during a golden age of Islamic history. In a six-volume work on knowledge, politics, economics and urban life, he analysed cycles of conflict between desert nomads and city states. He described the astonishing power of small kinship and sympathy groups, which used religious fervour to win power over decadent townspeople. Coalescing groups of conquerors would sow the seeds of their own destruction through wealth, corruption and political conflict. The cycle would start again when new groups of desert nomads attacked. The nomads stuck together through *asibayah* (solidarity) whereas townies simply looked after themselves. Contemporary observers of the rapid progress of Islamic State aggressors seeking a caliphate in Syria and Iraq might see this as a recurring theme. But the important point was that Khaldun recognised the power of small, cohesive sympathy groups, whether for good or bad. They could brutally attack as well as heroically defend.

In modern times a sympathy group created the internet, another the smart-phone and tablet. One sympathy group of Saudi terrorists blew up the Twin Towers of the World Trade Center. Another group of US Marines captured and killed Osama bin Laden. A constellation of these groups led to the abolition of slavery and to the destruction of apartheid. Sympathy groups helped create Impressionism, pop art and post-modernism, others the music of jazz, soul and rap. Many great films enjoyed sympathy groups of assistance facilitated by great directors.

The oldest form of an expressive sympathy group is in theatre. At least five thousand years old, theatre grew out of the rituals and ceremonies of social life as an interpretation of power, pleasure or duty. Theatre is, as director Peter Brook describes it, 'a small world' created in an empty space[7]. For people living in open-ended urban or imagined communities, theatre reminds us of our social edge. "The theatre community stays the same: the cast of a play is still the size that it has always been," writes Brook. In Renaissance England, companies of actors, like William Shakespeare's the King's Men at the Globe Theatre and the Admiral's Men at the Fortune Theatre, comprised 10-12 'shareholders'. They managed and performed the plays with the help of hired hands who made scenery and play minor parts. In the 16th and 17th centuries, small companies like these spread across the whole of Europe. Theatrical companies are a classic sympathy group: a facilitator (director), a shared purpose, creative tension and a dramatic gift to the community.

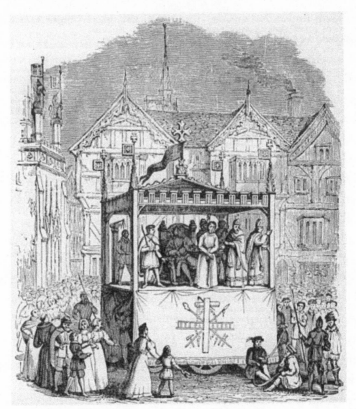

Figure 5. An early Chester Mystery Play

Figure 6. Peter Brook directing the Tightrope with Yoshi Oida (gesturing), 2012

Figure 7. Barnum theatre troupe, Menier Chocolate Factory,
London 2018. Photo: the author

A similar edginess between individual greed and small group solidarity underlies modern economics. Okun's Law, proposed by the American economist, Arthur M Okun, describes the traction between market forces and market containment. "Institutions in a capitalist democracy," he wrote in his social policy opus Equality and Efficiency, "prod us to get ahead of our neighbours economically after telling us to stay in line socially. This double standard lauds an egalitarian political system while generating gaping disparities in economic well-being."[8] Individual competition, he believed, marginalises the weakest or least powerful.

Someone who saw particular value in small sympathy groups to restore the confidence of marginalised people was Frantz Fanon, the Martinique-Algerian psychiatrist and political scientist.[9] He observed the effects of colonialism every day in his clinic. Neuroses in 1950s Algeria were the product, he observed, of the humiliation, low self-esteem and everyday racism that blighted the lives of the colonially oppressed. He didn't see national liberation as the simple answer. Post-colonial nations would quickly replace colonial oppressors with other political and economic elites unless attention was paid to 'individual liberation', which would allow people to rediscover their confidence, self-esteem and brio. "Superiority? Inferiority? Why not simply try to touch the other, feel the other, discover each other?" In the right circumstances, sympathy groups provide a nurturing space for oppressed people to learn to take decisions, to challenge authority and to enjoy the strength and confidence that comes from solidarity.

More broadly, we all crave another side to our medical care – a relationship, intimate conversation, empathy and kindness. Group solidarity can play a pivotal role in ensuring that kindness remains a key part of caring. Sadly, medicine remains inimical to ideas that health care is more than skilled workers, drugs, vaccines and techniques for passive and grateful patients. For example, a 2017 World Health Organisation conference in Geneva on neglected tropical diseases brought pharmaceutical companies and governments to discuss efforts to tackle leishmaniasis, guinea worm, dengue fever, trypanosomiasis and zika virus. All remain widely prevalent in neglected populations. A Lancet blog described key elements for success: research and innovation, capacity building, surveillance and evaluation, integration and logistical support for drug delivery.[10] All well and good, but no mention of communities. No priority given to community groups sharing information or tackling the underlying causes of their neglect. Nothing on claiming rights to receive appropriate care.

By the same token, the US political scientist Murray Bookchin saw our ecological crisis as rooted in the loss of power in local communities.[11] "Hierarchy at a local level inspired a contempt for our natural environment. This repression then extends outward to external nature as a mere object of rule and later of exploitation." Bookchin renounced Marxism to seek a social ecology to address our environmental crisis. "The overriding problem is to change the structure of society so that people gain power. The best arena to do that is the municipality – the city, town, and village – where we have an opportunity to create a face-to-face democracy."

Strangely, after his death, Bookchin's rather neglected ideas inspired, quite recently, an astonishing political movement in northern Syria, led by Abdullah Ocalan, a Kurdish leader in the autonomous state of Rojava, home to 4.6 million Kurds. Ocalan had also renounced Marxism. Just a few kilometres from the emergent state of Isis he established a radical democracy where women were leaders, the law protected the environment, and local groups came together to decide their defensive and governance strategies. In Qamishli, the capital, the Mesopotamian Social Sciences Academy runs courses for young men and women about how to build a secular non-hierarchical society, and how to defend their land against the terror of Isis and their Wahhabist-inspired medieval theocracy. A secular utopia to match the ideology of the Islamist jihadists, Rojava is an oasis of feminist equality. It lives within a desert region in flames under the bombs of big powers and the suicide vests of insurgents.

The argument of this book is that sympathy groups tackling their own health, organisation and environmental challenges is not an optional, 'nice' extra. It is central, profoundly important, and ignored. Broader issues of rights and democracy are, of course, central to a tolerant, progressive state. But the philosopher Onora O'Neill, in her analysis of the Northern Ireland peace process, hit the nail on the head. "Human rights and democracy are not the basis of trust: on the contrary, trust is the basis for human rights and democracy."[12]

And groups are not collections of individuals. When we use the word sympathy to describe small group solidarity we don't mean groups that promote 'self-help' for individual members. Biologists wouldn't label mitochondria in cells as a self-help energy source or the heart as a self-help organ. They are part of a larger whole. Self-help as a label makes sympathy groups seem like an optional extra. But like mitochondria to cells, and hearts to vertebrates, sympathy groups are essential to human society, a driving force behind social energy. If we accept human altruism we might call them 'mutual-help groups'. Less crucial for immediate survival than the clique of kinship in your family, they are more important in our everyday politics of ward or district.

And they're ubiquitous. In isolated hamlets, small towns, and metropolitan Manhattan, Mayfair or Mumbai. Ancestral sympathy groups are like a visual illusion which, stared at long enough, disappears from view. They occupy a blind spot for many contemporary historians and social scientists. Anthropologist Margaret Mead's observation was prescient. "Never doubt that a small group of thoughtful, committed people can change the world. Indeed it is the only thing that ever has." We can do far more to analyse and experiment with sympathy groups to build a better world. Can we experiment to create healthy, wealthy, more equal and sustainable communities?

Yet in all communities we have the essentials – beneficiaries, enablers, neighbours, focus, iteration, trust and strategies – which create the acronymic qualities, BENEFITS, of sympathy groups. Every reader will have their own case histories to illustrate their power. Examples abound in our workplace and social networks. As a junior paediatrician, trained in London to treat medical problems in individual children in hospital, I rarely considered a social and group approach to health. I worried about diagnoses and drugs and drips. I knew, of course, about the different backgrounds of my clients: single, white, teenaged mothers who lived chaotic lives on the Grahame Park estate in Edgware; the purdahed lives of adolescent, illiterate Sylheti mothers in King's Cross, imported as wives by older Bengali waiters from the hills of eastern Bangladesh. Nonetheless my world was curative not preventive, reactive not proactive. In medicine and science we find that case histories and chance observations may change perspective, and create the agenda for further experiments. Stories illustrate, embroider and create hypotheses. I had no concept of sympathy groups or community participation in creating health but my education was about to change. It began in the 1980s, on a plateau town in the middle hills of Nepal, 20 hours' walk from a road, above the deepest gorge on earth between Dhaulagiri and Annapurna.

A LINE OF TIGERS

When, in 1984, we left our damp basement studio in London's Notting Hill to work in rural west Nepal, I knew we would travel through time. I had just finished two years of hothouse research in newborn intensive care. Before leaving, I imagined our new small town of Baglung, two days' walk from a road, as a trip to the Wessex of Thomas Hardy. "Far away, from the files of formal houses, by the bough the firstling browses, lives a Sweet: no merchants meet, no man barters, no man sells, where she dwells." We didn't imagine we would travel back in time quite so far. Nor learn the value of collective trust in our tiny hill town.

After we arrived in Kathmandu and learnt rudimentary Nepali for a month, we made our long march for two days from Pokhara to Baglung. We trudged through the monsoon mud and waded the rivers of the middle hills. In Baglung district we found the true nature of rural life and Nepalese society. Most homesteads, outside the redbrick small town of 7000 people, were like mediaeval English peasant cruck houses, a wooden frame on to which women plastered wattle and daub. The English would have used oak and a mixture of clay, straw and manure. Nepalis used bamboo and the ubiquitous, warm, red ferrous-rich mud of a younger geology. In subsistence hamlets near fragile terraces sculpted for rice and maize we met simply dressed families. They hunted, gathered in forests and used common land to augment their staple crops with beans or soy.

Rural Nepal, in the words of King Prithvi Narayan Shah, was "a garden of many flowers". He united the modern state from multiple hill Rajas in the eighteenth century. Tibeto-Burman ethnic groups – Gurungs, Magars, Newars, Tamangs, Rais, Limbus – lived alongside the Indo-Aryan tribes, arrivistes from India, drawn from a Hindu caste structure classified by ritual pollution and segmented by their labour. Living side by side, in apparent harmony, the groups hardly ever inter-married. Within their clans, they protected themselves from the risk of incest by arranged marriages. Astrologically approved families were genetically separated by at least five generations.

We were welcomed into a strange, warm and open world, where personal space deferred to the group. All rural Nepalis, regardless of ethnicity or caste, offered open house not only to wandering monks and *sadhus* but also to casual travellers like us. If you arrived at a small hamlet in the evening and needed food and a bed, they provided. It was Nepali tradition, without charge, even if donations were readily accepted. Villagers smiled and shared. They sought shamanic health care. They sang in harmony as they winnowed and planted. Their weddings, carefully preserving caste purity, were public, noisy and inclusive (though they involved barely adult brides). When we received old newspapers and books in the postbag each week from Kathmandu, a world and a half away, we read about an absolute monarch. He ruled a whimsical and rickety government structure more concerned with obeisance than law. We'd already learned in Kathmandu about the networks of charming and elegant spies from the King's court. And that Nepal was a land of few taxes, of royalist newspapers and no television.

Quickly I reset our time machine from William Cobbett to the Middle Ages. The Cambridge social anthropologist and historian, Alan Macfarlane, who completed two PhDs, one on English medieval witchcraft, the other on the Gurungs of western Nepal, placed rural Nepal a millennium earlier than Hardy's Wessex. "Two things especially struck me when comparing it [a Gurung village] to England in the past. The first was the very great difference in per capita wealth in the two societies . . . When I compared the technology, the inventories of possessions and the budgets of the contemporary Asian society with those for English sixteenth century villagers, I found that there was already an enormous gap. The English were, on the whole, an immeasurably wealthier people, with a far higher investment in tools and other productive forces. To think of India or China in the early twentieth century as directly comparable to England just before the Industrial Revolution appeared to be a serious mistake."[13]

Certainly Baglung villagers were poor, and the tensions and 'hidden violence' of family life were not so obscure. Poverty was absolute as well as relative. Daily we witnessed discrimination against women and the crudest exploitation of young boys and girls working in kitchens. We watched low caste families breaking stones. Occasional tribal or inter-caste tension flared up. We witnessed government officers being '*gheraoed*', surrounded by a pressure sympathy group of angry litigants. Most families strictly separated gender roles. They maintained the discipline of respect for someone your 'senior', or absorbed new daughters-in-law into servitude, isolation and fear. They would gossip about domestic fights, drunkenness and affairs. At parties we squatted in circles, eating popcorn and nuts, drinking *raksi* (rice wine) and *chhaang* (millet beer). We whispered tittle-tattle or rumours, until the *daal bhaat* was ready to be served.

As a young wife, a woman became isolated, a servant to her husband and her mother-in-law (*sasu*). Once she produced children, especially sons, she gained a higher status and voice. Women had to conform to the household hierarchy but most Nepali women did accrue hidden power. The life course of many women was a roller coaster: from young princess to teenage domestic servant; from married dowry slave to fecund mother, to queen regent. The assumption that all women in Nepal suffered disempowerment and oppression needed qualification. The World Health Organisation suggests "girls and women suffer systematic discrimination in access to power, prestige and resources". All did suffer, but not to the same extent over time. At the start and end of the life course women had relative dominion over households. These periods coincided with times when they had stronger peer group contact.

A villager's work was tough and relentless, within a sine curve of seasonal privations. Rural Nepal gave us an insight into how humans evolved to co-operate. For the poorer clans, the distinction between agriculture and hunter-gathering was blurred. The Majhi (fishermen) and the Chepang (forest dwellers) lived almost solely from hunting, and the occasional trade of their kill. Others, like low-caste *dalits* and the poorest Magar families, would hunt and fish and practise broadcast sowing and rudimentary agriculture on common land to gather green vegetables and soyabean. Most other families survived on subsistence agriculture, owning or working one to two acres of rice terrace and maize field, hand tilled and sculpted, fertilised by the dung of cows and water buffalo.

Women faced a daily grind of fetching and carrying, smoke-filled kitchens and heavy agricultural work. Everywhere was intensely collective. Extended families wandered in and out of neighbours' houses, with stray children and chickens. On market stalls, low-caste meat cutters displayed their lean joints and yellow, leathery, villous buffalo stomachs. Yet they parlayed happily with higher caste customers. Women, in ethnic dress, squatted with their sisters and mothers-in-law. Together they picked nits, sifted rice, scrubbed pots, smoked *chillums*, brewed tea.

Education was also sporadic. Many scraggy, wild-haired working children carrying sticks or pots just stared into empty space, with no hope of any schooling. A few smarter children, with brushed hair and laundered blue uniforms, marched hand in hand to the English boarding school. The school had no boarders and didn't teach in English. For the lucky children who could attend school, they joined a crush of 60 or more crammed into a classroom without furniture, just a blackboard without chalk. They listened obediently to despotic and didactic teachers. Or chatted when staff disappeared for long periods to smoke or read the newspapers. By diktat and recitation the children learnt English passages they couldn't understand or pronounce.

Baglung was not what we expected in another way. People were happier than they should have been. We became inured to our simple lifestyle and rural rhythms. We lost our cravings for sugary fixes. A plate of boiled rice and *daal* and a few strands of leathery spinach, acidified by the juice of a lime, was a banquet. A glass of iodinated water tasted as refreshing as coconut milk or champagne. Rural Nepal was a land of strange social contrasts, linear and circular, rigid and rhythmic, oppressive and tolerant. Within gender and generational peer groups we found humour and generosity and friendship. Across groups there was formality and strict adherence to codes of respect and obeisance. To an outsider their interactions seemed sometimes cold and abusive.

Above all, villagers were not solitary. Their social life was complex, sophisticated, funny, humane, long term, sustainable, embracing and cultured. They sang and danced and gossiped and loved, usually in co-ordinated groups. In the small towns we found traditional family crafts: musicians and painters, goldsmiths and glassblowers, oil pressers and hairdressers and beauticians. In rural hamlets, sympathy groups came together for farming, forestry, funerals and family fora. They grieved for their dead and ancestors in ways we have forgotten. People would assemble for funerals at which corpses were wreathed and bound in white or yellow cloth, strewn with flower petals. They cremated bodies communally on a wood pyre by the fast-flowing Kali Gandaki. When a parent died, men would shave their heads and wear only white garments for a year. Then they'd call a party of celebration and remembrance for hundreds of their tribe and neighbours. And when they needed to build or farm or migrate, or decide whether to seek help in a crisis, they did so in ancestral groups. These were the nexi of 'beyond-family beneficiaries' who, since the dawn of mankind, would have met in sympathy.

For the most part, the Nepalese lived beyond bureaucracy and political control. Villages and hamlets had their own de facto monarchs, a local kind of mayor called the *pradhan pancha*. But his influence was intermittent and often ignored. Their poverty was less about oppression and more about exclusion. The state was not even an imagined presence. Even in London and New York today, the poorest live beyond the recognition of state structures, as illegal immigrants or vagrants. They are victims of what the sociologist Saskia Sassen calls expulsion rather than exclusion.[14]

Of course Alan Macfarlane was right from an economic perspective. Rural subsistence households were barely different from the earliest stages of human agriculture. Or even from those hunter-gatherers of prehistory who depended rather more on plants than animals. With less than an acre to produce their rice, lentils and vegetables, families gathered wood, fruits and herbs from meadows and forests. They picked citrus fruits. At festivals they might sacrifice a chicken. They expected nothing from the state and gave nothing, apart from the occasional son to the security forces. They lived in splendid isolation, amid the silence and noise of rurality. They were not disturbed by internal combustion engines, apart perhaps from the distant drone of aircraft, or the use of a generator by a bazaar shopkeeper showing a video. The biggest threats to their livelihood were predators and climate. In Baglung we awakened more than once to the cries of "Baag! Baag!" which spread like a message from Paul Revere, hamlet to hamlet. In the evergreen conifer forests that covered the hills, the habitat was a leopard's paradise. The name Baglung meant "a line of tigers".

The Nepalese did suffer the malnutrition of poor hygiene rather than hunger (except in the poorest households). The average life expectancy was then less than 60 years. South Asians are not genetically small, they become severely stunted in infancy. Their environment curtails their genetic potential. During the first 18 months of life, they faced the weanling's dilemma: whether to remain on safe, sterile breastmilk, or to boost their calories with denser, solid foods with the risk of contamination with microbes that cause diarrhoea and weight loss. And stunting of growth reflected stunting of the brain. Elfin children would do worse at school, with lower employment prospects than their better nourished peers. Most children followed their parents into subsistence agriculture, so the social disability of poor education was muted. But the cycle of deprivation would turn.

Yet despite all the hardships, Helen and I learned quickly that in most respects the English philosopher Thomas Hobbes was wrong. The natural condition of mankind, outside of political authority, was not an abomination. Hobbes believed that without a government and civil society governed by a social contract there would be a "war of all against all". But to call the lives of the Nepalese "solitary, poor, nasty, brutish, and short" was way off the mark. Their lives had meaning and beauty. They were touched with a panoply of tender human emotions. Despite the threats from poor hygiene, more often than not, if they survived infancy, their bodies were healthy and vibrant. Most families ate a good enough balanced diet, and experienced the highs of festivals and feasts. In times of plenty after the harvest, the richer shared with the poorer families. Juvenal, the Stoic philosopher, said that rather than for wealth, power or children, men should pray for a "sound mind in a sound body" (*mens sana in corpore sano*). The rural Nepalese, apart from the poorest households, had a lifestyle often closer to the gods than our own.[15]

Figures 8 A. With our clinic team in Baglung

B. The day of King Birendra's visit to Baglung

DHAMJA GROUPS

We learned much about sympathy groups in the daily life of Nepal from our arduous monthly health post support trips. Our small teams of doctor or health assistant, nurse, educator and porter would walk for hours over mountain trails to distant health centres. One was to the ramshackle stone health post at Dhamja, on the snowline edge of a rhododendron forest, a 10-hour walk from Baglung. The trek to Dhamja, endorphin infused, was tough but staggeringly beautiful. As we edged up over a ridge with spectacular views of Dhaulagiri, the Himalayan foothills were populated, like their people, by forests of native trees and historic intruders. Many of the most attractive trees and plants of the world's gardens were brought from these forests: deodar cedars, magnolias, rhododendron, *simal, phaledo, spirea*, barberry and varieties of primrose and mountain poppy. The beautiful banyan and peepul trees, members of the fig family, were planted, often together, by the aristocratic Ranas in their ornamental gardens. Villagers tended them at *chautaras*, the shady, stone resting places encircling the huge tree trunks, at which travellers and porters rested, ate snacks and cooked communal meals. But invaders proliferated – eucalyptus, bottlebrush and silky oak from Australia, bougainvillea, poinsettia and monkey puzzle trees from south America, blue wisteria from China, and many garden flowers from Europe. The ubiquitous yellow marigolds, which adorn every religious *puja*, originated from eastern Europe. Vegetables too: peppers, maize, potatoes, tomatoes and beans arrived from America and Europe.

Near the top of the Dhamja ridge, as light faded after our full-day trek, our small team were greeted by Dil Bahadur, the health post in charge and his staff. His peon had cooked *daal bhaat* and the temperature was falling. So, after a few pleasantries, a trip to the bushes and a slurpy pile of rice and lentils, we climbed into our sleeping bags on bamboo mats in the cold waiting room. When conversation petered out Dil switched on his plastic portable radio to listen to BBC World Service news.

Next morning, the clinic was spectacularly busy. Usually they expected to see between five and 30 patients. Today there were 120 of the very poorest come to receive care, for a change, on their own doorstep. They were friendly, open people around Dhamja, chiefly Magars and Chhetris. Many families eked out a desperately vulnerable subsistence and almost all children showed signs of malnutrition. One skeletal child I advised to be sent immediately to our nutrition unit in Baglung.

"Maybe next month," said the mother.

"Next month will be too late."

"But what can I do? My husband is in India, I must tend the rice, the millet and maize, feed the buffalo, make the food. There are four others to feed."

"What about your daughter?" I suggested, pointing at the child's elder sister who was 14 years old but looked about eight. "She is deaf and dumb," said the mother. She laughed casually, in the almost shocking way that many people did in Nepal, faced with similar distress. We had many conversations with parents of severely malnourished infants, dying babies or crippled children. Mothers in terrible distress, or grinding, absolute poverty, punctuated their faltering interviews with laughter as well as tears. It was more than a mannerism, a way to cope. It was the acceptable face of Hinduism. Everyone at all times has a position and a place in the meaning of life, and there must be hope and happiness. To observers, like writer VS Naipaul,[16] it's a philosophy of complacency and stagnation; in a society where the only changes in a century have been the cycles of the seasons, where development is little more than a dusty five-year plan on the shelf of the district officer, and stagnation carries no pejorative meaning.

In the evening, we sipped hot lemon and rum and led a formal education session. We talked about nutrition with our impromptu sympathy group of health workers, 12 in all, from Baglung and Dhamja. Dil Bahadur was polite and kind but his demeanour expressed resignation and fatalism. He accepted the disinterest of his district superior, never doubting the inevitable lack of opportunity in his career, never believing that things could really change, and never wishing to embrace the risk of innovation and failure. Despite prompts, only Baglung staff did the talking. The Dhamja team maintained a respectful silence. With every workshop, every training day, we learned that Nepal health care was not weak through a lack of knowledge and skills but a loss of hope and motivation. We were going through the motions of training. Our seeds of wisdom fell on stony soil. Outside, a group of dogs erupted at intervals into frenzied negotiations about dominance and subordination. The education ended. Deflated, we went to our sleeping bags on the hard, cold wooden floor.

In Dhamja the immanent power of village sympathy groups emerged unexpectedly. Next morning, our refreshed and smiling in-charge Dil Bahadur showed us his empty diagnostic room, with cardboard boxes full of bronze bottles of gentian violet and paracetamol syrup. Smaller white boxes of foiled condoms were labelled, in one of the better Nepali mis-spellings, 'electronically tasted'. His registration book revealed sparse attendance and a prescription routine of analgesia and cheap antisepsis. Then he took us outside, beyond the peon quarters and the latrine, to a small patch of ground 20 yards behind the post, close to the scrub that bordered the alpine woods. A strange contraption had been assembled, like a small wooden hen coop, or perhaps a punishment cell in a concentration camp. A raised wooden-framed meshed door closed the tunnel at either end. Each door opened vertically and fell like a guillotine when a trap was sprung. Inside, close to the door at the far end was tied a baby goat, sitting patiently, chewing on a pile of grass.

"What is it?" I asked.

"A leopard trap," said Dil Bahadur. "The Magar men come and bait it every night. There were several attacks last month. One family lost a water buffalo calf, another a couple of goats."

A group of about 15 householders, from families living in this small snowline hamlet, had come together to discuss the threat to their livestock from *Panthera pardus*, the reclusive leopard. They debated the problem and considered their options. No point, they agreed, to hunt the leopard in the forest even if Mr Pun said he could borrow a gun. Leopards are solitary night-time assassins, masters of disguise, as quick as lightning. Even a trained sniper would struggle. No point either in waiting for huntsmen or wildlife rangers sent by the royal consul who ruled the district panchayats. Even if he was lobbied, and rangers could be found, Magar hamlets would not be first in line to receive scarce municipal largesse. And even if the leopard was killed, another might soon move into the vacant territory. So a baited trap was the best option. When it came to predators, the community were in sympathy. They were focused, creative and strategic. A common threat needed a group solution. The design and execution of a trap was part of folk tradition, so the group's decision led to rapid construction. A dead leopard also had value, for its aphrodisiac and healing properties, as well as its skin and meat. Later I learned the local village convened other sympathy groups, to help at harvest, to respond to landslides and to organise funerals.

But no sympathy group existed for the health post. Somehow it was peripheral to their needs, the obligatory creation of an indifferent and distant administrative centre. The village health committee was inactive, and the staff were largely ignored. Without community involvement, the morale and skills of the health assistants, working in remote isolation, faded. Two months earlier we had walked for six hours to another health post at Kusmi Sera. The young Yadav Maithili-speaking health worker from the heat of the *terai*, the Gangetic plains that border India, had loathed his appointment to a remote, chilly hill village. In turn the locals despised and ignored him. Like a Mexican in Winnipeg, or a Greek in Finland, he felt alienated and foreign. Like Dil Bahadur he had listened politely to our training and nodded frequently, with empty eyes. Soon after our visit he took extended sick leave, presumably to lobby for a transfer. He hadn't returned.

After the tour of the leopard trap, our busy clinic and our final training session on diarrhoea and vitamin A deficiency (Dil Bahadur and his two assistants had stayed awake but again said little), the sky turned red then black. The temperature plummeted and we sought warmth in our bags. Dil Bahadur lay on the wood floor wearing a woolly hat and sipped hot rum and lemon. "What do you do up here?" I asked, "evenings".

"I listen to the World BBC Service," he said. "I heard yesterday that Srimati Totchaire told the Europeans No! No! No!"[17] It took me a while to work out he was speaking of the Iron Lady Mrs Thatcher. "I like the news and the Sandi Jones request show."

"What kind of music do you like?"

"Tina Turner. She's the best."

I admired his cheerfulness, isolated in a cold mountain health post. He waited for his transfer, unable to treat more than the mundane, and referred sick villagers to the district hospital a day's walk away. I felt sorry for him and sympathised with his steadfast resilience.

On our return trip from Dhamja, we walked down the slippery, precipitous trail as our team shouted regular warnings. "*Raato maato, chiplo baato!*" ("red mud, slippery road") they cried through the clouds that clung like fungus to the hillsides. Conversations with nurse Laxmi and auxiliary health worker Ujar became cross-culturally complex.

"How far is it to walk from your village to Helen's village?" asked Laxmi. It took me a minute or two to respond. Answer: about 11 days from Lewisham in south London to Goole in south Yorkshire, assuming you cannot walk alongside the M1 motorway. Ujar got more personal. "Was it a love marriage or arranged?" he asked knowingly. This required careful diplomacy. Answer: Half and half. My mother-in-law arranged the wedding but aspects of pre-marital love arose.

Serendipitously we discovered more sympathy groups. An hour down the mountain, as we skipped through a crossroads, where the trail went right to Resa and left to Baglung, a dozen women sat on a bamboo mat under a tree. This sympathy group chatted about community forestry with an extension worker. Further on, we passed a funeral party. They came from Sigana, where there were many beautifully carved traditional Newar houses. This was a Maharjan *guthi* group, from the agricultural sub-clan of Newars. A *guthi* is a traditional co-operative method, about sympathy group size, which protects their rituals, monuments, lands and shared resources like water spouts and *chautaras*. The eldest member of the group, the *thakali*, guides its norms and charity. His most important role is to ensure that the transition from this life to the next is seamless. A straggle of mourners, fewer than 20, led by the *thakali*, trailed behind a corpse. He was bound in white cloth, strewn with yellow marigolds, borne aloft on bamboo poles by four men with red *tikka*ed foreheads, shaven heads, white lungis and yellow headscarves. The man had died that morning. They were heading down to the river, because all rivers are sacred and lead to the Ganges. The body would be cremated, attended by his sons, and the ashes cast. Without this speedy ritual, or in the absence of a son, the dead cannot pass to heaven. They will remain to plague the living as an evil spirit.

Offerings would be made to the dead man's spirit, and perhaps to a crow, which represents ancestors, and to a dog, which symbolises the god of death. Newars are syncretist, they practise both Hinduism and Buddhism. So if the sub-clan has strong Buddhist leanings, the women might, on the third day after death, make a *mandala* from coloured sand, usually of Lord Buddha, which they would keep in the house for four days. Afterwards, mourning rites would be observed. Heads shaved, salt and meat avoided for 13 days, the wearing of white *topis* and white clothes. A complex series of social and religious rituals would follow, astrologically guided, at four, seven, 13 and 45 days following death. After 13 days, food and gifts for the dead in heaven would be given to the priest, and a feast held. On the anniversary, the entire extended clan, perhaps several hundred people, would be invited for a memorial feast. Such a complex series of events demanded an organised group and regular meetings.

The funerals, leopard traps, community groups and health post visits were our social education in Nepal. Three days later, back in Baglung, Helen scribbled a blue aerogramme to Sandi Jones and asked her to play Private Dancer for Dil Bahadur of Dhamja health post in Nepal. She tucked it into the postbag that the *Majhi* porter Yamy carried to Balewa airstrip for the perilous journey to Bush House, and we forgot about it. Two months later, with our support team, we reprised our long trek to Dhamja. As we walked, altitude breathless, into his empty stone health post Dil Bahadur was wreathed in smiles.

"Doctor sahib! Helen didi! Sandi Jones. She played it for Dil Bahadur in Dhamja. From my heart, I thank you, doctor sahib."

He had told the entire neighbourhood. Others, too, had heard the startling mention of Dhamja by the British Broadcasting Corporation.

His morale had never been higher. Our group visit had brought him recognition and a sense of belonging. Emotional and team support go a long way. Dil Bahadur didn't set up a formal strategy group, *comme le leopard*, but gradually broadened the ownership and decision-making by his staff at the health post, trained his auxiliaries and improved the management of his pharmacy. He renewed meetings with the *Pradhan Pancha* and the panchayat committee. After a year, we analysed the attendances at the five district health posts we had supported and compared them with the four that we hadn't. To my surprise, attendances had risen dramatically – by 75% for all patients and 226% for children under five in the supported health posts.[18] The management principle developed by Hewlett Packard in the 1970s of MBWA, "management by wandering around" had been put to good use. By wandering around the district to create local teams, we had not only supported Dil Bahadur and colleagues, but also improved their performance. Hundreds of families enjoyed better care.

I didn't see Dil Bahadur again for nearly 20 years, when our hair colour had matured in grey harmony. I was visiting the Ministry of Health in Ram Shah Path for an appointment with the Additional Secretary. In the ante-room sat a knot of health workers, there to do *chakuri* (creeping) in the hope of a transfer from yet another remote and undesired posting. Immediately I recognised his cheery, optimistic face. "Dil Bahadur?" I said without thinking.

"Doctor sahib!"

I pointed at him. "Dhamja health post, Baglung!"

He pointed back. "Tina Turner!"

Figure 9. Dhamja health post. Dil Bahadur is far right

Ancestral Benefits

ESSENTIAL FEATURES

Sympathy groups, creating and implementing good ideas, were a central driver of historical and economic development. They have endured from slavery, through serfdom and peasantry, to the industrial and communication revolutions. In our era, a social and political question of more than trivial importance is how sympathy groups, in a frantic, complex global world, can help to transform lives and communities. It may seem strange to argue for more scientific exploration of ancient social structures when, in the twenty-first century, we can speak with almost anyone on the planet. In a second, we can search the world's library on our smartphones. Shouldn't we just accept we spend hours alone, in a virtual, isolated world of facts, news and entertainment. Perhaps greater than at any time in human history we live more alone than together. Is this a bad thing or simply inevitable?

Or is it a summons to manage modern technology to help us redesign our world to support sympathetic human relationships? How can our workplace, neighbourhood and public services have more of a human face? Science, perhaps, can teach us the best way to do it. How we can unleash positive energy and manage their use of time. How modern states might organise policies and institutions to support sympathy groups. The climate and consumption crisis is a case in point. Can the sinister thought of an impending climate catastrophe be tempered by the optimism of human group innovation? Bill Clinton speaks about the power of networks of co-operation and that "People can do anything as long as they feel they can make the future better."[19] Clinton believes the reason why some states in America are more successful than others is largely because they have better networks of co-operation. So can we harness our primeval networks of co-operation, and unlock the power of everyday politics to bring about sustainable social transformation?

Let's consider in more detail the essential features of a sympathy group. This ancestral process for collective survival originated, we think, from the grooming cliques of primates. Grooming reduces the stress of individuals and families living in much larger populations.[20] An individual in a large crowd of strangers is highly stressed, within a smaller group of friends much less so. The strength of ties between sympathy group members lies between the close ties of family and the weak ties of affinity band members. In essence, members are beneficiaries, enablers or neighbours. Group processes involve a focus for action, iteration, the development of trust and the fulfilment of strategies.

Beneficiaries within sympathy groups are people with a direct interest in a specific utility such as survival, income or recreation. Or they want a change in behaviour, better quality services or a successful trade. Famously, Adam Smith realised that individual self-interest, not altruism, governs trade: "It is not from the benevolence of the butcher, the brewer, or the baker, that we expect our dinner, but from their regard to their own interest. We address ourselves, not to their humanity but to their self-love, and never talk to them of our necessities but of their advantages."[21] The Adam Smith principle applies to sympathy groups, which act for the most pressing interests of their members. Direct beneficiaries lead or join sympathy groups. They don't include those who have no personal interest in what happens locally, such as civil servants or outsiders from headquarters. The groups might invite them as an occasional guest.

When sympathy groups work well they do so because people with facilitation skills – enablers – ensure they meet regularly and build trust to solve a problem. Rather than becoming pre-occupied with gossip or local conflicts, the group learns ways to collaborate. The members use games to solve immediate and underlying problems, in their own interest. Groups bring together older and younger generations. They allow neighbours to become allies. They energise a workplace. Members may focus on a special interest, like a choir or a sports team, or maybe a savings, environment or antenatal group. Outside advocates or politicians play no part unless consulted for a specific purpose, or if happenstance makes them a neighbour.

To be successful, groups concentrate on specific challenges. How to change a local organisation or improve an amenity, how to get through a liminal event like childbirth, a wedding or funeral, how to resolve a contest or a dispute, or how to make the most of opportunities in agriculture, business or communications. Facilitators hold repeated meetings to build consensus, conversation and problem-solving skills. They analyse, innovate, copy and assess solutions. They are not a passive 'focus group', as used by spin doctors, psephologists or advertisers. These people extract quick data about voter opinions, party political preferences or washing powder. Nor are they the groups used by social scientists and anthropologists to study community beliefs or sexual attitudes, or complex cultural identities. Focus groups provide valuable insights but aren't catalysts for change. The sympathy group work takes time, has a structure, a facilitator and demands commitment.

A level of trust and confidentiality emerges within a successful group. An obvious proviso is that human nature means groups might absorb rivals, spies, opponents or perceived inferiors. All of us retain a modicum of suspicion of sibling and neighbour, but trust becomes a critical factor in group success. Strategies are key outputs. How the strategies are accomplished is critical for success. Farmers' groups might decide to share labour and skills, sports groups to fundraise or commit to more rigorous fitness, church groups to start outreach action or retreats. Across the world, pregnancy groups share birth plans and relaxation techniques, and workplace groups organise quality circles or sabbatical cover. Musicians work in groups to build and exchange ideas, activists in groups to build their solidarity and advocacy campaigns.

The acronym BENEFITS is a useful aide memoire: beneficiaries, enablers, neighbours, focus, iteration and interaction, trust and strategies. As we shall see later, our own social experiments with sympathy women's groups in poor villages in Bangladesh, India, Malawi and Nepal showed how women could co-operate to ensure the survival of their children. These BENEFITS, established as the groups became rooted and proliferated, led to astonishing health outcomes – way beyond anything we expected.

Figure 10. Duke Ellington and his Orchestra, 1938

Figure 11. Sports sympathy groups
A. Barcelona football club – the club has sympathy group teams at many age levels below the senior team

B. Jardine's cricket team at Welbeck Abbey

Figure 12. Women's suffrage group, New South Wales, 1892

INDIVIDUALISM AND POWER ELITES

The dominant narrative of our human story over the past two millennia has been about individuals and mass movements. Historians study great and weak leaders, their luck and ill fortune. They analyse states, empires, governments, parties, armies, churches and courts. They argue over ideologies of capitalism, communism or anarchism. They bracket time into identifiable epochs like the Dark Ages, the Renaissance, the Enlightenment and the end of history. Essayist Thomas Carlyle even proposed a 'great men' theory of history whereby chronicled shifts occurred when dynamic males challenged the status quo. But the history of small groups, clubs, everyday politics and sympathy is rarely mentioned.

Why has the power of the sympathy group been ignored in analyses of our social past? One reason is that individualism has much to commend it. The modern era of technologically driven economic success has consecrated the importance of the individual like no other. A selfish world view dominates behind a presumption of state power and support. Western individualism seems irresistible. In Anglo-Saxon economies, the history of individual rights goes back eight hundred years to Magna Carta. English individualism and first-born inheritance led to an accumulation of wealth, capital and land in a manner different from European and Asian peasantries. In part, this capital stock fuelled the Industrial Revolution. European pioneers who colonised North America built the individual ethic. They enshrined it in the US constitution and the cultural evolution of the American dream. Free markets and capitalism are now dominant everywhere.

Over the past five centuries, the medical, biological and psychological sciences also focused triumphantly on individuals and their component parts, from organs to cells to the genetic code: Leonardo da Vinci's anatomical studies, William Harvey's discovery of the circulation of blood and Claude Bernard's homeostasis − the constancy of the internal environment as a condition for a free life. Other examples include Robert Koch and Louis Pasteur's bacterial infections, Lord

Adrian's nerve conduction as a frequency code, and Watson and Crick's decoding of genetic replication. Science ignited an explosion of cellular and molecular knowledge. Biological innovation and national immunisation campaigns have almost eliminated polio, smallpox, diphtheria, measles, whooping cough and tetanus.

An individualist mindset was finally cemented by Charles Darwin's theory of evolution. Natural selection of random mutations leads to the survival of the fittest. Our selfish genes dictate which characteristics of the current generation will leave their mark on future generations. The strongest individual characteristics are selected. Our reproductive success derives from conflict and self-interest, from chance and necessity, and from selfish genes. The natural world is pitiless and ruthless, but produces the best available genotype to survive what the environment will throw at us. Ancestral groups would appear to be an evolutionary irrelevance.

We also prefer to measure economic success based on delayed reward and competition in myriad rat races. Anglo-Saxon markets unwittingly draw breath from philosopher Ayn Rand and her virtue of selfishness. Even our behavioural economic analysis of human interaction emphasises networks of individuals rather than the collective power of the group. The decisions of individual company leaders and the performance of large corporations dominate the business media. In macroeconomics, the opinions of austerity and deficit hawks, Keynesians, free marketeers, structuralists and creative destructionists debate the shifts and cycles of growth and recessions across nation states. Economists and traders pore over financial flows, commodity prices, market confidence, currency exchanges and stock analyses to understand collective fear and greed. For smaller businesses a plethora of self-help books analyse the key individual traits of leadership, good marketing, individual accounts, decision making and individual consultant inputs for organisational change. Our daily experience of working together in smallish groups, the lifeblood of an economy, is rarely analysed or mentioned.

And since the 1960s our demands for individual gratification have multiplied. Author Tom Wolfe labelled the 1970s the Me decade.[22]

Novelist Kurt Andersen wrote about liberty: "It's all of a piece. For hippies and bohemians as for businesspeople and investors, extreme individualism has been triumphant. Selfishness won".[23] Even psychology has ignored the interaction of humans in groups. In psychotherapy, Freudians and their heirs focused on the interactions of superego and id upon the ego of introspective individuals. Cognitive theorists unpick our individual development, motivation, memory and learning. Behaviourists believe we are a sophisticated collection of Pavlovian reflexes. Our disturbances of mind are treated by drugs and individual cognitive or psychoanalytic therapies, not group conversation and solidarity. The work of SH Foulkes, Wilfred Bion and Carl Rogers, who founded the group therapy movement, is little more than a footnote in modern psychiatry.

Attention to the stress of isolation and the therapeutic value of group contact remains marginal, outside the mainstream of health care. Scientists and doctors, entranced by the power of their laboratories, forget our social core. Medicine focuses obsessively on the development and delivery of magical drugs, silver bullets and vaccines to revolutionise survival. We celebrate individual success and careers. We test our children endlessly on cognitive tasks, but rarely their ability to co-operate, support and be neighbourly.

Historians are not much better. They have disregarded small human groups because of a fascination with the emergence of nation states. Since the 1648 Treaty of Westphalia, history has documented the struggle between the ascendancy of government taxation and citizen rights. State taxes are essential if governments are to protect citizens against private violence and to mount military operations. Ever since Roman times the right to extract taxes has been a key feature of a sovereign state. But the consent to pay taxes became enshrined in a legal system that protected other citizen rights, our security, our honour and protection of property. With democracy, the rights of citizens became stronger, but equally the burden of taxation grew.

Taxes and citizen rights are directly correlated, but at either ends of the spectrum the relationship goes awry. With totalitarianism, taxes may not lead to any strengthening of citizen services – indeed the experience of North Korea, Haiti and other modern dictatorships suggests otherwise. By contrast, 'neoliberalism', a phrase invented at the Walter Lippmann Colloque of 1938 for a movement to oppose the centralised planning of communism through "the priority of the price mechanism, the free enterprise, the system of competition and a strong and impartial state", released a force that threatened citizen rights. When Ronald Reagan and Margaret Thatcher wanted to reduce the burden of taxation, the corollary was a decline in citizens' rights and protection by the state. Crony capitalists profited and oligarchs enjoyed special protection. Health care, transport, education and even policing were to be 'privatised' for better performance, despite rising inequality between rich and poor. The debasement of social protection through lack of investment led to visible, preventable disasters like the New Orleans floods and the Grenfell Tower fire disaster in west London.

So, make no mistake, we espouse individualism for perfectly good reasons. It brought utility, advantage and freedoms. Markets of free-thinking 'rational' consumers and entrepreneurs have generated wealth and survival. Individual human rights legislation has undermined dictatorships and oppression. Medical research on cellular and organ systems has relieved suffering, unparalleled in human history. Evolutionary theory based on a selfish gene has brought a profound understanding of biology and ecosystems. Political science has documented struggles between capital and labour, democracy and communism, state and private sector performance, freedom of expression and surveillance for security.

Kindness and sharing is seen by constitutionalists, human rights agencies, and economists studying rational individual consumers, as little more than an epiphenomenon. One reason is because most of the communities we observe or analyse are much larger than 'primordial villages of face-to-face contact'. They are not an immediate and real presence, but part of our imagination.[24] Political scientist Benedict Anderson described a town, district or city as an imagined political community, complex, limited and sovereign. "It is imagined because the members of even the smallest nation will never know most of their fellow-members, meet them, or even hear of them, yet in the minds of each lives the image of their communion." Imagined communities emerge as kaleidoscopic collections of individuals, layered within hierarchies, rather than the coherent gestalt of a solid small group or conglomeration of groups.

Yet even at state level, the influence of sympathy groups is seriously underplayed. Every modern state has power networks that include extremely influential sympathy group circles around a leader. After he won the election, a sympathy group of trusted advisers encircled Donald Trump to help organise his transition to the Presidency. His inner circle included Kellyanne Conway (campaign manager), Steve Bannon (chief strategist), Jeff Sessions (national security chair), Walid Phares (counter-terrorism advisor) Ivanka (daughter), Don Jr (son), Eric (son), Jared Kushner (son-in-law), Dan Scavino Jr (social media director), Ann Coulter, Sean Hannity, Laura Ingraham, Roger Stone, Roger Ailes and Rebekah Mercer. None of them were grandees of the Republican Party, nor sycophants on the make. All 15 of his sympathy group were considered loyal and trusted for their ideas or financial support. Later, some fell by the wayside.

Russia is perhaps the best example of how sympathy circles overlap to run a state. Russia didn't benefit from the legacy of Roman Empire administrative structures. From a western perspective, it still has rudimentary democratic institutions. The *sistema* of Vladimir Putin refers to a melange of formal government rules and informal norms, opaque to outsiders but clearly understood by insiders. Political scientist Alena Ledeneva calls it "a co-dependence of parasitic power elites and parasitic masses".[25] She describes an inner circle sympathy group of key advisers to Putin. In President Putin's first terms they included Igor Sechin of the St Petersburg security group from which Putin originated, who controls Rosneft, the largest state conglomerate in the country. The inner circle also included Nikolai Patrushev, Aleksander Bortnikov, Viktor Ivanov and Aleksander Bastrykin; a counterbalancing security group including Viktor Cherkesov, and Viktor Molotov; Prosecutor General Yuri Chaika, former President Dmitry Medvedev, finance minister Aleksei Kudrin; and a bevy of industrialists including Putin's long-time friend Yuri Koval'chuk who controls Bank Rossiya, Gennady Timchenko owner of the oil trader

Gunvor, Mayor of Moscow Sergei Sobyanin, former Kremlin chief of staff Aleksander Voloshin and Putin's closest and favourite billionaire, the owner of Chelsea Football club, Roman Abramovich. They were another perfect 15 for Putin's core sympathy group.

Outside this circle, Ledeneva describes a band of 'useful friends', and a wider circle of weaker ties made up of 'core and mediated contacts'. In all administrations these networks have stabilising and corrupting functions. For Putin, his closest group provides social comfort and emotional support for routine domestic work. They can mobilise resources speedily through extended networks. They're a survival kit. They allocate resources for market and state decisions and for 'self-provisioning and coercive appropriations'. Group decisions protect because responsibility is shared and reduces the threat of rivals. The inner group network is a safety net which ensures trusted people will monitor and implement policy.

A precarious risk is the potential for groupthink. Groups display a 'lock-in' effect, which reduces adaptive capacity and thinking outside the box. Ledeneva suggests the inner group acts as a 'buffer' that protects against external threats and increases flexibility in dealing with constraints. In countries such as Russia, with poorly developed systems of state trust, interpersonal systems become much more important. Social capital can make things happen quickly. It helps entrepreneurs and start-up businesses everywhere. Later, though, groups run the risk of becoming 'path dependent,' i.e. unnecessarily restrictive when systems should be transparent, competitive and price-sensitive.

Groups of determinedly powerful people are especially dangerous when wedded to theories of superiority. Curiously, in both Trump and Putin administrations the work of Julius Evola, an Italian poet and painter of the Dada School, influences key advisers. Evola dabbled in esotericism and mysticism and wrote a book Synthesis of the Doctrine of Race which inspired Benito Mussolini. He subscribed to "the law of the regression of the castes", claiming that civilisations have a Hindu-type structure of four castes: sacred leaders, noble warriors, bourgeois merchants and slaves. Countries fail when traditional caste structures break down. Alt-right

Figure 13. President Vladimir Putin, centre, at a cabinet of ministers conference, 2006

advisers like former White House strategist Stephen Bannon and traditionalists in the Putin government wish to preserve strong caste identity and power in the Christian tradition.

We could do the same group analysis for British, German, Indian, Chinese and any other government. At the centre will be a key sympathy group. Each member will be a beneficiary, an enabler or a political neighbour. And the President chooses people he is confident will discharge his instructions. So sympathy groups in government have both positive and negative effects. The balance of their impact depends upon the context, the values and ideology of the group, and the facilitation skills of the leader.

Counterintuitively, grand analysis of international political strategy also reveals persistent small group principles. The 'grand strategy' of US foreign policy in some ways closely parallels the features of sympathy groups. President Woodrow Wilson lauded grand and noble aims of peace, democracy and trade. Nicholas Spykman, Yale Professor of International Relations, concluded that American intention was less noble, to achieve a balance of power heavily stacked in its favour. The methods were fourfold: persuasion, purchase, barter and coercion.[26] Similarly, small group solutions to local problems invariably focus on strategies of negotiation, doing deals, making transactions, or using the threat of symbolic coercion or withdrawal of support. In the US response to the 9/11 attacks by Al Qaeda, Walter Russell Mead saw something similar.[27] Three predominant forms of American power emerged: sweet influence with friends (cultural influences like movies, universities, charities, international organisations); sticky diplomacy with doubter countries (economic and trade relations that bind countries together); and sharp (military force or sanctions) with hostile states. Likewise sympathy groups share cultural interests, are stuck together through shared trade and interests, and occasionally use collective threats to ensure access to rights and resources.

SELF HELP OR GROUP HELP?

Most of us, covertly, look for tips to improve our life. We wish for a better career, to lose extra pounds, to reduce our stress or enjoy happy relationships. Self-help guides with catchy titles dominate the non-fiction section of bookshops. Two of the earliest bestsellers Man's Search For Meaning by Viktor E. Frankl and How to Win Friends and Influence People by Dale Carnegie were superior to many imitators. Stephen Covey's The 7 Habits of Highly Successful People still tops the bestseller charts two decades after publication. Imitator authors are legion.

Social and network phenomena have become popular. Malcolm Gladwell's Tipping Point unpicked the origins of social epidemics. He described a sudden craze for wearing Hush Puppies, a surge in sexually transmitted infections, and a sharp decline in violent crime in New York City. Curiously he saw most tipping points caused by a few individuals. His 'Law of the Few' involved three types of people. Connectors know lots of people, mavens accumulate knowledge obsessionally to create market data banks, and salesmen persuade others to buy a new product. Gladwell saw the start of the American Revolution, for example, as a word-of-mouth epidemic spread by a few salesmen. A single man, Paul Revere, acted as both maven and connector. This is odd because he obscures the social context that preceded Revere's role. He doesn't mention that Paul Revere had built group links over several years with artisan members of the 'Loyal Nine'. This rebel group organised protests against the Stamp Act. Nor that Revere also met regularly in a public house, the Green Dragon, with a sympathy group of 'Mechanics'. They monitored and shared intelligence about British troop movements. Nor does he explore the role of women like Mercy Otis Warren, who held group meetings in her house. She staged sympathy group plays and histories about the defence of patriot rights and the infringement of those rights by the British colonists. Revere's midnight ride on April 18th 1775 to alarm the countryside between Boston and Cambridge that 'the British are coming' was not the act of a random individual and a few salesmen. In his heroic ride to stop the British, Revere catalysed a network of activated groups, built up over years.

David Brooks in The Social Animal also highlighted the importance of social interactions in affecting the life-course of two fictional characters. And Pulitzer prize-winner Tina Rosenberg's Join the Club described how peer pressure can 'transform the world'. But neither mentions the sympathy group. Steven Johnson, a media theorist, comes closest. He argued that the best places ever found for ideas and innovation were in the London coffee houses of the mid-17th century.[28] Coffee replaced the routine of beer at breakfast, wine at lunch and gin in the evening as the social lubricant of choice. A stimulant replaced a depressant. The result was the most innovative forum for the Enlightenment, the coffee house. New ideas were born. Hogarth's picture of a London coffee house gives an idea of its attraction. The space was important and the group size ideal for originating good ideas, innovations and deals. Coffee house sympathy spawned a tribal assortment of groups.[29] For businessmen, the Jamaican Coffee house attracted West Indian traders, exchange brokers sat at Jonathan's and Oriental merchants went to the Jerusalem. Tea and coffee traders congregated at Garraways and the Virginia and Baltic. Writers preferred Buttons, Dick's, St. George's, the Somerset, the Grecian and Don Salterno's. Poets and critics met at Will's in Covent Garden, founded by Will Urwin in 1660. Writers and printers also used the Chapterhouse, where Charlotte and Anne Brontë stayed when they visited their publisher.

Politicians met closer to Parliament in places like White's Chocolate House. The Whigs used James's. Truby's serviced the clergy, Rawhmell's the scientists and philanthropists, foreigners went to the Orange Coffeehouse in Haymarket. Tom's in Covent Garden served a mix of actors, artists and doctors.

Men dominated the discussions and many women were not happy. A 1674 pamphlet, 'The Women's Petition against Coffee', complains that "we find them not capable of performing those Devoirs which their *Duty*, and our *Expectations* Exact . . .(which) we can Attribute to nothing more than the Excessive use of that Newfangled, Abominable, Heathenish Liquor called COFFEE, which Riffling Nature of her Choicest *Treasures*, and *Drying* up the *Radical Moisture*, has so *Eunucht* our Husbands, and Cripple our more kind *Gallants*, that they are become as *Impotent* as Age . . ."[30] But passions were still aroused. In Bedford coffee house, close to my university, the Reverend Hackman, overcome with jealousy, shot Miss Ray, a singer and mistress of Lord Sandwich. The emotional but indecisive vicar then failed to kill himself successfully so the state stepped in to help. At Tyburn the following week he was hanged in public.

Figure 14 Interior of a London Coffee-house, 17th century

In the first half of the eighteenth century, the number of sympathy group clubs went viral. Every parish, every interest, every wacky group had its own club. Clubs for philosophers, fox-hunters, hackney-cab drivers, wigmakers, shoemakers, clock-makers, for literature and music.[31] And a Terrible Club, a Silent Club, a Lazy Club, the club of Ugly Faces and even a Farter's Club. London, with a population of 700,000, had 3000 clubs. Bristol had 250 in a population of 50,000. In other words, a club existed for about every 200-250 people. For men in seventeenth century British towns, clubs and sympathy groups, after the working day was over, were a central part of social life.

How to protect individual rights but also encourage social commitments has been a central question for philosophers, politicians and economists. Jean-Jacques Rousseau in the Social Contract worried about how groups might affect individual liberty. "How to find a form of association which will defend the person or goods of each member with the collective force of all, and under which each individual, while uniting himself with the others, obeys no one but himself, and remains as free as before." The social contract was a key solution. "If, then, we eliminate from the social pact everything that is not essential to it, we find it comes down to this: Each one of us puts into the community his person and all his powers under the supreme direction of the general will; and as a body, we incorporate every member as an indivisible part of the whole."

This concept of 'civil society' goes back to Aristotle and Greek philosophy. The world's religions enjoin. In Christianity, the Gospel of Matthew emphasised "Blessed are the poor in spirit, for theirs is the kingdom of heaven . . . .You are the light of the world . . . .. let your light shine before men, that they may see your good deeds."[32] At a spiritual level too, sympathy groups play a fundamental role. Deep in the Jesuit philosophy of St Ignatius Loyola are the concepts of consolation, moving towards God, and of desolation, moving away from Him. Desolation makes us negative, isolated, cut off from our community. It saps our energy. Consolation, like compassion, shares our joy and despair with other people. It creates new bonds, gives us inspiration, energy and ideas.

The Quran speaks similarly of the sympathy function of righteousness. Beyond a belief in Allah, worshippers should show love "for your kin, for orphans, for the needy, for the wayfarer, for those who ask; and for the ransom of slaves; to be steadfast in prayers and practise regular charity; to fulfil the contracts which you made."[33] Further, the first pillar of Islamic organisational structure is "that no community of Muslims, large or small, should be without *ul al-amr* or a decision-making body". The second pillar is that "this body must be chosen by the community" and must consult. The fifth pillar is the iterative function of the sympathy group. "Muslims are expected to organise their collective life in a process of continuous correction, reform and improvement through education and public criticism.' Vital to the interests of the local community there must be "many knowledgeable persons who raise responsible voices when a wrong begins to establish or when a right thing does not get established". These moderate Muslim groups are the best way to address rare and violent forms of Wahabbist Islam and jihadist aggression.

The Buddhist concept of compassion, especially in the Mahayana tradition found in Tibet, India and Japan, embraces the importance of social engagement to alleviate suffering. Buddhism is characterised in the west as a process of introspection and contemplation which brings tranquillity to disturbed minds. In Asia the practice is different. The social and the individual demands of Buddhist practice are intertwined. Indeed the split between Mahayana and Nirvana Buddhism arose precisely because Mahayana (greater Vehicle) Buddhists believed enlightenment could only be achieved through a selfless practice: to help the less fortunate, to join community discussions for a better ecology, agriculture or urban space. Indeed, when Dr Ambedkar, in the 1950s, advised the untouchable *dalits* of India to convert to Buddhism, he did so to challenge the caste system. For him, conversion was not simply introspective or spiritual but a chance to challenge social inequalities and to gain a political voice. He wanted *dalits*, unshackled from their Hindu caste status, to join groups as equals. They should join the process of local and national decision-making.

Within the Hindu tradition, groups coming together to offer *pujas* to the Gods are an everyday part of routine and ritual. In 2015, in Godavari,

Kathmandu, soon after the destructive earthquakes, I sat in an open-air circle of priests and women devotees offering prayers and flowers to appease the earth and nature gods they believed had brought the quake. The mantras, burnt incense and flowers reassured us. And the group brought a peaceful solidarity. It came as no surprise.

Figure 15. Religious sympathy group appeasing the
Gods after the Nepal earthquake, 2015

Individualism alone cannot explain human progress. Evolutionary theory supports survival of the fittest but Darwin also believed in parochial altruism. Getting together in groups protected the survival of individuals within them. "Groups where the members are altruistic towards their own group and aggressive towards other groups," he wrote, "have a greater chance of survival than groups where there is a lack of such altruism."[34] Why does group co-operation succeed in everyday life? Doesn't selflessness contravene the harsh principles of Darwin's natural selection? Darwinists can partly explain it. As we shall see in our discussion of relatedness, our genes remain selfish because primitive groups are based on families. If I sacrifice my life for my sister, the family genes will still be protected. WD Hamilton called this process 'pedigree kinship' and 'inclusive fitness'. But why might our success or survival depend upon group co-operation of unrelated individuals? Naturally sacrifice for (or sharing with) a non-related in-law will have benefit for future offspring and therefore great evolutionary value, but what about others who offer no reproductive benefit?

Edward Wilson summarises this tension for the few species that exhibit social behaviour, like bees, ants, wasps, primates and humans. "Cheaters may win within the colony, variously acquiring a larger share of resources, avoiding dangerous tasks, or breaking rules; but colonies of cheaters lose to colonies of co-operators. How tightly organised and regulated a colony is depends on the number of co-operators as opposed to cheaters, which in turn depends on both the history of the species and the relative intensities of individual selection versus group selection that had occurred."

The evolutionary struggle between group and individual survival traits led to humans showing intense competition both within and between groups. Instability of group composition leads to fission to create new groups. Wilson sees humanity as in a perpetual contest that pits the products of group selection, honour, duty and virtue, against the products of individual selection, selfishness, cowardice and hypocrisy. Group skills include the expert reading of intention in others, and our culture and creative arts express the clash between group and individual needs. Both processes give us joy. Our individual happiness and wellbeing come from sleep, food, some kinds of work, exercise, sex, cognitive improvement and competition. Our five or so close family members also usually provide nurture, love and unconditional care. But much of our happiness and skills come from sympathy groups, gatherings of perhaps three times that number in social meetings – through the workplace, religion, farms, gardens, hunting, clans, books, sport, choirs, politics, loans, dance, games, nature, conservation, investment, hobbies, theatre and voluntary action.

GROUPS ARE NOT COLLECTIONS
OF INDIVIDUALS

The fallacy of group composition is that "because something is true of members of a group, it is true of the group as a whole".[35] Thinking about groups in this way leads to serious policy errors. For example, individual women in Malawi are not aware of many problems they face during maternity care, like haemorrhage, obstructed labour, convulsions or infection. But when we brought groups of 15-20 Malawian women together to discuss childbirth, their collective memory and experience of complications allowed them to identify and prioritise maternity problems as effectively as a World Health Organisation survey.[36] While governments might design expensive and unscalable policies for health education to be targeted at individual mothers, by contrast, a policy that works through local groups will not only be cheaper but also more effective because sharing of information and memories adds value continuously. Sharing through a group response after a shock or emergency protects individuals more effectively.

The policy response to the 2008 global financial crisis was a good example of the fallacy of composition. The crisis and its solution were often linked, especially by centre-right politicians and economists, to the need to tackle high levels of national and household debt. Then British Prime Minister David Cameron said repeatedly "you don't solve a debt problem by creating more debt". He won the 2015 general election so his story was widely believed. Certainly government and private debt above a certain level is probably a cause of declining economic growth. But centre-left opponents and Keynesian economists argue that the fundamental problem is one of poor demand, not simply debt, which underpins weak growth and therefore requires stimulus policies from government. Governments throughout history have ensured that their economies do not collapse because of what John Maynard Keynes called the 'paradox of thrift'. If all individual households start saving and stop spending, lack of demand means the economy will spiral downwards into a recession or slump. Keynes advised that policies for growth were needed to tackle debt even if, in the short term, these policies increased the national debt. The needs of the group conflict with those of the individual.

In fact, the US Federal Reserve and the Bank of England, and latterly the European Central Bank, have done a substitution job for governments. They embarked upon a policy of 'quantitative easing' (QE), a process of buying bonds from banks to increase liquidity in markets and to keep bond yields, and therefore interest rates, low. Right-wing observers like Niall Ferguson and Brian Riedl predicted such policies would lead to rampant inflation. They also quoted the advice of the Harvard economists Kenneth Rogoff and Carmen Reinhart, whose historical studies suggested debt levels above a threshold of 80%-90% of gross domestic product would have a negative impact on growth – until their evidence was discredited by the discovery of errors in their spreadsheets. Up to 2018, the economic evidence supported those arguing for stimulus to resist the paradox of thrift, like Nobel Prize winners Joseph Stiglitz and Paul Krugman, and Larry Summers and Martin Wolf in the Financial Times. Interest rates and inflation have remained low, and the eurozone, which initially resisted QE because of German Bundesbank fears of inflation, slipped into deflation. Where practised, fiscal austerity in countries has enhanced the economic recession in the same way that the 'rugged individualism' policies of Herbert Hoover did in the USA in the 1930s.

Vaccination is another policy area which balances the rights and benefits of individuals compared with groups. Take immunisation to protect girls from the effects of rubella. In childhood, rubella is a relatively benign disease. Many children will become infected without any expression of illness, others at worst experience a mild fever and rash. In endemic societies, more than 90% of the population will catch the disease before their fifth birthday and develop lifelong immunity. So why vaccinate? The reason is to protect the few vulnerable girls who remain uninfected. They will not be immune to the disease when they enter their childbearing years. Rubella infection during pregnancy has catastrophic effects on the foetus, causing severe, lifelong disability such as blindness, poor brain growth, learning difficulties and congenital abnormalities.

So when the MMR vaccine, combined measles, mumps and rubella, was introduced in 1988, experts knew that a high coverage, above 90%, with the new vaccine was essential. A shortfall in coverage, say to 50% or less, could actually increase the numbers of infants damaged by congenital rubella in pregnancy. That doesn't seem to make sense. If 90% coverage of a population group has almost total benefit in eradication of the problem, it would seem logical that 50% coverage would at least halve the problem. Not so. If only half the population is vaccinated early, the pool of infected children is certainly halved. But improved herd immunity means that many unvaccinated girls are less likely to get the illness in childhood, so more will be vulnerable when they become pregnant. So numbers of rubella-affected foetuses may actually increase. This tension between the needs of individuals and the community recurs in vaccination policy. For example, whooping cough (pertussis) vaccine does not protect children adequately until about 3-4 months of age. Yet infants of 1-2 months of age are at their most vulnerable to the infection. In some ways, vaccination against pertussis aims to build herd immunity. In other words, your child is vaccinated in order to protect your neighbour's children, and vice versa.

The fallacy of division is the converse fallacy of arguing that if something is true of a group, then it is also true of individuals belonging to it. For example, Article 2 of the American Bill of Rights states that 'a well-regulated militia, being necessary to the security of a free state, the right of the people to keep and bear arms shall not be infringed'. The statement is ambiguous, though, over whether what is being created is the right of the citizens collectively to keep and bear arms (i.e. to organise themselves militarily, or to sustain a militia), or the right of each individual separately, and not well regulated, to amass his or her own arsenal.[37] Such an ambiguity has plagued US politics over gun control for two centuries and arguably has led to the deaths of millions of American citizens. Homicide rates in the US are much higher than in countries where individual gun ownership is restricted. In 2014, the Centers for Disease Control and Prevention reported that 33,736 US citizens died from firearms either through homicide or suicide. Having a gun in the home does not make you safer – it doubles your risk of murder and trebles your risk of suicide.[38] Despite National Rifle Association propaganda, gun control works. Unequivocally. In Australia, Former Premier John Howard brought in strict gun control legislation after one massacre (defined as more than four people killed), the thirteenth mass shooting in 18 years. In the 18 years after strict gun control was introduced in Australia there was no massacre, and suicides and homicides involving guns fell dramatically. After all-too-frequent gun massacres, President Obama would regularly wring his hands in despair as Congress continually blocked sensible legislation to restrict gun ownership.

Further we must not confuse the value of individual rights and talents with a belief that progress results primarily from individual actions. Groups are more than networks of individuals. Their size, bonds and trust make them different in their modus operandi. The Harvard psychologists, Nicholas Christakis and James Fowler, beautifully describe modern network theories but make no reference to sympathy groups.[39] Their own research points up the difference.[40] They studied how to improve the delivery of two public health interventions – chlorine for water purification and multivitamins for micronutrient deficiencies – in Honduran villages. They wanted to understand how information and behaviour can spread through interpersonal ties so they allocated villagers randomly to one of three groups. In the first group they chose villagers at random and in the second they chose villagers with the most social ties. In the third group they targeted nominated friends of random villagers, a strategy to exploit the so-called friendship paradox of social networks whereby the friends of randomly selected individuals are more central in the network than the individuals who named them.

The nominated friend method worked best. Targeting nominated friends increased adoption of the nutritional intervention by 12% compared with random targeting. Curiously though they interpreted the results only in terms of 'interconnected individuals' without reference to village group structures or to whether or not nominated individuals might be leaders of local groups. They concluded that policymakers should "efficiently identify structurally influential individuals, as well as the people around them who are likely to be influenced, for more cost-effective campaigns". They might be right but it's a good example of a blind spot in analysis that ignores the complexity of groups, facilitators and altruism. They see behaviour change as passive dissemination of information from selected individuals rather than active mobilisation of small, positively reinforcing groups.

Psychotherapists see it differently. We might be biological individuals but psychologically we belong to groups. Our lives are a continual process of communicating with different groups interspersed with periods of being alone. Our group interactions allow us the space to consider new ideas. "Competing discourses come into conflict, with the aim to free each group member from being stuck in one's own discourse, one's own experience of the self and the world, and opens up the possibility of connecting with other discourses, other ways of being and experiencing to which one did not have previous access."[41] A group allows us to mirror each other, to share with others while, at the same time, perceiving how we are different from them. We can sort out our similarities and differences.

In 1954, Harvard's eminent psychologist Gordon Allport suggested that contact between groups could reduce inter-group prejudice. But the effect only worked as long as certain conditions were met – groups would need equal status, a common goal, a commitment to co-operation and the support of authorities and the law.[42] In 2006, a review of 515 studies by Thomas Pettigrew and Linda Tropp confirmed that inter-group contact across racial and ethnic lines did indeed reduce prejudice, even in the absence of Allport's conditions, although the effects were much greater if they were present. Group connections worked beyond racial prejudice, for example for religious, gender and educational groups. If we think for a moment, these findings have enormous social implications in a world where retreat into nationalism and xenophobia has become epidemic.

We can also tap into both the positive and negative forces within a group. Psychoanalyst Morris Nitsun refers to destructive forces as the 'anti-group.'[43] Groups contain the seeds of both constructive and destructive forces, a tension between the group and the anti-group. In psychotherapy, this tension is seen as a struggle between the social instinct and the individual super-ego. In reality, destructive forces or fantasies are not always negative. They allow group members to move on, to get through the period of 'storming' after the group is formed, and move on to the creative stages of 'norming' and 'performing'. Once the group deals with its fears and threats, and sees group members as simply others, with different ideas and their own rights and vulnerabilities, a sense of maturity sets in and the group can move on. Indeed diverse groups are invariably stronger than homogeneous ones. A recent study looked at the research literature on diversity. Homogeneity of group membership may lead to an avoidance of disagreement, less use of unique information, and overconfidence about performance. Maybe there will be more of a social than task focus, and less sensitivity to relationship conflict in a community than might be warranted.[44]

Another social reality, that we physicians like to forget, is that apparent survival gains from modern medicine arguably owe as much to social resilience as to individual technologies. Between 1900 and 1960 in western societies, over 90% of the fall in prevalence and death rates from tuberculosis and measles happened before the two vaccines were introduced. Social reorganisation, and growing household wealth and better nutrition, brought about resilience to infection through lower rates of transmission and better immunity.

Social resilience, though, is complex and hard to measure. In November 1970, cyclone Bhola hit the entire coast of Bangladesh, affecting the southern states from Chittagong to Haringhata. Officially the death toll was reported at 500,000 but the number was probably higher. Within a day or two, one million cattle, 20,000 fishing boats, 400,000 houses and

3,500 schools and college were destroyed. Maximum wind speed reached 138 miles per hour and the storm surge was nearly 11 metres high. In November 1997, disturbed weather developed south of the Andaman Islands forming tropical cyclone Sidr, of similar severity to Bhola, which once again assaulted the southern Bangladesh coastline with sustained winds of 135mph. There was much physical damage but the death toll was around 5000 people. What explains this hundredfold mortality difference between two similar cyclones? In part, group resilience. Since 1971, the newly independent Bangladesh had built early warning systems, mobilised communities and strengthened village communications. The government made people aware about what to do when a cyclone arrived and how to seek rescue and care. Their actions were political and social, much of the protection coming from everyday politics and communication through village groups.

RELATEDNESS, SELF-ORGANISATION AND CO-PRODUCTION

By sympathy we don't mean pity. In the eighteenth century, physicians and social theorists wrote about sympathy as harmony.[45] In 1772, John Gregory, the Edinburgh philosopher and professor of medicine (not a common combination today) considered sympathy "a distinguishing principle of mankind . . . which unites them into societies and attaches them to one another".[46] He was part of the school of Scottish social theorists who saw sympathy as "the great cement of human society".[47] At that time doctors used the term to mean the communication between different organs of the body. Francis Bacon, the philosopher, reported the unsympathetic effects through a mother on her baby from diet, alcohol, tobacco, too much thinking, beans and onions. He also observed that coriander consumption led to ingenuity in offspring.[48] The mood of one individual could infect others. Mothers were in sympathy with their developing fetus.[49] Oliver Sacks reports that sympathy disorders in Regency England were also thought to cause epilepsy and migraine. Seguin Henry Jackson, an Edinburgh physician, wrote A Treatise on Sympathy, described as often involuntary, like yawning or infectious laughing.[50] Sympathy could create superstition but also value during labour, with pregnant women highly sensitive to "tender and sympathetic feelings". Women who witnessed another in labour often went into labour themselves.[51] Scottish surgeon John Hunter saw the human body as "a mirror of a commercial society whose health depended upon the free movement of self-motivated entities contributing towards the larger well-being".[52] Physiology and society were in harmony when they displayed 'sympathy'.

Certainly it drove Adam Smith's theory of moral sentiments. He conceived sympathy as the observations by one person of another that would create their own morality, for better or worse. If we are MPs who operate within an expense-fiddling culture, we are more likely to fiddle our own. If we're bankers who see others getting huge bonuses we demand one for ourselves. If we are wealthy and discover that John Carnegie, Bill Gates or Warren Buffett give their fortunes away, we might do the same. The prominence given by Adam Smith to sympathy as a driving force of human behaviour is largely forgotten. His Wealth of Nations is universally quoted for his concept of 'self-interest' as a driver of economic relations. But he embraced wider notions of sympathy and co-operation, which raised human behaviour to a higher moral level and addressed situations above and beyond transactions with butchers and bakers. Scottish philosopher David Hume also resisted the moral pessimism of Thomas Hobbes and his brutish view of humanity, that "the condition of man . . . is a condition of everyone against everyone". Through our sympathy with others, said Hume, "we are taken out of ourselves". He endorsed Smith's description of the critical human faculty of 'fellow feeling'.[53]

Evolutionary theorists, though, faced a new challenge when asked to explain social and selfless behaviour. Under classical models of 'selfish genes' the only social behaviour needed to preserve the species is for humans to come together for sex and for parental care to ensure children survive. So genes that promote the fitness of an individual to gain a mate, or to ensure a child survives into adulthood and reproduces successfully, will leave replicas in the next generation. Genes that are counterproductive will be counterselected. Soon the evolutionary gang began to realise that social interaction with neighbours may also affect reproductive and survival outcomes. Selfish behaviour will, of course, mean that neighbours' genes lose out, but altruistic behaviour may mean they benefit. Given that near neighbours or relatives share a gene pool this must be factored into any theory of evolution. For example, an alarm call by a bird increases the risk of predator attack to that individual but may safeguard the wider gene pool by protecting nearby birds, some of them related.

So how can genetics explain altruistic scenarios? In 1964, WD Hamilton proposed a 'model of inclusive fitness' which suggested "no one is prepared to sacrifice his life for any single person but that everyone will sacrifice it when he can thereby save more than two brothers, or four half-brothers, or eight first cousins . . ." Conversely, while selfish behaviour against immediate siblings or close relatives will not evolve, from a gene's point of view, "it is worthwhile to deprive a large number of distant relatives in order to extract a small reproductive advantage."[54] Hamilton's theory emphasised the importance of relatedness in promoting selfless behaviour. An individual will assess his neighbour's fitness against his own according to how close his relationship is. The level of genetic relatedness is often uncertain, so the perception rather than the actuality of a neighbour's relatedness is critical. Social hierarchies and grooming behaviour help make a relatedness assessment. But other cues matter. In human societies, similarity of appearance, use of language or dialect, clothing, humour and song, and shared cultural behaviours all play a part. Strangers, or community members who change their appearance, will be attacked or relegated to a lower status. Zoologists have found many such examples. Herring gulls previously caught in nets are treated with hostility by their colony. A hive of wasps reject a colony member who has been removed and then returned in a 'wet and bedraggled condition'.[55] In modern societies we need no reminders about how immigrants are the first to face blame, rejection or attack, especially at times of economic stress or austerity. Nor that people who suffer discrimination are often 'different' in their sexual orientation, religious allegiance and disability, or because they contravene cultural norms: teetotallers, vegetarians, transgender people or supporters of the wrong football team.

If relatedness is a critical determinant of altruism and social co-operation, then the closer our social ties, the more effective and prevalent will be our selfless behaviour. A sympathy group is based on close social ties. Information is shared, decisions made collectively and strategies implemented. Trust is far greater within sympathy groups than between distant acquaintances or strangers. There are one or two variations to this rule: a post-reproductive animal or human can afford to be totally altruistic from a genetic point of view. Grandmas and elderly spinster aunts have great evolutionary value. (We shall return to the role of grandmothers in co-operative nurturing of children.) And the menopause gives a human mother more time to perform her child-rearing and educational role, freed from the duties of reproduction, which tend to limit her selfless streak.

Another threat to a selfless disposition is modern economic theory, which emphasises the virtue of selfishness in a free market of individual consumers, producing a kind of rational economic Darwinism. Many writers suggest, persuasively, that selfish economics has made the world get steadily better.[56] Almost everywhere income per head is rising, death rates falling, life expectancy increasing. They dismiss pessimists who say we are threatened by climate change and environmental threats. The future is rosy, isn't it, because of the virtue of selfishness? Not necessarily. Prosperity has broader dimensions than just the accumulation of monetary wealth expressed as the gross domestic product of nations.

Two cautionary tales undermine our hubristic belief in a selfishly, successful species. The first hinges on our understanding of the difference between stocks and flows. As the economist Sir Partha Dasgupta says: "Wealth is a stock, income (GDP) is a flow." A society's productive base comprises different types of capital wealth: manufacturing (buildings, machinery, transport), human (our health, education and skills), our knowledge (science, libraries, culture), institutions (laws, banks, professional organisations) and nature (our ecosystems, atmosphere, oceans, land). The combination of these stocks adds up to the totality of our society's wealth.

We could imagine, though, a scenario where we see improvements in the flows of the first four, but still end up less prosperous if our natural capital is so eroded that it threatens our future. In its fundamental essence our economy depends upon the natural world – the irreversible destruction of which, through rampant and selfish over-consumption, could eventually undo us. Likewise we might consider sustainable health as a stock, and life expectancy as a flow. We might enjoy a life span of around 80 years right now because of our recent past. But it might not be sustained if, in future, our stocks of productivity collapse through abuse of nature and support systems. "Civilisations die from suicide, not murder,"[57] wrote Arnold Toynbee, aware of the historical hubris of earlier empires. So a sharing, selfless approach to the 'commons' might prevent longer term catastrophe – indeed most species that abuse or over-tax their environment generally pay the price.

The second point of caution about selfishness as a determinant of wealth was beautifully phrased by Robert Kennedy in one of the great American political speeches. "The gross national product does not allow for the health of our children, the quality of their education, or the joy of their play. It does not include the beauty of our poetry or the strength of our marriages; the intelligence of our public debate or the integrity of our public officials. It measures neither our wit nor our courage; neither our wisdom nor our learning; neither our compassion nor our devotion to our country; it measures everything, in short, except that which makes life worthwhile. And it tells us everything about America except why we are proud that we are Americans."

Beyond relatedness, a critical feature of human sympathy groups is self-organisation. Self-organisation is a ubiquitous process in nature. Wherever there is chaos, islands of predictable order emerge. After the Big Bang, matter coalesced into stars, planets and galaxies. When the temperature drops below zero, water freezes into beautiful, highly ordered crystals. In living cells, proteins self-assemble using the blueprint of the genetic code held in DNA molecules. Mammals thrive using mechanisms of homeostasis, the self-organisation of a constant internal environment that protects against the vagaries of heat, cold and external threat. And to ensure survival, birds flock, bees swarm, fish shoal and primates nurture in groups.

The idea of a self-organising system as a key to cognition and social adaptation was first proposed by psychiatrist W Ross Ashby after the Second World War. Ashby was an early guru in the new science of systems, cybernetics, which applied the principles of physics and engineering to explain human intelligence. The word cybernetics is derived from the Greek meaning 'to steer' or 'to govern' and Ashby saw it as the 'art of steermanship', bringing a new science to the complexity of human behaviour and organisation. The mathematician Norbert Wiener developed the idea of 'feedback' in systems, and computer scientist Alan Turing almost managed to link cybernetics with his Automatic Computing Engine (ACE). Ashby had written to Turing asking for help. Turing wrote back to Ashby telling him that "it would be quite possible for the machine to try out variations of behaviour and accept or reject them in the manner you describe". He offered his ACE to conduct further systems experiments but sadly died before they could collaborate.

Recent studies of cognition and brain function have led to a fascinating new theory of how the mind works and how humans, indeed all living things, self-organise. All living systems must actively resist a natural tendency for disorder. By definition, they must self-organise. Neuroscientist Karl Friston and his colleagues see the brain as one part of a biological system that at every level (cell, organ, brain, and even social interaction) finds ways to minimise the use of 'free energy'.[58] The free energy principle "applies to any . . . system that resists a tendency to disorder; from single-cell organisms to social networks". The laws of thermodynamics explain how chemical and physical systems respond to changes in their environment to get the right balance between heat and work from free energy. Friston suggests living systems "negotiate a changing . . . environment in a way that allows them to endure over substantial periods of time". Biological and cognitive systems alike handle multiple and complex information flows. Like energy we can define information thermodynamically. At each level, 'active inference' is a statistical method used by a cell, organ or brain to minimise any 'surprise' arising from sensory evidence received. When the inference and sensory evidence are not aligned, a correction is made and the cell, organ or brain modifies its active inferences so as to minimise uncertainty and shocks in future. Friston applies this theory to psychiatry. Psychosis arises when brains are faulty in making active inferences about reality, what he calls the 'dysconnection hypothesis'.[59] He also suggests that a biological system does not create a model from sensory information but rather *is* a model of its local environment. For the philosopher Michael Kirchhoff, "life and mind co-emerge within the broader class of processes pertaining to the minimization of uncertainty."[60] Using this analogy we might speculate that sympathy groups are the way in which humans at the social edge maximise their efficiency (and minimise their use of social energy and uncertainty) to achieve their goals. Sympathy groups collect their own evidence to test and improve the inferences, assumptions and judgments they hold, and to deal with unpleasant surprises.

The American statistician W Edwards Deming also applied the principles of self-organisation and cybernetics when he invented the concept of total quality management, which he used to transform the post-war Japanese economy. Deming loathed the idea of industrial productivity being related to individual incentives and management by objectives. For Deming, the team was everything. If team processes were equitable and self-organising, linked to an agreed strategy, high quality outcomes would follow. In the 1950s, after the Japanese government had taken Deming's advice, the quality of their manufactured goods soared. By the 1970s, Japan had outstripped US and European industrial productivity. Japanese products from companies like Sony, Toyota and Panasonic had become market leaders.

In modern parlance, a sympathy group creates the conditions for 'co-production', a phenomenon where public servants perform better when they create an equal and reciprocal relationship with the people they serve. The Nobel Prize-winning economist, Elinor Ostrom introduced the term 'co-production' when she observed that crime rates in Chicago shot up when policemen retreated from their neighbourhood beat into their squad cars.[61] Losing their relationship with the community, and the insider knowledge it brought, meant the police were far less effective in fighting crime.

Very gradually, the idea of co-production and group care is gaining ground in the health profession, for conditions like diabetes and antenatal care.[62] In Massachusetts, doctors replaced individual appointments with group sessions, eight to 15 diabetics at a time, who shared a meal, a conversation and brief individual check-ups over two hours. It transformed the balance of power in the doctor-patient relationship. One medical resident observed: "The group has shown . . . diabetes from a patient perspective. We see . . . lab values, dietary plans, medication regimens [as] commonplace and . . . don't think twice about them. For patients, some of these things carry an enormous stigma . . . Hearing their perspective and fears has made me more aware."[63]

Sympathy groups also play a critical role in increasing the performance of economic institutions, whether in traditional societies or in complex modern multinational companies. We have moved on from the idea of classical economics being simply about prices and quantities, supply and demand, labour and incentives. Oliver Williamson won his Nobel Prize by analysing distinct social levels of influence on the economics of institutions.[64] He described four layers, and a zero layer, which help us to interpret our economic systems. The zero layer is our state of mind, how we think, the nature of our brains – whether we are male or female, young or old. We can't change this level easily. The first layer, the next level, is our organisational culture, what Williamson calls 'embeddedness'. 'Culture eats strategy for breakfast' is a growing refrain in successful companies, and brings a focus on how to create a social environment where people perform best. Sympathy groups have tremendous potential to influence this layer of our economic life, and to speed up the process of change. They also have the power to be regressive. Culture in traditional societies appears relatively slow to change, though not always. Desired family size can shift dramatically in just a generation once younger people realise the advantages of wealth and education in transforming their own prospects, which alters their perception from having many children as an asset to seeing them as a liability. Likewise, cultures can turn in on themselves. The rise of reactionary Islamic movements like Isis in Syria and Iraq, and Boko Haram in Nigeria are, in part, drawn from the desire to resist the influence of alien cultures. They resent western approaches to religion, education and female empowerment.

Williamson's second layer is the rules of the game, especially around property rights and how these are agreed and legislated. These may take years to reform through relatively slow political processes but sympathy groups may play their part in ensuring rights are enforced for marginalised and powerless people. The institutions of government, regulations, contract laws and political systems form a third layer, again heavily influenced by culture and groups. In Nepal, the constituent assembly formed in 2007 after the peace agreement between the Maoists and the political parties struggled for eight years to create a new constitution. The final version, in 2017, remains contested widely. Many groups see the old, high-caste patriarchal powers simply reinforcing their dominance.

Only then do we get to the traditional fourth layer of economics working through prices, supply quantities and incentives. Sympathy groups also remain critical at this lowest layer of production and consumption. They do not follow a rigid classical score of notes and tempo guides. Groups self-organise like jazz around a loose improvisation framework of chords and progressions. They can increase or impede economic efficiency, taking account of traditions, religious beliefs and cultural tastes. And they may also be the best way to stimulate change in productivity and consumption patterns through sympathy group practices such as quality circles or viral marketing.

Immediate Return Societies

CIRCLES OF ACQUAINTANCE

Our modern pre-occupation with individualism, ideology and statism leaves a big hole in our understanding of the human condition. The story of the past five millennia is only a brief fraction of the emergence of humanity. During human prehistory egalitarian groups of gatherers and hunters shared and co-operated for survival. Social evolution progressed through stages from nomadic band, to tribe, to chiefdom, to state. Only in the past ten milliennia did cultures become more complex and hier-archical, with rising social inequality and the emergence of towns and state.[65] Hunter-gatherer bands, egalitarian in nature, were the basic unit and style of social existence for most of our progress over the past 200,000 years. Selfishness was socially taboo. We survived through groups managing meagre rations collectively. The argument about whether humans are essentially selfish or kind arose only with civilised history and with the formation of more complex governance structures and states.

Archaic Homo sapiens species, including *Homo heidelbergensis*, *Homo rhodesiensis* and *Homo neanderthalensis*, emerged over 500,000 years ago, and modern Homo sapiens about 200,000 years ago. We occasionally mated with our cousins: new genetic studies suggest modern man inter-bred with two groups of ancient humans, Neanderthals and the Denisovans, a group who lived in Russia and East Asia and were genetically distinct from the Neanderthals. In Europe, Neanderthals survived until about 40,000 years ago,[66] probably wiped out by a combination of genocide and infection. Another Homo variant, the Red Deer Cave people of China, survived until 11,500 years ago.

So what accounts for the success of modern humans? How did we manage to endure repeated climate catastrophes which, 70,000 years ago, reduced the human population to only 10,000 people in East Africa, with as few as 1000-2000 breeding pairs. Why is it that Neanderthals and other Homo variants died out? What accounted for the great breakout, 70,000 or so years ago, when modern humans left their small, vulnerable population base in Africa, and migrated out to global reach and dominance? Can technology and innovation alone explain our rise? Or did our social skills drive our success, aided and abetted by emergent technologies?

In the 21st century we have discovered much more about the pre-agricultural era of the cultural and social development of Homo sapiens. Whether the breakout of humans from Africa to India and Europe took place before a massive volcanic eruption 74,000 years ago, or in the aftermath during the next 10,000-15,000 years, is a matter of dispute. Stephen Oppenheimer from Oxford University believes the migration via southern Arabia happened probably before the Toba eruption in Indonesia.[67] This natural disaster caused six years of a volcanic winter, a collapse in our population, and a 'bottleneck' in human evolution. The eruption further exacerbated climate change. Sea levels fell by 200 feet below their present level as glaciation advanced. The forests of Africa declined, the deserts expanded, and the bitter cold dried out the savannahs.

Robert Foley and Marta Mirazón Lahr from Cambridge University disagree with Oppenheimer.[68] They suggest that the first migration via a southern route into India did not happen until much later, nearer 60,000 years ago. Neither estimate affects the consensus that this breakout coincided with clear evidence of a rapid advance in human culture, socialisation, and innovation. Writer Richard Klein called it the cultural 'Big Bang'. Sceptical academics preferred that cultural evolution progressed steadily, with new strategies and solutions developed by social processes on an 'as needed basis'.[69] One view is that a series of random pre-adaptations came together in a glorious sequence. An expanded forebrain to retain memories, a prehensile thumb to allow skilled manipulation, the skill to use fire, hunting in groups with tools and weapons, discovering how to cook digestible, high protein food, and the development of simple agriculture were critical steps along our evolutionary path. But they were not key ingredients for our cultural success. The Neanderthals who lived alongside us until 40,000 years ago had even larger brains, similar prehensility, our upright posture, simple tools, use of fire and basic agriculture. But they didn't progress. In almost 200,000 years their social progress was almost static. Eventually they disappeared, in the same way as their paleontologically fleeting predecessors.

For the biologist Edward Wilson, the secret of our success lay in our capacity for group thinking and altruism, which allowed a more rapid method of social evolution. Altruism became part of our division of labour. Social groups that crossed gender and generational boundaries came together, with surprising equality, to address local challenges. This onset of 'eusociality' allowed enormous expansion of *H.sapiens* from a fragile population base in East Africa to a current global population of over seven billion, living in every continent and climatic region. "The pathway to eusociality was charted by a contest between selection based on the relative success of individuals within groups versus relative success among groups. The strategies of this game were written as a complicated mix of closely calibrated altruism, co-operation, competition, domination, reciprocity, defection, and deceit."[70]

Altruism and eusociality are surprisingly rare among animal species. Humans, some primates, ants, wasps, bees, termites and voles are among the few to succeed. Social co-operation and division of labour arise primarily to defend a nest. For this to happen, an unusual confluence of chance, necessity, and pre-adaptation must arise. When it does happen it confers a massive evolutionary advantage. We must not forget that we have Stone Age brains. There's no reason to believe our brains have changed anatomically in the past 100,000 years. So altruism is probably ancient. A recent study played a variation on the ultimatum game with children and chimpanzees.[71] The ultimatum is that both partners must agree on the distribution of a reward if they are both to receive it. Humans are typically generous. Primates aren't. But the variation of the ultimatum game enabled individuals to choose between two tokens that, with their partner's co-operation, could be exchanged for rewards, one providing equal rewards, the other favouring the chooser. Children and chimpanzees behaved the same. If their partner's co-operation was required, they split the rewards equally. With passive partners they preferred the selfish option. These results suggest our human sense of fairness must have a longer history than we thought.

Figure 16. Namibia, Eastern Bushmanland, Tsumkwe. A band of !Kung hunter-gath-erers makes a stealthy approach towards an antelope

Humans have always lived in groups. They give us many evolutionary advantages. Our ancestor hunters shared crucial information with group members when stalking deer or hunting down birds or monkeys. When the world was colder, before Lake Huron flooded 8000 years ago, groups of Stone Age hunters herded caribou through long parapets of stones towards boulders, behind which archers lay in waiting.[72] Extended family groups improved not only hunting but also the ability to farm for food.

They acquired capital or pooled resources for new economic opportunities. Groups also provided access to a broader selection of partners for reproduction, and maintained social taboos around consanguinous marriage to prevent inbreeding. They played a central role in protecting ethnic or tribal identity, and political and union groups would nurture the solidarity needed to stand up to landlords, exploitative employers and aristocrats.

Sympathy groups, made up of those neighbours you might meet regularly, were critical for hunting, forest gathering, harvesting, singing or collective decision-making and problem solving. Their size was manageable, they brought diversity of generation and skill and background, and relative egalitarianism. They brought a huge range of evolutionary social advantages. They co-ordinated tribal activities, developed leadership and followership, divided up extrovert and introvert roles, brought masculine skills to warfare, feminine skills to peacemaking, built an oral transactional memory, and developed a theory of mind based on an empathy with others. Groups organised the exchange of products and people, and created status through signalling, emotions, self-esteem, and competitive altruism.

Of course, groups could create disaster as well. Groupthink is a problem where cohesion and loyalty override the sharing or debate of accurate information. For example, the financial collapse of 2008 was caused by bankers' 'irrational exuberance' in valuing mortgage credit derivatives way too high, partly through miscalculation or malpractice, but largely because others did the same. Groupthink among western leaders (French President Jacques Chirac a notable exception) led to the 2003 Iraq invasion, with insufficient consideration of the potential for a post-Saddam implosion of tribal conflict. And the Nepal earthquake of 2015 had been predicted by seismologists for two decades but groupthink among elites in Nepal created a fatalistic assumption it might never happen, or that building resilience would be ineffective.

Tremendous social and biological pressures ensure we remain loyal to the group through tribality, custom, religion, music, dance, and laughter. Collective decision-making in sympathy groups was central to hunter-gatherer groups. Later they became a key, if less noticeable, element of the governance structures of modern civilisation and the formation of the nation state. Fear of strangers and ethnocentrism may have arisen through the protective need to avoid pathogens carried by foreigners, but group diplomacy also mediated peacemaking and reconciliation.

One intriguing debate is whether human language emerged primarily for social bonding rather than for the exchange of information. Most analysts assumed that information sharing drove its evolution but language is essential for the formation and maintenance of social groups. Three possible mechanisms are offered for the evolutionary advantage from social bonding. The 'gossip hypothesis' proposes that sharing information about others makes living in large groups far more practical than if we had to have individual one-to-one interactions with everybody.[73] Gossip ensures social news is transmitted more effectively and that judgments about potential mates cover a wider range of options. The 'social contract' hypothesis suggests that language-mediated contracts over marriage offered some protection for those hunting men worried about having their women and paternity stolen by rivals when they were away.[74] The ability to arrange a marriage verbally confers evolutionary advantage. The 'Scheherazade' hypothesis, in contrast, sees language as an aphrodisiac. Flamboyant and amusing language by both men and women is a strong indicator of intelligence, and a powerful reason for sexual selection.[75] Being charming guarantees your genetic line continues.

Whatever the mechanism, the social bonding theory of the emergence of language is supported by snippets of evidence. In memory experiments, people remember social stories far better than ones that simply contain technical information.[76] Second, if language was primarily about information exchange, why does language fragment so easily into dialects and eventually form new mother tongues? Dialects are a mark of community and tribe, indicating quickly and clearly to others the social group to which you belong. In Nancy Mitford's The Pursuit of Love, a coruscating novel about the landed gentry of England in the 1930s, language is repeatedly used as a hallmark of class and suitability for marriage. The preservation of wealth and aristocratic status through betrothal is paramount. The Radletts, headed by Lord Alconleigh, use their circles of acquaintance with family (five), weekend guests (15), the hunt (50) and coming out balls during the deb season (150 or 500) to ensure that marriage of daughters is appropriate, socially acceptable and virginal. Later analysed as the use of U (upper class) and non-U language (middle class), the heroine's uncle Matthew, Lord Alconleigh, disapproves of non-U suitors who use the word lounge instead of drawing room, dinner instead of lunch, glasses instead of spectacles, and radio instead of wireless.

What is more, language distribution varies with geography. In high latitudes, where the growing season is short, the need to trade for resources becomes more important, so a common language covers a broader area and population. In the tropics, where food is abundant, languages are more parochial and diverse, reflecting the lesser need in ancient times for social trade over distances.

We prefer to believe otherwise but social stratification in marriage remains alive and kicking. One has only to read the society pages of Hello magazine and the Tatler in the UK, Town & Country in the USA, and The Hindu in India to witness the hunt for tribal union. A recent survey in India revealed that an astonishing 95% of people still marry along caste lines. Social flexibility in the west seems greater but not as much as we think. In fact, in Britain marriage across classes is in decline. A 2013 report from the Institute for Public Policy Research showed that one third of women born in 1958 had a partner from the same class as themselves whereas 38% married up and 23% married down.[77] But 45% of women born in 1970 married into the same class; and 56% of those born between 1976 and 1981 married into the same class, with only 16% marrying up. It's noteworthy that women appear to find generous and trustworthy men sexually more attractive.[78] Of course, men might be faking it. A recent study showed single men adopt co-operative behaviours as a way to successfully attract a mate, which means that co-operation is partly sexually selected.[79]

For so-called primitive hunter-gatherer groups, equality, sharing and 'immediate return' living are universal features. Anthropologist James Woodburn highlights the nature of immediate return cultures: "A system of material production for immediate use without significant storage or investment; an egalitarian ideology and an egalitarian practice in which even intergenerational relationships are nearly equal; a system of social relations and social groupings minimising dependence and stressing direct individual access to material resources, to knowledge and skills with these resources, this knowledge and these skills not controlled or allocated by people of senior generation; an emphasis on individual freedom to select on a day-to-day basis one's residential and other associates; a system of transactions focused on entitlement to share other people's recognised property, the recognised yield of other people's labour."[80] Co-operation among hunter-gatherers was a more dominant characteristic than competition. The success of this system, over tens of thousands of years, was not fundamentally based on predation, entrepreneurship and competition. Indeed such a system would probably not have survived. Hunter-gatherers, by and large, prized the fact that societies were made of equals: "Equals in wealth, equals in power, equality is perceived as meritorious, as worthy, as honourable, and inequality as unacceptable, as disreputable and even as evil and dangerous."

Though their style of life appears 'simple' and is often described as 'primitive', hunter-gatherers have their own complex patterns of work, inheritance, marriage rules, polygamy, polyandry (in high Himalayan groups), matriliny and patriarchy. And their societies survived through managed sympathy groups that exhibited astonishing equality. Even in the early Upper Paleolithic of the Cro-Magnon Aurignacian culture, hunting by men contributed far less to daily calorie intake than the gathering of wild fruit, fungi and vegetables by women in groups. Most ate a diet largely of plant material, fruit, vegetables and nuts, supplemented by occasional feasts of animal fat and protein. The American anthropologist, Marshall Sahlin, threw new light on the hunter-gatherer when, in 1966, he described them controversially as the original affluent society,[81] with a "marvellously varied diet" based on local flora and fauna, and better nutrition and more leisure time than most people in the industrial era. Their society was the "Zen road to affluence, which states that human material wants are finite and few, and technical means unchanging but on the whole adequate." Indeed Sahlin saw poverty based on social relations rather than a lack of goods. "The world's most 'primitive' people have few possessions, but they are not poor. Poverty is not a certain small amount of goods, nor is it just a relation between means and ends; above all it is a relation between people. Poverty is a social status. As such it is the invention of civilisation. It has grown with civilisation, at once as an invidious distinction between classes and more importantly as a tributary relation."

Sahlin calculated from comparative studies of contemporary hunter-gatherer groups, like the !Kung, a San people living in the Kalahari Desert in southern Africa, that working patterns were relatively light, somewhere between 20 and 40 hours a week. The tribes showed equality of the sexes, freedom of expression, much laughter, a lack of hierarchy, and violence only when tribal groups encroached upon each other's territory or resources.

The anthropologist Catherine Panter-Brick showed something similar in her studies of physical activity among the agricultural Tamang peoples in rural Nepal, with long periods of relative leisure in the post-harvest season. Women, though, always worked harder than men for the collection of fodder and water and household chores and their days were relentless and arduous when the planting season came.[82] Just as hunter-gatherers are characterised by relative equality of the sexes, we found shared decision-making in groups, individual freedoms and laxity in sexual choice and behaviour, and a strong ethic of nurturing for others within the tribal, lower caste or ethnic groups we worked with in Nepal. Groups like the Tamang and Magars were often outwardly happier in their quotidian lives than the higher castes.

FOOD, WINE, WOMEN AND SONG

The transition from hunter-gatherer to farmer as our livelihood was neither sudden nor smooth. Agriculture started 12000 years ago in the Levant, in west Asia and later south-east Europe and the Americas, when seven 'founder crops', wheat, barley, peas, lentils, flax, chick peas and bitter vetch emerged in the archaeological record. Today, two billion people depend upon subsistence farming or landlessness, livelihoods where the gathering of wild fruits and herbs and hunting of wild animals provide supplementary food or income. The transition shifted our mindset much more than how we ate or used implements, profoundly affecting our daily lives in ways we may not realise. For 95% or more of our evolutionary history we had lived in 'immediate return' social systems. Modern hunter-gatherer and aboriginal groups still practise immediate return with encroaching 'delayed return' habits. Many problems they face in making a transition to agricultural or industrial lifestyles stem from the psychological imprint of 'immediate return' thinking.

The transition to farming enabled humans to have a larger and more stable source of food through storage of staple crops. But it had a price. With changing nutrition, our growth and development deteriorated and the risk of infection rose. Diversity of diets fell. Some 10,000 to 7,000 years before present – defined as 1950 - during the early Holocene period, the average stature of adult foragers in the Indian region was 178-180 cms. In the period 6500-2900 years before present, as agriculture took hold, average stature fell by around 8 cms. By the middle of the twentieth century, after the colonial period of impoverishment and exploitation, Indian women's stature reached its nadir at around 160-162 cms, almost 20 cms less than their hunter-gatherer forebears.[83] Smaller mothers have smaller pelvises so they bear smaller babies. Average birth weights fell by as much as 500 grammes or more. This weight loss had short-term survival advantages for adaptation to a more thrifty world, but longer-term metabolic consequences which we see in our modern world. Greater longevity of low birth weight babies sees their short-term advantage for survival converted into a longer-term vulnerability to degenerative diseases like diabetes, high blood pressure, heart attacks and strokes. In south Asia today these diseases have reached epidemic proportions, exacerbated by the carbo-rush of confectionery and junk food, the sedentary lifestyle of urban migrants and the appeal of fossil fuel transport over Shanks's pony or bicycle.

Women's groups hold a collective knowledge of foraging in rural societies like Baglung but it has died out in urban populations. Group foraging skills and knowledge generate an astonishingly varied diet: clover dandelion, alfalfa, large burdock leaves, wild asparagus, cat-tails with their juicy roots and their soft stems collected down by the marshy banks of a river, amaranth, and chicory with its pale blue flowers and edible roots which makes a hot drink as an alternative to coffee. We can add chicory's cousin the curly endive, chickweed, curled dock, boiled dandelion, pennycress and watercress, purple fireweed, green seaweed and kelp for coastal populations, broadleafed marsh plantain, wood and sheep sorrel, clovers and white mustard. In the Middle Paleolithic, Aurignacian family groups would burn woodfires in shallow pits to heat large stones, keeping a store of energy for up to 48 hours. Broths and stews and infusions could be made in hide containers heated over stones. Food would be flavoured with wild herbs: rosemary, mint, lavender, sweet cicely, comfrey and yarrow. Freshwater crayfish and shrimp, newts and frogs and snails, grubs and caterpillars, and many kinds of insect provided wild, collectible animal protein. Biscuits were cooked from mixtures of pollen and nuts such as almonds. Recently my colleague Naomi Saville studied the poorest of poor groups in southern Nepal to ask pregnant women about their common foods. She found that snails were their largest source of animal protein, and foraging for wild vegetables provided much of their dietary diversity.

Another role of sympathy groups is to celebrate culture in song, dance and painting. Since 1990, archaeological research has rewritten our description of 'prehistory' and the lives of pre-agricultural peoples, and transformed our understanding of the origins of culture, art and language. Archaeologists found rich evidence for cultural diversity from the Upper Paleolithic, during the millennia between 60,000 and 10,000 years ago, after human migration from Africa into Europe, the eastern Mediterranean, Asia, the Americas and Australasia.[84] Our distant ancestors played musical instruments in the form of bone flutes, painted their bodies and used cosmetics for rituals and celebrations. Music is often the first expression of sympathy groups coming together around a task. When foraging, sympathy groups of women sing to relax, to bond and sometimes to scare off predators. One can watch Baka women from Gbiné in the Cameroon singing their traditional polyphonic 'Yelli' songs, or the singing of their relatives, Aka Pygmies of central African tropical forests in the Congo.[85] Polyphony is a texture of two or more melodic voices, rather than homophony music with just one voice or with a voice accompanied by chords. Studies of 'cantometrics' by ethnomusicologists like Alan Lomax and Victor Grauer track ancestral singing styles to these hunter-gatherer songs.[86] They describe the songs as "interlocked, with maximum vocal blend, polyphony, precisely co-ordinated rhythms, yodelled, with open, relaxed throats, no embellishment, short phrases and meaningless vocables". Genetically, the Bushmen of west Africa and tropical Pygmies of the Congo diverged from a common African ancestor, around 70,000-100,000 years ago. Yet their singing styles in sympathy groups are too similar to have been independently invented. Likewise, singing styles of Northern Eurasian Paleosiberian hunter groups, from the Samis of Lapland to the Ainu of northern Japan, share several characteristics with Pygmies, Bushmen and each other: repetitive texts, wide intervals, relatively open voices. Improvised group singing goes back to the earliest stages of human evolution and echoes reverberate in the twenty-first century.

Figure 17. Group of Naro bushman (San) women digging up an edible root, Central Kalahari, Botswana

Art was expressed in the form of ivory or ceramic Venus figurines, or therianthropic carvings showing the metamorphosis of humans into animals. Rituals of the forms used by shamans today were evident in funeral relics. Shamanism may have been a solitary profession not just because resident groups were small but to justify behaviour that is considered psychotic in modern communities.[87] Shamanism is often the chosen profession for psychologically troubled members of communities. For tens of millennia shamans were the diplomats to the spirit world and to sister species. Using psychoactives, trances and self-hypnosis, they took on the subtle and dangerous task to align and appease hidden and supernatural forces. As village organisation progressed, from chiefdoms and hill rajas to cities and states, and trade and migration expanded, the individual shaman was absorbed into castes of priests with a hierarchy and code of conduct, usually sanctioned by leaders.

Bone relics illustrate the 'lunarchy' of early European hunter-gatherers. Some bones marked with lunar calendar signs indicate a mature understanding of the seasons, and the waxing and waning of success in animal kills with the visibility of the full moon. Early hunter-gatherers kept lunar calendars carved on bone or cave walls. In 2005 in Scotland a 10,000-year-old array of 12 pits and arc was discovered at Warren Field in Aberdeenshire. The site aligns along the midwinter solstice, and was calibrated annually to adjust for the passage of time indicated by the Moon, the solar year and its seasons.[88] Hunting reached its zenith with the full moon, when night-time visibility enabled skilled sympathy groups of men to encircle bison, reindeer and the odd mammoth.

We can't know for sure how groups of the pre-agricultural Paleolithic took decisions. But we know that contemporary hunter-gatherers and marginalised rural people use sympathy groups to organise collectively, practise customary law, and defend in groups against predators and rivals. Decisions about food and fodder and harvest and water are within the kinship of the house. But, without state governance, individual rights or taxation, they take important decisions through ancestral sympathy groups. In rural Nepal these matters included a horoscope to decide the most auspicious time of a betrothment or wedding, and how to respond to a death, flood, or health crisis, and the underlying bewitchment that caused the problem. One critical decision was when to plant, once early rains arrived, to maximise the yield of a harvest. Plant too early and the seedlings lack vigour, grow poorly or attract water mould and predatory birds. Too late and the plants suffer from high temperature panicle blight, more pest diseases and lower grain quality. Farming groups consult and share ideas. The sacrifice of a valuable goat as rain-maker was costly but sometimes necessary.

In animist and tribal communities in the Nepal middle hills, many sympathy groups remain within the clan. A shaman, (lama or bombo or dhami-jhankri) is accompanied by other clan members and leaders. For Hindu caste groups, the hierarchy is led by a Brahmin priest, perhaps a Chettri or Newar bureaucrat, and assorted neighbours, moneylenders or skilled labour. Mats are brought, tea or rice wine (raksi) served, and matters discussed on clay verandahs or on a stone chautara in the shade of a pipal tree. And the functionality of groups varies. Sometimes a headstrong or drunken household head would tyrannise and rant. In the partyless panchayat era of King Birendra political tensions were unspoken but often present. Supporters of Indian-style Congress democracy (kangresis) and royalists were wary of one another. More often, mothers-in-laws dominated and cajoled. Sometimes relatives would take charge, or occasionally a literate son, returned from the army or an education. Groups gossiped about local scandal, elopements, separations and fights, or even the occasional murder or suicide, before getting down to business.

In evolutionary terms, women do gain sexual advantages from sympathy groups and overnight bands. In a campsite band of maybe 50 humans, reproductive-aged women would naturally synchronise their menstrual cycles around the exact rhythm of the moon at 29 days. This length is the precise multiple times nine of the gestational period of a full-term infant. Synchrony has advantages for women. No woman wants a partner who will get her pregnant only to disappear for another conquest.[89] Groups of women want to resist philanderers. Reproductive synchrony enables reproductive levelling, so that men are around at the same time and improve a woman's chance of choosing a generous and trustworthy monogamous partner.[90]

An interesting feature of our sympathy groups of women in Africa and south Asia was that, once shyness dissipated, meetings began with laughter, gossip and, often, a song. Once I stayed overnight in the house of a village headman in a remote village of Mchinji district in Malawi. After dusk, there was an impromptu choral performance by a 'band' of about 15 women. They arrived, swaying in unison, laughing and ululating. Then, in the moonlight, they sang beautiful synchronised and euphonic songs in the Chichewa language. They would sway, step and sidle in perfect time. I had long wondered whether the inherent rhythms and incomparable dancing of African villagers was instinctive. This proved it. Women called from their houses without warning had launched themselves into a musical ensemble of sophisticated harmonies comparable to a cathedral chorale.

I asked the headman how they did it, was it something that Malawian women were born with?

"No I don't think so," he said. "Maybe it's because they practise four or five times a week."

I hadn't realised the centrality of the choir in village and ecumenical life for these Catholic, Protestant and Evangelical churchgoers.

So why are laughter and singing so important? Relaxed social laughter generates feelings of wellbeing and emotional comfort. In experiments, Dunbar's group studied the biology of laughing and showed that pain thresholds (used as a measure of endorphin release) were elevated after laughter, compared with control subjects who didn't laugh. They wrote: "Because humans do not laugh readily when watching even the funniest performances alone, and laughter is 30 times more likely to occur in social contexts than when alone, all subjects were tested in groups".[91] Endorphins buffer humans against the effects of physiological and psychological stress. Group laughter plays a central role in social bonding through the opiate effect of endorphins released within the brain.

Laughter also affects other brain chemicals such as dopamine and oxytocin, the most fashionable of hormones. Oxytocin controls childbirth through contractions of the uterus, regulates breastfeeding through let-down of milk, and bathes a mother's brain to change her behaviour. Under the influence of oxytocin, breastfeeding animals such as bitches or cows will nurture their litter but attack outsiders who come too close, a good example of Darwin's 'parochial altruism'. But oxytocin is not simply the cuddle or love hormone. It might also promote group-serving dishonesty. In one experiment, giving oxytocin or placebo to volunteers revealed that those receiving the drug lied more to benefit their groups, even without expecting a favour in return.[92] The neurochemistry of bonding and co-operation might also shape dishonesty, and turn collaboration into corruption. Another study by the same group showed a rise in ethnocentrism. Volunteers given oxytocin expressed more in-group favouritism and derogatory remarks about non-group outsiders.[93] Maybe our fashionable hormone supports inter-group violence - or an urge to build inter-tribal walls in China, Berlin, the Scottish border and, quite soon, Mexico.

Nonetheless the social advantages of groups are obvious. Religious or therapy groups have always offered solace and peace and relaxation and friendship. They help us in our spiritual quest for meaning and wellbeing. Church groups and choirs, and recreation groups for sport and dance, yoga and meditation bring harmony and relaxation to tired minds. Much of what I enjoy for recreation takes place in small groups, gatherings with extended family, football matches with my children to join a small group of regular supporters, yoga classes with my wife, a book group of seven local, lonely men (active for 17 years, 180 books read, and endless, pointless discussion about our football clubs), third saxophone in the Blue Frogs soul band (until it broke up) and a social cricket team called the Jardines as autocratic president. Only walking and cycling are individual pleasures. And yoga alone in a hotel room to recover from jet lag is less enjoyable than yoga in a group with a teacher. I'm told the prana flows differently when yoga is practised in a group.

CO-OPERATIVE NURTURING

A popular fallacy is that hunter-gatherer groups had brutal levels of inter-group conflict. Murder, cannibalism or death in battle were posited as the commonest causes of short life expectancy. Anthropologists proposed that group skills in fighting were the main evolutionary mechanism for selection and survival. Groups, especially those sub-groups that focus on fighting and security, provide protection from other groups. A well-trained battalion with its focused aggression is much better than disorganised vigilantes or hooligans. Large mobs of testosterone-fuelled supporters fighting after a Boston Bruins ice-hockey match, or an Eagles v Dallas NFL game, or a Millwall v West Ham local derby, would stand little chance against a small and focused platoon of Marines or a troop from the Brigade of Gurkhas. Discipline counts for more than naked aggression.

But little evidence shows violent death as the dominant driver of poor survival among our ancestors, or of chronic conflict before 15,000 years ago. For tens of thousands of years, human hunter-gatherers operated in small bands of families, with primitive weaponry, and no ability to support an army. By and large, hunter-gatherers are peaceful with adequate access to territory. When population pressure caused encroachment of agriculture, violent conflict became more common. Then groups would fight with the flexibility, courage and ferocity of modern insurgents. In India and Nepal many feared the forest dwellers, whose legendary terror and demonic behaviour created a pantheon of demons for the caste stories of the agrarians. Forest dwellers themselves had a hierarchy of survival methods, from pure hunting to shifting cultivation, with varying degrees of skilful horticulture and sedentary cultivation. The Chepang of Nepal and the numerous tribal groups across India, like the Santal and the Ho, display this spectrum of livelihood today, albeit with a big shift towards sedentary cultivation. Native Americans, the Mbuti Pygmies of the Congo and the Batek of Malaysia practise forest-based agriculture but none show particular aggression.

A more persuasive argument is that co-operation has greater evolutionary advantage in nurturing children for survival than winning battles to the death. As we've seen, equality does not mean that everyone necessarily does the same work. Women gather and nurture, men hunt and protect. A picture emerges less of solitary mothers quietly rearing their children while their men are away chasing a kill, than a 'village raising a child'. The Harvard anthropologist Sarah Hrdy writes of co-operative breeding, where the presence of grandmothers, sisters, group women, fathers and 'as if' kin provide collective care and support for child-rearing, each, to a greater or lesser extent, contributing to child survival.[94] She believes child-rearing style is more important than intergroup conflict to explain the evolutionary power of groups. Altruism's midwife was not warfare but nurture in the dangerous months of infancy. Is child-rearing the origin of our intense, social world? Does the risk of child mortality explain why hunter-gatherers avoid competition and protect social fabric by "reflexively shunning, humiliating, even ostracising or executing those who behave in stingy, boastful or anti-social ways".

For sure, co-operative nurturing in the animal kingdom is uncommon. Only 9% of birds and 3%-4% of mammals practise it. African wild dogs do. They return to a nest with pre-digested meat that they regurgitate to several pups, including not only their own. Co-operative animals buffer their young from starvation, which permits long periods of post-weaning or fledging. Human childhood is long. Our ancestors faced a more pressing challenge than being wiped out by neighbours. Our larger brains, body size and cognitive development meant the nutritional price tag for rearing a child, about 13 million calories, is more than a mother can provide. Furthermore, our inter-birth interval at three to four years is about half what you find in other apes, so the nutritional demands of siblings can double or treble the calories a family needs. Sole care by a mother, without shared care and provisions, cannot produce young who survive. She needs help.

A quarter of primates practise some kind of shared care but only in tamarins and marmosets (callitrichids) do we find extensive provisioning by others.[95] Members of the callitrichid troupe will hunt for beetles and frogs – as much as 90% of baby food may come from other 'alloparents'. Their babies, often twins, are carried by adult males while mothers and others forage for food. Other apes, though, like chimpanzees, show no maternal tolerance to others taking their babies. Chimp mothers remain in skin-to-skin contact with their infants for six months and attack other troupe members who interfere. Generally chimps are indifferent to the wellbeing of others, especially unrelated group members. For chimps, sharing is simply scrounging or tolerated theft.[96]

Studies among the Efe tribes in the Congo show babies are held by between five and 24 allomothers, 14 different caretakers, and spend 39% of their time with others from birth.[97] Ethnographer Paula Ivey Henry suggests infants with the most allomothers are more likely to survive to the age of three.[98] Anthropologists Ruth Mace and Rebecca Sear went back to the records of Mandinka horticulturist families who had been studied for 50 years at a Medical Research Council field site in the Gambia, West Africa.[99] Of 2300 children under five, almost 40% had died. If the child had older sisters or a grandmother living nearby, death rates of children halved. And after the age of two, death of a mother did not threaten survival. Sisters, grandmas and neighbours could now cope with an orphan.

We should note that context is important. When Sear studied women in Malawi from matrilineal villages (those with the unusual inheritance system which passes property down the female line, from mother to daughter) she found that related grandmothers had no effect on child mortality; indeed girl infants died more in families where the grandmother was present.[100] Sear speculates that where a grandmother must think about all her grandchildren, resource allocation is at the expense of some, particularly girls, who, in this matrilineal setting, create greater competition for resources within the family than boys.

Grandmas do deliver the goods when it comes to foraging. Among Hadza hunter-gatherers in the eastern Rift Valley of Tanzania the most prolific food gatherers were elderly, hard-working grandmothers.[101] Grandmothers are of particular importance for child-rearing.[102] In most species female longevity is the same as their fertile period. In humans, post-menopausal women live for several more decades. When grandmas are present at home, they build a greater sensitivity of mothers to infant needs, to more secure infant attachment,[103] and to better cognitive outcomes for the child at four years.[104]

And a mother's absence may be crucial, so she can forage or trade to ensure stability of food supplies. Hunters often fail. When they do, women foragers maintain food security. Two thirds of hunter-gatherer possessions

94

– clothes, beads, knives, pots – are transitory, so when times are hard, women travel to trade their possessions for food. Women were dead keen to exchange with particularly good hunters because meat would always be shared. A classic anthropological treatise Marcel Mauss's 'Essai sur le don' (The Gift)[105] showed that long distance gift exchange cycles between groups, not simply to share but to maintain crucial social networks, were common as early as the Middle Stone Age, from 50,000 to 130,000 years ago. "In the systems of the past we do not find simple exchange of goods, wealth and produce through markets established among individuals. For it is groups, and not individuals, which carry on exchange, make contracts, and are bound by obligations; the persons represented in the contracts are moral persons, clans, tribes, and families; the groups, or the chiefs as intermediaries for the groups, confront and oppose each other. Further, what they exchange is not exclusively goods and wealth, real and personal property, and things of economic value. They exchange rather courtesies, entertainments, ritual, military assistance, women, children, dances, and feasts."

After death, the networks of the parental group were maintained and gifts exchanged. "Every human society depends on some system of exchange and mutual aid, but foragers have elevated exchange to a core value and an elaborate art form.' To expand networks of exchange, foragers would trace their relatedness and kinship through both mothers and fathers. In ancient days, therefore, a woman without relatives would be a less advantageous mate. We might observe that twenty-first century humans accumulate things, whereas our ancestors accumulated social relations.

Men also did their share in child-care activities. Hunter-gatherer men spend more time in nurturing their children than modern fathers. The American anthropologist Barry Hewlett observed that Aka Pygmies in the Congo spent almost half their time within reach of their young infants. And children themselves bring powerful social genes to the party. We might share 98% of our genetic code with other apes, chimps and bonobos, but Esther Hermann and her colleagues found that although the cognitive skills of two-and-a-half-year-old children and chimpanzees were comparable for the physical world, the children were far more sophisticated than chimps when dealing with their social world.[106]

Co-operative nurturing ensures that social skills needed in the next generation are firmly imprinted in children. Multiple carers build capacity for a child to take multiple perspectives. The ability of children to understand that others have their own intentions and perspectives is contagious. If older siblings are present, children appear to have a more sophisticated 'theory of mind' by the age of three and improved social skills at older ages.[107] Natural selection would tend to favour children with perspective taking, mutual tolerance, social learning and sharing. There is a price to pay though for the co-operative nature of humans, tamarins and marmosets. If a mother has access to babysitters there's a risk she won't return. Both callitrichids and humans can abandon their babies at birth. They are also the only primates where mothers may harm their own newborn infants, if they lack social support.

So why is it just us, human primates, who have the tremendous benefits of co-operation? Babies are born to connect. The basic wiring for identifying with others is certainly present in newborn apes but they remain rather autistic. Human babies who imitate and show interactive engagement are rewarded with smiles and cuddles whereas adult apes lose interest in their infant at about 12 weeks of age. All human groups share in the nurture of a baby. Our neurophysiology shows we have an urge and happiness in sharing whereas among non-human apes sharing is very uncommon.

The Other Side of Silence

History is meagre with the saga of social progress mediated by sympathy and civic groups, clubs and guilds. In her novel, Middlemarch, George Eliot suggests that: "If we had a keen vision and feeling of all ordinary human life, it would be like hearing the grass grow and the squirrel's heart beat, and we should die of that roar which lies on the other side of silence.' Every day millions of groups come together unnoticed for benefit. So it is necessary to consider briefly the neglected role that sympathy groups have played in several major historical transitions, with examples chosen from Greek and Roman antiquity, Medieval change, English pre-industrial transition, the American Dream, and the Chinese Red Revolution.

GREEK AND ROMAN PHILOSOPHY

Despite colossal cultural progress during antiquity, when Greek city states and the Roman empire flourished, precious little kindness was found outside the social elites of the landowners. The main form of livelihood in both eras was slavery with shocking numbers of slaves as a proportion of the population. In the fifth century in Athens, the largest Hellenic city state, 30,000–40,000 citizens were serviced by 80,000–100,000 slaves.[108] Urban centres were based on rural wealth production through corn, wine and olives and added little value in production apart from textiles, jewellery and furniture.

In many ways, the advance of political groups and craftsmen associations reflected the rise of civilisation. In Greece, after the Persian Wars and before the Peloponnesian War, from 448 to 431 BC, many political clubs of the unenslaved, called *hetairiai,* surfaced to secure legal redress in courts or to win elections. Clubs were attached to both democratic and oligarchic sympathisers, and subversive groups later tried to undermine democracy in the cities of the Delian league. Craftsmen organisations called *koinon* in Greece and *collegia* in the Roman Empire spread across Europe. In China, the *hanghui* guilds developed during the Han (206BC – AD 220) and Sui (589-618AD) dynasties, and in India, during the Gupta period (AD 300-600), when associations called *shreni* represented different caste and craft groups.

In the time of Socrates and Plato, a sympathy group meeting at a symposium was the most popular form of social interaction for the landed gentry and aristocrats. Plato's book Symposium presents a typical event.[109] Male friends would gather in an Athenian dining room with seven to nine couches arranged in a circle, two persons to a couch. Around the outside, slaves waited upon the guests, whose left arms rested on cushions allowing them space to reach low tables for food and alcohol. After dinner, the host arranged entertainment by slaves, women pipe players, dancers, singers and acrobats. Later, the women or young male slaves became optional sexual partners for the guests. Athenian women had few rights and were given in arranged and often loveless marriages to raise children and manage households. For their dilettante husbands, prostitution, or homoeroticism with male slaves and boys, was a common form of entertainment, accepted as normal in Athenian society. Plato suggests that Socrates was attracted to adolescents and young boys.

After dinner, wine and cabaret, followed by ritual libations and songs to Zeus, discussions began, addressing matters of love, goodness and philosophy. Greek philosophy, which arose from these sympathy group discussions, still informs the ethics and norms of our modern life. Plato opposed the principles of Athenian democracy. Plato's dialogues, for example, report the words of Socrates, and his own analysis that states are structured by castes to reflect the human qualities of appetite, spirit and reason. The productive and menial class of labour address our appetite, the warrior caste or army reflect our spirit of adventure and bravery, and the highest caste of wise rulers make decisions on behalf of the community. Ideal city states should be ruled by philosopher kings who are trained to be just and wise. Aristotle, in contrast, believed in democracy and empirical evidence. A life of virtue (*eudaimonia*) arose from the intellectual skills (*theoria*) we use to understand the universe, balanced by a practical wisdom (*phronesis*) with which we deal with our ever-changing social world. Unlike Plato and Socrates he did not believe in any absolute moral rules related to love and goodness. Ethical agency was the product of the values and political life of the community.[110]

Figure 18. The symposium of Plato

The Roman empire took slavery to new depths: with the success of the Punic, Macedonian, and Gallic campaigns, multitudes of captured soldiers were put to agricultural work on the expanded estates of the Roman city aristocrats. Slaves had virtually no freedoms and were kept in barrack quarters without conjugal partners. In such an asocial and repressive world, it's not surprising that the Epicureans saw a person's desire for friendship as selfish. Humanity was a group of individuals seeking their own dose of pleasure.

The Roman Stoic philosophers, like Seneca, drawn from the unenslaved population, saw it differently. They proposed a moral psychology based on *oikeiosis*, the attachment of self to other.[111] Constructing a scheme remarkably similar to the circles of acquaintance described by modern evolutionary anthropologists, Seneca believed the self was at the centre of a series of concentric circles, from family, to neighbours and friends, radiating outwards to broader society. The closer the connection, the stronger the feelings of affection, and the greater the chances of co-operation. Sociologist Mark Granovetter's twentieth century concept of strong and weak ties has echoes of Seneca.[112]

MEDIEVAL CHANGE

The insecurity of the ninth and tenth centuries in western Europe led to widespread rule by castellans, governors who acted as majordomos for staff and as local military administrators, backed up by vigilante groups. In England, continuous raids by Norwegian pirates along the Kent and Essex coasts reached into London, leading to the gradual formation of walled towns. Townsfolk behind communal walls had physical protection from the noble-led gangs or bandits in open countryside. These medieval communes, which multiplied throughout the tenth and eleventh centuries, saw town sympathy groups spring up, which enabled poorer people to win rights to market goods, to manage systems of exchange and to develop external trade. Because there was no centralised national authority, towns became self-governing corporations that guaranteed systems of mutual defence and developed their own charters of law. Communes or cantons would form alliances, although they usually had to pay taxes to a king or emperor, and often to a liege lord. Life expectancy increased from a Roman average of 25 years to about 35 years by 1350 and the population of western Europe doubled from around 20 million in 950 to 45 million in 1350.

A new urban class formed guilds from landless wage earners who earned their living in crafts or service. Towns were led by nobles in Italy and Holland, and by lords in England. Gold coinage re-emerged in Genoa and Florence and usury provided the credit for extravagant expansion. Gradually, a few independent 'communes' in Lombardy, Flanders, and, later, the Rhineland challenged the ubiquitous hierarchy of monarch to liege lord, to serf. The power of the new metropolitan centres to some extent emancipated them. New communes formed from federations that signed treaties of mutual support in a kind of social contract. Urban populations formed more complex sympathy groups drawn from a wider population than the few families of a rural hamlet. By the early Middle Ages there were craft guilds in England, *metiers* in France, *Zünfte* in Germany, *senf* in Iran, and *futuwwah* in Turkey. Even in west Africa, in the area of present-day Nigeria and Benin during the Oyo Empire, guilds appeared for dancers, mask carvers and musicians such as the *egbe* and *efako*.

The dominance of the church and the development of urban communes made northern Italy the most socially advanced region of western Europe. During the 12th and 13th centuries, community groups in Italy helped people to obtain credit and insurance.[113] Infringements of credit contracts were dealt with collectively. If an individual broke an agreement, the group of people to which he belonged was penalised. In this way the community, not the individual, built a reputation for honesty. Social co-operation was heavily incentivised by a low discount rate for future co-operation, and community leaders watched out for cheaters within their midst. These origins of social trust in Medieval Italy formed the bedrock for credit expansion and the development of national institutions. We might say that sympathy groups laid the groundwork for modernity.

By the early Middle Ages, a free market of sympathy groups flourished.[114] There was no concept of society, but rather a territory of stratified groups. The word 'society' is a later construct, which emerged only in the eight-eenth century. Indeed the word 'group' first appeared in the Middle Ages, probably deriving from the English word crop, or the German Krippe.[115] In Medieval sympathy groups, achievement of individual personal goals was not the main criterion of success. By joining a group, and forming a close bond, individuals happily pursued the interest of that group. Unless people were enslaved, they had the opportunity, even in serf or peasant-dominated societies, to join many different groups. If anyone disagreed with a group decision they could leave and join another. People simultaneously belonged to kin and neighbourhood groups, groups established by contracts and fiefs, political, social, religious, farming and identity groups. Age and totem groups were less common. Most people had multiple group identities and shifted allegiances according to taste.

The modes of thinking that pre-literate people brought to group decision-making were influenced by the seasons and the life-giving and destructive energy of weather and nature. Groups formed to appease pagan deities, the Christian Trinity, bishops and monks, witches and other superhuman agents, monarchs and lords, ancestors and the local dead, healers and shamans, rival groups, and senior members of their community. The local terrain always presented threats, from predators to forest inhabitants, to the risks attendant on any family migration.

By the fourteenth century, western Europe faced a growing economic crisis which accelerated the progression from serfdom to peasantry. Population growth outstripped the productivity of rural agriculture and climate shocks precipitated famines in Europe, most severely in 1315-16. Rural wages fell at a time when shortages of silver from the collapse of mining led to great money inflation. Many peasant groups revolted, causing social upheaval across Europe. (Rebellions had occurred much earlier in advanced metropolitan areas of Italy. In Bologna, serfs had gained their freedom as early as 1257). The European peasant revolts increased emancipation in rural areas, where lords, with Thatcherite alacrity, cut their losses and sold their land rights, which converted bonded serfs into free peasants.

In 1348, the Black Death arrived from Asia, bringing epidemic death rates and population collapse. The plague led to a massive fall in the price of livestock and a surge in the cost of labour. To keep labour rates down, the lords introduced legislation in the form of a parliamentary Statute of

Labour obliging labourers to accept employment at the rates paid in 1346. Refusal led to imprisonment. But the crisis created much greater freedom of association and more intense sympathy groupings emerged in rural populations, with social mobilisation in towns. Many peasants bought and accumulated land to become yeoman farmers, peasant smallholders with up to 100 acres of land. The final straw came when John of Gaunt imposed three crippling poll taxes to fund the war against France. Myriad village discussions involving peasant sympathy groups led to the first large Peasants Revolt. In 1381, Wat Tyler, the preacher John Ball and Jack Straw led a mass violent uprising from Kent and marched into London, capturing the Tower of London. The young King Richard II, aged 14, promised to address their grievances. At their second meeting on Blackheath, after Wat Tyler was murdered, the angry mob at last agreed to disperse and leave London alone. Nonetheless, the economic turmoil and epidemics of disease after the Black Death unleashed two centuries of insecurity, with gangsterism and baronial conflict reaching a new peak as lords tried to protect their dwindling assets. Villages mobilised sporadically through sympathy group action to defend their interests.

ENGLISH PRE-INDUSTRIAL TRANSITION

Hierarchical societies materialised once written instructions and legal codes were used to inform orders and planning. The power of local groups, based on sympathy as a driver of action, was emulated by a new space occupied by a ladder of command and control. Decision-making shifted from perceptions that were group-centred to those that were space-centred. Spatial centres of decision-making were in local castles on hills or within urban patriciates of traders and craftsmen, or by monarchs in distant palaces. Our representational arts, from the thirteenth century onwards, changed to reflect this development. The long transition to an industrial economy was led by England, closely followed by economies in north-west Europe and the USA. After the Inclosure Act was passed in 1773, large farmers, landlords and landowners dominated agriculture and used hired wage labour. Migration to towns by displaced peasant families was rapid. Historian Eric Hobsbawm suggests that "Agricultural England in the nineteenth century presented a unique and amazing spectacle to the enquiring foreigner, it had no peasants".[116] Other European economies took much longer to make the transition. French rural agricultural households, according to historian Eugen Weber only switched from an isolated and backward peasant subsistence agriculture to modern French nationhood in the late nineteenth and early twentieth century.[117]

Social historian Harold Perkin identified the major cause of the British Industrial Revolution as "the unique nature and structure of English society as it had evolved by the eighteenth century", and "the openness of the hierarchy, the freedom of movement up and down the scale, and above all the absence of legal or customary barriers between the landed aristocracy and the rest".[118] English agriculture became "individualistic" while French agriculture remained "communal". English villeinage was different from French servage: "Villeinage is in fact a specifically English institution." From at least the second half of the twelfth century the whole system of centralised royal justice and the Common Law set the English agrarian structure on a different course than France.[119]

Certainly England's success with industrialisation did not arise from a nurturing social structure. As early as 1500, foreign ambassadors and their staff reported on the odd nature of English society. One Italian observer noted that the English were out for themselves compared with Italian society. The English have no "sincere and solid friendships amongst themselves, insomuch that they do not trust each other to discuss either public or private affairs together, in the confidential manner we do in Italy". He went on to observe "the want of affection in the English is strongly manifested towards their children; for after having kept them at home till they arrived at the age of seven or nine years at the utmost, they put them out, both males and females, to hard service in the houses of other people, binding them generally for another seven to nine years. And these are called apprentices".[120]

Nonetheless sympathy groups played a crucial part in English village governance. The historian Ron Green describes organisation in the eighteenth century in the Yorkshire coastal village of Flamborough.[121] The village had two distinct communities, fish and farm, and after land owner-ship by lords of the manor shifted to multiple private land enclosures, civic leadership was taken over by groups of tenant farmers. Although answerable to the laws of Westminster, the maintenance of village services, protection of roads and markets, upkeep of the church, supplements to the chronically poor, water protection and policing, were organised by a sympathy group committee of villagers called the vestry. The group comprised around 12 elected members. Every year jobs changed routinely to eliminate the risk of corruption. Vestry members served a year as churchwarden, then as constable, overseer, surveyor and so on. They were respected members of the community, drawn from the wealthier land-owners who paid the most in rates and taxes, which provided insurance, because any profligacy or waste would cost vestry members the most. Alehouse licences approved by local magistrates required the written support of vestry members. On the other hand, local vestry members were held to account by local justices if community members complained about a road or surveying problem. So there was two-way accountability.

Figure 19. Satirical cartoon of the select vestry of St. Paul's, Covent Garden.
Thomas Jones 1828

A central feature of English social structure from mediaeval times emphasised the rights and privileges of individuals, including women, compared with larger groups or the state. "After the Norman Conquest the woman of full age who has no husband is in England a fully competent person for all the purposes of private law; she sues and is sued, makes feoffments,[122] seals bonds, and all without any guardian . . .".[123] The evidence for a sudden social change sometime between the sixteenth and seventeenth centuries, assumed by Karl Marx, Max Weber and many historians, is weak. The stereotype of a peasant society was not present in England as early as the fourteenth century. Individual rights in law created the context for the Anglo-Saxon economies that led industrialisation, but the function of sympathy groups and self-organisation within these economies was central to their success.

THE AMERICAN DREAM

The origins of the American Dream, to a large extent, derive from English individualism. The history of English law and practice has influenced much of the world through its former colonies in Asia, Africa, Australia and Canada. The only areas that never had a peasantry were nations colonised by England: North America, Australia, New Zealand and Canada. When American founding father Thomas Jefferson wrote: "We hold these truths to be self-evident, that all men are created equal, that they are endowed by their Creator with certain unalienable Rights, that among these are Life, Liberty and the pursuit of Happiness," he put into words a view of the individual and society with roots in thirteenth century England or earlier.[124] So is there a difference in attitude to group rather than individual initiatives in Anglo-Saxon economies?

In the 16th and 17th centuries the Puritans, a group of English Protestants, with Calvinists in their midst, sought an even greater emphasis on daily worship and doctrine than the English Reformation of theology had brought. Together with Scottish Presbyterians, who shared their views, they briefly came to power after the English Civil War (1642–46), before being deposed with the Restoration of the English monarchy. Just before these revolutionary changes happened, in 1629, four hundred Puritan pilgrims left the English coastal town of Plymouth to cross the Atlantic and establish the Massachusetts Bay Colony. These early settlers sought to create a redeemed nation, based on a pure religious movement in the New World. Within a decade 20,000 had arrived and other Puritan colonies were set up in New Haven, Saybrook, and Connecticut.

The Puritans brought Calvinist beliefs to America, a focus on daily worship and hard work, and tightly knit social groups around self-sufficient homesteads. They led a new approach to activist democracy that still informs modern political behaviour in the United States. Protestant work, English individualism and neighbourhood sympathy groups forged the American Dream. Throwing off the shackles of colonialism, the New World built the greatest economy on earth. Self-help and duty to God merged with the individual property rights of the Magna Carta and the principles of free association. In Europe, the old order of monarchies and elites still had to be dismantled. The rise of their industrial capitalist states created disparities of wealth and privilege, the new urban poor having progressed only from peasantry to proletariat. Theories of state reconstruction to manage Old World inequality emerged after the French Revolution, when the New World celebrated its freedom.

So the New World sought a selfish form of salvation and wealth, whereas the Old World governments sought prosperity from expansionary colonial conquests. But the focus on selfishness or sharing, asceticism or action, combined in odd ways on both sides of the Atlantic. The simplest non-family form of co-operation, the sympathy group, grew beneath the radar of both types of ideology. The final common pathway of whichever state of government is chosen is through families and their neighbours. Statecraft and models of democracy did not always determine whether sympathy groups would flourish or not. Nineteenth century radicals everywhere sought social models of co-operation to distribute the products of industrial labour more equitably. The battle of ideas between New World Anglo-Saxon free market selfishness and emergent European socialism of the Old World, with centralised regulation and 'welfare', still has resonance today.

Protestant reformism, though inspired by the individual path to salvation, was far from being a selfish standpoint. It merged with early ecological movements based on local groups which aimed to share and be self-sufficient. Those Protestants who rebelled against the wealth and corruption of the Renaissance church, which offered quick and easy salvation purchased in a free market of plenary indulgences, emphasised not only the rigours of Christian family life but also the importance of fellow feeling and simplicity of lifestyle. The Anabaptists in Ulster, the Cathars in France, the Puritans in America and the Levellers in England came from the same stock. Gerrard Winstanley, the leader of the Digger or True Leveller movement at the time of Oliver Cromwell, tried to create smallholder and egalitarian social groups, which farmed on common land. Together with 14 others (a perfect sympathy group) Winstanley published The New Law of Righteousness, a pamphlet based on Biblical teaching expressing views little different to those of modern permaculturists. Levellers believed that man's freedom lay close to the land which provided him or her with "nourishment and preservation". Another leader, John Lilbourne, was a Puritan, later a Quaker, and a passionate advocate for 'freeborn' rights as opposed to the rights of government or the law. These included freedom of speech and freedom to publish without licence. He was tried and imprisoned for high treason as he was considered a Leveller and so a threat to the monarchy. During his sojourn in the Tower of London, he wrote with others An Agreement of the Free People of England. Tendered as a Peace Offering to this distressed Nation, which later inspired the fifth amendment of the US constitution.

When the Diggers took over common land in several counties of southern England, local landowners took fright and sent thugs to beat them up. Hostility to common land dwellers like Gypsies, especially in the conservative counties of southern England, remains a powerful force today.[125] Radical movements like the San Francisco Diggers of the 1960s took their inspiration from Winstanley but hippy communes which sprung up among the Woodstock generation lasted little longer than the Levellers, sadly, dissolved by the attractions of affluence.

Figure 20. John Lilburne, Leveller leader

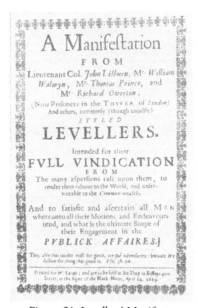

Figure 21. Levellers' Manifesto

In 1831, a young Frenchman called Alexis de Tocqueville travelled to America to study the way in which prisons were organised. An aristocrat and political scientist, he was blown away by the unusual interpretation of democracy in America compared with governance in his native France. Four years later, his classic Democracy in America compared and contrasted the management of power in the New World with European states.[126] He tried to understand why Americans were so passionate about decentralised power and how it affected their systems of state. How did local democracy influence the intellectual life of Americans, their feelings, their manners, their ambitions, and their approach to the equality of the sexes? His comparative analysis has more than a little relevance today.

De Tocqueville recognised the central importance of sympathy groups and of small-scale political associations in the United States. "In no country in the world," he wrote, "has the principle of association been more successfully used, or applied to a greater multitude of objects, than in America. Besides the permanent associations, established by law, under the names of townships, cities, and counties, a vast number of others are formed and maintained by the agency of private individuals . . . The citizen of the United States," he went on, "is taught from infancy to rely upon his own exertions, in order to resist the evils and the difficulties of life; he looks upon the social authority with an eye of mistrust and anxiety, and he claims its assistance only when he is unable to do without it." For example, he observed that if a road was blocked in America neighbours would immediately form themselves into a deliberative body to solve the problem. Not like France, where appeals to a central authority would not be resolved for weeks or months. Throughout his nine-month stay in America he was astonished by the energy of sympathy and other forms of local groups.

"No sooner do you set foot upon American ground, then you are stunned by a kind of tumult . . . a thousand simultaneous voices demand the satisfaction of their social wants. Everything is in motion around you; here, the people of one quarter of the town are met to decide upon the building of the church; there, the election of a representative is going on; a little further, the delegates of a district are posting to the town in order

Figure 22. Alexis de Tocqueville

to consult someone on local improvements; in another place, the labourers of a village quit their ploughs to deliberate upon the project of a road or a public school." He saw the political agitation of American legislative bodies as a "mere episode", in contrast to "that universal movement which originates in the lowest classes of the people, and extends successively to all the ranks of society. It is impossible to spend more effort in the pursuit of happiness." He saw all manner of small societies for the management and enhancement of "public pleasure", for the prevention of intemperance, to promote public safety, for commerce, industry, morality, and religion.

In his analysis of local political association, de Tocqueville recorded key principles of a sympathy group. First, the power of engagement, so that when people come together and "become acquainted . . . their zeal is increased by the number". Second, the power of meeting, which brings local people "the opportunity of seeing each other; means of execution are combined; and opinions are maintained with a warmth and energy which written language can never attain." Finally he recognised the political power of small groups such that partisans of an opinion in a small group could unite with others to join electoral bodies. Informality and sympathy at a local level was quickly translated into political action in America. The nineteenth century saw progressive development of missionary groups, post-Civil War relief organisations, professional bodies like the American Medical Association, formed in 1847, immigrant societies like the Irish Ancient Order of Hibernians, farmers' societies like the Grange, which linked up isolated rural farmers, recreational clubs focusing on hobbies and bicycling, study groups, especially for women, and an early trade union movement. In the late nineteenth century, women's groups laid the seeds for the women's rights struggle which continued until the present day. One example was the work of a Rhode Island high school teacher, Sarah Doyle. She was outraged that Brown University, founded in 1764, was an all-male preserve at a time when New York's Columbia University in 1889 had created Barnard College, and Boston club women had persuaded Harvard University to create Radcliffe College in 1894. In 1897 she rallied women to raise the staggering sum of $37,601 to build Pembroke Hall.

The zenith of civic participation was reached just prior to the 1930s Depression. Clubs, societies and voluntary organisations engineered a social revolution in the USA. As historian Karen Blair documents: "The evidence is everywhere: in institutions (including parks and playgrounds, settlement houses, retirement homes, children's museums, community theatres); municipal amenities (benches, streetlights, water fountains, flagpoles, public art, memorials to veterans); services (scholarships, advice to gardeners); prohibitions (speed limits, restrictions on billboards); entertainments (Easter egg hunts for children, book discussions, barbershop quartet summertime concerts in the town square); and social services (free health clinics, food banks, women's shelters, winter coats for children)."[127]

The Depression and the Second World War halted abruptly the advance of civic participation. The Cold War and the liberation movement of the 1960s did ignite a new style of engagement around feminism, pacifism, civil rights, justice for American Indians, the Black Panthers, gay rights, environmentalism, and pro-democracy groups. But the decline in civic participation and social capital, documented by Robert Putnam in his classic work Bowling Alone, began a more rapid descent in the 1970s.

The astonishing development of the USA punctures the common and false assumption that community groups are a phenomenon of left-leaning political systems rather than free market economies. A decline in social capital has happened in many western countries but not necessarily linked with the ideology of free markets. Some capitalist economies preserve strong community traditions; others less so. Likewise, communist economies that start with dynamic people's movements may observe decline and disinterest as the motivation for their success and institutional support dissipates.

Nonetheless, the apparent primacy of the individual in Anglo-Saxon countries has been successfully exported worldwide. Individual betterment is a key part of the American Dream. And not only in America: modern democracies share the deeply held belief about the principles of meritocracy, individualism and equal opportunity. James Truslow Adams in his 1931 Epic of America described the phrase somewhat differently than contemporary right-wing politicians: "that dream of a land in which life should be better and richer and fuller for every man (sic), with opportunity for each according to his ability or achievement. It is a difficult dream for the European upper classes to interpret adequately . . . a dream of social order in which each man and each woman shall be able to attain to the fullest stature of which they are innately capable, and be recognised by others for what they are, regardless of the fortuitous circumstances of birth or position."

Even Ayn Rand, who promoted the virtue of selfishness, did not oppose group action as long as the principles of individual property rights, and the freedom to operate in one's own self interest, are protected. If independent men and women trade with one another, whether it be goods or knowledge or labour, then she believed happiness will ensue. From Rand's perspective, social interaction in sympathy groups is just fine. "The two great values to be gained from social existence are: knowledge and trade . . . the knowledge potentially available to man is greater than any one man could begin to acquire in his own life-span . . . The second great benefit is the division of labour: it enables a man to devote his effort to a particular field of work and to trade with others who specialize in other fields. This form of cooperation allows all men who take part in it to achieve a greater knowledge, skill and productive return on their effort than they could achieve . . . on a desert island or on a self-sustaining farm."[128]

Little different indeed from Benjamin Franklin who, in 1727, launched Junto, a secret group made up of 12 artisans and tradesmen to discuss contemporary political issues, one of the earliest voluntary organisations in the country. The Masonic fraternal order was set up in Boston in 1735, and the Sons of Liberty in 1765, which drew together patriots who were angry about the British Stamp Act. The War of Independence led to the formation of an active women's society, the Daughters of Liberty, which raised money for soldiers' clothing. And the 1773 Bostonian protest against British tea taxes, a key event in the US Revolution, was orchestrated by the Whig politician Samuel Adams and a sympathy group of protesters at the Old South Meeting House. They rebelled against British colonial arrogance and the infringement of their right to be taxed only by their elected representatives. 'No taxation without representation' emerged as a powerful political motto. After the revolutionary war, benevolence organisations multiplied to assist with children, widows and war orphans. Groups linked to new political parties proliferated.

Generally the far left and far right express some scepticism of small group action. On the left, action by civil society and voluntary self-help groups risks removing the pressure on the state to address social and economic inequalities. On the right, conservatives cherry-pick certain group activities they consider as 'socialist', arguing that these threaten America's concept of freedom. The Tea Party movement sees big government initiatives like Medicare and community health as a cause of debt and state control in an area best left to the private sector. But right and left use sympathy groups extensively to promote their political agendas.

Figure 23. The Boston Tea Party: Colonists dressed as Mohawk Indians dump British imported tea into the Boston Harbour, angry at the British government for taxing the colonies

CHINESE RED REVOLUTION

Arguably the greatest, most rapid political and demographic transition in human history was the emergence of modern China. Both phases of its communist revolution, the initial bravery and idealism of village sympathy to overthrow local oppression, followed by totalitarian collectivisation that killed more people than Stalin and Hitler combined, were led by the same person, Mao Tse-tung. In the first three decades of the twentieth century China was in political turmoil. After the 1911 collapse of the Qing dynasty, China was divided by warlords and emergent nationalist political parties. Mao's early success as a political leader was grounded in his brilliance as an organiser of small, local revolutionary groups to gain the support of peasant populations. The groups galvanised Red Army soldiers who, against formidable odds, fought the Kuomintang nationalists of Chiang Kai-shek.

Mao reflected that as a youth, "my mind was a curious mixture of ideas of liberalism, democratic reformism and Utopian socialism . . . I was definitely an antimilitarist and anti-imperialist."[129] Mao was close to his mother and a devout Buddhist. His peasant father, "a hot-tempered man who frequently beat both me and my brothers," scorned his subscriptions to newspapers and his spending on books. Mao read avidly, the Wealth of Nations, the Origin of Species, John Stuart Mill on Ethics, Spencer's Logic and a book on law by Montesquieu. He sought intellectual refuge in a sympathy group of school friends, which talked about "large matters . . . the nature of men, of human society, of China, the world and the universe!"

The group became ardent body trainers, going on long treks, camping out and swimming in cold rivers in winter, building endurance skills that would prove invaluable during the Long March. In 1917, when Mao was 24, his school group formed the nucleus of an influential society, the Hsin Min Hsueh Hui or the New People's Study Society, which attracted up to 80 members. Many were later killed in the 1927 counter-revolution when Chiang Kai-shek's Kuomintang (Nationalist party) turned on the communists after they had agreed an alliance.

Mao attributed his conversion from social democrat to Marxist primarily to Lenin and the Russian Revolution. He was also influenced by an event in Hunan that he never forgot. During a severe famine in Changsha, capital of his home province, starving peasants begged for relief from the governor, who told them the city had plenty of food. They held mass meetings, demonstrated and drove him out. The Emperor sent in a new governor who ordered the arrest of the peasant leaders, beheaded them and displayed their heads on poles as a warning to future malcontents. Mao and his friends were outraged but powerless to intervene. His rebellious political views were further honed by Japanese occupation of Korea, Formosa, Indo-China, Burma and the threat of China's dismemberment.

Mao went to work in the university library in Peking, where a leftist librarian Li-Ta Chao gave him Marxist literature and introduced him to the Journalism Society and the Society of Philosophy. After returning to Changsha, Mao formed the Wen-hua Shu Hui (Cultural Book Society) and agitated against the *tuchun* of Hunan, a vicious man called Chang

Ching-yao. Mao was a strong supporter of America's Monroe Doctrine, that opposed European colonialism, and argued that the southern province of Hunan should separate from Peking. His sympathy group demanded equal rights for men and women, representative government and approved "a platform for a bourgeois democracy".

Police repression ended their struggle and Mao decided that "only mass political power, secured through mass action, could guarantee the realisation of dynamic reforms". After meeting in Shanghai with Ch'en Tu-hsiu, later the first leader of the party, Mao read the Communist manifesto, Class Struggle by Karl Kautsky and the History of Socialism by Thomas Kirkup.[130] In May 1921, he joined sympathy group meetings of 12 nationally prominent leftist agitators in Shanghai, including his old librarian boss Li-Ta Chao. They formed the foundational meeting of the Communist Party of China. Simultaneously, a Chinese Communist Party was founded in Paris, which included Zhou Enlai, later the first Premier of the People's Republic of China, and Shang Chen-yu, the only woman founder of the Party.

From 1927 to 1930, six million peasants died of starvation from famine in north west China, a disaster unnoticed in the western world. Malnutrition rates exploded, corpses littered the streets, and money-lenders and crop hoarders, guarded by private security, made fortunes buying thousands of acres from starving farmers for a few cents per acre. They held the land for when the rains came, when they could rent it to the new landless. The passivity of the starving farmers perplexed Edgar Snow, an American journalist who travelled with the Red Army on its Long March, because he knew them to be brave. If they were to counter the exploitation, corruption and abuse they suffered under the Kuomintang, they needed a method, leadership, organisational skills and the support of armed insurgents.

Within five years the communists and Red Army provided it. Their economic reforms were popular: land redistribution, abolition of exploit-ative money lending and taxes, and removal of protection for privileged groups. But their organisational skills using community groups were pivotal. Representative government began from the bottom up with elections to village committees. These village representatives fed into a district administration, which set up committees for education, co-operatives, public health, land, agrarian mutual aid, land-tilling, military training and defence. Civil society organisations included children's brigades, the Young Vanguards, poor people's societies and nurse training schools. They wanted every person to be a member of something, usually a sympathy group, as member of a larger society or a council. The Red Army were careful to engage with women and to ensure that peasants felt respected and would retain their independence. Their approach was different from the totalitarian communes during the Great Leap Forward 25 years later.

All their groups were 'three-in-one', with economic, cultural and political objectives. They committed to eliminate opium, abolish begging, foot-binding, prostitution, child slavery, infanticide and polygamy, and cut unemployment. Offering women's rights in matters of marriage, divorce, inheritance and property was a priority. Education would be free and a universal right, although parents had to pay for books and clothes. They committed to private enterprise, competition and industry, a new currency was printed, and state capitalism through co-operatives would promote credit and help with production and sales.

The Red administration recognised the power of theatre. From 1931 they trained 60 classic sympathy groups, theatrical troupes of about 15 members each. The troupes fanned out to every district to organise Saturday night shows, three hours of playlets, dance, pantomime, propaganda and music. The evenings touched on social and political problems, different from classical Chinese cymbals and soprano songs. The audiences participated. Performers were paid little but received food, hospitality and lodging from grateful onlookers. Hundreds of peasants travelled in from surrounding villages to sit on the grass and enjoy these shows, a mixture of art, fun and propaganda. Snow attended one show where Mao and his fellow leaders sat among villagers on the grass with no preferment and little attention paid to them. The Reds recognised that Saturday shows run by trained sympathy troupes were the best method by far to explain their intentions.

Mao followed 1930's world politics on the radio and in newspapers.

Figures 24 A and B: Red China Theatre on the Long March, and a theatrical troupe from the Red Army

The British Labour Party intrigued him because it had not formed a workers' government. He called Prime Minister Ramsay MacDonald a *han-chien*, a traitor to his people. He was more impressed by President Franklin D Roosevelt and his New Deal but "regarded Hitler and Mussolini as mountebanks".[131] Mao was already showing signs of the paranoia and ruthlessness of his later years. He led the civil war, the Long March, and the tricky alliance with the Kuomintang to fight Japan. After the Japanese were defeated, he resumed civil hostilities, negotiated with General Marshall and the Americans, expelled Chiang Kai-shek and his nationalists, and formed the People's Republic.

If Mao had stepped down in 1956 and handed power to Chou Enlai or Deng Xiaoping, he would be revered as the father of modern China, a leader who masterminded the greatest ever transition out of poverty. But he didn't. By 1958 Mao was a paranoid and repressive communist leader, obsessed by his rivalry with Russian leaders, Josef Stalin and Nikita Khrushchev. He decided to suppress village initiatives and impose collective farms and artificial people's communes as part of a Great Leap Forward. This policy catastrophe, opposed by the people, led to the worst famine in history. He abandoned village sympathy groups as drivers of social improvement. From the winter of 1957, after a visit to Moscow to learn from Russian communism, he aimed to match Khrushchev's ambition for Russia and to outstrip the US economy within 15 years. Mao believed that mass mobilisation through gigantic communes of 20,000 households, and collectivisation of rural agriculture, would do it. Communal dining, boarding kindergartens, abolition of money and the imposition of production targets by party cadres who led the communes guaranteed a farming catastrophe. In party conferences he publicly admonished Chou Enlai and other senior party officials who opposed his totalitarian policies.

Over the next four years, as production collapsed, Mao's policies caused the deaths of up to 45 million Chinese peasants and workers from famine, violence and suicide.[132] By October 1960, tens of millions had died and Mao was presented with a famine report from Xinyang region in Henan province written by Li Fuchun, a close acolyte and head of the planning commission. A million peasants died in Xinyang during 1960. Mass graves and infanticide were widespread. Party cadres clubbed to death 67,000 people.[133] Mao saw plots and conspiracies everywhere, but recognised he had to backtrack. Emergency policies reduced the power of the communes and restored private plots. Mao imported food from the west on a massive scale. By 1962, the blame for the disaster was put on party officials, rather than Mao, but his reputation was tarnished. In 1966, he purged opponents in the Cultural Revolution to maintain ideological purity, adding millions more to the death toll. Over Mao's rule, China achieved the most rapid and spectacular improvement in fertility decline, population public health and literacy. And the worst famine in history. The structures of sympathy in everyday politics played an important role in the triumph, and their abolition a key element of the disaster.

Part 2.

Trials of Wicked Women

Makwanpur

INTO KATHMANDU

Just after dawn, in the late monsoon, with harvest underway, the Indian Airlines plane skimmed over a patchwork tapestry of green, mauve and tan fields. The first signs of the city were the solar stalactites of smoking brickwork kilns at the valley perimeter. As we reached the runway at Tribhuvan airport, the egrets wafted across the paddies like white tissues in a breeze. Smells elicit memory and emotion. I love the first scent of a new country. In Kathmandu, you descend steps to tarmac and inhale the mountain air, flavoured with wood smoke and a touch of diesel. In Dhaka, as you walk the aircraft plank into the brash neon of the airport, a whiff of damp suffuses the reception, as though floods and rain have touched every carpet, curtain and corridor. In Mumbai, a night-time mix of salty sea-breeze with a niff of sweet sewage is not unpleasant. In Lilongwe, you sense the cool altitude of the Rift Valley plateau and the fragrance of honeysuckle blended with tints of jet kerosene.

I had the jitters. I yearned for my quieter days in Baglung, a decade earlier. Tomorrow I would chair a meeting to plan our Nepal women's group study. Everything about it made me anxious. The ridiculous ambition, the delegation of district local politicians arriving after a seven-hour journey, and the sceptical Ministry of Health people. The chances that our doctors and social scientists would agree among themselves were slight. The last thing we needed was a public squabble among our carefully assembled "multidisciplinary" team.

And we were desperate for a winner. Our previous study in the mid-1990s, in Kalimati, a slum area in the no-man's-land between Kathmandu municipality and the ancient kingdom of Patan, had ended 'badly' i.e. with a negative result. We'd tested whether trained women health educators, who gave information to pregnant, illiterate women about infant care, danger signs, vaccination, breastfeeding and family planning, would bring about preventive 'behaviour change'. To prove this apparently blindingly obvious proposition, we'd used a randomised controlled trial design. Surprisingly, a recent review of health education programmes conducted by the World Bank had shown that only four of the 500 studies reviewed had had a rigorous randomised design.[134] On arrival at the Prasuti Griha maternity hospital, mothers were assigned randomly to a health education 'intervention arm', or to a control arm where they simply received routine care. In the health education group, they sat with a local trained women educator for a 45-minute one-to-one session before they were discharged. Another session followed at their home within the next month. With embarrassment, we had published in the British Medical Journal no observable differences between the mothers in the health education and the control groups. Our measures of knowledge and behaviour, vaccination rates, and duration of exclusive breastfeeding were the same in both groups.

Strictly, a negative result is not actually a bad one. You learn as much from negative studies as from positive. But it feels bad. Worse, at medical conferences they received the news with a yawn. Everyone was into cytokines and vaccines and the new genetics. Health education was a turn-off, a negative study more so. Then, one day, after my presentation of our findings at the medical school a woman stood up and asked a difficult question. "You didn't seriously think you would change behaviour, did you?" she said. She was a psychologist.

' Well ... er ... as a doctor we're expected to give information to help our patients, to help them change their behaviour," I said, lamely.

"Aren't you aware of Bandura's social cognitive model?"

I mumbled incoherently. "I think I might have read it somewhere."

She expounded. "Bandura believes that we only change our behaviour by learning from peer groups. They help build our own 'self-efficacy'. They give us the confidence to change less healthy behaviours, like smoking or taking no exercise or eating cakes." She seemed to know, intuitively, I was still smoking, had stopped running, and had a penchant for cream horns. After the lecture she was more gracious. "Don't worry," she said, "every doctor and nurse think it's their duty to tell people what to do. It doesn't work. Most patients don't even take the drugs you give them." She had a point.

A week later I attended a lecture in London by Robert Chambers, whose books were mandatory reading for any aspiring development worker. His Rural Development: Putting The Last First argued that the poor, the marginalised and the destitute were mostly excluded from development plans and projects. Foreign experts and consultants had a knack of avoiding the worst months when the rains and floods came, and preferred to visit show villages near the capital rather than the poorest and most remote areas. They listened to and socialised with ministry and international NGO elites who controlled state and donor budgets. He reminded us do-gooders in civil society that development tourism, and unequal power relations between aid organisations and those they professed to help, were the reason why aid was ineffective and got a bad name.

Chambers echoed Graham Hancock's Lords of Poverty, another devastating critique of the aid industry, which described how taxes and donations from the poor of rich countries ended up supporting the rich in poor countries. "After the multi-billion-dollar 'financial flows' . . . have been filtered in the deep pockets of hundreds of thousands of foreign experts and aid agency staff, skimmed off by dishonest commission agents, and stolen by corrupt Ministers and Presidents, there is really very little left to go around."[135] William Easterly has produced a modern version of this argument in his Tyranny of Experts.[136] Development depends much less on technical solutions and the inputs of foreign 'experts', far more on ensuring poor people's rights.

In his lecture in 1997, Chambers spoke about a quiet revolution, a new wave of programmes which invited local people to assess their own problems in agriculture, forestry or water supplies and sanitation. He described a process of self-organisation or "participatory learning", where local people built their own social capital. They mapped village resources, discussed problems, planned initiatives, mobilised support from local authorities, and evaluated what they did. Participation was low-cost, avoided the kick-backs of major infrastructure projects like roads and bridges, and respected the autonomy and dignity of local villagers. "We are in the middle of a silent development revolution," he said. The relevance to health seemed obvious. I felt inspired.

On the way home, my inner scepticism took over. Was there any experimental evidence that participation was a cost-effective way to bring measurable changes in survival and health? The omission seemed odd given the trend from intuitive to evidence-based medicine. One could admire Chambers' optimism and humanity. His work with poor people away from well-meaning but deluded planners in New York and Geneva resonated with my own experience in rural Nepal. But could the success of participation in a few villages, led by charismatic men like Chambers, show benefits at scale? The development and social science world seemed unencumbered by the need to prove benefit according to the rigorous criteria for a medical treatment.

Soon after I rang Hilary Standing, a social anthropologist who worked with Chambers at Sussex University Institute of Development Studies. She had just seen a report from Bolivia where, in remote Andean villages, they had used participatory agriculture and forestry methods for reproductive health programmes. Women in remote mountain villages met monthly, in groups, to discuss pregnancy and newborn care. Preliminary evaluation had shown quite large falls in perinatal death rates, albeit on a small sample size and without a randomised or controlled design.

We found a copy of the excellent Bolivian facilitation manual designed by the American psychologist Lisa Howard-Grabman and her team. The sceptical psychologist who'd taken me down a peg or two had suggested peer groups. They appeared more scalable and sustainable, and ideal for remote middle hill villages many hours' walk from a hospital. But would women's groups across hundreds of villages measurably improve the survival of mothers and babies? And was it feasible to do a randomised controlled study to assess their impact on death rates? Warm village meetings which produced handmade maps and photogenic smiles might impress charity-givers, but not hard-nosed economists at the World Bank, epidemiologists at the World Health Organisation, or an editorial panel at the Lancet. They would want solid evidence that women's groups actually saved lives.

After discussions with our Nepali partners, Professor Dharma Manandhar and his colleagues, we decided to do the study. With death rates as a primary outcome it would have to be a large study in a population of perhaps 200,000. "Why not do a smaller study and just measure the impact on breastfeeding or use of clinics?" suggested a friend. I said "no". A small study would end up in an obscure journal unread. A large-scale evaluation of impact on deaths would answer the critics of small-scale approaches who said the developing world was "awash with pilot projects". To change international policy we needed convincing evidence about survival. As Sir Richard Doll, the great epidemiologist who unravelled the links between smoking and multiple causes of death, once said: "Death is unambiguous. And of over-riding interest to the individual." A large cluster randomised trial would be difficult to fund and set up. It ran the risk of a negative outcome. But Chambers' arguments about the power of community groups was powerful and persuasive. It was an important question to answer.

We chose to work in Makwanpur district, seven hours' drive from Kathmandu. With only two motorable roads, it covers nearly 2000 square kilometres of rugged, steep hills and deep valleys. More than half the population are Tamangs, the Tibeto-Burman Buddhist group of 'non-enslavable alcohol drinkers.' I knew the former district health officer, Jyoti Shrestha, and it turned out he'd been in Dharma's card playing sympathy group when they both worked, 20 years earlier, in the steamy heat of Nepalganj hospital. When we got together for a *daal bhaat*, Jyoti gave us a quick district tour and persuaded us that Makwanpur was perfect for a research study. Next we wrote a proposal and received a positive commitment for funds from a large donor.

Nonetheless my nerves were frayed. Our Kathmandu meeting was to plan a study one hundred times more complex than a trial of women educators and flip charts for 1000 women in the maternity hospital. Our women's groups study needed a surveillance system to monitor births and deaths across murderous mountains and vertiginous ravines. We would employ 400 women to cover scattered villages and incredibly remote hamlets. We needed money, political permission, community consent, active support from leaders and local women, and a new manual for the women's group meetings. We calculated a population of 160,000 would generate just enough births within the timeframe to compare newborn death rates between the two arms of clusters, those with women's groups and those without. Above all, we needed a positive commitment from the investigators and collaborators, from the doctors and social scientists and fieldworkers.

I could think of 30 reasons why a women's group trial would fail as spectacularly as our health education study in the slums of Kalimati: matriarchy and the oppressive dominance of mothers-in-laws, the problems of joining a group, the fatalism of Nepali households, the cultural barriers to sharing, the likelihood of women not staying in the groups, the perennial challenge of coverage, how to sustain the desire to keep going when the going got tough, and the possibility of reversion to bad habits after the women's group programme ended. My anxiety was inwardly contagious.

The restorative chaos of Kathmandu airport calmed me down. Custom officials gossiped over Yeti cigarettes, while the spluttering luggage conveyor belts snaked between crowds of tired tourists, who duelled with wonky-wheeled trolleys. The arrivals hall was a menagerie of humanity. Newari and Rana businessmen, Tibetan refugees in saffron smocks, sweaty Russian pilots in need of a drink, ageing Peace Corps veterans in well-worn khaki shorts back for a wistful retreat, Italian package tourists in shock. In the queue for customs were Indian salesmen in shades, the odd Norwegian or Japanese mountaineer buried under sacks of equipment, and assorted UN aid officials. Next to me stood a World Bank consultant in regulation blue blazer and slacks, tie-loosened through jet-lag, vaguely irritated that business class luggage received no special treatment from the low-caste luggage handlers chatting behind the frayed flaps. At the money change and taxi desks, I saw weekend Buddhists, Gurkha officers in civvies on furlough, perhaps a Ladakhi, a Bhutani, or a Humli, and a knot of timid Magars on the Dhaka run, overdressed in smuggled sweaters, wristwatches and overcoats. On the benches sat Delhi *sasus* in saris, skinny Tamil *sadhus* in ivory lungis, and a bearded ethnographer (or maybe a water engineer) chatting in Nepali.

I bluffed my way past the green channel with a phrase or two in Nepali. The trick I learnt as a teenager walking back from Millwall home games was to confront a potential hooligan head on before they started to cause trouble. "Got a light, mate? Crap game wonnit." I did the same with the surly customs men, to avoid them peering into my suitcase stuffed with undutied medical supplies.

"*Namaste. Sanchai? Maph garnos, tora ma sita computer chha. Tikkai?*

A smile, a smudge of chalk, a scribble in the passport, a drag on the Yeti, and Mr Rajendra Karki waved me through, without a glance at the suitcase or my money belt stuffed with conference dollar per diems. I wobbled through the doors into another scrum of hotel and taxi touts, grappling porters and missionary relatives. Beyond sat queues of aid wallah four-wheel drives and rusty taxis. After a timid fare negotiation I headed off in a wobbly Maruti to my guesthouse in Patan.

NEWARS

Kathmandu is a kidney dish sanctuary, a high altitude valley surrounded by dark green wooded hills, with a haze halo hovering above the expanding honeycomb of city houses which spill out beyond the ring road into the rice paddies. Once an ancestral lake, an ancient Buddhist text, the Swayambhu Purana, dated to 1558, reported that a huge inland sea (*Naga vasa hrada*, the home of the God of Serpents) was drained when the Bodhisattva Manjushri took his sword and cut the southern hills of the valley, near the Chobhar gorge, to release the waters. The land became inhabitable and freed from serpentine monsters. A Hindu version of the myth attributes this action to Pradyumna, a son of Lord Krishna.[137] Certainly the geological record supports the mythology of a lake. In 2007, Japanese geologists showed that detritus from hill slopes, and lacustrine sediments deposited as the waters rose and fell, were evident in the late Pleistocene. Only 30,000 years ago a placid loch filled the entire valley basin. The Bagmati river, now a putrid dribble in the dry season, was the probable route of drainage rather than the sword of a deity.[138]

Kathmandu is a modern and medieval mix, the valley now home to over three million people. The city struggles to maintain water and energy for the migrants who have steadily swelled the indigenous population. The Newari indigenes, more related to Tibeto-Burman groups, live alongside the old hill (*pahaad*) families descended from the Rajput troops and bureaucrats brought by King Prithvi Narayan Shah after 1768. Both groups, Newar and *pahaad*, tut and harrumph at the growing numbers of Terai carpet workers, Bihari traders, Tamang taxi-drivers and low-caste landless immigrants who come to eke out their livelihoods rather than seek their fortunes. Load shedding leads to 16-hour power cuts, and water lorries trundle round the city selling to those who can afford it. The stench of sewage from the Bagmati river slum dwellers makes commuters nauseous. Older residents look back to a golden era when the valley was largely agricultural, traffic was bullock carts, and the views of Mount Manaslu were unimpeded by lorry exhaust.

That evening, in 1999, we dined at Madan's in Kopundol. As Deputy Director of the Nepal Administrative Staff College, armed with a PhD in management from Birmingham University, he had worked with bureaucrats from all 75 districts in Nepal. He had invited Giridha, his wife's brother, the son of Thakur Lal Manandhar, the late professor of literature and author of the standard Newari-English dictionary. Our conversation reminded me once again of the complexity of Nepali society and politics. Giri described the political "context" of our planned women's group experiment. After 15 years working in the British Council and then at Roche, he had set up his own drug company. "The border is open only to people, not goods," he said. "I cannot export my drugs to India." We moved on to Newari and Manandhar culture. His father knew the famous Austrian anthropologist Christoph von Fürer-Haimendorf, the favourite student of Sylvain Lévi, author of the classic *Le Népal: Étude Historique d'un Royaume Hindou*.[139] He declared that Newari language is infinitely richer and more poetic than Nepali, which had been brought in by the Parbatiyan Gorkhalis. After a 24-year siege they had invaded the valley in 1768 when their leader King Prithvi Narayan Shah united modern Nepal. Newars like Madan, Giridha and Dharma remain openly resentful at the loss of control of the three kingdoms of the valley, Kathmandu, Patan and Bhaktapur. Quickly, the frayed social edge of caste was exposed.

"The Brahmins have distorted the true meaning of Hinduism," Giridha said." We Newars always saw that we were classless but differentiated by profession – the Manandhars were oil merchants, the Citrakar painters, the Maharjan farmers, and Nai the barbers. But we always lacked administrative and political skills, and that's when the trouble began, with our own Shresthas.[140] They came in from India, and led us into the trouble with the Parbatiyans (the hill castes), and brought in their Rajopadhya Brahman priests."

We talked about the factionalisation of politics and the rise of the Maoists under the reputedly brilliant Baburam Bhattarai. Now in hiding, Bhattarai was an academic economist and architect of the underground movement. Three years into their insurgency, the Maoists targeted banks, corrupt politicians and the Pajeros of politicians and international organisations. Dharma, usually conservative, seemed almost enthusiastic.

"They never target civil servants and the people, only the sources of corruption like the politicians. This is good," he said.

"And the police, and the vehicles on the road," I added provocatively, "and some foreigners?"

"The police, yes, that is true, but their vehicles are also Pajeros."

"What about Land Cruisers?"

"They're OK," said Dharma.

"You mean a Mitsubishi Pajero is a target for Maoist militants but not a Toyota Land Cruiser? Are you telling me that political acceptability is based on fuel consumption or engine size? And why Pajeros anyway?"

"Because it's the vehicle chosen by the MPs. They import and sell them under parliamentary privilege."

"And only Pajeros have been stoned and burnt?"

"Er . . .no. They burnt another in Kathmandu, belonging to the Save the Children Fund."

"Which make?"

"Well they thought it was a Pajero but they misread the make. In fact it was a Toyota Prado."

We moved on to the feasibility of managing a huge new project in rural Nepal under such a political cloud. Dharma, the paediatrician, sipped cardamon tea and reclined on his wooden chair beneath a photo of Madan's father. He was gloomy about the political class. He had chatted with the Royal physician who told him: "I can rise no further in the medical hierarchy of Nepal. Yet I am nothing more than the glow of the moon. My weak light depends on the reflected power of another, and soon it may fade. My astrologer tells me the light will soon fade."

For Dharma, the system was irredeemable and corrupt. "There is no need for any capability, you understand. What is needed I shall tell you: only *chakari* and *chukeri*. To pay respect to those above and to spread rumours."

Madan was more circumspect. He defended our proposed study. We drank more *raksi,* a powerful rice wine, somewhere between vodka and paint stripper. I remained despondent about making anything work. Suddenly, to my astonishment, Giridha recited, word perfect, the first stanza of TS Eliot's The Love Song of J Alfred Prufrock:

Let us go then, you and I,
When the evening is spread out against the sky
Like a patient etherised upon a table;
Let us go, through certain half-deserted streets,

The muttering retreats
Of restless nights in one-night cheap hotels
And sawdust restaurants with oyster-shells:
Streets that follow like a tedious argument
Of insidious intent
To lead you to an overwhelming question . . .
Oh, do not ask, "What is it?"
Let us go and make our visit."

The poem made me as calm as I'd felt all day. We finished our meal and left promptly, the custom in Nepal. Talk precedes the meal. On my slow walk back to my guesthouse after dinner, I detoured through the historic stupas and temples of lamp-lit Patan Durbar square. I larked about with a knot of Nepali college students who sat and chatted on the red brick perimeter seats outside the Patan museum. They looked like Newari Shakyas, the highest Newar Buddhist priestly caste. We talked football.

"Who did you support in the World Cup?" I asked.

"Nepal", shouted a wag. Hoots of laughter.

"Did you like England?"

"You have my clown!" said one tikkaed boy cheerfully.

"My clown?"

"Yes he's the best!"

I tuned in.

"Oh Michael Owen!"

I demonstrated his goal against Argentina with a peanut bag and a bench as goal. The drink was kicking in.

"You know what . . ." I slurred, "I think the two most beautiful cities in the world are London . . . and Kathmandu".

"This isn't Kathmandu," said one student with attitude, "this is Lalitpur". It was a sober reminder that the historical division of the valley into three kingdoms, Kathmandu, Patan/Lalitpur and Bhaktapur, despite the merging of the first two through urban sprawl, and invasion more than 250 years ago, remained a forceful political reality. The angry young men of Patan knew their heritage and resented their loss of independence.

THE SHANKER PROPOSITION

Our meeting was in the chandeliered banquet room of the Hotel Shanker. The Shanker was one of the first white stucco fin de siècle palaces in the valley. Built by a Rana merchant from a cloistered and Anglophile elite family, who had travelled to Europe in the 1890s, his penchant for French architecture and Victorian bric-a-brac was obvious. With moulded icing sugar ceilings, carved wood bas reliefs, bejewelled stained mirrors, copper pots and elaborate ornamental gardens, the Shanker is a glorious but fading remnant of the Rana dynasty. In 1999, every aspect of the hotel was living on borrowed time. Porters in ill-fitting, torn scarlet livery scurried for tips. Waiters with tuberculous coughs served stewed coffee and plastic marmalade at breakfast, and hovered intrusively as I read the Rising Nepal. They were incredulous and offended when, each morning, I declined an egg.

"An egg sir?"

"No thank you."

"Are you sure, sir? Why, everyone must eat eggs at breakfast. A chilli omelette perhaps?"

"No."

"Fried egg?"

"No! I don't want any eggs!"

Corridors were perfumed with incense to combat the odours of organic acids and sulphurs from the fungi and bacteria that thrived in the faulty plumbing. The bedrooms were dark and creaky and the walls a gloriously Victorian mix of dark brown, saffron and yellow paint. Receptionists wrote countless receipts and bills through 10 layers of carbon paper. Check-out took half an hour. In the Kunti Bar, the barmen served musty, aflatoxin-rich peanuts and damp prawn crackers with the drinks. Maharjan women weeded the driveway in their mauve and white traditional dress, their lower backs supported by red *patukas*, long shawls wrapped around their waist. Squatting, they smoked tobacco *bidis* held, like a chillum pipe, between thumb and forefinger.

The Shanker was cheap, friendly and uniquely Nepali. Much later, the son of the owner took a tourism degree in Australia and upgraded the entire offering, so it's now among the most sought-after hotels in the Valley. A few years later, in its updated format, I would enjoy a monsoon breakfast in the garden with Sting. He showed me his diary, his broken finger and a bag of Tibetan antiquarian clothes, all accrued from a trek in Mustang.

Thirty people arrived for the workshop – Makwanpur district council members, the Ministry of Health officers, charity wallahs, midwives, doctors, social scientists and local women. We discussed the big research idea – whether women's groups in remote mountain villages, coming together to chat about mother and baby care, would improve their chances in pregnancy and at delivery and cut newborn infant deaths. We wanted to know what they thought. Would women's groups be easy to set up? Would different castes and ethnic groups sit together? Would mothers-in-law allow the new mothers out of their homes? How could we randomise villages or wards into the 'intervention' and 'control' areas? Who would give us approval?

I prayed the discussion would be cool and scientific. I reminded myself that science is neutral. We generate ideas, propose a hypothesis, and test it by experiment. The experiment produces results that are positive or negative. Regardless, we write the findings in a scientific paper, send it to a medical or science journal, and, after review, answer the constructive criticism of our peers. If the study is well designed, follows international procedures, uses correct sampling, collects enough data, and applies appro-priate statistical methods, the paper will be accepted. Positive and negative findings are equally important. The editor will want to avoid publication bias. After fast-track publication, and wide media interest, the study find-ings will be read by professionals and policymakers, who, fascinated and persuaded by the new evidence, will rapidly change clinical practice or population programmes for everyone's benefit.

Except it's not like that. Experiments are messy and the results often unclear. Peer reviewers might be compassionate; more often, they are hard-nosed competitors keen to rubbish your methods. And everyone loves a winner, especially editors seeking headlines for a medical break-through. "New drug has no effect on child cancer!" is not a common headline. So publication bias is inevitable. Even if findings are positive and dramatic, few show much interest. Attempts to change routine prac-tice in medicine are agonisingly slow. New drugs, with proven advantages, take 10 years to get into a general practitioner's drill. Physicians and GPs think they know best. Civil servants, especially in feudal monarchies or British ministries, are programmed to be risk averse. Doing nothing new is always the safe option. Important decisions get passed upwards.

About an hour into the workshop, after Dharma, my Nepali lead collaborator, had overseen the welcome and the incense *pujas*, the skir-mishes started. I was in the chair. The social scientists had summarised the women's group method.

"It won't work," announced Dharma, now a backbencher. It wasn't a good start. The participants looked surprised. Dharma was a paediatrician who spoke his mind.

"I'm sure that chatting is useful and helps the women in different ways, but you can't save lives without drugs. The babies die from infection and the mothers from haemorrhage. What about antibiotics and oxytocin for the mothers? Where are the health workers? Only 10 per cent of the women reach a hospital. Many health centres have no drugs. Simply talking in groups will not change things. This is not correct."

The atmosphere soured.

"Better to have it out in the open," I said, weakly.

A social science trained Nepali nurse courageously argued the alter-native. "Of course the drugs will be important, doctor sahib, but the women can help get the drugs. And there will be other benefits. They can discuss things like hygiene, and breastfeeding and cutting the cord cleanly, and make plans for their births."

Dharma turned his mouth downwards and shook his head slowly.

"It won't work," he said gloomily.

The rest of the day was spent discussing, in a warm, rambling Nepali way, three questions that have dogged my career for decades. First, how can we balance the medical and the social in bringing about health improvement in poor communities? Would our groups add value or should we simply target mothers or community health workers with drugs and messages? Second, do we need experiments to prove things work or simply rely on common sense? Are complex interventions like women's groups amenable to the same kind of experiment as drugs for hypertension? Maternal and newborn care is itself extremely complex – it's not like treating malaria or pneumonia – so maybe an experiment would not be the right approach. Finally, even if we showed some benefit in a trial, would the groups be sustainable and scalable? Would the government take it on, would it lose effectiveness when rolled out to millions, would it simply be too expensive? And even if they worked in some areas like rural Nepal, would women's groups work in other settings like near neighbours India and Bangladesh, or in Africa? In fact, Dharma's negativity was a useful first step. It built, in the words of Bertrand Russell, our "firm foundation of unyielding despair". The battle-lines were clear between the medics and the socials, the quants and the quals, so our discussions sought compromise and solutions.

The district council members assuredly impressed. Four members of the ruling United Marxist Leninist democracy party attended, and a lone 'kangresi' (loyal to Nepali Congress). Local government permitted better relations between UML and Congress Party opponents. Rameshwar Rana, the district UML committee chairman, a committed and baby-faced thirty-something Magar, led the delegation. He sat bolt upright with an intense stare. He wore an open-necked white starched shirt, a brown sports jacket, and a multicoloured *topi* as a mark of his senior government status. He told the meeting how he had followed our plans from inception and understood the rationale. He thought the project was sound. We had his full support. Babies were dying unnecessarily and he wanted action. Women could be mobilised. During the election he had walked for days across mountain paths and met farmers' families in remote hamlets. He had heard many stories about babies being stillborn or dying in infancy. Some families gave graphic accounts of mothers who, after their labour in the house or cowshed, had bled to death.

Then he told us about a Tamang woman who, late at night in her mud and wattle house, had collapsed in shock after delivery of a baby girl. She was 17. It was her first pregnancy. Her husband had called his shaman, a Tamang *bombo*, who drummed and chanted and sacrificed a chicken. The young mother became more breathless and distressed. The *bombo* eventually advised her family to move her to hospital. At 2am her mother-in-law rounded up a posse of local men. She needed help for her son to carry his wife on a makeshift canvas stretcher for the six-hour journey across mountain paths to the road-head. From there, they could get a bus or truck to the hospital, an hour's drive away in Hetauda. The mountain men were nimble and hardy, and they made good progress, even in the dark. By dawn, they got her through Namtaar to a teashop where she took a few sips of water. Along the flat riverbank they speeded up, criss-crossing the edge of paddies with the daintiness of ballerinas. As they walked up through the forested path, about an hour from the road, they realised she was dead. There was no option but to turn back to the nearest village where they found a lama, a local Buddhist priest. He did his rituals and, after they collected wood from the forest, they cremated her at dawn by the river.

There was a brief silence in the meeting. His story was compelling. It brought energy and removed scepticism. I was deeply impressed. One evening, two months before, in the bar of the Motel Avocado in Makwanpur, Dharma, Jyoti and I had met with Mr Rana and his polit-buro. After two hours of increasingly jolly discussion, I felt confident enough to ask him why he, the district chairman, being a Magar, from a tribe famous for serious drunkenness during festivals, was drinking a Diet Coke. Meanwhile his four Brahmin politburo members, teetotal wearers of the sacred thread, had just emptied a bottle of Red Label at my expense. The Brahmins exploded with laughter. Backs were slapped, red eyes rubbed. Marlboro cigarettes were offered round and another bottle ordered.

Rana had smiled lugubriously. He had always been teetotal. He was a Marxist but a democrat. Was the project a sensible idea, I wondered? Yes, he said, mother and baby care was a big problem, many babies died, local women needed work, and he wanted to know whether investing in our mother and baby groups plan worked. Without prompting, he understood clearly why we needed a comparison group of villages without new women's groups. The comparison would tell us if the programme lowered death rates. And he liked the lottery method for choosing which village development areas would get the groups, or not. He was pressurised by the village development committee chairmen for favours. It would make his life easier if we did it by lottery.

Although Rana's story was inspiring, and the political vibe of the Shanker meeting excellent, I remained worried. In hamlets scattered over a vast expanse of rugged mountain terrain how would we reliably count the births and deaths? In Nepal gatherings, the formidable is dismissed as simple, and the simple as formidably difficult. Men would eagerly walk for 10 hours to explain a consent form or organise a village meeting. But they would take a month to write a paragraph for a report. Births and deaths? No worry. Nepali staff were confident we could recruit women enumerators in every ward. They would document the deaths and assist a smaller band of interviewers to collect the details of pregnancy, delivery and newborn care. The discussion lasted 15 minutes. And yes, if there was a stillbirth, or maternal or newborn death there would be no problems doing a 'verbal autopsy'. The families would be happy to chat.

I couldn't quite believe this confidence. When we lived in Nepal we had walked for days across the hills to the remotest hamlets and health posts, visiting tiny homesteads high above their crop terraces. To survey 2000 square kilometres of mountains, and to do it repeatedly, month by month, seemed a formidable challenge. But it turned out our Nepali friends were right. We learnt once again about the hardiness and adaptation of hill dwellers. They had got around the mountains for centuries. Writing a report on time was another matter.

The mood had lifted. Sniping continued *sotto voce*, as I expected, between the social scientists and the doctors. The social clique wanted women to decide themselves what to do. There could be no imposition of education. That was the mistake we had made in our last 'top-down' negative trial, where we imposed, hegemonically, our ideas about health education. The groups needed to develop a critical consciousness, according

141

to the principles of the liberation philosopher Paulo Freire. That's all very well, said the medical men, led by Dharma, but no deaths will be saved unless we can supply more antibiotics and provide them at the houses where the babies are born. Chatting is OK but it won't ensure survival. The social scientists chanted autonomy. The medics pleaded drugs. Tempers again frayed.

I looked towards Madan, my gentle facilitator, for help. "Let me test my understanding," he said. "I think we can see things from both angles." He calmly persuaded the workshop that working with community groups was enriching. We should remember the principles of participation, and learn lessons from Robert Chambers.[141] As chairperson, I reassured the medics that we'd make sure that all the health posts, in all the study areas, had a steady supply of antibiotics and essential drugs. And, of course, women would not be patronised. We had to demonstrate any benefits of women's groups to doctors and health planners, because, naturally, they were committed mainly to vaccines and drugs, hence the need for a proper trial.

Another less obvious reason to do the study was to address the anthropological debate about whether human survival depends more upon superior conflict skills or more effective co-operative nurturing? The evidence to date was observational and associative. But the first rule of science is that an association does not necessarily mean a cause. To test the co-operative breeding hypothesis properly we needed to set up an evolutionary experiment. In populations where death rates of infants remain high we could assess whether improved co-operation within women's sympathy groups, bringing 'alloparental skills' to help new mothers during pregnancy, delivery, nurturing and feeding, would ensure greater survival. If the conflict hypothesis was the main reason for human survival, then whether a mother breeds individually or co-operatively may not matter too much; if on the other hand co-operative breeding is critical, attempts to strengthen group solidarity could make a big difference to infant survival.

Quite serendipitously, that's exactly what we did. Frustrated by failed attempts to cut infant death rates in poor Nepali mountain villages we planned our experiment to explore the use of women's groups to improve birth outcomes. Our purpose was medical benefit, not evolutionary hypothesis testing, but our experiment with women in the mountainous villages of Makwanpur district, through happenstance, cast light on the power of social behaviour for survival. It would stimulate coeval experiments in far-flung farming and forest communities in India, Bangladesh and Malawi.

Our results would suggest we have made two serious errors in tackling the reproductive casualty across the developing world. First, we've focused almost exclusively on treatments for individuals rather than groups. And second, we haven't done enough experiments. As the Nobel prizewinner Sir Paul Nurse put it: "We need to emphasise why the scientific process is such a reliable generator of knowledge with its respect for evidence, for scepticism, for consistency of approach, for the constant testing of ideas." We wanted to make the case for the power of sympathy groups. And we argued for experiments to test when, where and how they might unleash benefit, and how to minimise their risks.

The Shanker meeting ended with smiles, through clenched teeth, and a kind of agreement. I should have been relieved, but I hadn't yet told Dharma about a shortfall in cash from the funders. His Asian approach to saving, making sure that every penny is spent meticulously, meant he always saved some for a rainy day. I wasn't sure he would agree to start an under-funded project.

After the workshop, David, our clinical epidemiologist, took me to the Swyambhunath stupa, near to his apartment in a Sherpa ghetto. He and Susie enjoyed stunning views over the valley. During our long evenings in Thamel, or on seven-hour jeep journeys to the projects, we competed to find the best mis-spellings on hoardings and pirate products. David specialised in posters like the 40 foot advert for whisky labelled "Everybody's fiend". In the pirate CD shops I had scored well with a couple of memorable CDs – the English Concert by Duck Ellington, and my trump card, Van Morrison's classic "Hymens to the Silence". Now he was smug and triumphant. He led me along a muddy path to the foot of the stupa where the local ice-cream sellers peddled their dubious concoctions.

"Look," he said.

I saw an ice-cream seller with a green wooden vat on wheels. The painted sign read "Perish Ice Cream"

I didn't get it.

David quickly pointed out the phonetic error of the Nepali accent. "He thinks it spells . . . Fresh."

THE GROUP TREK

The day after the Shanker workshop we wound our way over the mountain passes of Makwanpur for a group trek with our staff. We wanted to bond as a team and form our own sympathy group. We sought to explore the social edge in our new district, and learn more about village life. After a restful night at the Motel Avocado, the team gathered belongings and crammed into vehicles. We headed off up along the narrow valley towards the cement and boulder conveyor rigs perched precariously 3000 feet above us on the western ridge of Bhaise, one of our village development committee areas.

Our guide was Mohan, an impeccably suited but surprisingly ectomorphic Newar from the bazaar, whose suave style was marred by the wool scarf wrapped coronally around his head. He'd been a classmate of Madan when they were eight years old at Shanti Niwas school in Kathmandu. Mohan was a magnificent guide, quiet, calm, polite, knowledgeable, imperturbable. After dusk, the team played Bluff, a card game where the object was to blindly pass on pairs, triplets and more to your neighbour, who must accept the accumulated stack of cards if they wrongly called your bluff, or pass them on with additions to the next in line. Mohan's qualities gave him a huge advantage. The most unexpected team members were accomplished liars. Mohan triumphed, inscrutably.

We bumped along a dusty track up and beyond the cement rigging, to where the valley opened out into a trident of scrubby forested and partly cultivated new ridges. We left the vehicle at about 2000 metres, where the road ran out, and walked up towards the highest Tamang settlement at Kiteni. A local Tamang man emerged as a guide. He circled us around marigold-edged terraces of mustard and millet and a beautiful pink flowering crop called *phapa*. A Diwali ping, a festival bamboo swing, was being assembled by a group of Tamang boys, and the burnt brown faces of smiling Tamang girls carrying fodder and water, and occasional scrappy exercise books, emerged from the whitewashed wooden houses, with their recently *lipnued* ochre mud floors. The verandahs subsided with pale maize stacks, fat pumpkins and crumpled dried washing. The roofs were covered in millet heads, drying mustard leaves and coriander. Tibetan terriers barked amicably, quite unlike the packs of Patan mongrels. Old women calmly wove their *ghundris* (straw matting) or squatted and smoked, with cupped hands, nostril gold glinting in the afternoon sun. There was a humbling simplicity and ultimate sustainability to these high Tamang villages. The late afternoon sun lit up a panorama of timeless rural utopia.

"This is a girl trafficking area," said Jyoti, puncturing my idyll.

In the evening we ate *daal bhaat* with village leaders and enjoyed a musical soirée of traditional Nepali songs accompanied by Bhim on a goat's hide *maadal* drum, and a young boy on bamboo flute. The foreigners, invited to return the compliment, sang a ham-fisted version of Let it Be.

The next day we walked to Namtaar, and stumbled upon a meeting of the local women's savings group. Madan summoned an impromptu gathering for the village development committee (VDC) leaders to meet these local women on the grass outside the health facility. Chairs were brought out for the *toulo manchis* (big shots), but Madan cleverly and firmly declined. He wanted us to squat on the grass to level our status. The women explained why they needed money. Health services for women were derisory. Even safe delivery kits were unavailable. They told us about the forest produce they sold and their monthly stipend to accumulate a fund. We visited a nearby prim mud and wattle sub-health post staffed by a young, well-groomed mother-and-child health worker. He was blithely unaware of most clinical health problems. In the early evening, I climbed up the ridge for a buffalo-milking lesson from the ward chairman's wife while her children fashioned walking sticks with small knives.

She offered me reward for my labour, a brass mug of rich buffalo milk supernatant, the ghee already removed.

Back at the office, the team was gelling nicely, chatting and laughing together. As we ate *baat* in the only foodshop in Namtaar, our group was disturbed by a drunkard who had witnessed a Maoist attack on the local bank. He warned us to be careful. After ablutions in the river, scene of a terrible flood in 1994 when the old bazaar was washed away and many locals died, we visited the school headmaster. He said that families were reluctant to keep their children boarding at the school because of the risk of violence. This started a debate within the team about whether to exclude any of the VDC population clusters from our study because of threats from the Maoists. Jyoti was worried about working in Dadakharka, the most remote VDC in the western part of Makwanpur, six hours' walk away. One of the remote VDCs in the east, Betini, was mentioned by the district superintendent of police as a safe haven for insurgents. By this time, more than 1000 had been killed in the national insurgency, mainly police, Congress workers, civil servants and the Maoists themselves. The shadowy Maoist leader Prachanda, formerly a Brahmin agricultural technician, was an iconic figure much discussed in the broadsheets, Himal, Face to Face, and the Independent.

To my surprise it was Madan, our facilitator and management guru, who pitched in with sense and balance on the issue of VDC selection and randomisation. "I don't think we should change our selection of VDCs at all. Why? I'll tell you. First it will look very bad to our scientific friends if we seem to pick and choose the VDCs we like. Randomisation should be a lottery, not a pick and mix. Second, I like randomisation because it makes us go to the remote and poorer VDCs in equal measure. Jyoti agrees that the problem in Dadakharka is mainly grinding poverty. If we come to help them and keep a low profile they will welcome us, as in Namtaar. They are good, kind people and none of the other NGOs go there. Always the agencies end up in the VDCs closest to the road, and the distant parts are neglected. And third, you know," Madan quietened his voice and looked around, "these Maoists have never attacked the local people. Their argument is with the police and the Congress workers, not with the people. When the 25 men came in their hoods and ransacked the bank at Namtaar, someone shouted that the building was privately owned so they didn't burn it down."

"What about the attack on the PLAN office?"

"Let me tell you," said Madan, his calm, smiling face now animated, "they say that their argument was not with the foreigners. The local project officer was a man of bad character who had taken . . ." he paused and looked around again," . . . nude photos of women in the project. Nude photos!" Immediately the company sighed and whistled in sympathy with the Maoists. Jyoti nodded with a sad finality, like a judge. Pornography was the ultimate justification for an insurgent attack.

On our wanderings through Chuniya we met with female community health volunteers and traditional birth attendants (*sudehni*) and Tamang *bombos* and *lamas* (healers and priests). A well-known local *dhami-jhankri* (Hindu shaman) showed us his snakeskin drum and, by the roadside, discussed his healing methods of *phuknu*, blowing evil spirits away, and *tantra-mantra*, going into a trance to combat the evil spirit causing the illness.

For our final evening with our sympathy group team who would manage the study, we drove up the winding road to Daman, one of our selected VDCs in the north of the district. As we climbed up through the millet and cabbage terraces of Tamang villages, and mushroom shacks made from bamboo and canvas, we crossed a ridge to reveal Bhimphedi and its defunct military encampment in a distant valley to the east. Further up we visited a new school designed and funded by Japanese aid, beautifully laid out on the southern forested slopes just below the peak of Daman ridge. After a school tour, anointment of the impeccable toilets, brass mugs of sweet tea and a game of table tennis, we headed on up through the blue pine, oaks, orchids and rhododendrons. Suddenly a vista emerged at the astonishing viewpoint that opens out the Himalayan range from Everest in the east to beyond Dhaulagiri in the west. We had to stay high in this forest to catch the dawn view. The only options were the touristy Daman View guest house at an exorbitant and unobtainable 50 dollars per night, or to trek up to the prayer flags below the Buddhist monastery and trust to our blessings.

Jyoti suggested we settle for one of the tatty Sherpa lodges down by the roadside. We could walk up to the viewing point in the early morning. Madan and Mohan murmured conspiratorially in Newari and started to giggle. "Turn here," ordered Madan to Buddharaj, the driver, who swerved on to a dirt track at the summit. After 200 metres he found a clearing amidst the pine and oaks. Stone steps led up to a splendid, obscured wooden guest house at the very peak of the ridge, opposite a Buddhist temple. A large lounge, two large bunk bedrooms, a communal kitchen, hot showers, and no one in sight. A smouldering wood fire outside on a piece of corrugated roofing suggested the *chowkidar* (caretaker) was nearby.

"What is this place?" I asked

"It's government," said Madan. "It's OK. Mohan rang ahead to let the cook know we are coming. What do you think?"

Directly ahead the Himalayan range was bathed in the glow of dusk, a panorama that made me hold my breath.

"Madan. I can't speak."

He chuckled.

"Actually it's owned by the Department of Soil Conservation, but we should be OK as long as no one comes. We don't have any letter of authorisation. There are just enough beds for all of us."

The team were thrilled by Madan and Mohan's bravado. Dej went to bed with a fever, Parang went into the forest to find me an orchid, the computer boys snapped away with their long lenses, Jyoti made tea, and Chandra digested my copy of India Today. Madan disappeared with Laxmi to quartermaster our evening meal. We were keen to get on with our management meeting so we drank our tea, and got down to business as dusk fell.

As we nibbled nuts and drank whisky and lemon, we heard voices at the main entrance and Madan disappeared for a few minutes.

"Who was that?" I asked.

"Oh nothing."

"What do you mean?"

To Jyoti and Mohan, Madan declared: "I don't think they had good intentions!"

"Who were they?" I asked, concerned they were insurgents.

"There were five of them. Two of them were women," he said, "I don't think their intentions were correct. I told them to go down the hill to the horticultural station where there are three slots, and put the *kethis* (young women) in the sherpa lodge."

"Why were they here?"

"They were from the Department of Soil Conservation."

"You mean you evicted government officers from their own guest house."

"Yes. But their intentions were not good."

Madan had hardly finished before we collapsed into a fit of whisky giggles which continued over cards into the night.

We had begun the group trek as strangers and employees. We ended it as friends in a sympathy group.

METHODS FOR WICKED SOLUTIONS

Wickedness means different things to different people: 'malignant' (in contrast to 'benign') or 'vicious' (like a circle) or 'tricky' (like a leprechaun) or 'aggressive' (like a fox). In modern slang it also means amazing, wonderful or cool. In 1973, Horst Rittel, a designer, and Melvin Webber, a city planner, applied the word 'wicked' to general planning problems.[142] "The kinds of problems that planners deal with – societal problems – are inherently different from the problems that scientists and perhaps some classes of engineers deal with. Planning problems are inherently wicked ... The problems that scientists and engineers have usually focused on are mostly 'tame' or 'benign' ones." They proposed that wicked problems don't end. They can be addressed but not solved. The answers are not true or false, simply better or worse. Apparent solutions generate new kinds of problems, because the wickedness of one problem may be a symptom of another.

Examples of wicked problems are manifold – obesity, climate change, nuclear waste, prison rehabilitation, mental health care, loneliness, survival at childbirth. If we introduce a policy to reduce the availability and intake of high sugar drinks to combat obesity in schools we might find that children seek other stimulants like e-cigarettes. Or maybe they'll create a black market in cola or sugary snacks so that consumption won't change. If we introduce a carbon tax to shift investment away from companies that burn fossil fuels, funds might divert into biomass energy companies that grow crops for fuel not food. And if we pay families incentives to go to poor quality hospitals we might damage confidence in health services without any measurable health gain. There is always a rush to act. "The problem in India," says Nachiket Mor, a distinguished banker and social entrepreneur, "is that everyone wants to do something, rather than to think about why things haven't worked".

Maybe wicked problems need wicked solutions – non-linear creativity to address non-linear complexity. While childbirth in rural Nepal seems a classic resistant and wicked problem, targeted social interventions might still work. Wicked solutions attempt to test the ultimate wickedness of a problem. By conducting trials of solutions to apparently intractable problems, we can discover whether the assumption of wickedness and intractability is actually true. Sympathy groups, one might argue, have the best chance to work because they harness the oldest motivation and creativity of human endeavour.

Certainly our Makwanpur study would surprise us. Women's groups met once a month to discuss the problems they faced in pregnancy, childbirth and afterwards. After three meetings they discussed how they might tackle them. At the planning stage we had worried that group facilitators wouldn't understand or manage the community action cycle, the four stages of conversations about problems, planning of strategies, their implementation and final evaluation. Even if they did, would the women and their community respond? In reality, the facilitators learnt quickly and the groups followed the cycle carefully, enjoying the structure it brought to their two to three-hour meetings.

We had also worried about random selection of village clusters. Despite its scientific power and beauty, many people have an irrational prejudice against a random punt. Would the local Marxist-Leninist politburo share

Rameshwar Rana's enthusiasm to use a kind of bingo? Our droll surveil-lance manager, Kirti, a Limbu with dubious claims to ethnic royalty in Ilam, reassured me that the meeting with the communists went well. "They fully understood the lottery method and thought it was fair," he said, "but the chair of the local development office asked me how it could be scien-tific to pick a number on a piece of paper out of an earthen pot?"

"What did you say?"

He smiled. "I told him we get the British to do it."

And what about getting the local people to accept the groups? Acceptance was much less difficult than we supposed. Entry to villages to explain the study and take consent was organised with aplomb by Bhim, Kirti, Rita and the team. In public health, a tension often arises between the benefits to the community and the autonomy of individuals to give consent to take part. Initially, we sought formal approval from cluster guardians and the village development committee chiefs, who enjoyed a day's discussion about the project and finally gave their signed agreement. Some asked for benefits and employment favours but we were clear, firm and resilient. We were also backed by Mr Rana, the district chair, who sanctioned open community meetings in every cluster to gain local buy-in.

Mothers and their families were visited at home by Nepali field staff and told about the women's groups and how they'd operate. Attendance was, of course, voluntary. They were free to decline interviews. In control clusters, women were told about the study, that they were a 'control area' by chance, they could opt out of interviews, and that only information on pregnancy, delivery, births and deaths was being collected for now. Once the first phase of the trial was over, if results were positive, we would bring it to their villages, which eventually we did.

Staff also explained the benefits for all families whichever cluster they lived in. Health workers, local volunteers and traditional birth attendants would be trained in newborn care in all areas of the district. New equip-ment and essential drugs would be given to the hospital, primary health centres and health posts. The community response was mature and posi-tive. Some families made a pitch for water supplies, for food supplements or a new bridge across a river, so we explained that our programme aimed to create self-organisation rather than to distribute aid. Besides we didn't have funds for infrastructure.

The next challenge was to set up a reliable system to monitor births and deaths. With brilliant innovation and logistical skill, Bhim and Kirti established surveillance across an immense and precipitous territory. Wards of up to 1500 people living in 200-300 houses were divided into four sectors. Local women, recruited as ward enumerators, drew large coloured maps of their ward, with help from neighbours, and marked every household, hamlet, track, school, shrine, health post and thicket. Every week the enumerator would visit all the houses in one sector and ask about births or signs of pregnancy. If there was a stillbirth or death she informed a senior interviewer to come and do a confidential verbal autopsy, a sensitive interview with the family about their loss and the events leading up to the death of the mother or baby. Once a month she met with the interviewer and eight other ward enumerators from the same VDC cluster to share her information for the four sectors of her ward.

So far, so good. After the women's groups had been running for three months I came back to see how things were going. Tension in Kathmandu was palpable as the Maoists had broken away from the third round of negotiations with Prime Minister Sher Bahadur Deuba. The next day they set off explosions in many districts (breaking three windows at the Lever factory in Hetauda, Makwanpur's capital). In Ghorahi they attacked the army barracks, killing an army major and 12 troops. This was the first time the army had been attacked, a deliberate, almost suicidal ploy by Prachanda and Baburam Bhattarai, the Maoist leaders. A huge Maoist attack in the Everest region of Solu Khumbu ended with more than 200 dead, mainly Maoist, which included the chief district officer and several soldiers. The cabinet, predictably, after consultations with all opposition parties, obtained permission from the King to declare a state of emergency. In Makwanpur, staff were nervous about the profile of our visit, and wanted meetings with village supervisors and VDC chairmen moved from the Avocado motel to the district hospital.

Nevertheless, the women's sympathy groups were a revelation. Some groups were already established for annual immunisation campaigns but none had met regularly. Now they did. Put simply, the women loved the meetings. Group size varied, settling at around 15-20. If groups were too big they split into two. The women assembled, chatted and laughed as others arrived. They squatted on bamboo mats with their babies and small children, and usually sang songs as icebreakers. The local woman facilitator had been recruited by interview with competitive criteria, and trained for a few days in participatory methods. Quite deliberately she was not a health worker so as to avoid an instructional and didactic approach. She also learnt about common health problems during pregnancy and child-birth. When leading the structured discussions she had a licence to improvise. Her simple pictorial training manual gave her the broad struc-ture of our 'action cycle'.

At first, only one or two confident or senior women would venture opinions in the group, but the facilitator invited all to speak. As the meeting cycle progressed, most women lost their shyness (*laaj*) and became animated and engaged. To my great surprise, attendance and interest in the groups didn't wane. On the contrary, women were loyal and steadfast. Many walked for one to two hours to attend. They welcomed the chance to sit, chat, gossip, laugh, learn, share, debate and plan. It was a rare inter-ruption from their daily humdrum of fuel, fodder and water collection. A pause from the endless demands of husbandry, cooking and childcare. They saw the groups as appropriate within their culture. The facilitator was one of their own, a respected friend who would help them with their fears around childbirth. This solidarity was addictive. Many young women had felt isolated and controlled. The groups provided an intimate liberation.

After the gossip and introductions, the groups got down to work. They debated the spiritual and medical causes of illness and death, and were comfortable with both. Most Nepali villagers when sick, including our own staff, would consult both health workers and shamans. The first tackled the problem, the second the underlying cause of the problem. The facilitator would help them to play games, use picture cards to link solutions to clinical problems and act out role plays. The women voted on their priorities for action, and asked deeper questions about why they faced problems in pregnancy and the puerperium. Participatory methods showed the value of a group rather an individual way of creating health. Sharing stories about tragedies and successes made a powerful impression. Many were moved to tears by a neighbour's bereavement or near-miss experience. For young women who attended with their mothers-in-law (*sasus*), a subtle shift evolved in their power relations. Traditional total obedience to their *sasu* was diluted. Group discussions allowed third party ideas from informed neighbours in making decisions about seeking care.

Figure 25. Makwanpur womens group, Nepal
A. A women's group in facilitated conversation. Courtesy Thomas Kelly
B. Kirti Tumbahamphe. Photo, the author
C. Women's group receiving revolving fund payments
D. Making their own safe delivery kits

The development world talks about how to increase agency and empowerment, especially for women. Agency refers to an individual's ability to take control of her life. Empowerment is a broader concept that embraces both changes in agency and in the structure of her social environment. Structural opportunity includes whether she can learn how to read and use numbers, make decisions about finances or personal health, take a loan, or work outside the home. The Brazilian educator Paulo Freire believed empowerment derived from what he called 'critical consciousness'.[143] Understanding and taking ownership of one's own problems is the backbone of empowerment. The women in our groups visibly grew in confidence, learnt how to plan, to solve problems and to negotiate with others. Groups debated their own priorities, sought their own strategies and self-organised to put them into practice, often helped by menfolk and ward officers. Revolving funds were popular and bound the group together. In a medical emergency, access to money in cashless subsistence households is critical, for transport, for replacement labour, for escorts and the costs of care. Three quarters of groups adopted some kind of fund.

Other strategies included transport schemes using community stretchers and local volunteer porters. Kitchen gardens could provide a more diverse diet and cash from sales. Groups made and distributed their own clean delivery kits. Senior group members visited marginalised or remote households, or first-time younger mothers forbidden to join the groups, to share information about antenatal services, state supplements or immunisation campaigns. Men were press-ganged into water protection. Some groups became active with family planning, forestry and even film-making.

THE TRIAL VERDICT

Early on we calculated from group registers that only 8% of women of reproductive age in the population had joined our groups. How could we cut deaths if so few women were mobilised? A vaccination coverage of 8% would be considered a disaster. David and I suppressed our gloom.

Figure 26. Gathering of two womens' groups, Bhimphedi, Makwanpur.

At that time we didn't realise the fraction of newly pregnant women who joined the groups, around 40%, was much higher. Word had spread. Older women didn't need to come but they made sure the younger ones did, especially if pregnant. So exposure to the groups of our target audience, pregnant women, was high. And the young, first time primigravidae mothers who were stuck at home, forbidden to attend, through purdah or parental pressure, often received impromptu visits from older women to share the group discussions and strategies.

In 2003, I arrived in Kathmandu to discuss the results. I wasn't optimistic. David had been working intensively with the Nepal data team. As we left the airport in a wobbly taxi, David, with a curly grin, said: "I have a surprise for you." In the office he showed me the analysis. We had monitored birth outcomes in a cohort of 28,931 women drawn from villages scattered over the rugged mountains. Our primary outcome was deaths of newborn babies. From 2001 to 2003, after the groups had started, the newborn mortality rate was 26.2 deaths per 1000 live births in the clusters of villages with our women's groups, compared with 36.9 per 1000 in control areas, a reduction of almost one third.

We were shocked and delighted. Even better, after making adjustments for differences in education and economic status between the clusters at baseline, the result remained statistically significant. Stillbirth rates, though, didn't change. Maternal deaths were 69 per 100,000 births (two deaths per 2899 live births) in women's group clusters, compared with 341 per 100,000 (11 deaths per 3226 live births) in control clusters. We were cautious. The numbers of maternal deaths were few, might have arisen by chance, and maternal deaths were not our primary hypothesis or outcome. From a low baseline, women in the group areas were more likely to receive antenatal care, trained birth attendance (though the increase was small) and hygienic care. Attendance at hospitals or clinics though remained uncommon. The biggest differences were in home care practices. The five cleans at delivery, a clean surface, attendants washing hands, use of a plastic sheet, cutting the cord with a clean razor, and cord care, improved. Mothers and their assistants kept babies warm through prompt drying and wrapping. Immediate breastfeeding rates rose and mothers stopped throwing away the first yellowish colostrum. Traditionally colostrum is seen as stale and unhealthy by the older generation. But it's immensely rich in immunoglobulins, which protect against infection after birth.

We wrote the paper speedily. If you follow prescribed guidelines for doing a randomised controlled trial, the format of publication is straight-forward. We were thrilled when the reviewers were generous and the Lancet accepted the paper. We felt confident we'd stumbled upon a new way to cut preventable deaths of mothers and babies. We awaited reaction from academics and policymakers. The silence was deafening. Reactions we did get varied from "Well, I could have told you that women's groups were a good thing – didn't need a trial," to "are you seriously suggesting that women chatting will cut the deaths of mothers and babies?" and "the priority is a hospital delivery and midwives", as if mobilising women and providing a midwife were mutually exclusive options. We were back to the arguments at the Hotel Shanker four years before.

We'd also realised that sceptics, quite rightly, would never change their minds or policies from a single trial. Was there something special about

Makwanpur? Would it work in tribal India or Muslim Bangladesh or rural Africa? Would urban communities show similar loyalty to groups? In development speak, were our women's groups generalisable, sustainable and scalable? We hadn't really got much further. But we'd already decided to repeat the studies in different settings working with reliable friends and colleagues in India, Bangladesh and Malawi.

Replicants

INDIA EKJUT

Science is an odd mix of competition and collaboration, where the chess games of the fittest and cleverest boffins interweave with magnanimous teamwork. Although we felt offended, the scepticism of professionals who read our Makwanpur study was the right response. No global or national policy should change on the basis of one experiment. We needed more experiments. And stories as well. Why might our groups work? What was the breadth of their benefits and risks? The phrase 'social capital' was being bandied around in development circles. What did it mean? Could it be measured? Were groups affecting social capital in ways that made them more resilient? And what were the conditions for them to listen and become more powerful?

The Ekjut study in Jharkhand and Orissa, India, led by Prasanta and Nirmala, took over three years. The population of 228,000 was rural, largely tribal, and included over 400 villages and 500 hamlets. The Ekjut team identified 36 clusters of villages, each cluster with a target population of over 6000. Some 244 groups in 18 clusters received the cycle of women's group meetings, within three bordering districts of Jharkhand (West Singhbhum and Saraikela Kharsawan) and the neighbouring state of Orissa (Keonjhar).[144] Mostly tribal or *adivasi* (indigenous) groups lived here including Ho, Santhal, Juang, Bhuiyan, Oraon and Munda communities.

Figure 27 A and B. Adivasi women work in groups to create
health promotion materials. Orissa State, India.
C. Adivasi elder in Jharkhand forest.

Adivasi groups have their own identities and fiercely protect their local
associations and ancestral territories. They worship nature and pay ritual
respect to supernatural beings that protect or threaten their homes and
forest. They survive through subsistence farming and foraging in forests,
increasingly supplemented by wage labour from men migrating to brick
kilns or mines in the hilly terrain. For villages close to conurbations, men
and women take jobs in cleaning, security and service. Generally though,
physical isolation in 12 out of the 18 clusters meant villagers had very

limited access to health services. Traditional birth attendants carried out over one third of home deliveries. A higher proportion were overseen by mothers-in-law, husbands, relatives or neighbours.

The social edge of our groups in Jharkhand displayed many stories of solidarity. A typical member of a woman's group was Archana. Married at 13, she had her first child within a year, born at home because Archana knew nothing about health facilities or available care. As a new women's group member, she learnt about the importance of taking iron tablets, good nutrition, tetanus injections, and the national scheme that provides financial help for women to give birth in hospital. She also carried a note of the phone number of the vehicle that would take her there, and even kept a new delivery kit at home. And she trusted the facilitator. "She is from our community, she is a friend, she helps us in solving our problems and makes us aware of the problems we suffer from by using picture cards and games. We consider her as a part of us and trust her." She realised the value of the group meetings. Attendance stayed high and few slipped away. "We could not do much as individuals but as a group we could find a way to solve each other's problems."[145]

The newborn death rate during the baseline period (2004-2005) was 58 per 1000 live births, at a time when 80% of women delivered their newborns at home without skilled attendance. When we analysed the final results we found that in women's group areas (compared with controls) we observed a 32% fall in newborn deaths (adjusted for clustering, stratification, and baseline differences) over three years.[146] It had taken the groups up to a year to get established so we were pleased to find an even greater reduction in deaths (45%) over the last two years of the study. We also measured levels of maternal depression. Maybe being exposed to groups in pregnancy would be protective, we wondered? Although we did not find a significant effect on all maternal depression, whether mild, moderate or severe, the moderate depression rates fell 57% in year three among the mothers in women's group areas, suggestive of a longer term protective effect.

To our surprise, women in the clusters with groups, as in Nepal, showed no greater care-seeking behaviour than those in control clusters. Only

14% of women in the women's group areas went to an institution to deliver their baby, compared with 20% in control areas. Again what was markedly different was better hygiene behaviour in the home – hand-washing by birth attendants, use of soap, use of a safe delivery kit, a clean plastic sheet to lie on, the umbilical cord tied with a boiled thread and cut with a new or boiled blade. Decisions in the home about cleanliness, and informed choices about soliciting specialist support in the face of limited options, seemed to explain our dramatic finding. We were quietly delighted. Here was replication on a grand scale. The Nepal study results could no longer be explained purely by chance. Bigger benefits, a different country, a larger study, more clusters and a larger sample. We turned now to Bangladesh to await the results from what we hoped would be a confirmatory study.

BANGLADESH

The Bangladesh study was led by Kishwar, a wonderfully feisty paediatrician entitled to her aristocratic nickname, the Begum. We planned the trial design over three exhausting days in her humid Dhaka hospital office, her staff contributing opinions under her high command. Kishu and her husband Azad had rented a Corbusier-influenced lakeside house on the edge of the lake in Gulshan. Designed by the professor of architecture at Dhaka University, the plain white three-storey building was an unusual modern masterpiece, with sunken rectangular windows, from fat oblongs to mediaeval castle slits, and bulging verandahs at each corner of the upper storeys. Much later, in the absence of planning rules or listed buildings, a developer brutally bulldozed it in order to invest in rental apartments.

At dinner I wore my latest gift from the Begum, a magnificent red silk panjabi and paijama. We ate fried flounder, coconut prawns, snake gourd with egg, rice, roti, *amra* leaves and a mysterious savoury mango-like vegetable with a fibrous seed you should not chew. Azad had given me a woven wool hat in the style of Mohammad Ali Jinnah to wear.

"You know how these hats are made?" he asked. "They separate the lambs at birth so the mothers cannot lick away the amniotic fluid. It dries and fixes the wool in this wavy style. The animals grow and are killed in adulthood with their wool in the same style."

Azad, one of the country's leading physicians, is an expert on botany and Bengali history. We got on to Bengal in the late eighteenth century. He told me that corruption was as rife as it is today.

"Macaulay wrote that Robert Clive was challenged in court about his corruption. Clive said: 'All I received was gifts, which is the tradition of the Bengalis'. You know what the prosecutor said? 'Dogs bark, rats bite and Bengalis lie'."

He grinned. "Clive was found guilty, and killed himself in prison."

The kitchen team hovered and tried to force feed me with rice and the prawn curry.

"By the way do you know how the Nawab of Ayodhya was caught at the siege of Calcutta? He was completely naked, barefoot and his servants had fled. He couldn't go out and escape."

Azad chuckled. "He had never learnt how to put his clothes on. And it wasn't the East India Company which founded Calcutta you know . . . it was a lone Scotsman, Job Charnock, who decided there should be a bazaar to trade his goods. He rescued a young widow being dragged through the streets towards *suttidar*, (burning of a widow) married her, remained faithful and had two children. When he died, the wife and children returned to England, but later came back to build his mausoleum in the city."

Bangladesh is a geographer's dream and a farmer's nightmare. In the north-west, droughts and river erosion threaten hamlets in the hills of Sylhet and Moulvibazar. The north-eastern Hoor lowlands are swampy, waterlogged or flooded. The central regions, where most of the people live, on smallholdings and ribbon urbanities, are prone to seasonal flooding which can devastate crops and bring epidemics of cholera. Most vulnerable are the southern states, at sea level, with silent salinity poisoning their soil, and the annual risk of terrifying cyclones and storm surges. The river channels change constantly with silt forming temporary *char* lands, where the destitute chance their arm to get a crop or two in before storms rearrange the topography. If they survive the floods, they jump ship to a new silt char that has sprung up from nowhere in the Bay of Bengal. *Monga* is a Bengali word to summarise their vulnerability. It means the prospect of feast and famine, of food shortages and empty pockets. But the southern coastline facing the Bay of Bengal has one massive line of defence, the mangrove forests of the Sundarbans. Blocking the monsoon storms as they sweep in without warning, the mangroves act as shock absorbers. They are like an infantry that suffers heavy casualties but holds the frontline and saves the lives of innocent millions behind.

The innocent, though, are innovative, not helpless. They can think and adapt. They diversify their crops, plant cereals in the dry season and multi-crop. They can change the dates of planting and harvesting, make floating farms, create shrimp and fish farms, and rear ducks. They build houses on stilts or shore up the plinth of mud (*bithi*) they sit upon, or tie the roofs to trees. They welcome new rice seed varieties that are salt resistant or grow in a shorter period. They take micro-credit, barter their produce, share labour, and give food relief to relatives or neighbours. In times of stress, the Imams and the Pandits provide comfort and solidarity. Women go to see the *kabiraj* or the fakirs or perhaps a mullah. They engineer cheap solutions to harvest rainwater when the wells are flooded. For centuries, the villagers near the mangroves have used sealed earthenware stores of water, which they bury in the clay for a rainy day. Now they use plastic containers. In coastal communities, clever horticulturists build floating gardens, stacked above a thicket of water hyacinth, in protected natural harbours. Soil and manure are layered on to the hyacinth raft where short-cycle vegetables and fruits are grown.

Ironically the landless poor who migrate from rural peril to urban protection may find themselves in a more precarious position. A storm can undo their shanty security. In the ensuing chaos they fear eviction or relocation. And if their job as a rickshaw puller, garment factory hand, security guard or sweeper suddenly stops, their nuclear family is without a safety net. They will fall back on meagre savings or into the hands of loan sharks. Income insecurity may be compounded by blocked drains, lack of water, fear of crime, threats of violence and decrepit shelter. In the heat of the pre-monsoon, the urban heat island effect also makes shanties intolerably hot. Stores of food and water are not common. Borrowing often leads to deeper debt. Extended family networks are hours away in their natal village, so they may depend solely on *zakat*, the charity of the local mosque or a wealthy Islamic benefactor.

After dinner, Azad took me up on to their verandah. The Begum was surrounded by her Alsatians, corgi, Siamese cats and servants. In the sticky heat of the monsoon their roof garden was rampant with the seductive perfume of frangipani, the amra trees, delicate orchids and a plethora of latex-oozing architecturals.

"What's this?" he asked, raising his arm.

"Your hand."

"How many digits?"

"Five."

"Now look at this," he said pointing at a flower. "How many petals?"

"Five."

"Why? What is the evolutionary significance of the number five? And why do coloured flowers, with the exception of roses, never smell? Only the white varieties are aromatic. Why?"

He smiled and didn't wait for my reply.

"And why are flowers coloured anyway? What is the evolutionary value? Scientists cannot satisfactorily explain these things."

In the 1970s, Azad had worked with gastroenterologist Sidney Truelove in Oxford on the development of the drug salazopyrine for ulcerative colitis. He was the first to recommend the chemical composition for the enema suppository, now used routinely.

"Did you get a patent?" I asked.

He shook his head.

"Shame . . . you would be very rich now."

"It was not the practice. In Oxford it was looked down upon to seek patents, to not share your findings freely with the wider scientific community."

The Begum stroked one of the Siamese, and we looked out over the lake where the shanty huts seemed to grow out of the water hyacinth. "My friends complain that our lake has no walkway to prevent the locals from shitting there," she said. "But I don't want people walking around the lake whilst I'm on the verandah. And as for shitting, there is no worse smell here than anywhere else. And if you want to see real shitting, go to Delhi on an express train arriving in the morning. Thousands evacuating on to the tracks, oblivious to everything. That's shitting for you."

Bombs had gone off in cinemas in Mymensingh, killing 20 and injuring 200. Mystery surrounded the perpetrators or motive. The Bangladesh Nationalist Party government blamed the opposition Awami League, and promptly rounded up large numbers of Awami League activists. The Awami League responded by calling a national strike, blaming local fundamentalists with links to Al Qaeda. The American Embassy had cautiously denied evidence of Al Qaeda cells in Bangladesh. In any case, I wondered, would Al Qaeda really trouble themselves with the cinemas of Mymensingh?

Azad saw darker forces. "It could be the military wanting to destabilise the country in order to take over." I'm usually sceptical of the south Asian tendency to over-egg the pudding of conspiracy. Later I talked with waiters at the Dhaka Club, unanimous in their renewed support for General Ershad and the military, ironically to rid the country of corruption, so maybe Azad had a point.

The next day we recruited the project team. Interviews for the project staff brought charming Banglish. One application letter said: "I look forward to your welcome knock." The first candidate Mr Ali was asked whether he had written any reports or publications for a journal during his 15-year career. He shook his head sadly. "Why did you not manage to publish?" asked Azad gently. Mr Ali looked crestfallen, a man whose moral fibre had been exposed. "I don't know, sir. Idleness I suppose."

Another woman, Mrs Farid, was asked the three qualities she might bring to the job of a training officer. "My experience in mother and child health, my hard work and a fascination."

"A fascination?" I asked.

"Yes, I have such a fascination, sir."

"Oh . . . thank you."

The weakest candidate arrived near the end. His response to the 'three qualities he might bring to the job' was a blank stare followed by "Well, sir, I'm unemployed. I want a salary. I want to better my position. These are the three things." He smiled with satisfaction that he had negotiated the question well. Kishu rolled her eyes and passed me a note which read "Aaaargh!" But by then we'd already found a strong and balanced management team, two male, two female, one Hindu, one Muslim, one Christian and one Buddhist.

Our Bangladesh study faced even greater money constraints than in Nepal or India so we chose cheap and cheerful options. We picked three districts, Faridpur (west), Bogra (north) and Moulvibazar (northeast), where Azad's Bangladesh Diabetic Association had a strong presence. Azad is a brilliant administrator, leader of the biggest non-government health service provider in the country, runs hospitals in every district, and is a believer in collective leadership and personal propriety.

"We look after our people but not to the extent of the big NGOs. I tell my staff that on field visits we should live in comfort not style."

He told me of the rivalry between The Bangladesh Rural Advancement Committee (BRAC), the world's largest non-government organisation with over 120,000 employees, and the Grameen Bank. Sir Fazle Hasan Abed versus Professor Muhammad Yunus. Abed believed that Yunus had stolen his ideas and achieved unjustified international recognition when he won the Nobel Prize. Azad agrees they should have shared it. BRAC seems the better run organisation and Azad supported Abed as a brilliant manager.

"But I'm worried what will happen when Abed goes. Do they have the governance to sustain this scale of operation? I believe in collective leadership. Abed asked me how I managed with such dominant people on the Diabetic Association board. I have co-opted all the best business brains. But I told him they were no trouble. They provide us with the leadership and skills we need . . . we must remain successful long after I have left . . ."

Figure 28. Azad Khan and Kishwar Azad

Our Bangladesh study ran for four years. With a small budget and half a million people to cover, we created a shoestring scheme to monitor births and deaths using respected local women, one per 200 homes, as key informants. Every month each woman met our interviewers, who would follow up all the births and deaths she reported. In some ways, the method proved more accurate and less intrusive to families than our gold standard systems in Nepal and India. Households were only visited when something occurred like a birth or a death. People don't like being disturbed and interrogated every month.

But accidents still happened. A few months into the project the Begum phoned me.

"Tony, we cannot use one of our unions in Faridpur. It's a real pain."

"Why not?"

"Two of the three wards in one union cluster have gone."

"Gone? Gone where? Have they emigrated?"

"No, they were washed away." The monsoon had been heavy. The disappearance of whole villages seemed pretty routine to her.

"Luckily we have another union nearby. Can we use it?" I consulted the statistician and we agreed.

The women's groups got going, the group sizes were good, the facilitators liked their jobs. After three years of hard community work we had enrolled a large sample of 36,000 births. The women's stories had encouraged us. Jyosna, 20, had not been an official member of the women's group but went to the meetings regularly because she enjoyed being with the other women. She learnt to do all the right things during her pregnancy – took iron tablets, and had tetanus injections and regular check-ups. Her family made sure she had a good diet and plenty of rest. But at eight months she developed a sudden, severe headache and, soon after, convulsions. Her family was in shock. Luckily a neighbour, Shameem, a fellow women's group member came by. She recognised the symptoms of severe pre-eclampsia and that Jyosna needed immediate medical help. Shameem gave Jyosna's husband 5,000 taka from the women's group fund so the could take her to the hospital immediately. Two hours later, her baby was safely delivered by C-section. The doctor told them any longer and Jyosna wouldn't have survived. Without the women's group she and baby Nurani would not be alive today.

Anju, 27, was another enthusiastic recruit to her local women's group. Despite having only primary education, she quickly became a leading member and encouraged other women in the village to attend. At one meeting, Anju made an influential speech about the care of newborn babies and the importance of nutrition and hygiene for mothers. The group encouraged her to stand for election to the Union Parishad. They mobilised others to help her campaign and she won her local government seat in Bhatra with a large majority. Since becoming a representative in the local council, she had helped to organise the building of a road and 10 toilets. She also encouraged all women in the 19 villages she represents to attend women's groups and to send their children to school.

In 2009, I flew back to Dhaka. Sarah, our epidemiologist, was extracting the preliminary results from our data team. We had death rates from

36,113 births over three years in a population of 503,163. Cluster-level mean newborn death rate (adjusted for stratification and clustering) was 34 deaths per 1000 live births in the intervention clusters compared with 36.5 per 1000 in the control clusters. A small effect (7%), but not statistically significant. The study had shown no real impact.[147]

We sat together in silent shock. The Begum swore and the rest of the team cried. They had failed. The Nepalis and Indians had delivered and Bangladesh had aborted. Heads hung in shame. Juniors feared retribution but none came. I tried to be motivational.

"Guys, that's why we do scientific trials. Negative results are as important as positive. If we knew the result we wouldn't do it. We must learn what the data is telling us." It didn't seem to help. The smudged mascara symbolised a collective sense of guilt.

"OK, lets go for a meal and celebrate what you did. You set up hundreds of women's groups. It wasn't a waste of time."

Over a Chinese meal in Gulshan I laid out some explanations. "I can think of three reasons it didn't work. First, perhaps the women's groups weren't as lively or effective as in India or Nepal."

"Rubbish," said the Begum. "I visited Makwanpur and Ekjut. Our groups were just as good. Bengali women can talk, you know."

"OK. Well maybe the groups chatted but afterwards the members commingled less in the villages. Especially the repressed conservative ones up in Moulvibazar."

"But there's no difference in death rates between the districts. And women have ways of networking, even up there. I don't believe it."

"Then it must be the coverage. We got the dose wrong. We reached too few pregnant women compared with India and Nepal. You Bengalis are too densely populated."

"That's true."

"Which means we need to work out the coverage of pregnant women attending groups and repeat the study with a much higher dose of groups. If it's something to do with Bengali social networking then changing the dose won't work. If it's simply down to too few groups we should show an impact."

Figure 29. Bengali women's group

The Begum looked daggers. This meant another study.

In fact, our coverage of women of reproductive age turned out to be less than half the rate in the other countries and the numbers of pregnant women reached was much lower. Luckily, we had support for group expansion from the good old National Lottery so we decided to build in a new evaluation study: more groups, a greater effort to mobilise pregnant women, and another three years. The Begum's team were happy because they kept their jobs and believed my explanation. Azad saw the logic.

"Yes it makes sense. We can do better in reaching the primigravidae. Lets do it. Treble the number of groups."

But the Begum was sceptical. She looked me in the eyes.

"If it doesn't work, I'll kill you." I half believed her.

Three and a half years later I passed an open office door at the UCL Institute for Global Health.

"Hang on," said Ed, our new epidemiologist. "Those new PCP results. Do you want the bad news?

"Don't. I can't bear it. Kishu'll have my guts for garters."

"Control cluster newborn death rate, er . . . 30.1 per 1000."

"Yes. And the intervention?"

"Intervention clusters . . ." a long pause, " . . . 21.3 per 1000 live births."

"No! What's the effect size?"

"38% cut in deaths. Risk ratio 0.62 with a 95% confidence interval of, er, 0.43 to 0.89.

"I love you."

"And better hygiene, fewer cold baths on the first day, and earlier initiation of breastfeeding."

"Unbelievable. I'll buy you a cappuccino."

We flew to Dhaka feeling smug. The Begum and her entourage were triumphant.

"It's the same as a drug," she explained to her staff, "we had to get the dose right."

In India there was a post-script. In order to demonstrate that facilitated women's groups could be scaled up through the government, the Ekjut team repeated a large community trial using government-approved Accredited Social Health Activists (ASHAs) as leaders of participatory women's groups.[148] In India, over 900,000 ASHAs are in post, each covering a population of over 1000. Initially their role was as volunteer social activists, but quickly they were transformed into unpaid community health workers to carry the burden of promoting birth in hospitals, immunising children, advocating for family planning and sterilisation, improving village sanitation, treating simple illnesses like diarrhoea with oral rehydration sachets, anaemia with iron and folic acid tablets, malaria with chloroquine, and storing disposable delivery kits (DDK), contraceptive pills and condoms. This is a huge burden for a volunteer who might reasonably be expected to work only a few hours a week.

Ekjut wanted to see whether using ASHAs in their original role to facilitate women's groups might be the way to scale up the approach. Between 2009 and 2012, they enrolled 30 population clusters (estimated population 156,519) to the women's group intervention (15 clusters, estimated population 82,702) or control (15 clusters, 73,817). The newborn mortality rate during this period was 30 per 1000 live births in the intervention group and 44 per 1000 live births in the control group, a highly significant cut in deaths of 31%. The intervention was highly cost-effective according to the WHO threshold, as the cost per life year saved was less than India's GDP per capita[149]. Needless to say, immediately after the analysis, Prasanta, Nirmala and the Ekjut team started similar women's groups in the control clusters. And the Indian government has now instructed eight states to roll out the women's group programme, run by the ASHAs.

MALAWI

Our studies in impoverished rural Malawi teased us. We faced real world research problems of unpredictable context, the twists and turns of 'field research', and how to interpret data changes in relation to moving baselines. We learnt how to run a social analysis of the groups alongside our measures of death rates. We developed theories of change, measures of implementation strength, integrated measures of poverty and empowerment, and new ways to analyse results.

In Malawi's Mchinji district, villagers eked out a precarious subsistence, their fragile food security garrisoned by meagre tobacco cash crops. Here we set up a field study in 48 population clusters, each cluster of up to three villages or around 3000 people. In Lilongwe, the capital, the study was led by two paediatricians, Peter Kazembe and Charles Mwansambo, whose wise counsel and cool experience steered us through the rapids of officialdom. Both worked long, long hours as clinicians, researchers and leaders but both had a hinterland. Charles moonlighted as a DJ. Peter was a connoisseur of the local music scene, though in his keen support for Manchester United he lacked serious judgment about Premier League football.

One evening, Sonia, our resident epidemiologist, took me to Harry's bar to listen to the Makanbale Brothers, a band of shoeless, village boys, two of them playing makeshift guitars created from five-litre oil cans, a spliced wooden bridge and steel wire strung tightly up to the frets. The single string bass player used a 10-gallon can lying lengthways on the floor. The neck leaned at an angle of 30 degrees stretching up to a chair. The bassist played it like a keyboard and supported the timpani with bursts of bass drum by beating the oil drum. The drummer used two cane sticks to thrash a small beaten saucepan lid cymbal and two improvised small leather drums. The rhythm was hypnotic, lashed by taut guitar repeats and glorious voice harmonies. This was pure African music, the roots of the blues, of soul and jazz. Here were the repetitive phrases and pulse of improvisation, the core of modern music, where a harmonic conversation developed within a miniature sympathy group. We needed no reminder that deep culture is found amid poverty and deprivation.

When we started our women's group study in 2003, the rampant AIDS epidemic had brought death to almost every family. At Sam's Motel in Mchinji, a five dollar a night guesthouse where we played pool and watched Premier League football with the locals, I gave my condolences to Sam. His 14-year-old stepdaughter, admitted to Lilongwe Central Hospital with meningitis the week before, had died despite full treatment. It sounded odd.

"She had a problem with her liver," said Sam, who himself would die a few months later.

"For a long time?"

"Yes."

Even odder. Meningitis and a long standing liver problem didn't seem to be linked unless she had cerebral malaria, but Charles had told me she didn't have malaria. Back at the hospital I asked Peter about the case.

"She had cryptococcal meningitis and didn't respond to any of the drugs. It was very sudden, but we had known she was positive for some time."

"But how does a 14-year-old die of AIDS? It couldn't have been perinatal transmission because she would have been dead by now."

"True," said Peter.

"And she must have acquired the infection at least two years ago, unless she was one of those cases who deteriorated very rapidly."

"True."

"So are we concluding that this was sexual transmission at an age below 12? Was she pubertally advanced?"

"Not at all. She was barely pubertal when she died?"

"So how is it explained?"

"She might have been scarified or tattooed," said Peter. It's quite common in the villages . . . on their cheeks or chest or their inner thighs."

But we could not rule out sexual transmission. The songs in the villages are intensely sexual. Girls are taught by aunts and mothers from the age of eight or nine how to be sexual, how to attract and obey the man, and how to please and congratulate him during and after intercourse. The girls must never refuse sex. Inevitably, uncles or neighbours may abuse young girls. And after AIDS arrived it got even worse. Many infected men believed that sex with a young virgin would cleanse them of the virus.

By and large, Malawians are joyous, friendly people. But undercurrents of violence run close to the surface. In the night-time capital, in the wealthier areas, security jeep teams, wearing outsized uniforms and tin hats, carrying rusty rifles, patrol the barbed wire compounds. In the newspaper we read of a minor league footballer macheted to death in Mangochi by opposition fans. And in Mchinji the day before, when auditors arrived to check the annual accounts, the hospital accountant was found hanged from a tree. Seven million kwacha was missing, almost the annual budget for the hospital. Others were thought to be involved, possibly high up in the district council.

At Sonia's bungalow, not far from Mchinji hospital, ringed by bamboo fences, the gardener's wife had died of AIDS six months earlier. We were surprised to find another 15-year-old girl living with him, a new wife he had brought from his village soon after the funeral. Sonia had spent time counselling him and left boxes of condoms in his hut and every toilet in the house. To no avail. The young woman was pregnant already, and almost certainly she, the baby and her new husband would die from AIDS in the next few years. (At this time no antiretroviral drugs were available). His new wife was a strong, straight-backed woman, bright and competent. I saw her whispering instructions to him behind the flame trees, probably helping him to negotiate better severance terms when they decided to go back to their village to open a small business.

Our MaiMwana (mother and infants) women's group study faced the usual formidable problems with surveillance, staff and supervision. The women though were quick to mobilise around their maternal health challenges. Karonga village women's group, for example, considered anaemia a serious problem in pregnancy. They suggested pig farming as one way to address the problem. They planned to sell pigs and raise money to promote a more diverse diet for pregnant women. They bought pigs through members' contributions and, with local hired hands, erected a shelter. Subsequently, they persuaded the village headman to give them an acre of common land for a potager garden. Here they planted different varieties of vegetables rich in iron and vitamins. They also lobbied the health centre midwife to come and run a village clinic once a month, to spare the pregnant women their six-mile hike. The solidarity of group members helped them to know who to turn to in an emergency. And, after many months of lobbying their district council, one of the Karonga group, along with several other group reps, managed to get a consignment of insecticide-treated bed nets provided under the shamefully inaccessible national distribution programme.

In three other districts, Kasungu, Salima and Lilongwe rural, we took advantage of another large scale expansion of community women groups, allied to quality improvement initiatives at hospitals and health centres. We helped to create the MaiKhanda (mother and child) study. We built in a randomised evaluation of the two initiatives and worked with an enthusiastic team led by Agnes Makhonda, with Charles Makwenda, Bejoy Nambiar, Tim Colbourn and a team of excellent women facilitators. The MaiMwana team generously shared their experiences in Mchinji. One visit by our funder was memorable. The officer had come out to review progress with the programme, which aimed to cut maternal and newborn deaths. After a couple of village visits, anxious for quick results, he was unhappy. He wanted to know why the women were not doing what he expected.

"They're doing kitchen gardening?" he said, acerbically.

"Yes," I said. "They're called *dimba* gardens"

"But we're funding a project to cut newborn deaths."

"Yes."

"So how will kitchen gardens reduce newborn deaths?"

I tried to think on my feet.

"Well, er, they grow spinach and other green leafy vegetables. The pregnant women eat better. It will boost their vitamin A."

"But what about the messages about hygiene and going to the hospital? They should be focusing on the main causes of death and their treatment."

"They'll get there. But it's important we let the women decide their own priorities."

He was sceptical. "We shall ask the team to set up task forces to support the groups and give them the right messages. I don't see how kitchen gardens can help." He turned and left.

Outsiders always think they know best. To be honest, I knew a benefit from green leafy vegetables would, at best, be small. Nonetheless a few weeks later I spoke with Florida, our brilliant field co-ordinator in our Mchinji office, in the westernmost district of Malawi. The gardens were the commonest strategy developed by the 201 women's groups. She felt the nutritional benefits were a bit of an irrelevance.

"The prime reason is money," she said, slightly nonplussed that I hadn't grasped the point. "The *dimba* gardens give them produce to sell. The chiefs don't mind to give them about one hectare of land. The women grow and sell their produce to generate cash for any emergency – a delivery, a bleed, or when their child is sick."

Gardens, vegetables, cash and power – the logic was impeccable, though not simple, nor necessarily linear. Unlike women's groups in south Asia, the African women had little experience of revolving cash funds. But the women were right. The funder and I were both wrong. Empowerment came from cash.

Figure 30. A. Women's group with observers, Mchinji, Malawi
B. One thousand villagers attend women's groups' festival watched
by local MP, Patience Zulu

In brief, the results our two Malawi studies showed significant newborn infant survival benefits of varying degrees. In MaiMwana we had used a more complex 'factorial' design whereby we tested two interventions for the price of one – using four arms of clusters, women's groups and peer counsellors separately, both together, or an arm with neither intervention. This created unexpected problems because baseline differences in death rates meant we had two ways to analyse the study. Using one method we found a large impact of women's groups (almost a 40% cut in newborn deaths), while with another analysis there was none. The truth was probably somewhere between the two.

In the other MaiKhanda study we showed a smaller 16% cut in perinatal deaths in the areas in which we ran the women's groups. The quality improvement initiatives showed little impact on care, probably because shortages of drugs and health workers were so common. The world is messy. Controlled experiments in the real world are always confounded, complicated and challenging. But they're important if we want to know what works and bring you closer to the real problems facing poor people,

179

teaching you about their humanity, ingenuity and compassion. And they're huge fun to do. The series of studies had generated differing results and we had to bring them together. We needed to think about why and how chatting in groups might bring about survival benefits, and how to present a scientific summary to the world of medical science and policy.

MUMBAI SLUMS

In India we were keen to study how women's groups might perform in a slum. As our world becomes more urban, with most poor people now living in the fragile state of a shanty town rather than a rural homestead, slum dwellers have become among the most vulnerable people on the planet. Our friend, the paediatrician Armida Fernandez, was just the person to do it. Armida's eminence as a child health specialist and Dean of a medical school in Mumbai meant she could indulge her real interest in community mother and child health. She gathered together a group of formidable women: Neena Shah More, Ujwala Bapat, Sushmita Das, Wasu Joshi and Nayreen Daruwalla, among others, from all kinds of backgrounds – social work, gender violence, community development, nutrition, newborn care – and started to raise money for a charity, SNEHA (the Society for Nutrition, Education and Health Action). They planned to provide appropriate care to the poorest in the city. As a scientist she also wanted to assess what might work best.

Armida had networking and fundraising skills like no other person I knew. She buzzed around her friends among the Mumbai fashion, film and finance elites to raise funds. Her team of acolytes were drawn to her like moths to a light. Her enthusiasm, warmth and humility were irresistible. We helped a little with money, but mainly supplied assistance with data collection. David had decided that seven years in Kathmandu was enough. The lure of the bright lights of Mumbai and the largest slum in the world, Dharavi, proved irresistible. Susie and David soon defected to Bandra West to join SNEHA (a Hindi word meaning friendship) and Armida's dynamic team.

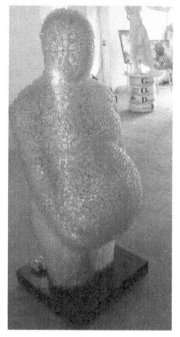

Figure 31: A. Dharavi Biennale Art Exhibition created by community groups, Mumbai
B. Women's health leader Nayreen Daruwalla persuades Mr Sinha, local announcer,
singer, mimic and video producer, to support the Biennale
C. Pregnant woman sculpture made from medicine bottles. Photos, the author[150]

So SNEHA planned another study. Women's groups would meet fortnightly to share their experiences, discuss problems, discover their strengths, consider what to do, act and reflect. Urban slum clusters of 1000–1500 households, 48 in total, were randomly selected, with 24 clusters assigned to the women's group programme and 24 as controls. Across every cluster, a programme of health facility strengthening was led by Wasu, who used novel 'appreciative inquiry' techniques to hypnotically transform demotivated staff into campaigning workaholics. So transformative, in fact, I invited her to London to do the same with our academic department, to fascinating effect.

Quickly the team learned that slums are distinctly different from rural hamlets. In the dark, smoky, cluttered alleys of Dharavi, women's meetings had to be much smaller, crammed into tiny slum bedrooms. They were briefer and more frequent, when every member could manage the time. Community solidarity was less than in quiet villages, suspicion greater and migration common. Further, Mumbai offers a chaotic but far richer mix of health care options, both public and private. And slum dweller incomes are generally higher than for the rural poor.

To our surprise, baseline death rate of newborns was about half what we had predicted, around 15 per 1000 births, except in the most marginalised and recently arrived families. This meant we were highly unlikely to detect a difference in deaths between the study arms unless the population, already large, was doubled in size. Financially, this was out of the question. The study continued, with deep learning about the slum dwellers, their illnesses, home care, family decision-making, and their use of clinics and hospitals. Domestic violence and alcohol abuse, a toxic mix, emerged as a primary concern to many women, so that refuge and rehabilitation, mediation and mentoring, came to the fore. One third of pregnant women experienced some kind of abuse. SNEHA became world leaders in ways to respond to gender violence. At completion of their women's group study after three years we were not surprised to learn that death rates across the two arms of the study were similar. But the study inaugurated an academic group that was to become a pioneer of health inquiry within slums and how to respond to the abuse that so many women suffer.

The Power of Conversation

HOW WOMEN'S GROUPS WORK

In one sense, a women's group is a therapeutic conversation. The psycho-
therapist Paul Gordon sees "therapy as a conversation about things that
matter".[151] There is speaking and listening. He shares the view of the
philosopher Karl Jaspers on the pernicious nature of solitude.[152] Humanity
is rooted in the application of reason to our lives, in 'interpersonal existential communication'. We react to 'boundary situations' such as suffering,
death and the daily struggle for power, for resources and social status at
the social edge. Existential communication is not so much exchange of
messages but more dimensions of intimacy, trust, openness, frankness, and
'loving struggle', a forum where "all kinds of power and superiority,
prejudice and calculating strategic reserve against the other are eliminated".[153] For young women in arranged marriages in patrilineal
households, low in the extended family hierarchy, a women's group acts
as a crucial outlet from the silence and stress of solitude. The nineteenth
century chronicler William Cobbett understood this. "Women are a
sisterhood. They make common cause on behalf of the sex; and, indeed,
this is natural enough, when we consider the vast power that the law
gives us over them."[154]

Gordon emphasises that conversation differs from discussion. In conversation you keep company, sit with others, what Jaspers calls an act of love

both nourishing and able to call into question. In discussion you analyse, break up. Discussion is like a game of ideas where the aim is to win. In a women's group, conversation walked all over discussion. The solidarity of the 'loving struggle' was ascendant.

Many medical scientists doubt the value and generalisability of social interventions. "Until you know the mechanism, you can't scale it up," was a common objection and non sequitur. In medicine, we don't know the precise mechanism of many of our treatments but we still use them if they are proven to work. Transcutaneous electrical nerve stimulation (TENS) for pain in labour, Alcoholics Anonymous meetings for our commonest addiction, social ties to protect mental health, even electro-convulsive therapy in severe depression. We send our children to school without understanding exactly how education works. We don't understand in detail how many drugs work, such as steroids for auto-immune disease, or chemotherapy for cancer. Artemisinin, our most effective anti-malarial, derived from *qinghao* or sweet wormwood, was a popular medicine in China for a millennium. Ditto for morphine in many countries. Use of a drug pre-dates an understanding of its mechanism.

Our groups increased women's power rather than just changing their behaviour. Prasanta, a community development expert, explains: "We never talk about messages. How can we tell mothers 'you must not bathe your baby until after the second day'. A bath on the first day in 45 degrees heat might cause no harm. A bath on the third day for a preterm infant in winter might cause severe hypothermia? We want to encourage problem-solving, for people to find solutions to their own problems." As the paediatrician and psychoanalyst Donald Winnicott put it, "training is for dogs, education is for people".

Still, promotion of 'messages' for 'behaviour change' remains the most popular mantra within aid agencies and ministries. Everyone believes mobile text messages, radio jingles and posters will exhort poor communities to healthier lives. In the west we tell people to stop smoking, cut down the drink, and eat fewer doughnuts. In poor villages, where deaths from infection are common, we hope that hygiene messages will prevent unnecessary child deaths. Messages are cheaper than doctors and nurses, and easier than the bother of organising sympathy groups. Now that every village in Africa or south Asia has a mobile phone, with or without an electricity supply, messaging is easy. But we over-simplify its power. Evidence for long-term impact is thin. Advertising works but in much more subtle ways than instructions to buy a product. Advertising makes customers aware of locations, say, for clinics or stores or dentists, and builds a sense of responsibility and integrity for the product and its manufacturer. Advertising highlights the research and information around a product, and shares emotions and stories of satisfied customers. It uses many methods of persuasion. And it requires repetition through accessible media to reach 'wealthy enough' audiences. For many poor families these methods work less well.

Behaviour change communication (BCC) is Pavlovian in its sensitivity. We are fat because we overeat and slurp our Coca-Cola. A quick educational medicine will fix an errant code in our programmed suite of behaviours. We'll change to fruit, carrots and bottled water. Without doubt, messages on mobiles for appointments to see the dentist are a useful nudge. Nudges, for sure, can work everywhere. In India, mobile phone messages sent to HIV patients increased adherence slightly to their anti-retroviral drugs, from 85% to 91%. In a trial conducted in South Africa and Uganda, where circumcision can cut the risk of HIV transmission by 60%, 750 out of 12,993 (6%) uncircumcised men who tested HIV negative enrolled into three groups. One group received simple clinic referral for circumcision, another text messages as reminders, and a third home visits by lay counsellors. Results showed that only 28% of men had a circumcision after simple clinic referral but rates doubled to 48% when men received text messages, or 47% after a home visit.[155]

The MOTIF trial (Mobile Technology for Improved Family Planning) in Cambodia showed that among women who attended safe abortion services, adding a series of messages delivered by mobile phone had a short-term effect on contraceptive uptake up to four months, and on long-acting contraceptive methods at one year. No change occurred though in pregnancy or abortion rates.[156] Further, the feasibility and cost of mobile phone messaging at scale, and the ethics and legality, raise many questions for policymakers. Most policy people and technical experts are sceptical though of togetherness as a therapy. "Are you seriously telling me that chatting reduces death rates?' said one representative from an international agency. "You're simply teaching them to seek care and gain access to drugs aren't you?" I reminded him that care-seeking barely changed in our studies.

Behaviour change programmes don't aim to patronise people, but they rarely consider the minds receiving the message, or their culture, commerce and environment. Stress entices a mind to prefer a sugar-intense doughnut to a couple of peaches. Why do cultures celebrate 20 or 30 ounce soda bottles more than water from a street drinking fountain? Companies don't plot the obesity of fellow citizens but they bombard them with unhealthy advertising because they have sales targets. Which councils spend tax funds to provide space for exercise, play areas for children, and easy access to cheap, locally produced fruit and vegetables? Or do they build car parks over social space, place fizzy drink dispensing machines in schools and allow scared citizens to cycle along main roads shuddering with juggernauts. In reality, lasting benefits come from changed minds and social structures; and from environmentally intelligent and subtle governance. No, we don't want a nanny state. But we do want an environment that makes life pleasant and safe; one that protects our right to a healthy diet and a space to grow. A key social engine for environmental engineering is the sympathy group.

The first preference for a women's group conversation over a message to a single woman is shared memory. If you ask any woman in a village in Malawi about the risks of being pregnant they won't score too well. At best they might know of anaemia or haemorrhage but not the full panoply of risk and prevention. Yet, place them in a group and the shared memories of family experiences produces an epidemiological analysis better than a WHO survey. When our women's groups in Malawi listed and weighted the problems of maternity they did spectacularly well. They missed only two conditions, HIV and sepsis. Women see HIV as a general problem, not of maternity, and sepsis is difficult to recognise even by doctors.

A second asset of groups is to build the 'self-efficacy' of women. Groups offer them confidence to change their newborn care, their regular diet or birth plans. They watch and learn from peers. I gave up smoking not because I learned the dangers. I'm sorry to say I smoked for 12 years after my medical training. But then my wife stopped smoking, my office banned it, my children arrived on the scene. Two friends gave up with the help of nicotine gum and charts. Self-efficacy takes time. Knowledge and ownership of one's own problems is the cornerstone. Each of us has personal experience of trying to lose weight, to stop boozing, take more exercise, improve time management or reduce stress. Introspect and ask why it happened. Think whether a friend or family member or colleague gave advice that made sense. Who inspired you to imitate their own success? Social interaction and mimicry of peers increases our confidence and self-efficacy to improve our negotiation, planning and problem-solving skills. Paulo Freire calls this building "critical consciousness".[157]

Another obvious pay-off for the groups was control over resources. In south Asia, groups knew how to set up a mutual revolving fund. Women were part of other credit groups for forestry or farming. In Malawi, women's groups managing their own cash reserves were unusual. Instead they took land for kitchen gardening and sold their produce for cash when a member faced an emergency.

So far, so good. But women's groups produce something more valuable than efficacy of the self. They're not linear. At risk of offence, women find groups easier than men. They prefer to work in circles, not on ladders. The American midwife Elizabeth Davis describes the women's circle of life – from maiden to lover to mother to midwife to Amazon to matriarch to crone.[158] Women's groups are holistic, not a 'platform for intervention'. In the west we reduce health care to capsules, drugs, health workers and messages. But an active group coming together is more than the sum of its parts. Non-linearities mean groups catalyse new ideas, reach tipping points, produce a cascade of change.

For example, women who share ideas with family amplify health. They might change the diet of their sisters and daughters. They harness the energy of husbands, sons and fathers. They address unspoken issues like alcohol or gambling, or even domestic violence. And they release emergent talents like literacy, artistry, craft, horticulture, negotiation skills, comedy and musicality. They can learn decision-making in a crisis so they can respond to an obstetric emergency, a family death, a landslide or a poor harvest. The group will bring rich experience to a decision, or help a family decide where to seek care. These are not peripheral or marginal benefits. Solidarity is central to sustained success.

The benefits of camaraderie are plain when it's missing. I've never forgotten one pregnant woman I met in an isolated village before our study started. I had assumed that small villages were always social and neighbourly. The woman I met, Grace, had moved to the village after she became pregnant and lost her first baby as a stillbirth. Three years on, she lived in isolated drudgery. Weary and depressed, she knew few of her neighbours living less than 100 yards away. She had joined no groups, no choir, and enjoyed no recreation. She was pregnant again and worried about losing another baby. Grace's husband lived away as a security guard. The natal family lived hours away. She cared for her in-laws each day, without friendship or the comfort of a partner. I worried for her future.

Groups can analyse the emotional and family ripples from a crisis. They help build resilience. If you live outside a cash economy, an emergency fund is vital. Transport, porters, drugs and food need money when a family must get to a hospital. Friendship and sisterhood reduce their stress. And groups set up what engineers call closed-loop systems, processes that can support themselves. If we see families as passive, always requiring a health worker for every health problem, we ignore our most vital talent. Health workers and hospitals are mandatory, but health and resilience start at home. A group of beneficiaries are the first responders, neighbours who will share and rally round in a crisis. They advocate for outside resources or consult district officials or health workers. Aid talks of institution building. A sympathy group is the simplest institution we have.

For the poorest families, we found resilience to shocks increased through what economists call 'consumption smoothing'. When you live at the economic edge of subsistence, a heatwave, a flood, a wedding, a landslide or an illness can precipitate a 'shock'. Loss of income or new expenses create a sudden debt. At such time isolation can be fatal. In Malawi we surveyed households to ask how much food they ate before and after any crop losses they had suffered. Under a full insurance model, household consumption should move one-to-one with other members of the population.[159] Consumption should not fall with household-level crop losses because they have insurance. But most village people are uninsured, so consumption falls after a crop loss. Adverse weather events are common in Malawi. Twenty eight per cent of Malawian houses reported crop losses, which on average represented a deficit of 93% of a month's food supply. Among those who suffered a crop loss, people in women's group areas were more likely to talk to a friend or relative than those living in control areas. In group villages, families shared with each other so that food consumption after a shock hardly changed, whereas families in non-group areas showed substantial falls. Presumably groups offer a safety net of sharing for this consumption smoothing.

This protective effect of the group mirrors the ecology of species-rich environments. In 1972, Robert May analysed how connected subsets of species, called modules, with intense connections between themselves but not with species from other modules, provided greater stability and food security. A shock affected just that module across a network of species.[160] Clustering of species into groups is protective in animal populations against food collapse and extinction. Likewise the modularity introduced by sympathy groups can contain most economic shocks and increase local resilience.

Another strange finding from our studies was that the poorest families benefited the most.[161] Among the most marginalised members of the tribal population (mothers who were illiterate, very poor, had little or no land and belonged to a Scheduled Tribe or Scheduled Caste), newborn death rates were 59% lower in intervention than in control clusters in years two and three (70%, year three), whereas among the less marginalised, death rates were 36% lower (35%, year three). The women's group effect on death rates appeared stronger for the most marginalised. This is a rare exception to Dr Julian Tudor-Hart's 'inverse care law', whereby those who need health care the most get it the least, and those that need it least get the most.[162] The inverse care law is ubiquitous in population health – the tilted spirit level of inequality to access between rich and poor. Yet participatory group conversations reduced socio-economic inequalities. Why?

Prasanta proposed an 'anything they can get' hypothesis for our newborn survival findings. Any scraps of information or help around hygiene, feeding, thermal care and support in a crisis can save a life. Prasanta himself suffers from retinitis pigmentosa and is partially blind. At night he stumbles and needs help to find his way. He understands disability, both physical and social.

"They're the same as me. I gain the most from a torchlight," he explained. "Even morsels of knowledge and support can make the poorest families more resilient. Their margins are so small that they benefit much more. They are real survivors."

This characteristic of a group touches upon an important issue in economics called information asymmetry. In economics, Gresham's law states that 'bad money will drive out the good', meaning that if two currencies are of equal value, one fake or unreliable and one good, those holding good currency will withdraw it from the market of exchange. In 1970, George Akerlof won the Nobel Prize for his paper in the Quarterly Journal of Economics called 'The Market for Lemons'.[163] The paper took Gresham's law a stage further and addressed the economics of quality and uncertainty, and how one might calculate the economic costs of dishonesty. How did used car markets work when buyers face a choice between good cars – peaches – and malfunctioning cars – lemons? Higher prices cannot guarantee people get a better quality car if users don't have information on the car. Bad cars will drive out the good because they sell at the same price as good cars. Buyers won't notice if the car is a dud or not. Only the seller will know.

Likewise health services, especially in poorer countries, cannot be easily assessed for quality. Information asymmetry abounds. How can a patient identify if a doctor is well trained or not? Whether the drugs are fake or real? And whether treatment is necessary or for the pocket of the doctor? Membership of a group will at least give you information on user experiences or help to make the best of a limited choice. This is important because private hospitals will only invest in better quality care if they start to lose patients because care is considered below standard. In free at the point of delivery care, systems of regulation must substitute for the price mechanism. But the principle of sharing information more widely through population groups, to reduce information asymmetry, still holds.

Indeed, competition, not privatisation, drives improvement. A recent study showed that the UK National Health Service benefited from a 2006 policy that patients had a choice of at least five hospitals for their referral consultation.[164] It saved the NHS $479 million per year. By contrast, many private health care markets in the United States are heading in the opposite direction, with consolidation and mergers of private hospitals. Will this reduce competition and the value of care provided? For health insurance, though, information asymmetry works for the patient. It explains why people over the age of 65 find it nigh on impossible to buy health insurance. As people age, and understand, along with their doctor, their medical problems and risks, the asymmetry of information works against the insurance company. So sicker patients are more likely to seek insurance as they age, a problem known as adverse selection. In response, insurance companies either raise their prices hugely for the elderly or refuse to insure.

Another mistake is to underestimate the transitional and transformative value of sympathy groups. Members learn that it takes time to do things, to plan strategies, that no magic solution exists. People learn that local effort counts. They need not be fatalistic. They grasp that diversity of group talent brings unexpected change and inspired solutions. The creativity and complexity of women's groups can transform the health of their families. Empowerment of women in almost any society is a sign of development. As Karl Marx said, "Social progress can be measured by the social position of the female sex."[165] Our groups helped women to discover the principles of hygiene, to reduce their stress, to build neighbourly trust, enhance their status, help with care-seeking, and protect their local environment. Groups started to tackle more chronic deep-seated problems such as emotional and physical abuse by a partner, often driven by alcohol. A group imbued women with quiet subversive power, the power to gain a loan or credit, to weigh up risks. They learned to ask why, to challenge a local decision, to reduce the shame and humiliation of marginalised and low caste groups. In the longer term, some members sought political office at elections.

So groups are far more than vehicles for the exchange of helpful messages. The jargon is closed loops, transitional plans, holistic philosophy, functional interconnections and multi-tasking to create and use by-products, to build resilience and diversity, and to reduce information asymmetry. The end product is empowerment, 'critical consciousness', the first leg along the path to greater freedoms. These qualities share the language of how to live 'green', and how to absorb lessons from the *modus operandi* of our ancestors to live sustainably in future. Environmentalists describe permaculture, how to manage sustainable agriculture and eco-systems, as a way to 'meet human needs through ecological and regenerative design'. To some extent all design decisions follow ethical principles and use the logic and beauty of natural systems. The social and health functions of sympathy groups echo this movement.

Many of the components of 'empowerment' are difficult to measure. Sceptics can legitimately aim their fire at an aid industry that focuses only on improving women's earning power through sewing machines and rearing chickens.[166] They argue that empowerment projects are 'depo-liticising, obscuring women's relationships to power and the state' and 'collapse their identity to the circumstances of their victimhood.' It's true that this can happen. But our women's groups were political with a small 'p'. And we must be careful not to extrapolate from rotten projects to a general rejection of programmes that give poor people a voice.

THE BUM'S RUSH OF META-ANALYSIS

In 2013, our research team of doctors, anthropologists, epidemiologists, social scientists and development workers published a scientific paper in the Lancet. It's the world's leading medical journal.[167] We presented summary results from our seven large scientific studies, which had engrossed us for 15 years. In population experiments covering millions of poor village people in Africa and Asia we had tested the impact of participatory women's sympathy groups. When women came together to solve problems, they saved lives in large numbers. Led by Dr Audrey Prost, our 'meta-analysis' showed that with the right number of pregnant women joining the groups, villages with groups saw a large fall in the deaths of mothers and their newborn infants compared with those where they were absent. Deaths fell by one third, massive by public health standards. Groups were of proven value, scalable, sustainable and cost-effective. They worked for the poorest families in the most distant villages. The data was transparent, precise, comprehensive and hedged with statistical caution. And the findings had relevance to national health systems because every government struggles to contain escalating costs of care. Self-organisation and empowerment methods, as in sympathy groups, can improve health and cut welfare bills and taxes.

On the day of publication we tweeted and blogged, released press statements and stories. We launched, packaged, webbed and promoted. We hired a room at the UK House of Commons and implored funders and donors to attend. Many politely declined. The editor of the Lancet, Richard Horton, was succinct and powerful with his soundbite: "It's not a drug. It's not a vaccine. It's not a device," he tweeted, "it's women, working together, solving problems, saving lives." A commentary in the journal by the eminent Brazilian epidemiologist, Professor Cesar Victora, called our study a breath of fresh air.[168] "People who promote somewhat ethereal ideas such as empowerment are seldom the same people as those who are keen on doing randomised controlled trials," he wrote. "The greatest accomplishment of this group of investigators is to combine both." We flushed with pride.

The trouble was that we didn't make the Kilburn Times or the Tryon Daily Bulletin, let alone the daily broadsheets or the tabloids. In fact, we didn't make the news media at all — nothing on TV, radio, or any popular blog or online newspaper. In the days after publication we found nothing in the BBC, the Huffington Post, the Voice of America, the Mail or

Guardian Online, or the Times of India. In our round-the-clock global media frenzy, where we had sought our 15 seconds of fame, the library police removed us. We were frog-marched, strait-jacketed and gagged, along a silent CCTV-free corridor, into the dark, dead bunker of the world's science archive. My kid brother, a theatre producer, read the tweeted paper. And read it again. "Let me get this right, bro," he said, perplexed, "is your life's work based on coffee mornings in Nepal?"

Most people are wary of the narrative of science or don't understand it. We enjoy science fiction or popular science books on the cosmos and evolution, and stories of famous scientists, their theories, breakthroughs and scandals. But the astonishing profusion of scientific papers goes unnoticed. Most scientific papers enter a vast silent cavern, housing the world library, guarded by gatekeepers and paywalls, written in unspoken or incomprehensible dialects. The average readership of a detailed scientific paper is only four or five people, which doesn't exclude the authors' parents. Only sensational snippets leak out into the popular media.

Scientists are largely to blame. Our language is as bright and resonant as a digital clock. We remove colour for the sake of precision. We anaesthetise readers with sterile measured doses. Scientific papers read like gadget manuals, necessary but unreadable. Our love of stories is colossal – fantasies, fairytales, novels, adventures, gossip, entertainment, travel and nature. The foibles of sports stars, celebrities, presidents, victims and recluses are so addictive we buy mountains of books, newspapers, and magazines. We are glued to screens of every size. Communications and entertainment industries dominate our economy. Our fantasy world is richer than ever. Yet our popular understanding of science and its methods is rarely more than rudimentary.

Worse, great scientists and thinkers show an obstinate determination not to be understood. Consider academic writing on three subjects of scientific importance for the social edge: epigenetics, the balance between objective and subjective evaluation in social policy, and the principles of 'critical realism'. The emerging science of epigenetics aims to unravel how our DNA and gene expression can be modified by our physical and social environment. It offers the possibility to enhance genes we want expressed and to suppress those we don't. But academic writing is opaque and impenetrable for the lay reader, even for the journalist advocate who must translate it. Epigeneticist Shelley Berger and colleagues, for example, offer a definition of epigenetics in a scientific review: "Epigenetic events in eukaryotic organisms have evolved to provide a more precise and stable control of gene expression and genomic regulation through multiple generations ... exemplified by the existence of sex-specific dosage compensation or the fine-tuning of allele-specific expression, as seen in imprinted loci."[169] Even science undergraduates might struggle with this.

Another challenge is how to combine the subjective and objective in social evaluations. The French social scientist Pierre Bourdieu re-interpreted modern science as a social and subjective construct, partly created by our educational systems. For example, he saw English private schools like Eton College, the school attended by former UK Prime Minister David Cameron, UK Foreign Secretary Boris Johnson, and Justin Welby, the Archbishop of Canterbury, as promoting form over content,[170] social domination over intellectual ideas. Their team sports, Bourdieu claimed, were "fed by the anti-intellectualism of the imperial elite which valued loyalty and group spirit over personal development and independence." He quoted Lord Plummer's speech to Old Etonians "They taught us nothing at Eton ... but I think they taught it very well."[171] The French grandes écoles were much the same.

Similarly, Bourdieu argued that we cannot understand science outside its social context. He introduced the idea of the 'habitus', the principle that negotiates between social structures and scientific practices. Bourdieu had a huge impact on social science but his writing infuriates: "The habitus, the durably installed generative principle of regulated improvisa-tions, produces practices which tend to reproduce the regularities immanent in the objective conditions of the production of their gener-ative principle, while adjusting to the demands inscribed as objective potentialities in the situation, as defined by the cognitive and motivating structures making up the habitus".[172] I did not get beyond the first chapter.

Even if the subjective and objective intertwine, a third question is how we preserve rational experimental methods for social policy. Roy Bhaskar,

Oxford professor of philosophy, espoused 'critical realism' to explain why we must defend experimental evaluation in social science. He refuted the attacks of 'post-modernists' Bourdieu and Michel Foucault, who saw truth as only subjective. He defended the peaceful co-existence of stories and experiments. But, sadly, Bhaskar's writing wins the gold medal for obscurantism. Here he attempted to define 'critical realism': "dialectical critical realism may be seen under the aspect of Foucaultian strategic reversal – of the unholy trinity of Parmenidean/Platonic/Aristotelean provenance; of the Cartesian-Lockean-Humean-Kantian paradigm, of foundationalisms (in practice, fideistic foundationalisms) and irrationalisms (in practice, capricious exercises of the will-to-power or some other ideologically and/ or psycho-somatically buried source) new and old alike; of the primordial failing of western philosophy, ontological monovalence, and its close ally, the epistemic fallacy with its ontic dual; of the analytic problematic laid down by Plato, which Hegel served only to replicate in his actualist monovalent analytic reinstatement in transfigurative reconciling dialectical connection, while in his hubristic claims for absolute idealism he inaugurated the Comtean, Kierkegaardian and Nietzschean eclipses of reason, replicating the fundament of positivism through its transmutation route to the super-idealism of a Baudrillard."[173] Enough said.

Despite our team's bum's rush with the media, further studies strengthened the evidence base. In east India, Ekjut used national Accredited Social Health Activists, drawn from the cadre of 900,000 volunteers across the whole country, to facilitate the groups.[174] We assumed that newborn survival would lessen when scaled up through women with less time and commitment. Not true. Newborn deaths fell by 31% compared to areas without groups, and by 46% when adjusted for baseline death rates. In the same region, they examined the power of participatory groups of pregnant mothers and home visits by nutrition workers to tackle the huge problem of childhood stunting. Stunting is growth failure of both body and brain. Some 160 million children worldwide suffer stunting by the age of two. One third live in India. Ekjut found groups and home visits improved home care and dietary diversity for both mothers and infants, but did not affect stunting rates.[175] Access to toilets in these communities was less than 2%. So infection and diarrhoea were common in infancy, which stunted their growth. Still, infant deaths in the first year (not just newborn deaths in the first month) fell from 64 to 51 per 1000 live births where groups were active.

Where data are absent, poor quality or disputed, experiments show the benefits or otherwise at the social edge. Policy decisions need evidence as well as ideology. Experiments are often unsuccessful, development projects frustrating and unsustainable, planning decisions built upon mistaken ideology. We must not be depressed. 'Fail faster, succeed sooner.' And a negative result is as important as a positive, because we learn the constraints and limitations of what we can do. Bertrand Russell believed in rational evidence: "Never let yourself be diverted either by what you wish to believe, or by what you think would have beneficent social effects if it were believed. But look only, and solely, at what are the facts."

We must educate people on scientific methods. Scientists take existing theory and understanding, set up a hypothesis, make observations or experiments to test it, and interpret results to confirm or refute the first theory. The cycle is repeated with a new hypothesis. But science is not just done in laboratories. Population and social science is more amenable to the experimental method than many people believe. Experiments emerge from non-scientific observations. Sometimes the most original science comes from a single story – that's how X-rays and penicillin were discovered, by Alexander Fleming and Marie Curie. James Watson and Francis Crick unravelled the genetic code after listening attentively to stories from rival groups. Over 50 years of stories, observations and experiments have created an array of new scientific 'omes': the genome (our genetic make-up), proteome (proteins), metabolome (metabolites), biome (our biology), connectome (nerve connections in the brain) and the exposome (environmental exposures we face during our lifetime). What about a science of the 'groupome' or 'sympatholome'? But first we test a hypothesis that human development comes not just from income, freedom or education, but fundamentally from social trust. And that sympathy groups are fundamental in creating social trust.

Part 3
Development as Trust

Keeping Promises

POROSHREEKATOR

"There is a word in Bengali which has no comparable word in English."

Azad Khan, wearing a Harris tweed jacket over a cream cotton panjabi, a Burberry cashmere scarf pirated in Inner Mongolia, and a faux-fur Kosygin hat, stood at the stern of the longboat. We were gliding up a creek in the Sunderbans, the mangrove wilderness of southern Bangladesh, between banks of Jurassic Nypa palms, which rose like parasols from the grey milky mud. The birds were reticent this morning. We had seen only a green heron and a ruddy brown kingfisher. Our ornithological safari silence had petered out. Azad was keen to chat.

"The word is 'poroshreekator'. It means poro, somebody else, shree, his or her beauty, and kator, to feel bad or to covet."

"So it means jealous."

"No it's not the same. More than jealousy. You people are happy when others make money or achieve success. Bengalis are different. There is a story that St Peter went to inspect the separate hells designed for the Americans, the Germans and the Bengalis. The American hell had armed guards, and a careful network of perimeter fences. They surrounded the German hell with barbed wire and machine guns to stop people escaping. When St Peter came to the Bengali hell it was open with no guards in sight. A Bengali sat nearby reading a newspaper.

"Why is this hell unprotected?" St Peter demanded.

"Simple," said the Bengali. "Because if anyone tries to escape, another Bengali will stop him."

Eminent physician, pharmacological researcher, social entrepreneur, chief executive of the largest national diabetic association in the world, and rector of a university he created in 2007, Azad brings a wry intelligence to the way development does and doesn't work. In highlighting *poroshreekator* he described not only a Bengali phenomenon but an intense non-sharing jealousy that features in most 'developing' societies, and recurs, unless regulated or educated, within the most 'advanced'. Academic departments and political parties are prone to *poroshreekator*.

This desire to stop your neighbour doing well has a mirror image called corruption, the desire for private gain from a public good, or even private gain from another's private good. The intense desire to prevent anyone else from becoming better than you transmutes into the drive to ensure you become better than your neighbour, whatever it takes, and whatever he or she might do to prevent it. Betterment requires secrecy, conspiracy, mistrust and corruption. All societies are corrupt, some more than others. Azad tells me a heavenly parable.

"The US President has an audience with God at which he can ask one question.

'Please God, when will my nation again be the unchallenged superpower on earth?'

God smiles. 'Not in your lifetime,' he replies.

Then the President of China meets God and asks his own question.

'Please God, when will my nation be the unchallenged dominant economic power on earth?'

'Not in your lifetime,' says God.

The Prime Minister of Bangladesh is called. 'Dear God, when will my nation be free from rampant corruption?' God smiles and says nothing.

Again she asks, and God just smiles. 'Please God, you must tell me, for the sake of our development.' At last God speaks. 'Not in my lifetime'."

Why do *poroshreekator* and corruption flourish if they retard social progress? Like bond prices and yields they are two sides of the same

Figure 32: Nirmala Nair, Dharma Manandhar, Kishwar Azad, Prasanta Tripathy, Shanthi Pantvaidya and the author

human investment. In the messy world of human social evolution, the tension and balance between self-interest and group support creates many varieties of organisational culture. Ultimately, cheaters are defeated by co-operators, argue evolutionary theorists and economists. But corruption is pivotal, ill-understood and taboo in development. Every society tolerates it to a degree. We promote 'social capital' and 'institution strengthening' to prevent corruption and to improve 'good governance'. They work, we hope, through 'mutual trust'.

Economist Partha Dasgupta defines social capital as "interpersonal networks whose members develop and maintain trust in one another to keep their promises by the device of 'mutual enforcement' of agreements."[176] Mutual trust between people and their institutions are fundamental not only to wellbeing and smooth governance but also to the success of an economy. Dasgupta shows through mathematical models that an increase in trust among people would lead to an increase in the economy's wealth. Indeed in one economic model, which compared two autarkic communities with the same population, identical physical capital, and working the same number of hours, the one with a co-operative culture showed, over time, greatly increased household income. Real-life surveys show the same.[177] In another model, where two communities in 1900 are given the same human capital, total productivity, savings, and no changes observed in these factors or demographics occurring over the next 70 years, the one with the greater co-operation had, in 1970, much greater output, wages and salaries, profits, consumption and wealth.

Why is this? Why does mutual trust confer economic and development benefits when measures of individual human development and productivity remain unchanged? Could the extraordinary improvements since 1960 in the life expectancy, incomes and death rates of China, Bangladesh, Brazil and most of Latin America, south-east Asia and southern states of India, be explained less by medicines, vaccines, aid and investment, and more by rising aggregate mutual trust between and within communities? Are successful developing countries those that learn to accept the mutual enforcement of promises? That doesn't mean corruption is less, just that more people keep their promises.

WORD AS BOND

How do we make and honour promises within our communities? We might agree on joint action to support a park, an irrigation system or a water supply. Or we create a committee to sustain a local family health practice, rural health centre or hospital. We might plan a communal garden, drainage channel or riverbank, or to combine resources for a business through labour, credit or insurance. Maybe we want to ally two families through marriage, or set up a local credit or investment group. Others might advocate for a political or environmental cause. Or just buy something over the counter from a local trader.

Whatever we do, we must honour our promises, for the seller of goods or labour to give the finished article or work on time, and the buyer to pay for the goods in full. If parties to a contract are to keep their promises, we need a system whereby at all times 1) it's in the interest of each party to plan to keep their word and 2) each party believes that all others would keep their word. [178] Both conditions are needed. Number 1 justifies for number 2.[179]

So how to meet these conditions? Mutual affection between the contractees through being members of the same family or clan might do it. Most of us believe that blood is thicker than water. But families are often volatile and unreliable. When family disputes erupt they are among the most bitter. In June 2001 in a fit of drug-filled paranoia and anger, Crown Prince Dipendra gunned down the Nepalese Royal Family – his father, mother, sister and younger brother – before turning the weapon on himself. Extended family and several bystanders witnessed the attack. On visits to Makwanpur, our staff gave me their conspiracy theories on the assassination of King Birendra and Queen Aishwarya. Everyone I spoke to, along with 90% of the population in opinion polls, believed Gyanendra, the King's brother and successor, who was 200 miles away at the time, orchestrated the assassination.

"But you're not looking at the evidence," I told them. "The prince was in a forbidden love affair with Devi. He was furious with his parents who blocked his marriage with a rival Rana family. He was unpredictable and volatile." My voice rose, as a barrister gains momentum. "I even spoke with Kedar Mathema, the Nepali Ambassador to Japan. He told me that only a month before the bloodbath he wrote to the Prime Minister about his worries for the Prince's state of mind during his visit to Tokyo. Dipendra smoked cannabis regularly, took cocaine, and had a fixation on guns, with his own private arsenal." I reach a climax. "Anger, motive, drugs and guns. It's obvious. I rest my case."

Kirti stroked his chin, a Nepalese Sherlock Holmes, with haughty scepticism. After a considered pause he spoke.

"That is the linear model."

Kirti well understood the murky world of Nepalese families, of fratricide, inter-caste marriage taboos and competitive inheritance of power and fortune. Linear explanations missed the point. Families seethed with mutual distrust. With broken promises they could explode. The linear explanation of Dipendra's motives might conceal more duplicitous conspiracies.

A second way in which promises might be kept occurs in a society where co-operation is valued. For example hunter-gatherers prize a co-operative economy, and Amish, Quaker, or monastic communities emphasise sharing and charity. In England, the historic notion of a gentleman was lauded through the phrase "an Englishman's word is his bond". Of course this didn't stop rampant corruption in colonial outposts right up to the twentieth century, but the durability of British trade overseas depended on them being perceived as more trustworthy than competitors.

Culture is a predictor of keeping a promise but we risk stereotyping groups. Cultures can change in both directions. Villages that traditionally share might be forced into selfishness by ecological pressures and climate shocks, or by political conflicts when historic grievances between ethnic or religious groups flare up. Northern Ireland, Rwanda, Yugoslavia and Kenya spring to mind. Conversely, some communities can flourish with strong leadership and values, even in nations where retail corruption is the norm.

Corruption was once rife in Britain. In 1726, the Craftsman, a London journal set up to publicise the rampant corruption of the government led by Sir Robert Walpole, wrote: "the mystery of State-Craft abounds with such innumerable frauds, prostitutions and enormities, in all shapes, and under all disguises, that it is an inexhaustible fund, an entire resource for satire and reprehension". During the early years of the East India Company, the British Raj in India was run by deeply corrupt administrators. Robert Clive, who joined the company as a clerk at 18, built his reputation in the company's army as a master of divide and rule. He went on to defeat the Nawab of Bengal at the Battle of Plassey. In 2003, Christie's auctioned rare Mughal treasures taken by Clive of India in bribes from local leaders. They fetched £4.7 million. A 17th century jewelled jade flask, once displayed at the Victoria and Albert Museum, sold for £2.9 million. Clive had looted it from the collection of Siraj ud-Daulah, the Nawab of Bengal, who had kept British soldiers in a dungeon (the black hole of Calcutta) and amassed a collection of objets d'art. Other 'gifts' to Clive included a flywhisk of agate studded with rubies, a bejewelled dagger, a hookah with blue enamel and sapphires, and a pale green nephrite jade bowl.[180] After Clive was finally charged with corruption, he committed suicide at the age of 49. But the tradition was established. His successor Warren Hastings, India's first Governor-General, was a villain who insisted on corrupt offerings from every nawab and prince. London was so embarrassed they impeached him. The system was slowly transformed. Political reformer Jeremy Bentham's principles of publicity and inspectability exposed bureaucrats to scrutiny after 1860. Until 1850, the government drew Indian colonial administrators largely from a single school, Haileybury. The introduction of civil service administration laws widened competition, the pool of talent and reduced nepotism.

A third incentive to honour a promise is the certainty of external enforcement from the law in transactions where the law applies. This pre-supposes a functioning legal system, a method to verify a breach of contract, access to an affordable judiciary, and a state that will see justice is done. In most countries, these conditions are rarely met, and contracts are managed informally.

But the most fundamental quality of strong contractual bonds is 'mutual enforcement'. Analogous to the Adam Smith principle that self-interest ensures economic benefits for both parties, mutual enforcement is the way social capital works. For any member of a group who breaks an agreement, a credible threat of sanctions will deter them from doing it.

So how can sanctions be imposed by a group? One method is to use accepted rules of behaviour to create mutual trust i.e. that co-operation will happen for as long as neither party breaks their word, but that if either party transgresses, co-operation will be permanently withdrawn. This is known as the 'grim strategy'. The economic risks for the cheater are huge. Economists can make clever models of contracts between creditors and debtors for mutual benefit, with assumptions of how highly the parties value or discount future gain from co-operation.

Discounting is a universal method in economics, often difficult to understand. For example, a graduate receives two offers of employment of a five-year contract, in a start-up business for $50,000 a year or in a blue chip company for $40,000 a year. Rationality suggests the first offer is better: over five years she earns $50,000 more. But the future is heavily discounted because the start-up might fail in the first year or two. The blue chip is a safer bet, with a low future risk or discount rate; a five-year contract nets $200,000 in earnings compared with only $100,000 in a start-up that goes bankrupt after two years.

Or a Dragon's Den example: a person agrees to loan money to someone to invest in a small business for a profit share. If the co-operation discount value, is low, i.e. each partner will lose heavily if she breaks the contract and will not enjoy future co-operation, both parties are likely to adopt the 'grim strategy' out of mutual self-interest. Indeed, the discount rate might need to be as high as 25% before either party considers it in their interest to cheat or break an agreement.

In the poorest countries, where law and justice are inaccessible, one expects the grim strategy as the method to ensure mutual trust. In reality, the harsh sanction of never co-operating with someone again if cheating on a contract occurs is rarely applied. People care about co-operation but they face daily realities of living long term in communities with variable degrees of contractual reliability. They cannot move from creditors, suppliers, labourers or even distant family members. Certainly a cheater will be sanctioned but penalties may be mild. They are graded and increased in severity if the cheater infringes again. With high autonomy, loyalty and inter-dependence among families and clans, people pay a high social price for permanent non-co-operation.

In low-income countries most people lack trust in state provision and performance. They face poor quality and unreliable services and utilities, low compliance with taxes by the rich, and an acceptance that one must game the system through obeisance and bribes to bureaucrats. They need a high tolerance in dealing with unreliable, unaccountable, unsupervised and cheating agents and principals. They know impunity for poor performance is the norm. If wealth allows, the functions of state are privatised. For instance, Gurgaon is a city of 1.5 million, 20 miles outside Delhi, where major global companies – Google, HSBC, Nokia and Intel – have built offices. Executives live in gated communities with golf courses and malls, side by side with slum dwellers who offer their services.[181] The companies wouldn't wait for the snail trail of bureaucracy, so water, electricity and road maintenance are managed privately. Sewage from septic tanks is dumped in rivers or waste sites.

By contrast, the hallmark of the most developed societies is one of less autonomy and loyalty within nuclear survival cliques, high trust in the state institutions and commercial delivery, in agents and principals, high compliance with tax, and absolute rejection of agents who fail to deliver or cheat. In other words, the grim strategy is absolutely enforced. Where companies don't deliver good quality products or services they lose consumers, who will simply buy elsewhere.

So we have vicious and virtuous circles. The question of mutual enforcement of promises, or trust, is fundamental if we want to create wealth, health or national development. Trust is essential if we manage common resources or want the state to serve its citizens well. The social norms of mutual trust work well when the future benefits of co-operation are highly prized. But people who live among many cheaters may have to accommodate them. If they form contracts and relationships with people they do not inherently trust, the discount rate of future benefits of co-operation increases greatly. They might renege on the agreement at the first sign of trouble. Within a vicious circle of mutual mistrust and a heavily discounted value of social co-operation (outside one's family), external aid, policy reform, or technical inputs from experts will not change the fundamental dynamic of contaminated social relations. Trust can dissipate quickly. It takes a long time to rebuild.

Sympathy groups are our first human forays into mutual trust. Depending on circumstance, sympathy groups can prevent, reduce, endorse or even create corruption. Working well, they reduce local domination and subordination, address power relationships, or challenge inequality. Over time, they shift ideology and norms and accelerate diffusion of innovation. They can strengthen the trust needed for social gain and cut anti-social corruption. They might influence broader political imbalances between the centre and periphery, or the unequal allocation of urban and rural resources.

At first glance, development as the creation of trust is somewhat at odds with economist Amartya Sen's view of development as freedom, "a process of expanding the real freedoms that people enjoy".[182] In fact, Sen is at pains to say development involves not only improvement in human capital, the economy and public services but also social modernisation. "With adequate social opportunities, individuals can effectively shape their own destiny and help each other. They need not be seen primarily as passive recipients of the benefits of cunning development programmes. There is indeed a strong rationale for recognising the positive role of free and sustainable agency – and even a constructive impatience."

Sen recognised the conflict between "the basic value that the people must be allowed to decide freely what traditions they wish or not wish to follow; and the insistence that established traditions be followed (no matter what), or alternatively, people must obey the decisions by religious or secular authorities who enforce traditions – real or imagined." Certainly, many international agencies see Sen's approach as focused on the needs of individuals. Sen said little on how groups might organise and resist. He is vague on social opportunities. The "individual's substantive freedom to live better" intensifies a view that he sees development primarily as building human not social capital.

For organisations, social trust raises a fundamental question of strategy. The place to start is at the social edge. Local champions can build mutual trust and autonomy through sympathy groups and civic participation. For companies, viral marketing and product clubs build a relationship with their customers. In countries where colonial or totalitarian government left a legacy of civic passivity, or destroyed customary structures for collective decision-making, parochial skills in co-operation and negotiation need long-term investment and support. Development aid for sympathy groups at the social edge seems a better option than gaming a corrupt centre. Vested interests within governments must be challenged. Do we have evidence-based strategies to strengthen confidence in the police, build acceptable education and health systems, make the judiciary work, and hold free and fair elections? It's a tall order and many countries are struggling.

While democracy has spread, so too has anocracy – regimes whose governments are unstable, corrupt and with barely functioning institutions. No real democratic state existed in the world as recently as 1800.[183] Since 1990, democracy has spread to over 90 countries, a doubling. Now only 20 totalitarian regimes remain. But anocracy has risen, concomitantly, from 20 to over 50 states. Many so-called democracies openly rig elections. States in transition stumble towards democracy as wealth and education rise, but the risks of a coup, conflict and a failed state are ever-present. Environmental change, precipitating conflicts over natural resources, can tip fragile democracies back into chaos or war.

Corruption and lack of trust is not just an unwelcome side-effect during development. For some countries it's an existential threat. In China, endemic corruption imperils the Communist regime. The current President and general secretary, Xi Jinping, scion of a prominent Communist family and the most powerful leader since Mao, understands too clearly the risks. His predecessor Hu Jintao wrote that corruption could "deal a body blow to the Party and even lead to the collapse of the Party and country."[184] Xi himself wrote that he would "persevere in our anti-corruption effort till we achieve final success rather than start off full of sound and fury and then taper off in a whimper". The strategy is to tackle corruption at the top and the bottom – the tigers and the flies. Senior officials have been sacked, fugitive officials repatriated, and tens of thousands of junior civil servants punished for breaking the eight-point anti-corruption rules. One senior member of the Politburo, Zhou Yongkang, received a life sentence. But the challenge is immense. And for Xi there are risks. Senior political and military colleagues are protective of their assets and could rebel. Millions of party cadres don't want their perks of party membership removed. And, as the economy falters, the regime is struggling to create the fervour of Mao's revolution to "serve the people", or Deng Xiaoping's mantra "to get rich is glorious". Xi might seek affection through other means, foreign adventures or a clean-up of environmental stress at home.

In free market economies, gated communities divide social trust. In India, where army, medics and engineers are ring-fenced in middle class private ghettoes, those inside and outside the gates are divided by more than wealth. In the US, the killing of Trayvon Martin by George Zimmerman, a neighbourhood watch volunteer in the Twin Lakes neighbourhood of Sanford, Florida, illustrates how mistrust led to an innocent young black pedestrian being seen as a threatening intruder.

The vicious circle of mistrust is also evident in climate change. Developing countries mistrust high-consumption developed countries. Most economists and climate scientists agree that to restrict global warming to around two degrees we need proactive global agreements on emission cuts, carbon taxes, and investment in carbon capture and renewable energy. Countries must make promises and keep them. But emissions climb relentlessly. Global agreements founder, carbon tax is taboo and investment in carbon capture and renewable energy is inadequate. Why? States don't trust others to comply. The political discount rate is way too high. Even green politicians won't fritter away their political capital when electorates face rises in energy prices and government spending. During austerity the policies for a distant global good is a hard sell, because voters know it won't materialise if other states cheat.

Nearly 300 years ago, Lucy Lockit in John Gay's The Beggar's Opera, the fictional daughter of the keeper of Newgate prison, distilled the human tension between trust and deceit. "Of all animals of prey, man is the only sociable one. Every one of us preys upon his neighbour, and yet we herd together."

Social Capital

BONDING, BRIDGING AND SOCIAL MEDIA

In 1916, an educational reformer named LJ Hanifan, a supervisor of schools in West Virginia, first used the phrase 'social capital'. "The individual is helpless socially, if left to himself . . ." he wrote. "If he comes into contact with his neighbour, and they with other neighbours, there will be an accumulation of social capital, which may immediately satisfy his social needs and which may bear a social potentiality sufficient to the substantial improvement of living conditions in the whole community . . . and the Fellowship of his neighbours."[185] At the time of the Great War, Hanifan was ignored, but the idea of social capital was born. His phrase touched upon the concept of group responsibility emphasised by philosophers and religious scholars throughout history.

After studying philosophy, Pierre Bourdieu, the French anthropologist and social commentator, moved to Algiers, where he did detailed field research and wrote a book, Le Sociologie d'Algérie, on the Kabyle people, the largest of the ethnic groups referred to as Berbers. His experience led Bourdieu to oppose the view, common at the time among Marxist theorists and intellectual philosophers like Jean-Paul Sartre, that rational, individual decisions based on economic judgments define social behaviour. He contested the primacy of economics in community interactions, or that social struggles were about class conflict over economic control. In

1972, he wrote his Outline of a Theory of Practice, in which he described two important ideas, habitus and field, related to social capital.[186] Habitus relates to the subjective sum of perceptions, thoughts, tastes and actions of people that arise from their social situation, their class, their family, employment and education. Much of a person's habitus is unconscious and defined by their upbringing and social history. Field comprises the objective social space that people find themselves in at a particular time. This space is made up of rules, opinions, taboos and schemes of domination enacted by the family, village, town, national political and legal system and so on. For Bourdieu, the duties of a social scientist or anthropologist were first to study the objective reality of the field in which a particular group of people found themselves, and second, to examine the way in which their habitus, or internal unconscious forces and social perceptions, interacted with their particular objective situation.

Bourdieu prized identifying symbolic capital, the honour and prestige of a father or village headman, or the power of a mother-in-law in relation to her son's new wife, or the separate dining arrangements for senior executives in a company. He described symbolic violence, the subtle disapproval of parents when faced with an unacceptable marital partner for their son or daughter, the hostility of a higher caste or class person towards lower caste or class people joining a club or micro-credit group, or the misogyny of testosterone-loaded traders in City financial firms.

Bourdieu saw social groups as more complex, nuanced and symbolic than economic analysts would allow. Group actions can lead to bonding (exclusive) and bridging (inclusive) capital. Some groups of people focus on bonding together, through a book group or old school reunion. But if bonding becomes the raison d'être of a group, the danger is that they will exclude marginalised people and widen social divisions. Bridging capital is where groups make explicit their wish to increase their circle of influence, such as health reaching out to environmental groups. Bonding capital is important for solidarity among ethnic or union groups, whereas bridging capital may be the explicit outcome of a health or literacy promotion effort.

Do bonding and bridging social capital have any place in the harsh world of markets and capitalism? Isn't capitalism based on selfishness, not altruism? Adam Smith explained wealth creation from the self-interest of the butcher, the brewer, or the baker. Although he did write: "How selfish soever man may be supposed, there are evidently some principles in his nature, which interest him in the fortune of others, and render their happiness necessary to him, though he derives nothing from it, except the pleasure of seeing it."

Ekkehart Schlicht from the Institutional Economics group in Munich disagrees that companies will derive nothing from the fortune of others. He believes employees respond to both economic incentives and to the culture and social interaction in the workplace. Firms should build " . . . an appropriate corporate culture, governed by reciprocity, fairness and commitment." Sceptics say this is a refined form of exploitation, making "an atmosphere of mutuality for profit . . ." He disagrees because "social evolution proposes that attitudes which entail successful behaviours will be adopted and maintained more readily than less successful variants, and will therefore spread and attain dominance over time".

Again, Schlicht, like Bourdieu, sees economic determinants, like salary levels, given an exaggerated importance in corporate and consumer behaviour: ". . . Most interaction – even in modern market economies – takes place within firms and families, that is, within institutions and organisations that do not rely on the price mechanism for purposes of internal coordination. People spend most of their time in such organisations, and a lesser time doing shopping."

Corporate culture that celebrates good citizenship – co-operation on tasks, sharing information, voicing concerns or allowing whistleblowing, making positive public statements, and encouraging corporate social responsibility – creates an atmosphere which enhances a company's performance. Employment is a social rather than a market exchange. If the firm is not greedy then staff will not see their contract in terms of greed either. Retailer John Lewis, among the UK's most successful companies, prides itself on a strong employee culture and fairness to customers and employees. It maintains a balance in pay differentials, gives rewards for long service, and emphasises customer care. Low rates of staff turnover

ANTHONY COSTELLO

reflect the public perception that its slogan "Never knowingly undersold" applies not just to price but also to its corporate culture.

When senior bankers, before the 2008 crash, ignored threats to the viability of their companies from huge leverage taken to trade in credit derivatives, they did so because they valued their employment in terms of large salaries and bonuses more than social exchange within their institutions. As Schlicht points out: "If the firm requires sales people to work with customers in a strictly profit-oriented and even in a deceitful way, its corporate culture will be perceived as strongly concerned with profits." Before 2008, high street banks changed from trusted, boring deposit and loan institutions into aggressive sales machines, where staff chased aggressive sales targets for loans, credit cards, and life insurance. Winners received cash, staff missing their targets were humiliated, sometimes with cabbages placed on tellers' desks. Have things changed? In 2012, a survey by consumer group Which? found 43% of staff in the largest five UK banks felt pressurised into selling. Almost half knew colleagues who had mis-sold products to meet targets.

Investment banks also defrauded. Goldman Sachs faces many lawsuits and paid $5 billion in fines for mis-selling toxic mortgage securities to wealthy clients. It secretly made money through credit default swaps when the mortgage bonds defaulted. Have the banks learnt their lessons? In a November 2015 lecture in Brussels, Robert W. Jenkins, senior fellow at Better Markets, listed continuing multiple malpractices of banks and financiers, mis-selling of bonds, securities and insurance, abusive practices with small business lending, tax evasion and money laundering, manipulation of markets in foreign exchange, gold, commodity and electricity markets; and Goldman Sachs' collusion with Greek authorities to mislead EU policymakers on meeting euro criteria.

"But no bank has lost its banking licence. No senior has gone to jail. No management team has been prosecuted. No board or supervising executive has been financially ruined . . .", said Jenkins. "I was once hopeful. I am no longer optimistic." Such a culture of impunity risks another crash much sooner than warranted.

Maybe the same thing happened at pharmaceuticals company GSK, which paid a $3 billion fine, the largest in US corporate history, after corruption among sales teams in the US and emerging markets. It faced litigation in six countries. So if institutions make trust and reliability their hallmark will they enjoy greater success? The big UK banks, Barclays, RBS, NatWest, HSBC, Lloyds and TSB, had low ethical scores and low switch scores of customers moving to them. In contrast, Metro Bank, Handelsbanken and Nationwide, with high ethics scores, attracted higher switch scores. Successful companies avoid the costs of monitoring and control over employees' performance by enhancing intrinsic motivation in the workplace. They build a culture where social exchange is more important than monetary reward, their social engagement genuine, not deceitful. Group activities are a key element.

The words selfishness and altruism are imbued with moral and political meaning. The first implies evil, the second moral superiority. But both are essential for human success. Both can be destructive and dangerous. Neither is better or worse, so neutral phrases like self-action and group co-operation are preferable. Social capital links with many good things – better child development and adolescent wellbeing, mental health, lower violent crime rates and youth delinquency, fewer deaths, less binge drinking and depression, and greater compliance with anti-smoking programmes.[187] It reduces stress. Social capital gives us control over our working conditions and home environment. We live longer and healthier.

Has our modern world of personal computers and mobile phones reduced or increased our social capital? In Bowling Alone, Robert Putnam, Harvard professor of political science, documented the apparent decline in social capital in modern America. He saw social capital as "civic virtue . . . most powerful when embedded in a dense network of reciprocal social relations. A society of many virtuous but isolated individuals is not necessarily rich in social capital." Social capital depends not only on connections between individuals, but also on the nature of their existing networks. Where networks are dense, the explosive power of the amplification of messages or behaviour change will be much greater than in societies where networks are poor or restricted by social taboos. Social capital allows "citizens to resolve collective problems more easily . . . greases the wheels that allow communities to advance smoothly . . .". Putnam recognised the difficulties in measuring social capital but speculated on the reasons for its decline since the 1960s, with guesstimates of their contribution: "First, the pressures of time and money, including the special pressures on to career families, . . . (10%) . . . Second suburbanisation, commuting, and sprawl (15%). Third, the effect of electronic entertainment – above all, television – in privatising our leisure time has been substantial. (25%) . . . Fourth and most important, generational change – the slow, steady, and ineluctable replacement of the long civic generation by their less involved children and grandchildren . . . (Perhaps half of the overall decline)."

And changing business practices reduced the inputs of companies to their local communities. "As Walmart replaces the corner or hardware store, Bank of America takes over the First National Bank, and local owners are succeeded by impersonal markets, the incentives for business elites to contribute to community life atrophy." The twenty-first century decline of the British high street, exacerbated by the global financial recession, is a case in point. The rise in internet shopping and restrictive planning laws have jeopardised high street shops, made worse by falling demand from austerity. Local versions of supermarket chains like Tesco, Sainsbury and Marks and Spencer reduce the viability of smaller stores. When Sainsbury opened a local store where I live in London I asked three local food and wine stores how it affected their takings. All reported declines of around £200 to £300 per day.

One assumption is that social media fills the gap created by declines in social capital. Facebook, LinkedIn and Twitter challenge Dunbar's idea[188] that "adult social network size correlates with the volume of core areas in the neocortex . . . associated with the 'theory of mind' network in humans, also true of monkeys".[189] Dunbar's team analysed two large surveys, one of social media users (2000) and another of adults in full-time employment (1345), not necessarily social media users. They asked them how many individuals they considered close friends and how many they would 'consider going to for advice or sympathy in times of great emotional or other distress'. These questions correlated with sympathy groups and survival cliques. The mean number of social media friends was 155 and 183 in the two samples, not significantly different from the social brain limit of 150. For the 2000 social media users, the numbers answering the questions about survival cliques and sympathy groups came in as 4.1 and 13.6, close to the values of 5 and 15.

The conclusions are surprising. Social media do not appear to circumvent the rules on the limits of social circles of trust. They sustain contact but in a manner intrinsically less satisfying than personal face-to-face meetings. If you don't meet an old college friend, your friendship with them will gradually decay over time, descending through Dunbar's layers. After many years he or she may fall off your 150 limit. Social media may delay that process, but not forever if you lose personal contact.

THE RADIUS OF TRUST

Political scientist Francis Fukuyama interprets social capital as "the cultural component of modern societies, which in other respects have been organised since the Enlightenment on the basis of formal institutions, the rule of law and rationality."[190] He adds two important observations about how social capital works. First that many authors do not separate social capital from its effects. For Fukuyama, social capital is not a vague public good but arises from specific personal relationships. "Social capital is an instantiated informal norm that promotes co-operation between two or more individuals . . . They must be instantiated in an actual human relationship . . . reciprocity exists in potential in my dealings with all people, but is actualised only in my dealings with my friends. By this definition, trust, networks, civil society, and the like, which have been associated with social capital, are all epiphenomenal, arising as a result of social capital but not constituting social capital itself."

So networks alone are not social capital; they arise from it. Further, he introduces the idea of a circle or radius of trust. "All groups embodying social capital have a certain radius of trust, that is, the circle of people among whom co-operative norms are operative. If a group's social capital produces positive externalities, the radius of trust can be larger than the group itself."

This is an important concept for sympathy groups. For example, a group of 15 women meeting in an African village to discuss pregnancy and newborn health, who build their own social capital through relationships established within the group, has a much wider influence on women outside the group through "friends and cliques, up through NGOs and religious groups". When I lecture to tropical medicine doctors about women's groups I put up a slide halfway through the talk to wake them up. The slide says that we have discovered a new PCR method for DNA. They wake up abruptly, nudge their neighbours and wonder what they have missed. How can we have discovered a new polymerase chain reaction to amplify the DNA message from bacteria in a sample of spit or stool? Did we miss something? Wasn't he talking about women's groups? My next slide defines PCR as 'participation in the community for reproductive health' and DNA as women in the community who 'do not attend' health services. They smile and go back to snooze mode.

But I make a serious point. Just as the polymerase chain reaction amplifies the message of a single DNA strand over and over, so might a women's group amplify messages and norms of behaviour within their radius of trust and beyond, not just in the present but in the future too. They provide new advice to their daughters and grand-daughters. This generational effect is important when comparing the relative cost-effectiveness of group interventions for health with one-off shots of medicine or vaccine or micronutrient supplements. The latter may have an immediate effect, but will not change longer term behaviour across generations to amplify benefit.

On the other hand, groups such as traditional extended families have a very narrow radius of trust, and group solidarity reduces the ability of group members to interact with outsiders. This inward looking characteristic may justify much of the corruption, both retail and wholesale, that is the norm in traditional (not hunter-gatherer) societies. Strangers are not the same as kin, requiring less strict moral codes, so one is entitled to steal on behalf of one's family group. This is not a trivial issue. As we've seen, corruption has a major impact on the economy, the justice system, security and a sense of well-being. So corruption and trust could be amenable to experiment.

Colonialism, Caste and Class

THE RELATIONS OF PRODUCTION

Modernity, defined by the rise of nation states and the power of industrial capitalism, brought irreversible and dramatic changes in social relations and the structures of trust. Modern sympathy groups mutated. The change in the predominant mode of production from rural peasantry to urban industry affected and attacked non-market values and "dissolved forms of cultural meaning and social solidarities that play an important role in sustaining daily life."[191] Millions of people living under caste and class rules, displaced from rural lands, migrating to cities, or colonised by invaders, suffered poverty, stress and a deep sense of loneliness. "What loneliness is more lonely than distrust?"[192] In the Communist Manifesto Marx and Engels understood the revolutionary nature of industrial power and the immense creativity of capitalism whose leaders "cannot exist without constantly revolutionising the instruments of production, and therefore the relations of production and with them the relations of society". They recognised that a revolution of production led to "uninterrupted disturbance of all social conditions, everlasting uncertainty and agitation", which distinguished the new epoch from all others.

This view was shared by the late historian Sir Christopher Bayly, who saw that colonial and institutional forces outside Europe meant that "the position of labourers in cities deteriorated more rapidly, and their

economic position became bleaker, even than that of the peasantry ...
workers in colonial and semi-colonial societies suffered from a structural
lack of entitlement to food, goods and services ... average life expectancy
for the poor of ... Shanghai, Bombay or Batavia may have been as low
as 28 years, lower even than that of surrounding peasantry."[193] Rapidly
growing cities throughout the nineteenth century were socially unstable,
with high rates of crime, vagrancy and infanticide, and rebellions by
emerging union movements. Outsiders and immigrants were targeted by
local ruffians and the police. In colonial cities, a large proportion of the
urban, young male population were imprisoned. Middle classes were
nervous of the 'problem of labour' and saw the lower class as a source
of crime and disease. Groups of shopkeepers, clerks, craftsmen and
labourers coalesced around grievances, forming marches or rallies or
petitions to demand their rights.

After the 18th century Enclosures Act removed strip cultivation on
common land, and landowners expanded their estates, forcing migration
of rural workers to new conurbations, gardens and allotments became
central to the lives of the British working class. Margaret Willes describes
how gardening clubs and allotments improved their nutrition and food
security.[194] By 1945, over 1.5 million allotments in Britain brought thousands of people into co-operative horticultural groups. During the wars,
production shifted from flowers to vegetables and fruit when the government called for a 'Dig for Victory', and afterwards when they imposed
rationing. In Britain gardening remains a prime interest, supported by
clubs, shows and prime-time TV.

Despite the social impacts, capitalism, red in tooth and claw, brought
great economic growth. Driven by creativity and competition, and based
on the rapid expansion of a new geography of cities, to facilitate production and consumption, the power of capital gave birth to a modern
demographic transition. Large numbers migrated from rural to urban
centres. Population expanded rapidly as birth rates exceeded falling death
rates and health gains prolonged the lives of consumers. Economic growth
rates soared and nation states used their surpluses to build military power
and extend the reach of mercantilism. Governments secured and extended

their taxation base. New markets absorbed surpluses from the compounding growth of capital. Colonialisation of unmarketised economies by rising European states provided the demand.

Marx was unconvinced by political economist David Ricardo, who postulated that capitalism would sow the seeds of its own destruction through falling profitability. Nor was he persuaded by Thomas Malthus, who wrote that capitalism created poverty because of a geometrically increasing population. Malthus thought it would destroy itself through a collapse in food supply and natural resources, unable to keep pace, because capital increased only at an arithmetic linear rate. Marx though believed that poverty arose from class relations and because owners of capital maintained an impoverished labouring class for efficient production.[195] He saw industrial innovation and the opening of new colonial markets as a solution to falling profits and limited resources within Europe. Marx foresaw continuing success for capitalism which would only be restricted by class conflict.

Colonialism also undermined the basic mechanisms of social sympathy and small group action. Colonial powers invariably justify their invasion by a stated desire to improve the lot of the colonised through better governance and removal of corruption. Napoleon believed that Italy was degenerate and corrupt and that French influence would create civil institutions to purge the old systems of nepotism, feudalism and lack of property rights. The East India company, and later the Raj, believed much the same. The decline of the Mughal empire allowed the English East India company, between 1757 and 1765, to take over Bengal, with its rich economy of multiple rice crops and textile production. By setting up a fixed tax system for their local agents, the *zamindar* landlords, the English colonisers professed to believe that social value would emerge from a stable and progressive administration. The truth on the ground in most colonial districts was quite different.[196] The impact of colonialisation was not just retarded development of national institutions but also pernicious destruction of social sympathy within districts and villages.

For example, Sir H. Ricketts, a colonial administrator, wrote of the people in Chittagong in 1848:[197] "I am afraid that the people of this district deserve the character they have so long borne for litigiousness . . . they will litigate, incurring certain loss, in order to disturb or injure a neighbour. It is impossible to mix with any class of people without observing the undisguised ill-will which they bear to each other. Mistrust, suspicion, uncharitableness prevail; misfortune can find no sympathy." He did at least understand the impact of the British-run network of under-paid, corrupt native government officers, employed to assess and collect land taxes. "There was corruption in every village, the inhabitants . . . divided between informers and victims, the bribing and bribed. What could ensue but general demoralisation? How could children fail to grow up . . . litigious, distrustful of each other, suspicious of our purposes and intentions, and prone to fraud." He didn't reflect further on what the 'purposes and intentions' of the British might be.

The local landlords, the *zamindar*, had been created to collect taxes for the British. Most colonial district collectors turned a blind eye to the oppression and exploitation of rural peasants (*raiyats*) by these agents. Any increase in crop prices did not benefit the peasants; they simply ensured a simultaneous rise in land rents, assuming the cultivator had any surplus to sell, which was often not the case. The *zamindar* class also levied on the peasants an astonishing array of impromptu and illegal taxes, 'turn a blind eye' cesses called *abwabs*. Some were routine, others ceremonial. Routine *abwabs* included *zamindar* expenses for post, telegraph, schools, income tax, account-keeping, clerical and administrative charges and land contracts.[198] Ceremonial cesses were levied on every conceivable activity: entertainment for when a British officer visited an estate, when regiments marched nearby, for *zamindar* visits to villages, for erection of temples or mosques, when a *raiyat's* daughter was married, for purchases of horses and elephants by the *zamindar*, for the work of peons in collecting the rents, for religious festivals, for feeding other *raiyats* in times of famine, for petty crime, for a *zamindar* family wedding, on honeycombs, for petitions, for court costs, for picking fruits called *ritta*, for liquidation of a debt, for cutting down a tree, or for making a census of inhabitants for the district collector. The cumulative burden of colonial local administration was paid from a massive burden of formal and illegal rents imposed on the peasant population.

By the end of the nineteenth century, one third of peasant households were indebted through jute bonds owed to *mahajan* moneylenders. Interest rates were between 25% and 75% and debts were collected when crops were harvested. Defaulters lost their land or the peasant was forced to become a share cropper. Or unpaid interest was added to the principal and the family went into a downward spiral of debt. District collector's reports to their superiors spoke of improving conditions in their locality but few referred to the informal burden of taxes that overwhelmed most peasant households.

We do not teach European schoolchildren about the impact that colonial rule had on the indigenous family and sympathy group life across the world. Colonialism destroyed social group structures that might, as in Britain, have evolved into the civic participation so essential for a modern state. Instead, across millions of households, and thousands of villages, the British Empire built colonial states based on informers and victims, the bribing and the bribed, and neutered the customary fabric of accountability, village and district sympathy groups that would have created a social ecology for progressive change.

Memories of empire and exploitation die hard. Recently, while on holiday in Navarra's *Murillo el Fruto*, I met an 83-year-old Spanish alumnus of the London School of Economics, who was on a short retreat at the local Basque Cistercian *Monasterio La Oliva*. He was there, he said, "to address some of the profound questions you must face at the end of your life". Chatting over breakfast I told him about my great-great-great-grandfather, an Irish squaddie, Ned Costello, who had fought in Wellington's 95th Rifles alongside the Spanish in the Peninsular War, and won the Forlorn Hope medal twice. In his published memoir, Adventures of a Soldier, Rifleman Edward Costello had lunched by the river running through this very village in 1813.[199] The economist looked sad. "That was one of the darkest periods in our history. Most of the treasures of Northern Spain - Rembrandt, Velázquez, Murillo - were stolen by the French and sold to collectors and museums." Two hundred years after the invasion he still spoke bitterly of France and its lack of reparations.

Such stories are common-place in the ancestral homes of many former colonial countries. A month later, my friends in Jharkhand, India, taught me about the history and repression of tribal populations in India. It brought home the extent to which colonialism disrupted the social fabric of poor people right up to the present day. On the road from Ranchi to Chakradharpur in the south of Jharkhand state, which seceded from Bihar in 2001, we bought mangoes in the forest from a tribal *adivasi* Ho family. The family survived by selling their forest produce: brooms, leaves for paan, tubers, kendu leaves, and herbs for potions and poultices. I asked them if they still hunted to supplement their mango gathering business. Yes, they hunted for wild poultry in groups using low rolled-up nets with stakes. Would they demonstrate their hunting? The household head was a short friendly moustachioed man, with matted dreadlocks, a white bandanna, cream cotton vest, chequered *lunghi* gathered in a knot at the waist, and two necklace amulets and pendants made of *rudraksha* beads from endocarps and red and yellow dyed jute fibres. He summoned his relatives and neighbours. The group proudly showed me how to trap a wild hen using group tactics and a small 10 metre net. The younger lads chased a squawking white chicken around for five minutes while the mango salesman displayed his hunter-gatherer credentials and rolled out the net as if we were about to play ground level table tennis. After several spills and giggles, the chicken careered into the net, where the man triumphantly held it aloft, upended. With a big grin he offered it for sale. We declined but bought two more kilos of mangoes for forty rupees.

In the jeep, Prasanta and Nirmala told me about *adivasi* history in their region. Mostly they were Santhals and Mundas and Hos, and a host of smaller tribes, part of the 104 million aboriginal and animist people who live in the dense forests of central India, scattered across the states of Orissa, Madhya Pradesh, Andhra Pradesh, Chhattisgarh and Jharkhand. Today tribal Indians, greater in number than the populations of Germany France or Britain, are found throughout India. One northern belt covers

Rajasthan, Himachal Pradesh, Jammu, Kashmir and Uttarakhand; in the north-east, tribes dominate the populations of Mizoram, Arunachal Pradesh and Nagaland, and form up to one third of the population of Assam, Sikkim and Tripura. Smaller numbers live in the south, in Tamil Nadu and Kerala and Karnataka. For centuries aboriginal tribes used their forest goods sustainably, left alone by the villagised Indo-Aryan castes, who saw the forest and their peoples as dark and haunted and spiritually threatening.

As British influence in India grew, *adivasi* land and forests were handed over to designated *zamindar* landlords by civil servants. Revolts by *adivasi* groups, such as the Santhal rebellion of 1855, were brutally crushed by the East India Company, and, after 1858, by the new Raj administration of the British government. The Santhal rebellion was led by four brothers, Sindhu, Kanhu, Chand and Bhairav Murmu. They were outraged by the exploitation of Santhal men, often locked into bonded labour and unre-payable loans. And even more bitter about the sexual exploitation of Santhal women by upper caste landowners, and about the slavery of the youngest Santhals. Up to thirty thousand Santhals took up arms against the British colonists and slaughtered many local *zamindars* and their families. The rebellion gathered momentum over six months, but the Nawab of Murshidabad, assisted by landowners, and the 7th and 40th Native Infantry Regiments, which brought heavy cannon and muskets, crushed all resistance. The brothers were killed, Santhal homes were systematically trampled by elephants, and British-led troops committed many atrocities.

The Santhals had a sense of collective honour when fighting, referred to by Charles Dickens in his Household Words. They used poisoned arrows to hunt but never against their foes. The British officer Major Jervis observed that when they beat their drums, the tribesmen would stand their ground with their unpoisoned arrows and accept being shot down. When they regrouped and the drums sounded again, they would not fire their arrows despite the fatal volleys of bullets fired at them. "There was not a *sepoy* in the war who did not feel ashamed of himself," said Jervis.

Figure 33. The Santhal Rebellion. Attack by 600 Santhals upon a party of 50 sepoys, 40th Native Infantry Regiment

In 1865, the British Raj introduced the first Forest Act which restricted tribal access to their traditional forest commons. Ostensibly the reason given was to manage resources more effectively but the decision enabled mass logging by the colonial government for the development of the Indian Railway system. At the stroke of a colonial bureaucrat's pen, the rights of millions of people to their tribal forests were removed. A few concessions were made to particular tribes and *adivasi* elites, but poorer displaced tribes were forced to migrate to work on tea estates as menial guards and servants, a process which continued until long after Indian independence. The Madras Forest Act 1882 and the 1927 Indian Forest Act maintained legal restrictions, and independence did not bring immediate restoration of *adivasi* forest lands. The Indian government's Forest Reservation Act of 1980 finally redressed the injustice, but tribal people still fight battles with state governments and large mining companies to protect their land from takeover and exploitation of mineral resources. In 2017, *adivasis* have the worst development indicators in India, many work in tea gardens on bonded labour contracts, malnutrition is rife and death rates remain high. Only in the past decade have we started to celebrate the richness and nobility of tribal culture and traditions, and the co-operative culture of these forest people, the original inhabitants of the sub-continent.[200]

It's difficult to be precise about the impact of colonial exploitation on the death rates of tribal, low caste and peasant peoples in India. The counterfactual scenario of an India developing from 1800 onwards under self rather than British rule is difficult to model. Maybe the Maharajahs and a self-grown class of *zamindar* landlords would have preserved their dominance and exploitative rule for many decades. We don't know. But the distinguished Cambridge economic historian Angus Maddison[201] esti-mated that the gross national income of India increased from $400 million (expressed in 1990 value dollars) in 1820 to only about $650 million by the time of independence in 1947. Allowing for population growth from 240 to 320 million, income per head barely changed. After independence, the Indian economy grew steadily to $2 billion (again 1990 value dollars) by 1998, and accelerated to $2073 billion by 2015 (in current value dollars). We must assume that things would have been immeasurably better if Indians had not been colonised. Yes, maybe fewer railways and less devotion to cricket, but self-determination, national pride and the right not to have one's commodities and labour stolen by outsiders, are rather more important. Adding together *adivasi,* low caste and peasant lives lost from colonial counter-insurgency, execution, confiscation of land, bonded labour, removal of access to the commons for hunting and gathering, nutritional deprivation and vulnerability to epidemics of infections like tuberculosis, cholera and measles, lack of health care, famine and the shame of sexual transgression and suicide, a conservative estimate, I'm sure, would put the colonial genocide over 150 years into the many tens of millions of deaths.

The American historian Mike Davis in his coruscating Late Victorian Holocausts came up with an estimate of tens of millions of Indian famine deaths alone over the colonial period.[202] The last decades of the nine-teenth century saw "the theological application of the sacred principles of Smith, Bentham and Mill". The economist Karl Polanyi suggested that millions "perished in large numbers because the Indian village community had been demolished", although Indian economist Amartya Sen considered this view a gross exaggeration. Perhaps a consensus view might be that the Indian village community was disrupted, if not demolished, by colonialism. Even conservative historians like Niall Ferguson, who paints a rosy picture of the benefits of British colonialism, concedes that "the British were zealous in the acquisition and exploitation of slaves" (one wonders which form of slavery is not exploitative), and "practised forms of racial discrimination and segregation that we today consider abhorrent".[203]

As a postscript, it is bizarre and offensive that the British civic honours system chooses to award gongs in the name of empire and colonial oppression. Twice a year, the state celebrates enrolment of deserving citizens as Member, Order, Commander and Knight or Dame of the British Empire. One wonders whether Russians would like to receive a Stalin medal, Germans an order of the Third Reich, or the Chinese a civil garter in memory of Mao and his famine of 1958? And how comfortable to receive these medals are the British second and third generation descendants of Asian, African and Caribbean peoples who suffered under colonial rule? I'm sure many white British feel that the colonial era is our historical blind spot, fogged over by the stories and films of EM Forster, Rudyard Kipling and James Ivory. How many deserving citizens politely decline these tainted honours? After all, awards are not set in stone. Charles II created the Forlorn Hope medal in 1643 and in 1856 Queen Victoria replaced it with the Victoria Cross to honour acts of valour during the Crimean War. The Order of the British Empire only appeared in 1917, when George V created the honours for service to business, education, the arts and sciences, public services outside the Civil Service, and work for charity, health and welfare. Is it really that difficult for the Royal Household and the Houses of Lords and Commons in the twenty first century to change the phrase 'the British empire' to a simpler 'British excellence'?

SUBALTERNS

A more important issue about sympathy arises from the study of 'subaltern classes', a term introduced by Antonio Gramsci, the Italian philosopher and political scientist. The subalterns are people with "a whole set of knowledges that have been disqualified as inadequate to their task or insufficiently elaborated: naive knowledges, located low down on the hierarchy, beneath the required level of cognition or scientificity".[204] Indian scholar Gayatri Spivak calls subaltern groups "the people exposed to this 'epistemic violence' who are the men and women among the illiterate peasantry, the tribals, the lowest strata of the urban subproletariat . . ."[205] We have a duty to bring everyday lives and voices of the poorest into our histories of the colonial era. In recent times, a new history of subaltern groups emerged to scratch the surface of colonial misery and oppression. Whether giving subalterns a voice in contemporary society through sympathy groups will expedite development more than institutional reform is another matter.

This tension between the desire to increase decision-making, participation and the civic voice of the poor, versus reform of the institutions of imperialism and oppressive capitalism, has been at the heart of debates on political development for two hundred years. Edward Said took the latter view and criticised Michel Foucault for a simplistic notion of power, one that allowed Gramsci to "obliterate the role of classes, the role of economics, the role of insurgency and rebellion".[206] Foucault saw power as more diffuse, with positives as well as negatives from the use of conversation. The aim was to detach the power of truth "from the forms of hegemony, social, economic, and cultural, within which it operates at the present time".[207] For Foucault, conversations may or may not have value, dependent upon the complexity and stability of local conditions. "Discourses are not once and for all subservient to power or raised up against it . . . We must make allowances for the complex and unstable process whereby a discourse can be both an instrument and an effect of power, but also a hindrance, a stumbling point of resistance and a starting point for an opposing strategy.

Discourse transmits and produces power; it reinforces it, but also undermines and exposes it, renders it fragile and makes it possible to thwart."[208]

The philosopher Jürgen Habermas is more emphatic. In his theory of communicative reason, he believes that informal and sympathetic communication between people, below the structures of state and law, underpins and informs the whole legal and political order within western society. Spivak disagrees and asks whether, despite the recent focus of anthropology and political science to study oppressed women, these studies will, like Edward Said's critique of Orientalism, mingle "epistemic violence with the advancement of learning and civilisation. And the subaltern women will be as mute as ever." She worries that "the possibility of collectivity itself is persistently foreclosed through the manipulation of female agency". And she is concerned that while philosophers like Foucault and Habermas believe that the oppressed can speak and know their conditions, the conditions of imperialist epistemic violence make her ask the question 'can the subaltern speak'?

Our womens' group experiments, without us knowing it, touched on these debates and tested the strengths and limitations of local sympathy. We explored the ways in which subaltern women could speak, and assessed their opportunity and ability to take power, or not, regardless of their class, economics and desire for rebellion. In terms of survival of their infants, our women's group conversations had positive benefits. Whether it changed their lives more fundamentally is another question.

VILLAGE SWARAJ AND THE IMPEDIMENT OF CASTE

In India, Mahatma Gandhi believed that "independence begins at the bottom . . . A society must be built in which every village has to be self-sustained and capable of managing its own affairs." He spoke of village *swaraj*. "In innumerable villages, there will be ever widening, never ascending circles. Growth will not be a pyramid with the apex sustained by the bottom. But it will be an oceanic circle whose centre will be the individual. Therefore the outermost circumference will not wield power to crush the inner circle but will give strength to all within and derive its own strength from it."[209]

When the British colonial era ended, Gandhi saw communities as the source of all power: "Every village will be a republic or panchayat having full powers." Village *swaraj* (self-rule) was a central plank in his movement. "[The end of the Raj] may bring mere home rule (the rule of the modern coercive state) but not true home rule (the rule of the just, limited state); in any case it will not bring about self-rule." Gandhi considered an independence based on top-down western-style parliamentary government as delusional. It would only be worth it if villages were part of the process.

But Indian independence and the social democracy of the Indian Congress Party did not lead to the emancipation of the rural poor. In 2017, poverty, illiteracy and social oppression remains the norm for many rural villagers. The country's politics were not forged by migrant settlers, nor from the disruption of an ideological revolution. Sympathy groups have driven change in agriculture, forestry, small business, large business, in politics and culture. But the energy of sympathy and groups everywhere is reflected and dissipated by the absorbent walls of caste. Hereditary status subtly poisons any attempt at social mutuality.

For Gandhi, the father of modern India, caste was a sempiternal feature of Hindu culture. He opposed untouchability but defended caste. When in 1932 the British Raj offered a separate electorate to untouchables, he chose to fast to death in protest, fearful that the caste structure of India would be irreversibly damaged. While opposed to the concept of 'untouchability', which he saw as a perversion of the ancient order, he supported the four classes of varna at birth as "not a human invention but an immutable law of nature itself". By virtue of past lives Indians are born as Brahmins (priests and scholars), Kshatriya (warriors, soldiers, even kings), Vaishyas (traders, artisans, farmers) or Shudras (low castes who do menial or polluted tasks such as labourers, cleaners and butchers). "The law of varna," said Gandhi, "teaches us that we have each one of us to earn our bread by following the ancestral calling". The *dalits*, or untouchables, were considered so lowly as to be outside the varna system, ostracised by all other castes, sometimes beaten for merely casting a shadow over a person of higher standing.

Dr Bhimrao Ramji Ambedkar, born into a low caste Mahar family, learned the privations of untouchability early in life. At school he was excluded from the classroom and learned by listening from outside. Prohibited from drinking water unless poured from a height by a pupil or peon of higher caste, he was often thirsty during the hot summers, unless a peon came by. A brilliant student, he won scholarships to attend a school in Bombay, to study law at Columbia University and, later, a Masters and doctorate at the London School of Economics. He could have stayed in the west, but he couldn't forget his origins and chose to return to law practice in Bombay. There he led campaigns to remove the stigma of untouchability, to share public drinking water resources and to allow access for *dalits* to Hindu temples.

Gandhi's hunger strike to defend the caste system, whilst in jail in Poona under British rule, came when the British offered *dalits* the right to elect their own MPs. He placed mighty pressure on Ambedkar who had supported Gandhi's earlier *satgrahaya* movements of non-violence, a tactic he used again in his campaign to lift untouchability. Ambedkar feared that his support for the British Raj proposal for an electorate for untouchables, in opposition to Gandhi, would lead to massive reprisals, possibly a pogrom of untouchable families by higher castes. With reluctance he signed the Poona pact which reserved seats for untouchables (referred to as the depressed class) elected by the population as a whole rather than by *dalits* themselves. Their electoral power was neutered. Ambedkar always regretted his decision. If he had stood firm, the Raj legislation might have expedited low caste emancipation. Even as the architect of the Indian constitution 20 years later, Ambedkar knew he was constrained by the dominance of higher Hindu castes. In 1946 in Pakistan or the Partition of India he wrote: "No matter what Hindus say, Hinduism is a menace to liberty, equality and fraternity."

In May 2014, the new BJP government of Narendra Modi committed to 'minimum government and maximum governance' underpinned by a devotion to Hindutva, a sectarian movement based on Hindu beliefs.

Nonetheless the spectre of caste still overshadows everyday political life. The "mental distance from the clan to community, the tehsil, the district, the state and the nation-state is wider than in most countries" observes Nepali publisher Kanak Mani Dixit, who argues for devolution in a nation state too big and diverse to function like modern European states. The centralising force of Indian government, and reluctance to devolve too much power to regions, comes from a fear of "communal tensions, the rise of local feudocracies, human rights abuses, the denigration of local governance . . . and the abandonment of equalisation, the policy under which poor states are subsidised by others".[210] While such fears are genuinely held, most of these problems already exist within an over-centralised state. Devolution might ameliorate rather than exacerbate them. In reality, state governments have clawed back power from the centre with varying degrees of success.

In the presence of caste can a state be secular? Can sympathy groups creating trust operate within caste society? The historian Perry Anderson suggests the idea of a secular India (and, by implication, Nepal) is based on pro-Congress romanticism. In reality, post-independence India behaved more often like a confessional Hindu state, with repressive laws and protection for an overwhelmingly Hindu police force and army. It fought a series of insurgencies against other religions in the Punjab (Sikh), Kashmir (Muslim), Nagaland and Mizoram (Christian and animist) and the Naxalite communists (largely tribal aboriginal peoples) in the northern and eastern states of Jharkhand, Andhra Pradesh, Chhattisgarh and Orissa.[211] With the BJP's 2014 electoral success, secularity faces further threats. In December 2014 one of Modi's Union Ministers, Sadhvi Niranjan Jyoti, a Hindu nationalist, at a local election rally in Delhi, told people to choose between candidates who were "sons of Ram and illegitimate sons". She was not asked to resign.

Hindu caste has preserved a discriminatory democracy by cutting and dicing working classes into thousands of sub-groups or *jatis*. Despite being protected by reservations, affirmative action and public sector job quotas, low castes preserve their own hierarchy of hereditary privilege. Even if less oppressive than before independence, caste remains as pervasive as ever in Indian and Nepali culture and politics. In 2014, the India Human Development Survey (IHDS) reported that 30% of rural and 20% of urban households said they practised untouchability.[212] More than half of Brahmin families and people in the state of Madhya Pradesh practised untouchability.

"The real remedy for breaking caste is intermarriage," wrote Ambedkar in a lecture he was due to give to the Jat-Pat Todak Mandal in Lahore, later cancelled because he challenged Hindu scripture. "Nothing else will serve as the solvent of caste." To their credit, the Indian authority for third party reproduction through IVF and gamete donation has resisted providing information about the caste of donors.[213] But in 2014 it is remarkable that only five % of marriages in India are inter-caste. "The capacity to appreciate merits in a man apart from his caste does not exist in a Hindu," wrote Ambedkar scornfully. "There is appreciation of virtue but only when the man is a fellow caste-man."

Sixty five years after caste was abolished by a constitution which affirms that every citizen is an Indian due an equal status in the eyes of the law, and that surname or ethnicity is of secondary cultural value, it remains as potent as invisible air pollution. The egalitarian nature of India is spoken about, debated, legalised and romanticised, but in most of the states of the union not practised. The broad genera of scheduled castes, other backward castes and tribals have a huge list of species and sub-species, each trying to protect caste identity in the queue for affirmative action. Anderson is blunt. "A rigid social hierarchy was the basis of original democratic stability, and its mutation into a compartmentalised identity politics has simultaneously defended parliamentary democracy and debauched it. Throughout, caste is the cage that has held Indian democracy together, and it has yet to escape".[214]

To some extent, free market economics offers opportunities for low caste entrepreneurs. Since 1991, free market reforms have increased the premium on price rather than social status. The Dalit Indian Chamber of Commerce and Industry (DICCI) has over 3,000 rupee millionaire members.[215] In cities *dalit*-run restaurants serve meals to upper caste customers, and some *dalit* landowners now employ higher caste workers.

Ownership of mobile phones, benefit registration and access to better housing has improved the connections of *dalit* households to the national economy.

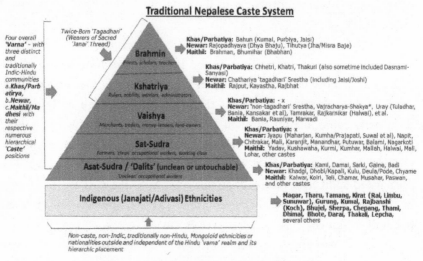

Traditional Nepalese Caste System

Figure 34. Traditional Nepal Caste Hierarchy,
courtesy Nepal Federalism Debate blog

But low caste and tribal groups still suffer terribly from discrimination, poverty and low self-esteem. Abuse and humiliation are routine in the street, the office and the hospital. Rapes, murders and 'witch hunting' are reported daily in newspapers, especially in the northern and eastern states of Uttar Pradesh, Uttarakhand, Bihar, Jharkhand, Orissa, Madhya Pradesh, Chhattisgarh, Rajasthan and Assam. And social discrimination has profound implications for health, with far higher rates of maternal and child deaths among low caste families. Caste bias is even seen in the mid–day meal scheme.[216] A Caring Citizens' Collective (CCC) survey showed that many higher caste parents object to their children being served by *dalit* women. Low caste children are frequently marginalised or excluded from meals by higher caste peers. Low caste women are also less likely to receive antenatal care or cash incentives after birth, and they fear using a higher caste birth attendant because of worries about disrespect and abuse. In coastal Andhra Pradesh, caste was the key factor in determining who has assets, who can access public facilities, who has political connections and who has supportive social networks. Women's participation in local groups could build resilience but only start to overcome the dominance of caste.[217]

CLASS

In the west we should not feel superior. Little has changed in our own hierarchies. In 2018, in England, the class system remains alive and well. The sympathy groups of the private elite 'public schools' are dominant. In Downing Street, the Etonian and elite schools 'chumocracy' cabinet of David Cameron, Nick Clegg, George Osborne, Boris Johnson, Jo Johnson, Jesse Norman, Ed Llewellyn, Oliver Letwin, and Sir George Young, surrounded by a club of school-mate advisers, took all major decisions before Brexit ousted Cameron. The royal princes and the Archbishop of Canterbury attended elitist Eton, so every pillar of the establishment was privileged. Even the conservative Daily Telegraph complained about the treatment of Shaun Bailey, a black, aspiring Tory politician brought in to advise Cameron on youth, crime and race issues.[218] The chumocracy, according to a friend, "tried to keep him away from Cameron" . . . and "being of a different class is probably equally, if not more, important than him being black". Bailey, not wishing to upset his career chances, refused to comment. The media are no different with independent school educated journalists dominating the BBC, ITV, Channel 4 and the broadsheets.

The ultimate cruelty of a caste or class is the determination to exclude others even when they try to join the club. Sympathy groups are by birthright, not by invitation. In Edward St Aubyn's novel Never Mind, a lacerating account of English upper class mores, he dissects the behaviour of local British aristocrats at a 1960s bohemian party in London given by an ambitious Peruvian mountaineer.[219]

"Nicholas and the other social peaks that the host was trying to scale stood together at one end of the room insulting the mountaineer as he scrambled about them attentively. When they had nothing better to do they allowed him to bribe them with his hospitality, on the understanding he would be swept away by an avalanche of invective if he ever treated them with familiarity at a party given by people who really mattered." The Peruvian might be rich and hospitable, but he was permanently ostracised from the English bourgeoisie.

In the so-called classless USA, neo-conservatives dominated the George W Bush administration. He chose senior administration officials from Texas oil networks or from the membership of the Project for a New American Century (PNAC) led by vice-president, Dick Cheney. Others included Richard Armitage, Zalmay Khalilzad, Lewis 'Scooter' Libby, Richard Perle, former US Secretary of Defense Donald Rumsfeld, and Paul Wolfowitz. White men with a college education dominate the heads of major corporates, and of law, education, civic organisations and foundations. Most are drawn from the Ivy League or the most prestigious and well-endowed universities.

Over one third of powerful elite men belong to exclusive clubs in Washington, New York, Boston and Chicago.[220] Most corporate boards comprise members of the American upper class elites and "those 15-20% of corporate directors who sit on two or more boards, who are called the 'inner circle' of the corporate directorate, unite 80-90% of the largest corporations in the United States into a well-connected "corporate community".[221] After the interlude of the Obama administration, the white male transition team of Donald Trump restored financial elitism and misogyny with a vengeance.

In France two highly selective academies, the Ecole Polytechnique and Ecole Nationale d'Administration, take in just 450 students every year. They're the finishing schools for almost the entire elite caste in government and business. "Nowhere else in the world does the question of where you go to school so utterly determine your professional career – and the destiny of an entire nation."[222] The social anthropologist Pierre Bourdieu castigated the lack of meritocracy in these schools. Far from being selective they were an exclusive caste that cloned its members. The alumni live in the same part of Paris, their children attend the same schools and become friends. They progress from 'classmates' to 'caste mates' according to sociologist Monique Pinçon-Charlot.[223] Needless to say, François Hollande and Emmanuel Macron were both graduates. But so were Jacques Chirac, Ségolène Royal, Alain Juppé, Valery Giscard d'Estaing, Lionel Jospin, Laurent Fabius, Michel Rocard, Edouard Balladur, Bruno Le Maire, Dominique de Villepin, Pascal Lamy, Jean-Claude Trichet, Florence Parly and Martine Aubry. It's almost easier to list the elite French politicians who didn't attend this small postgraduate school. The vast majority of students at the Grandes Ecoles are from wealthy elite families, a far more lop-sided distribution than for the Ivy League schools in America.

And the new business elites of modern India and Nepal have not dramatically changed caste domination. An aspiring young executive in India knows that whatever the brilliance of her knowledge about corporate strategy or six-sigma quality, or her distinction in her MBA or outstanding performance as a company star, links to family and caste will decide her promotion to the highest level of her company. Although social mobility loosens through education, 'being one of us' applies widely to aspiring politicians, doctors, engineers and journalists.

Figure 35 Ecole Nationale Superieure

THE POST-MODERN

The historian Arnold Toynbee wrote that the post-modern age started with the Franco-Prussian War when nationalism and industrial capitalism came into shuddering conflict and led to the First World War. By the end of the Second World War, the political landscape was so changed that others took this descriptor for a new epoch.[224] The old European world of great powers was in economic disarray. With new ideologies in Russia, China and Japan challenging the hegemony of the west colonialism came to an end. The industrial working class had greater power and the rise of universal suffrage was broadening democratic capitalism, strengthened by post-war changes in the emancipation and voice of women in the workplace. New Zealand introduced voting for women in 1893, followed by Australia in 1902, Norway in 1913, the Netherlands in 1919 and the Irish Free State in 1922. The USA introduced suffrage for women in 1920 but only removed discriminatory legislation against black voters in 1965. The UK gave votes for women in 1928 and France in 1944. The emergence of electronic innovation, especially television, transformed the post-war era into one of mass communication. The power of images and political exposure in every household, combined with the most rapid economic growth in a century, allowed social relations in the 1950s and 1960s to change dramatically. In the west our populations were transfixed by the 'sugar rush of commodities' which saved time, gave status and provided entertainment. Families became nuclear and the politics of right and left drifted into the centre.

The oil crises of the 1970s brought post-war optimism to a juddering halt. The victories of right wing leaders like Margaret Thatcher and Ronald Reagan meant neo-liberal economics dominated. In the 1980s came "the battering down of labour in core regions, outsourcing of plants to cheap wage locations in the periphery, displacement of investments into services and communications, expansion of military expenditure, and vertiginous rise in the relative weight of financial speculation at the expense of innovative production".[225] Newly independent former colonies found themselves with huge debts in an era of rising interest rates. The International Monetary Fund and World Bank insisted on harsh structural adjustment policies which attempted to 'get the prices right'. They compelled governments, desperate for loans, to remove the safety nets of food subsidies and charge for access to health, welfare and education, previously free at the point of delivery. In the 1990s, personal computer technology, as powerful as television, transformed access to communication and information, through the internet and the explosive uptake of mobile phones.

Since the millennium, human greenhouse gas pollution and climate change have led archaeologists and climate scientists to report a new geological era, a transition from the holocene into the 'anthropocene'. Modern politics has not yet caught on. The anthropocene will require a new altruism, sharing and regulation of the commons, governance beyond national boundaries and international trust for collective adherence to international regulations. Political leaders must temper a better tomorrow with responsibility and justice today. John Rawls's A Theory of Justice argued for two fundamental principles: provision of equal political rights and liberties for all, and acceptance of only those social and economic inequalities compatible with equal opportunity and which favour the poor. He didn't clarify the level of social inequalities permitted for the state to achieve its duty of favouring the poor. Perhaps that is why Rawls attracts support from both left and right. His methods to monitor favouring the poor and holding the state accountable were left open. Legal systems cannot be applied to such an ill-defined approach, so civil society must ensure justice and fairness and favour for the poor.

Within this space there is scope for much action at the social edge. Government can create spaces for civil society and sympathy groups to bring us closer to our environment, to share the happiness brought by 'biophilia', and to engage people in valuable tasks to protect a sustainable future for our children. What can we do to help politicians bring the power of sympathy groups into policy?

TAKE BACK CONTROL

Our social conquest of earth and the spread of civilised culture depended on circles of acquaintance we made from birth. Social groups, from families, to sympathy groups, larger overnight bands, villages, districts and more complex organisations of state created our emotional and cognitive environment. Our medicine, rights, politics, economy and development depended far more on our interaction within small groups than we give credit for. Yet in the twenty-first century of growing wealth and development, socially we face an epidemic of individual distress. Within small nuclear families, many separate or divorce. Children and older people face rippling repercussions of depression, insecurity and loneliness. We see a rising quantile of urban, single isolated parents. The co-operative nurture of rural extended families is in retreat. Most of us struggle with our inner demons of self while the complexity of modernity throws information at us in a mushrooming firestorm. Social sciences, history and microeconomics study kinship, hierarchies, networks and game theory as key elements of historical and cultural progress. But the literature on the sympathy group, Dunbar's 15 layer, is surprisingly thin.

In parallel, our four-decade enthusiasm for globalisation and neoliberalism is declining. Was 2016 a tipping point year, comparable to 1945, 1968 and 1979, when a 'new nationalism' emerged in many countries? In 2016 we saw Brexit, the election of Donald Trump, the rise of far-right parties in Europe, and the intensification of authoritarianism in Turkey, the Philippines, China, Russia and India. The reaction was, in part, a reaction to the unequal effects of globalisation and the repercussions of the global 2008 financial crash. Voters were disaffected. They relate more to their national polity than to broader alliances. Economic inequality arising from austerity economics is also a factor. The Gini coefficient, a measure of the gap between rich and poor, actually increased during Barack Obama's presidency. Apart from 2009, the wealth share of the richest 20% was higher than in any year that George W Bush was president, whereas the poorest 60% had a lower share throughout Obama's term in office.[226] Without doubt, voters are disgusted at the impunity of bankers and the tax evasion of the mega-rich. Their anger also reflects nascent racism as a reaction to surging refugee movements and jihadi violence, as well as to economic marginalisation.

But economics and xenophobia alone do not provide a comprehensive explanation. When people 'want their country back' or 'to take back control' there is a profound sense not so much of a meagreness of political voice but rather of not being listened to. Social engagement in communities appears to have declined and left feelings of learned helplessness. Many religious groups hanker after a return to 'traditional values'. 'Indigenes' and second generation migrants rail against excessive immigration, loss of cultural identity and urban ghettos. And hostility towards immigrant religions, especially Islam, has grown after terrorist acts by jihadist sympathisers. Such influences undoubtedly contributed to the electoral swing. Less discussed, and maybe more important as a cause of these reactions, was the emergent social vacuum in many people's lives. The loneliness of old people, the loss of neighbourhood decision-making, the separation of generations. Our young unemployed and the working poor are profoundly alienated. Their economic struggles are not compensated for by social identity or respect. We might add in the addictive isolation of our mobile screens, of online gaming and Facebook. And, as we urbanise, we witness the relative decline of the kinds of community engagement once enjoyed by our grandparents, through parish, choir, card evenings, amateur dramatics, sports clubs, fêtes, horticulture and village committees.

Part 4

Twenty Two Experiments at the Social Edge

Why experiment?

THE ROAD TO HELL

When I recall my early medical practice I get palpitations. A journalist might have reported my 1980s on-call weekend something like this: "Sunday morning, 6am, on the wards at University College maternity hospital, and the stream of phone calls to the paediatric team is relentless. Dr Anthony Costello, the newborn specialist in training, started his shift on Friday morning and will finish at lunchtime on Monday. Toyah, a tiny premature baby born yesterday, 17 weeks before her due date, and weighing just 450 grams, has meant Costello and his senior registrar have worked through the night. Toyah can only breathe with ventilator support, a tiny tube placed into her windpipe. She's fed through a fine catheter threaded up through her forearm into the right side of her heart. Over a coffee in the rest room, Costello enthuses about his long three-day shift. "I don't mind the on-call weekends. You learn so much. And the mothers enjoy seeing the same doctor throughout their care. I love the intensive work with the premmies, but we also do simple things. Every mother has an episiotomy (a planned cut in the vaginal wall just before delivery), which protects mums from a painful tear, and their babies from suffering trauma or brain damage. We advise mums to nurse their babies in the prone position. We know from our experience with the premmies that babies can regurgitate milk and choke if they lie on their backs. And we give first-time mothers a chance to establish breastfeeding through bed rest for seven days. If feeds are slow, I ask the midwives to top the baby up with some formula milk. It's just a precaution. I feel privileged to share these intense moments with couples. There is nothing more satisfying than a successful birth, and a happy and healthy mother and child."

This cameo reflects what I did. For a young doctor, maternity and newborn care was inspiring and fun. Weekend duty was part of the culture and vocation. We thrilled to its intensity and demands, a challenge of endurance, our rite of passage. Doctors who are well-trained, caring and available, as I tried to be, can also practise bad medicine. The care I gave as a junior – routine episiotomy, seven days of bed-rest for first time mothers, prone sleeping for newborn babies, and frequent formula top-ups for breastfeeding mothers – was not good clinical practice. Not just ineffective but dangerous. My training followed the guidelines of Lee and Jones's 1933 classic work, The Fundamentals of Good Medical Care " . . .the kind of medicine practised and taught by the recognised leaders of the medical profession".[227] Despite being textbook advice, the treatments I pushed derived from false premises and weak evidence. Worse, they risked serious complications, and broke a primary law of medicine, 'Primum non nocere, first do no harm'. As the American humorist HL Mencken put it, "the most common of all follies is to believe passionately in the palpably not true. It is the chief occupation of mankind."

Routine episiotomy cuts the vaginal wall with scissors to reduce the risk of a tear during the last stretching phase of labour. The practice subjects mothers to unnecessary trauma, serious discomfort for no measurable gain.[228] No strong evidence shows reduced risk of a third degree tear. The complications and pain caused by an unnecessary, ubiquitous practice have never been quantified. In many parts of the world routine episiotomy is still widely practised. Likewise, advice about first-time mothers resting for a week after birth was dangerous. Prolonged bed-rest after birth increases the risk of a deep vein thrombosis, which can cause a pulmonary embolus. A large clot of blood in the calf or pelvis dislodges and travels up through the heart and into the lung, where it blocks gas exchange. A large embolus causes death in minutes.

Most worrying, I gave terrible advice about sleeping position for babies. Prone, face-down sleeping arose because paediatricians in the 1970s learned that premature babies frequently regurgitate their milk feeds and can aspirate milk into their lungs, with catastrophic results. Nursing premature babies on their bellies rather than their backs reduced the risk of aspiration. This practice moved from premature baby units, with the blessing of paediatricians and midwives, to all term babies across the industrialised world. The result was disastrous.

Twenty years later, researchers in Auckland, New Zealand, Bristol, UK, the Netherlands, and Tasmania spotted an association between prone sleeping and an increased risk of cot death.[229] Word spread that the old midwife method of a baby sleeping face up was best. In 1994, an American Academy of Pediatrics review showed that where the fashion changed from prone to back or side sleeping, sudden infant deaths halved.[230] The epidemic of sudden infant deaths was, in no small way, caused by the medical profession. Well-intentioned neonatal paediatricians failed to realise that a premature baby is as different from a full-term baby as the full-termer is from a five-year-old. The same rules don't apply. A simple recommendation about how to nurse babies, against the instinct of their mothers, led to the deaths of thousands of children.

As for top-up formula feeds, the protective effects of exclusive breast-milk in early infancy are well researched. Introducing foreign milk protein early, even through one or two top-up feeds, increases the risks of allergy, and, in premature infants, of a nasty life-threatening inflammation of the intestines called necrotising enterocolitis. Everything we learn from new research on breastmilk confirms that a product perfected over 200 million years of mammalian evolution is the best and safest way to nourish an infant.

As a junior, I practised medicine based on stories, advice and text-books handed down from one generation to the next. It made me a bad doctor. Stories may be funny and inspiring, but are not good enough as evidence. "The fact that an opinion has been widely held is no evidence whatever that it is not utterly absurd," said Bertrand Russell. Take the strange case of antenatal corticosteroids. "The road to hell is paved with good intentions," said the late Bill Silverman, America's greatest paediatric epidemiologist. In the 1950s, Silverman had linked the use of oxygen for distressed premature infants with later blindness due to scarring of the retina. He also unravelled the link between sulphonamide antibiotics for newborn infection and writhing cerebral palsy from 'kernicterus' – staining of the lower brain basal ganglia, which control movement, with poisonous fat-soluble bilirubin, displaced from its protein-bound water-soluble safe form by the antibiotic. He realised that paediatricians who brought oxygen and sulphonamides to dying newborns acted with the best of intentions to save lives. But their use was fraught with danger. The care of premature newborn infants has to be right, day in and day out, to reduce the risks of later handicap.

In 2014, the United Nations Commission on Life-Saving Commodities announced a new life-saver – the use of antenatal steroids to reduce preterm birth in developing countries. They claimed the drug would save 400,000 lives each year. Use of the drug would "reduce incalculable suffering". International agencies and foundations leapt on to a new 'magic bullet' and called for immediate global scale-up.[231] Why? Most babies in developing countries die from being born too soon or too small. In the US, Europe and wealthy capital cities of emerging economies, the evidence is clear: an injection of antenatal steroids for a mother in premature labour will stimulate the preterm baby to produce a chemical surfactant which makes their lungs more pliable. A review of research studies showed steroids cut the risk of death by at least one quarter in babies born six weeks or more before term. Ergo, said the UN Commission, we can save the lives of tens of thousands of poor African and Asian babies by rolling out antenatal steroids.

My friend Kishwar Azad and I were sceptical. She knew from her work in Bangladesh that surfactant only works if premmies get round-the-clock specialised care. They must have skilled nursing, feeding and ventilation support, and blood tests to monitor the baby's biochemistry. In poor countries, special care is mostly absent and death rates are high. Would steroids bring any marginal benefit? Or might they increase the risks of disability even if babies survived? And could malnourished mothers face increased infection risks if they receive a steroid dose which suppresses their immunity? The Begum and I wrote a piece for the Lancet Global Health journal calling for extreme caution in scaling up steroids before the results of a proper evaluation.[232]

The letters column went red-hot. Some derided us as scaremongers. No evidence for a lack of safety, they claimed, thousands of babies will benefit, let's move ahead quickly. We responded by asking everyone to wait until results emerged from a multi-country research trial. We didn't have to wait long. The Argentinian obstetricians Dr Fernando Althabe and Dr José Belizán from the Institute for Clinical Effectiveness and Health Policy, Buenos Aires, led an international team in a study of almost 100,000 pregnant women in Argentina, Zambia, Guatemala, Pakistan, Kenya and Karnataka and Nagpur states in India.[233] They trained health workers to identify women in preterm labour and how to use antenatal corticosteroids. They compared the primary outcomes (newborn death, infection in mothers and use of steroids) between the mothers in areas where they had scaled up this training with mothers in areas that received only standard care.

The results shocked them. They discovered no effect on survival of small or preterm infants between the two arms of the trial. Worse, they observed a 12% increase in newborn deaths (term and preterm) in areas where steroids were being used on mothers. And mothers were harmed. Suspected maternal infection rates rose by a staggering 45%. Instead of unearthing a magic bullet, they had monitored a poison. But they had done a tremendous piece of research. Without this trial in poor populations, worldwide rollout of antenatal corticosteroids might have led to the deaths of thousands of infants and hundreds of mothers. Despite negative outcomes, the experimental trial would save lives in future by stopping a bad policy. Bill Silverman's warnings on 'the road to hell' were vindicated. Magic bullets in wealthy settings with high-quality care do not transfer into poor populations with the same risks and benefits. As the British paediatrician Sir Cyril Chantler wrote: "Medicine used to be simple, ineffective and relatively safe. It is now complex, effective and potentially dangerous."[234]

FROM STORY TO EXPERIMENT TO STORY

Experiment for social and political policy is not new. "Science requires a disputatious community of truth seekers," said the American sociologist Donald T Campbell in his book The Experimenting Society.[235] "If pure or applied social studies are to merit the term 'scientific', their problem areas will have to be colonised by the successful sciences." And philosopher Karl Popper himself had recommended that "a social technology is needed whose results can be tested by piecemeal social engineering".

In the early eighties, just qualified, I was unaware that world medicine would undergo a revolution: that would save countless lives and improve patient safety everywhere. A small band of medical academics drove the revolution. Alvan Feinstein in New York, David Sackett and Gordon Guyatt at McMaster University in Canada, and Kay Dickersin in Baltimore. And Iain Chalmers and Murray Enkin in Oxford transformed our understanding of effective care in pregnancy and childbirth. The Oxford group set up the Cochrane Collaboration to review all evidence in medicine. They put into practice a new approach from developments in philosophy, statistics and logic over 250 years. Their evidence-based movement transformed health care in less than a generation. With a strange mix of rigour and humility, they threw out ineffective treatments, the claims of quackery and the anecdotal commands of so-called experts. Today, claims for new discoveries and treatments receive pitiless scrutiny. Studies use agreed methods and protocols for experiment. The hocus-pocus of homeopathy and quackery face the ridicule of experimental scrutiny. For a fuller description of the pioneers and principles of randomised trials, please read the *Appendix*.

Should such scrutiny be restricted to medicine? Why not apply it to teachers, environmentalists, managers, economists, bankers and even politicians? Can we assess the practice of these professionals and hold them accountable? How can we know, for example, whether sympathy groups can really help us improve our health, wealth and a sustainable future? Bertrand Russell gave advice: "When you are studying any matter, or considering any philosophy, ask yourself only what are the facts and what is the truth that the facts bear out. Never let yourself be diverted either by what you wish to believe, or by what you think would have benefi-cent social effects if it were believed. But look only, and solely, at what are the facts." In medicine and social policy, evidence is more important than passion.

The experimental method, though flawed and not always applicable, is our most reliable source of evidence. Associations between two trends are misleading. A correlation between two variables, for example, tobacco and smoking, or low birth weight and the later risk of stroke, does not necessarily mean a cause. 'Post hoc ergo propter hoc' is the 'confusion of sequence and consequence; confusion of correlation and cause'.[236] An association between the Aries star sign and the risk of bronchiolitis at one year of age reflects the seasonal nature of a respiratory syncytial virus epidemic rather than any causal astrological configuration. Does bacon cause cancer? Or are people who eat bacon different from those who don't? With an association we must consider alternative explanations. Yet every news bulletin on TV, radio and the internet ignores this principle. "Almost every single nutrient imaginable has peer-reviewed publications associating it with almost any outcome," says John Ioannidis, Stanford Professor of Medicine, and "definitive solutions won't come from another million observational papers or small randomised trials".[237]

An experiment to assess a drug, education, or management strategy to change a business or social outcome should be rigorous and repeatable. The best way of knowing "the facts" is through experiment. Not just any old experiments but those that use the highest standards of practice agreed by international expert consensus. "Observation is a passive science, experimentation an active science," said Claude Bernard, the nineteenth century physiologist. "The true worth of an experimenter consists in his pursuing not only what he seeks in his experiment, but also what he did not seek."

Good experiments follow simple rules: a comparison group, to allocate the treatment or intervention in a random way, and precise measurement of outcomes, concealed from the investigators. That's it. Three simple ideas:

the need to experiment; recognise that an association does not mean a cause; and plan experiments that are randomised, controlled and blinded. These ideas help us make decisions based on the best facts, rather than what Russell called "the distorting medium of their own desires". If such evidence informs practice by our politicians, civil servants, managers, policemen, financiers, environmentalists, farmers and teachers, the world will be a better place. The good news is that, after a long delay, experiments are now used more in social policy, education and economics. The Campbell Collaboration, an international research network, is the social science niece of the medical Cochrane Collaboration. It provides distilled summaries of evidence in these areas as part of a 'third wave' of the evidence agenda.[238] It shows clearly the huge gaps in social science research and how much more could be done.

Don't mistake experimental principles for an attack on stories. The competition between stories and experiments is a false division. Stories tell you whether something might work. Experiments test the hypothesis that they do work. Alexander Fleming, the patient Scot, discovered the anti-bacterial action of penicillium at St Mary's Hospital in Paddington on Friday, September 28, 1928. He stared at a Petri dish of Staphylococci bacteria contaminated with penicillin mould and saw a ring of absent growth around the mould colonies. He was not the first witness. Ernest Duchesne, a French medical student, had made the same observation in 1896. But Fleming saw the point of the story, what it could mean. His interpretation led to experiments by Howard Florey and Ernst Chain, who studied how to mass-produce one of our most effective ever drugs.

Other stories can mislead. Emergency contraception prevents pregnancy and abortion doesn't it? For some individuals it does. But an expected big effect on pregnancy and abortion rates didn't materialise when it was scaled up. No effect was seen.[239] Women used it, but over-relied on the method and had unprotected sex in the same cycle, thinking they were safe.

Malaria treatment offers another example. Malaria scares the military big time. In the 1861-65 American Civil War, 1.3 million malaria cases caused thousands of deaths. Half of the Caucasian troops and a staggering

80% of African-American troops contracted malaria each year. They might have learnt from the British. In 1814-15, the British troops under Governor General Francis Rawdon-Hastings moved troops north from India to deal with rebellious Nepalese. To everyone's surprise, the Anglo-Nepalese war ended in stalemate. British troops contracted malaria as they marched up through the *Terai,* leaving them too weak to take on the hardy mountain defenders. In World War Two, 600,000 malaria cases emerged in the Pacific theatre. In some islands of the south, case attack rates were four per person per year.[240] In the Vietnam War, 100,000 soldiers contracted malaria. And in 2003, on a peacekeeping mission to Liberia, 80 out of 290 UN troops were evacuated with the mosquito-borne disease.

From the 1950s WHO campaigns to eradicate malaria failed. As chloroquine resistance grew, they saw a rebound in cases. In 1963, the US Military Malaria Research Program through the Walter Reed Institute aimed to develop new drugs, vaccines and to tackle drug resistance. Many new and useful drugs emerged but none had the power to replace chloroquine and the world struggled on. In 1970, China, also worried about chloroquine resistance, started a programme commissioned by Mao Tse-Tung. Dr Tu Youyou, head of the new malaria research group in Beijing, reviewed 2000 traditional herb preparations for antimalarial activity in a mouse model. One herb showed promise in inhibiting parasite growth. An intensive literature review revealed that *qinghaosu*, or sweet wormwood, a common herb named *Artemisia annua*, was described, along with 43 other treatments of malaria, in the Chinese Handbook for Prescriptions for Emergencies compiled by Ge Hong (284-346) in the fourth century: "a handful of qinghao immersed with two litres of water, wring out the juice and drink it all". But the experiments failed. They found no effect of the herb in the lab.

When Tu read the ancient text again she realised that the remedy was a cold extract. Her team had heated their extract, which probably destroyed the active ingredients. She wrote: "On 4 October 1971, we obtained a non-toxic, neutral extract that was 100% effective against parasitemia in mice infected with *Plasmodium berghei* and in monkeys infected with *Plasmodium cynomolgi.*"[241] Many experiments followed to assess the benefit, risks and dosages of artemisinin, but Tu's study of history books and her canny observation laid the basis for the discovery of modern medicine's most effective anti-malarial drug. Artemisinin in combination with other drugs is the first-line treatment across Africa and Asia. In 2015, not before time, Dr Tu received the Nobel Prize for medicine.

And stories go further. If an experiment shows a treatment works, but occasionally fails, stories of failure throw a torchlight of investigation into why that may be. From story, to experiment, to story. Stories propose a hypothesis, experiments dispose. Yet the amphitheatre of medicine still witnesses bloody battles between the gladiators of experiment and the lions of narrative. Gladiators have new names like quants and trialists and randomistas. Lions are quals, formatives and wickeds. George Bush Jnr taught us that humans can have a peaceful co-existence with the fish. So can gladiators and lions, if they meet rarely and without a baying crowd. Gladiators fight for their own survival. Lions live in their jungles and savannahs, balance the local ecosystem, and wonder at the beauty of it all. Science and humanities need each other, like predator and prey, to prevent us from destroying ourselves. We look at things from a different perspective. Would you ask your children which avatar of the 'presents' deity they believe in, Santa Claus or grandma? No. The answer is both.

Maxims and proverbs also have a place. They provide comfort and wisdom to complement an evidence-informed strategy. Sometimes they save you. On my first day as a clinical student at the Middlesex Hospital, Duncan Catterall, a gentle and wise pioneer of sexual health, told us that the physician should 'cure sometimes, relieve often and comfort always'. I've carried this maxim throughout my career. Another simple one is a Buddhist mantra, shared by the late David Harvey, the former royal paediatrician, a gay, Buddhist socialist and aesthete, taken from us too soon by Parkinson's disease. "When the neonatal unit gets frenetic I tell them to 'keep calm, keep going'." I use it every day.

And Einstein knew a thing or two. "Everything that can be counted does not necessarily count. Everything that counts cannot necessarily be counted." He was right. Evidence cannot substitute for an ideology based on justice and democracy. Even with good evidence we face dilemmas.

Effective drugs carry risks of side-effects. The eventual benefit from a powerful chemotherapy drug for cancer may be worth the short-term risks and side-effects for a young mother, but not for her elderly grand-mother. "The art of medicine lies in balancing probabilities," wrote Canadian physician Sir William Osler.

LEGITIMATE RESISTANCE TO EXPERIMENT

In the eighteenth century, Scottish physician James Lind reflected on why it is difficult for new evidence to challenge experts: " . . . it is no easy matter to root out old prejudices, or to overturn opinions established by time, custom and great authorities . . . it was necessary to remove a great deal of rubbish . . . Where I have been necessarily led, in this disagreeable part of the work, to criticise the sentiments of eminent and learned authors, I have not done it with a malignant view of depreciating their labours, or their names; but from a regard to truth, and to the good of mankind."

Resistance to accepted wisdom is as relevant today as in the time of Lind. Resistance to experiment arises from a toxic cocktail of anti-scientific prejudice and legitimate concerns about experimental rigour. The language of randomised controlled trials often makes non-scientists uncomfortable. The problem of complexity, that social interventions are not the same as drugs, is used to negate the value of a trial. Feasibility is questioned. How can a trial adjust for the ever-changing real world and the challenges of going to scale? For sceptical economists, who trawl through muddy national databases, experimental trials seem like a dangerous clear water illusion. For policymakers who want particular programmes unchallenged, a trial is an unnecessary and time-delaying obstacle. Some sceptics contest, with missionary zeal, the validity of social experimentation. In one meeting, a charity worker confronted me saying the use of any control group was unethical. Maybe scaling up unproven or harmful interventions, I suggested, is also unethical.

We experimentalists hurt ourselves. We use a disturbing dictionary of cold and brutal verbs. The language of security – monitoring and surveil-lance – replaces the language of care – recording health histories or biographies. We 'randomise' rather than draw lots or raffle. We enrol 'control' subjects rather than a voluntary group of equals. We conduct a 'trial' rather than a comparison. We evaluate rather than assess. Our tone is cold and neon. It alienates the people we come from. Language matters. If we create our authority with a professional priestly tongue we won't be emulated.

As scientists we must be alert to the risk of unrealised error. There are many pitfalls. We can do inappropriate statistical tests, misinterpret statis-tical significance, fail to adjust for clustering, mishandle missing data, get the effect size wrong, ignore confirmation bias (whereby we emphasise the positive findings that support our own hypothesis and dismiss the negative findings that falsify it), and report statistics poorly. A common problem is multiple testing of multiple outcomes for positive findings and 'P-value hacking'. The best trials have only one or two pre-specified primary outcomes to avoid this problem – other observed positive impacts on secondary outcome variables cannot have the same weight. Secondary impacts generate hypotheses for further trials, where they become primary outcomes.

Others argue that politics in the real world and the complexity of social initiatives limit the role of experiments. Their arguments are persua-sive. Research methodologists Ray Pawson and Nick Tilley propose an alternative of 'realist evaluation'.[242] They argue that we cannot simply experiment, we need a 'theory of change' about how any intervention might work. (Many trialists disagree. A trial decides impact, with or without a theory, although a theory of action helps in our explanations and analysis of causal chains). A theory creates an explanatory structure to measure postulated steps between intervention and outcome.

Social systems, they argue, differ in context for most physical experi-ments. They're fluid and ever changing so that social interventions cannot be "fully anticipated or entirely predictable". So 'realist' evaluators must "identify and explain the precise circumstances under which each theory holds". We must learn from many social situations and experiments to draw common lessons about hierarchies or groups or social processes. These criticisms don't de-legitimise a trial; rather they highlight that mixed methods are important and that social trials also have 'qualitative scientists' to observe the circumstances and performance of what is being tested. And trialists agree we do several experiments in different settings.

What about complexity?[243] Compound interventions within intricate social systems are difficult to evaluate. People enrolled into studies are active, not passive, recipients. They have minds of their own. High flyers and plodders, early and late adopters think differently. For example, a family practice initiative to reduce high blood pressure might comprise tests, visits, consultations, diagnoses, better compliance with treatment. Uniformity is impossible, with many opportunities for "inconsistency and reinterpretation, blockages, delays and unintended consequences".[244]

Location, location, location? The class, tribe or ethnic identity of a neighbourhood, people's relationships within a programme, the rules and customs of the institutions, available transport and amenities, levels of wealth, cultural restrictions on movement and so on produce a kaleido-scopic variety of circumstance. Great enthusiasm at the start of a programme wears off. For example, impressive short-term impacts of new diets don't lead to sustained weight loss after a year or more. Sequencing may be important. Anti-smoking legislation in public places had greater than expected compliance because measures were incremental and sequenced, first in public transport, then workplaces, then restaurants, and only finally bars and casinos. Smokers became inured to being bossed around.

Outcomes of social programmes are also more complex than, say, a new drug for a single variable like blood pressure or death. Evaluation may include multiple input like budget and staff time, to activities such as consultations or meetings or home visits, to outputs such as health promotion materials or use of services, to outcomes such as smoking or breastfeeding rates, or to reductions in death, illness or deviant behaviour. And results require interpretation. Do health service changes, such as reductions in waiting lists, always improve health or wellbeing?

How to handle confounders? In many communities a plethora of government services – health, employment, welfare and social care – run in parallel with third sector, charitable and non-government organisations. With similar aims, they are often unaware of each other's work. How to attribute impact for interventions introduced by one or other agency? And what if governments and policy change, or bureaucracies are restructured in wave after wave of reforms? Comparison areas exposed to the same broader change become more essential.

Evaluating advocacy programmes is a particular problem, for example, campaigns to reduce the deaths of mothers in poor countries or to cut cigarette smoking by young people. Components interact, resistance to behaviour change varies, many organisations are involved. And local culture affects the flexibility of community groups, and fidelity to the original plan. Political scientist Steven Teles in a lecture in Montreux reminded us that politics is strategic, iterative and unpredictable, so that experiments that track the impact of a political advocacy campaign on linear outcomes would seem to lack relevance. Stasis is the norm in politics, so getting something on to an agenda for public discussion might be the limit of our ambition. We face major challenges in measuring advocacy success. It doesn't necessarily result from the best people doing it. Further, the effectiveness of interventions is often regime-specific – lessons learned in the US might not transfer to Europe or vice versa. So Teles is sceptical. He believes that evaluation of advocacy is a legitimation ritual forced on civil servants by politicians who must justify their spending decisions. Advocacy agencies can also manipulate results, conceal negative information, and overstate their own importance.

Another key problem is timing of our chosen outcome. Many advocacy campaigns run with a long time horizon. Political change is a moving picture, not a single snapshot. If we want long-term changes in behaviour we must be sure it is durable and generative. We don't want to reward meaningless victories, nor to punish 'failure' based on interim outcomes. Do we aim to please the funder who wants quick wins over one to two years or sustainable change over five to 10 years? For instance, in the UK progress was slow in the first eight years of a national programme to cut teenage pregnancy rates with little change observed. Surprisingly the government took a long view and defended the programme. Many would have stopped funds. Over the next decade, as it became embedded in local councils and health services, pregnancy rates fell steeply.[245]

So how can advocacy be evaluated? In political advocacy, a person's private reputation for influence might be the best investment. In which case a good evaluator asks whether the advocate has real influence and seeks insider information on their relationships rather than data. An intelligence agent or person with undercover skills might be better than a scientist or consultant. Good evaluators realise things change. Programmes change both behaviour and "the conditions which make the programme work in the first place". Welfare provision may become welfare dependency. Group initiatives may lead to social exclusion as well as inclusion. Campaigns to distribute vitamin A supplements in poor populations suffering deficiency become redundant as dietary taboos and poor food choices are tackled and deficiency disappears.

In summary, adherents of the realist evaluation school are right to raise complexity, location, sustainability, multiple actors and change. Programmes may work only when "targeted at well-defined outcomes, for the right subjects, in appropriate circumstances. Large scale programmes often over-reach themselves so that impact falls, often to zero." In many ways realist evaluation complements the idea of experiments: They "ask not, 'what works?' or, 'does this program work?' but instead: 'What works for whom in what circumstances and in what respects, and how'?" [246]

We can agree that trial findings are interpreted carefully, informed by detailed process evaluations. But anti-trial scorn of realist evaluators and economists, including the Nobel Prize winner Angus Deaton, is too dogmatic. "Methinks they protesteth too much". Social science gains from a mix of experiment and analysis, as the great sociologist Professor Ann Oakley recognised two decades ago.[247] It isn't Us versus Them. The combination of an 'objective' impact experiment and careful 'subjective' observation of the process is possible and ideal. Philosophers agree. Roy Bhaskar, Oxford professor of philosophy, proposed a theory of science based on 'critical realism' that combined "the devil of empiricism and the deep blue sea of postmodernism".[248] His simple truth was to bind stories with experiments.

Science has transformed medical practice. Patients know their doctor will use a proven treatment. Randomised controlled trials show whether new drugs or practices work. Randomisation does a good job of getting rid of confounding factors, known and unknown, and, with enough statistical power, a trial measures the effectiveness of the intervention. Pooling results of several trials measures effectiveness and generalisability to different patient groups or populations.

But a failure to make comparative evaluations has blighted social evidence. Social science plays a central role in hypothesis generation and in analysing mechanisms of change in complex interventions. Social policy is rarely evidence-based, and, in many disciplines, randomised evaluations have hardly been used. Why is there reluctance to use elegant methods to improve decision-making for the lives of millions of families? Why have the principles of evidence been ignored by teachers, lawyers, financiers, economists and social scientists? Hopefully times are changing and a new wave of academics across disciplines are keen to experiment.

SYSTEMS THINKING AND RESILIENCE

We live and work in complex systems. Political and economic, health and education, ecological and cognitive, management and information, solar and galactic systems. A system is interdependent and connecting. It comprises many parts to make the whole. A system has boundaries in time and space and a social system is one in which communication is paramount. Systems thinkers and theorists consider the nature of social systems and how we might change them for sustainability, human development, economic benefit and so on. They look for deeper processes of change within complex systems than magic bullets or local heroes.

Environmental scientist Donella Meadows was a systems thinker who described leverage points where "a small shift in one thing can produce big changes in everything", probing points of power. Meadows was also on the MIT team in Boston that made the World3 computer model and a co-author of the influential 1972 Club of Rome report The Limits to

Growth.[249] The report predicted environmental consequences of continuing population and economic growth of which several, climate change, depletion of fisheries and ozone depletion, proved correct). She listed a hierarchy of leverage points to change a system. The top six, in increasing order of effectiveness, were:

6. The structure of information flows (who does and does not have access to information).
5. The rules of the system (such as incentives, punishments, constraints).
4. The power to add, change, evolve, or self-organise system structure.
3. The goals of the system.
2. The mindset out of which the system – its goals, structure, rules, delays, parameters – arises.
1. The power to transcend mindsets.

Studying the list, one is struck by the ways in which sympathy groups, more than most interventions, converse with these change points. Our women's groups increase the power of their members through flows of information from shared memory, health care experiences, rights, service quality, resources, networks and champions. By clarifying the rights and entitlements of members to things like food and fertiliser subsidies, cash transfers and supplies such as bed-nets, groups offer women the power of increased resilience.

Meadows' top three leverage points each contribute to Paulo Freire's 'critical consciousness'. Consider an antenatal first-time mother who lives in rural poverty, and whose traditional family have always had their births at home. Joining a woman's group with other pregnant women shows her the goals of a different system. One where preventive antenatal and delivery care is the norm, where seeking obstetric care in a crisis is subsidised, and where women have rights to cash and free medicines in pregnancy. She learns the value of registering her newborn child for entitlements, home-based records for immunisation and child development and growth monitoring. Her mindset of subsistence and self-sufficiency, locked into traditional practices, both good and harmful, will change as she communicates with mothers who changed their village expectations and culture of childbirth. When she learns about the value of exclusive breastfeeding she might resist the advice of local pharmacies and stores that push her to buy formula milk. When she learns about the value of not smoking or over-working in late pregnancy, she might discard cigarettes or ask permission to shift her workload within the household. Finally, if she's lucky, one or two members of her group might bring transformational ideas. Maybe her husband beats her after he gets drunk. Her group sisters tell her that domestic violence offends the law, her religion and her rights. The group offer her the solidarity to confront her husband, if she wants help, and pressure him to drink less and stop his violent behaviour.

Some sceptics tell me that complex systems cannot be changed by single interventions nor evaluated by randomised trials. My response is direct. Sympathy groups are not magic bullets or single interventions. They are complex, non-linear ways to generate solutions over an extended period. Non-linear complex problems need complex, non-linear solutions. If the focus of groups is well defined and deserves a social experiment, if the theory of change makes sense and the primary outcome indicators are carefully chosen, a randomised evaluation is appropriate and workable.

Sympathy groups also build resilience. Every day we hear of risk and threats in our everyday lives: the air we breathe, the hamburgers and Coke we enjoy, terrorist attacks at the station, smoking, drinking, sex, sun and sport. Medicine and public health exhort us to change our behaviour to cut our risks, to swallow statins for cholesterol, aspirin for stroke, vitamin A for child survival, or vape on nicotine to stop smoking. Medics call it secondary prevention. What we focus on far less is resilience. We let it happen by chance. As we get wealthier, better educated, more informed, face fewer bad options, we build our power and resilience to make preferable choices. But we don't analyse resilience, or only with broad variables we're unlikely to change, like our gender, social position, age or housing. But we can intervene to boost power and resilience, if we know what works. One hundred years ago my grandparents faced threats from infectious disease and warfare. In this century my children face different threats – long-term illness, depression, addictions, loneliness in old age, and environmental change. Our governments must deal with complex social and economic trends like youth unemployment, anti-social behaviour and domestic violence, or how to rehabilitate prisoners to stop re-offending and treat many more elderly people with dignity and compassion. Government must ensure our businesses compete through a skilled and flexible workforce. Whether making cars and computers, or providing design, entertainment or advice, organisational culture helps companies to flourish, be productive, and give great service quality.

Governments build resilience by protecting democracy, security, justice, freedoms, education, infrastructure, energy, social protection and the natural environment. Governments obey national boundaries but modernity requires cross-border, regional or global co-operation. Soon the world will have nine billion people with rising consumption and economic expectations. Governments, working together in global accord, must address overconsumption and carbon pollution, climate change and environmental damage. Corruption and inequality, far from a steady decline, have reached unparalleled heights. Sleaze and fraud threaten resilience by planting seeds of political instability. Corruption and credit, wood-boring larval twins, eat away at the foundations of our global financial system. Is another crash imminent? Social mechanisms to combat dishonesty in national institutions can stabilise economies. Credit traps the poor in vicious circles of hire purchase agreements or payday loans, with spiralling, unpayable debt. Thinking through mechanisms of resilient, good governance, from village to district to capital to state, from country to region, from continent to international summit, makes us think about the building blocks of success, and how we might do things better.

One neglected aspect of the communication revolution is the role that mobiles and social media play, and could play more, in sharing our learning about resilience. The collection, processing and dissemination of small and big data has never been easier. Curricula, action cycles, research findings and nudges towards resilience could feed into national networks of groups.

Maybe a link between the ancestral strengths of the sympathy group and the modern instantaneity of the SMS or tweet can create new synergies. Citizen science is possible. Citizens, like eighteenth century gentlemen scientists, can share, *en masse* and in groups, the ideas, energy and utility of groups to transform our world.

WHEN TO DO A SOCIAL EXPERIMENT

Epidemics of infectious disease such as HIV, tuberculosis, cholera, ebola and zika virus haven't disappeared. They remain regional and global threats. But we face rising epidemics of new non-infectious diseases, of loneliness, long-term conditions like depression and diabetes, anti-social behaviour, sexual violence, stunted children with impaired development, organisations that fail to be productive or caring or innovative, climate change that threatens our children's future, corruption and gridlock in government and commerce, and growing national inequality between rich and poor.

When we tackle daunting wicked problems we face thorny questions. First, how much exposure might our target population receive from a professional intervention? How much time can clinical or social welfare staff offer if we do something at scale? Compared with time spent with our families and friends at the social edge? With 5840 waking hours in a year, if we spend only two hours a day in the company of family, neighbours and friends, that amounts to 12% of our conscious existence. Even with a home visit from a care worker for half an hour twice a month (luxurious by most state provision standards), contact time is only 0.2% of conscious time, one sixtieth of the exposure to our circles of acquaintance.

The great epidemiologist Geoffrey Rose addressed coverage and exposure when he described the 'prevention paradox'.[250] It states that prevention strategies must reach the many to heal the few, and that a small shift in the population as a whole i.e. a small shift for any one individual, will have a larger effect on disease than targeting only those people at high risk. So reducing salt consumption overall in a population will have a larger effect on deaths from hypertension than medics targeting only those at high risk. Cutting population cholesterol levels with diet or statins, mass vaccination, compulsory seat belts and iodine-enriched salt to prevent thyroid deficiency in vulnerable areas are other examples of the paradox.

Second, professional one-to-one care is static and linear. What you see is what you get. The only circumstance in which professional care contact will boost itself is where a carer promotes patient support from local clubs and drop-ins. In practice, this solution is rare. Carers may not know the locality, their job description is clinical not social, and they lack resources or time to make it happen. A sympathy group is dynamic and non-linear. It creates its own voluntary resources, has local knowledge and a stronger sense of duty based on self-interest (if I help old people now, they'll look after me when I'm in the same position). Sympathy groups give the powerful endorphin and oxytocin kick that accompanies acts of compassion and the stimulus of friendship.

So how does the evidence and cost base for home visits compare with self-help groups for prevention of wicked social problems? Despite the enrichment of gurus, agony aunts and newspaper columnists, the evidence for health worker contact, or messaging at scale, to cut depression, addiction and antisocial behaviour is surprisingly thin. Smaller scale trials showed promise. Psychologist Daisy Singla and colleagues reviewed 27 proof-of-principle trials and found low cost treatments for depression worked in low and middle income countries.[251] Home treatment involved around 10 face-to-face sessions over two to three months to discuss behaviour, relationships, emotions, and thought patterns. Overall the treatments halved depression and post-traumatic stress. But governments lack the will and funds to go to scale. With a huge population, burden of depression and stress, 10 home visits to everyone affected is unrealistic.

A reasonable alternative hypothesis is that a benevolent state policy to tap into the self-interest of sympathy, and the positive feelings created by shared solutions, is more effective and less expensive. The role of the state shifts the balance from individual care towards an ecology for social action. The state might give incentives for volunteer training, free venues for groups and promotional campaigns on entitlements and meetings. Investment in research to study strategies at scale could, in theory, generate big economic returns. The ecological approach does not replace state clinical care but enhances it.

Third, can facilitated sympathy groups at scale, putting ideas into practice in unexpected ways, be tested and costed for a range of problems? Policy tends to pursue individual and professional treatment. Groups are ignored. Rigorous evaluation of sympathy group power is the exception, not the rule. We don't have reliable estimates of costs and effectiveness through randomised comparison studies. These would assess health outcomes while collecting the views of beneficiaries, how the groups worked, the coverage achieved, unforeseen benefits and risks, and whether things tailed off.

We shall next consider specific experiments to test the value of informal sympathy groups for a variety of twenty-first century social challenges. The 22 experiments presented here use sympathy group principles (beneficiaries, enablers, neighbours, focus, iteration, trust and strategies) for different target audiences. The meeting content varies as do the benefits we measure. I used seven criteria to choose these 22 experimental questions: the importance and size of the problem; the potential for social gain; the unclear nature of unintended consequences and costs of the groups (which make a trial necessary); the feasibility of doing the study; whether a group strategy is in existing policy (a trial is unethical if it is); the potential to change outcomes and policy; and finally, whimsy, whether I found the study interesting or not.

My experiments aim to test ways in which community groups can advance health, personal and social wellbeing, cut stress and anti-social behaviour, improve management and wealth creation, tackle climate change, enhance credit systems and reduce quiet corruption, strengthen good governance within public institutions, amplify lifestyle change within large populations, and speed up responses to humanitarian or epidemic emergencies. I have used a standard method to summarise the study design for each experiment – PICO – the Population we're aiming to reach, the design of the Intervention, the Comparison group and the Outcomes we shall measure. Outcomes will be primary and secondary. You build the hypothesis about the size of the effect you will have with the primary outcome. Secondary outcomes are those you're interested to measure. I haven't suggested hypotheses of the effect sizes for each experiment, but we want an effect that is policy-relevant, workable, and not so small as to need a huge sample size to detect a difference. The experiments I propose will use a simple randomised and controlled design, using population clusters, not individuals, as the unit of randomisation.

I shall assume that each experiment has an inbuilt assessment based on realist evaluation principles, to analyse the coverage and performance of the groups, drop-out rates, local conditions, and potential mechanisms by which changes in outcomes are explained. I assume that follow-up trials of the same intervention in different settings will test the generalisability of the findings and explore whether mechanisms of action might change in a different local milieu. Finally, the costs of running the programme will be analysed to give policymakers an idea of 'bang for their buck'.

Loneliness and
long-term conditions

LONELINESS: CASE STUDIES

In medical school we studied mnemonics, glossaries and fat textbooks on the pathology and treatment of individual patients. We learnt little about the therapeutic power of groups and nothing of the stress of human solitude. Early in my first house job at the Middlesex Hospital, in London's West End, two contrasting 'celebrity' admissions enlightened me.

One crisp February afternoon, in Wheelers Oyster Bar in Charlotte Street, Francis Bacon and M finished their lunch of crab, oysters and a bottle of cold Bollinger champagne. M loved her private lunches with Francis. She felt special, attended to, away from the smoky boisterousness of the Colony Room, where she was founder and proprietress of London's most famous and debauched salon for the arts. Francis adored M, his closest woman friend, whose raucous laughter and foul mouth never failed to cheer him up. Her hook nose and thick-set features, sweeping grey hair, and tall, upright frame gave her a physical dominance that matched her caustic wit and shameless obscenities. Francis considered his portrait of M a labour of love, not just any old commission, and one of his finest paintings. Much later, in 2007, after both were dead, his triptych of M sold at Sotheby's in Paris for 14 million euros, the proceeds of which went to a foundation for women's rights.

As the waiter brought petit fours and coffee, M leaned back in her chair, made a sudden gasp, held a rictus smile for several seconds, and then arced backwards on to the wooden floor, kicking out at the table from which a champagne flute fell and smashed on the floor. Francis was shocked into silence. M lay motionless, apart from a slight facial twitch, spreadeagled behind an adjacent table. The diners froze, assuming her to be drunk. They didn't like to interfere. Everyone knew Francis was a London celebrity, one of the world's greatest painters, but they didn't want to intrude. Slowly it dawned that something serious had happened. The proprietor rang for an ambulance, and M was ferried to the Middlesex Hospital casualty department just 300 yards away.

By the time, an hour later, the casualty officer called me to clerk the admission, M had regained consciousness but remained confused and aggressive. Her words were jumbled but not slurred, a left-sided facial twitch was evident every minute or two, and she seemed reluctant to move her left hand. She gazed to the right as if looking for something. Lawrence, my hyperactive South African registrar, thought her knee reflexes were brisk and her plantar reflex upgoing.

"She's hed a small strark, or perhaps just a transient ischaemic atteck. Tarm will tell. Do the usual work-up, with an ECG. She mart need a CT scan booked tomorrow."

As I took blood, M swore at me with football terrace venom, restrained by a staff nurse. I put it down to cortical disinhibition. The staff nurse, in turn, was an 'evil little bitch'. She put it down to the strong smell of alcohol from the stains of vomit and saliva on M's blouse. After another stream of invective, we got her up to Vaughan Morgan ward, away from the scared patients and staff in the casualty observation room. "Have we got a side-room Ruth?" I asked the ward sister on the phone. "I think she might be trouble." Ruth said No. She'd have to go on the open ward for observation.

The next few days were among the more memorable of my house registration year. M suffered the emotional lability and disinhibition found in stroke patients, but she did so from an Olympian base of unbounded, ill-disciplined offensiveness. The Colony club members loved her abuse.

Christopher Hitchens described her with pithy accuracy in his Hitch-22. "M, arguably the rudest person in England ('shut up c★★ty and order some more champagne'), almost never left her perch at the corner of the bar and was committed to that form of humour that insists on referring to all gentlemen as ladies."[252]

On the ward she cursed and ranted. With her attractive inability to pronounce her 'r's she screamed that the ward staff were a "lot of cwap". The horror of her sick neighbours, little old ladies from Belgravia with angina or faulty pacemakers, was Munchian. The nurses pleaded with me to get her out when she tried to discharge herself and fell over, semi-naked, in the middle of the ward. When my sober-suited consultant did his ward round and considered the case history, he sat on the bed to tell her gently that she'd had a little stroke and should be home in a few days. M told him he was an awwogant bastard and should contwol his vampire staff who had assaulted her for unnecessawy blood tests.

"I'm sure you'll be fine, Mrs B. You should be home in a few days."

"I'm not Mrs B, you arsehole. I'm a queer, and my best friend is Fwancis Bacon. And I'm not staying in this cemetery for a few days. As soon as Fwancis comes I'm going home."

"Well, we'll be as quick as we can."

"I'm going home, do you hear. NURSE! NURSE! Get this 'cking man away from me. NURSE! He's holding me AGAINST MY WILL. 'CK OFF! ALL OF YOU.

M continued to scream and curse throughout the ward round, and for much of the rest of the week. Only two things seemed to quieten her down. When the shouting became intolerable, I would sit on her bed and ask her about her club. She brightened and would tell me, scatter-gun, about her members, what they did, and how she needed a drink. The other calming influence was in the early afternoon when the Bacon entourage visited. His sympathy group was never less than 10 strong. Most smelt of booze after a liquid lunch in the Colony Room.

Bacon was the leader, a slight man with the most dysmorphic, asymmetric face I had ever seen, like two men glued together. He brought Fortnum and Mason's smoked salmon and hand-crafted chocolates. Around him were two bedraggled writers, a woman with cropped hair, dyed purple, and a tattoo on her neck, a few younger posh sycophants, and a pair of elderly ruddy-faced men who laughed uproariously every time M spoke. Another tall man wore orange leather trousers, a torn denim jacket, reeked of liquor and sported a fresh black eye, his left eyelid almost closed from bruising delivered by a punch.

Bacon was charming and polite. He loved M. As the formidable guardian of his temple, the Colony Room, he painted her, after her death, as a Greek Sphinx, part warm matron, part terrifying perched eagle. The distinguished neuroscientist, Semir Zeki, and his colleague Tomohiro Ishizu, refer to this painting in trying to understand the science behind the visual shock produced by Bacon's work.[253] In human perception, faces and bodies have a special place compared to objects like houses and chairs. *Prosopagnosia* refers to a syndrome of brain damage where individuals lack the capacity to recognise familiar faces. Bacon subverted our neurophysiology by 'violating the essential configuration of faces' while painting objects as he saw them, or by mixing animal faces with human bodies or vice versa. In his distorted portrait of M as a Sphinx he was rediscovering an ancient artistic method capable of shocking the viewer twice over, an echo of one of our earliest known sculptures, the Aurignacian lion-man (*Lowenmensch*), a figurine carbon-dated to the Upper Paleolithic, carved an astonishing 40,000 years ago.

Bacon took me aside. He wanted to know the nature of her condition and the underlying pathology. I explained about vascular accidents, and drew a crude outline of the cerebral circulation arising from the circle of Willis, a kind of arterial roundabout at the base of the brain. He was intrigued by clots and platelets and aneurysms and bleeds. He wanted to know about trauma to the brain, the damage done by boxing, and whether strokes recovered or not. The alcoholic with the black eye came over to join us.

"So how's she getting on?" he slurred. "Has she had any scans? Have you got the results from any tests?"

"I'm afraid I really can't say. I can only give information to her close relatives or a doctor."

"Yes that's me."

"Oh. Are you her brother?"

"No I'm her physician," he said, loftily. He worked in Soho, a notorious single-handed general practitioner and Colony Room aficionado.

The entourage visits increased rather than diminished. Bacon came every afternoon but several others returned in the evening. When they arrived M became fluent, radiant, charming and the centre of attention. She was the leader of the group, treated with deference by her artistes, and happy to be among her 'family'. After they left she would regale me with hilarious stories of wartime and the 1950s, and I grew to like her spirit and humour. In the mornings, when dishevelled and feeling old, she was abusive and threatening. I learnt later that Bacon had been a founder member of the Colony Room when M opened the doors in 1947. He was one of her 'daughters'.

Bacon's own survival clique had been unstable. His childhood had been profoundly unhappy. His father, a well-to-do Irish soldier and racehorse trainer, greeted his effeminacy with contempt. Reports say he had Bacon beaten by a groom after finding him dressed in his mother's underwear. Bacon absconded from schools, drifted abroad, and became part of the underworld and illegal homosexual scene in post-war London. His closest attachment was to his blind nanny, Jessie Lightfoot. When he set up his studio in a Chelsea flat she slept on the kitchen table and drew a hefty income during his illicit roulette parties, when she demanded exorbitant fees for invitees to use the loo. After she died in 1951, when Bacon was 42, he was so distraught he sold the house and its contents because he couldn't bear to live without her. He sought his comfort elsewhere and the Colony Room sympathy group of M, Henrietta Moraes, Frank Auerbach, Lucian Freud, Daniel Farson, Jeffrey Bernard and others became central to his life. M became Jessie.

After four days everyone on Vaughan Morgan ward had had enough. Under normal circumstances, M would have stayed longer for physiotherapy and rehabilitation. But her noise, willpower and Colony group identity gained her an early discharge. She wasn't obedient enough for allopathy. She was a renegade and needed her own space, the support of her members. They helped her out of the ward with a commotion. She failed to attend her outpatient appointments. Two months later I went to visit the Colony Room at lunchtime. M gave me a quadruple vodka and orange, gratis, and showered me with abuse about the Middlesex Hospital and doctors. She thrived for another couple of years before apoplexy claimed her. Her native habitat was a supportive and lively sympathy group. It kept her feeling healthy, in and out of hospital.

Figure 36. Francis Bacon

Another artist was less fortunate. Two months later, my registrar Lawrence was again in a hypomanic state, this time about a Mr H. My medical student training had created a veneer of diagnostic success, but I learned quickly how little we doctors know. My educators had focused on selected cases in which they had a diagnosis. In clinical practice, a firm diagnosis is less common, and applied retrospectively 'for the records'. H had arrived in casualty drowsy. After extensive blood tests and X-rays we were none the wiser about his diagnosis. He was now unresponsive, his tests were all normal, and the consultant ward round was imminent. Lawrence interrogated me.

"What's his cortisol?"

"Normal."

"Thyroid function?"

"Normal."

"Lumbar puncture?"

"Clear."

"For chris'sake, go check his neuro obs again."

I went back to examine the long, thin bedraggled poet. He had written one of my 'O' level set poems about the inhumanity of the military, from an anthology of the Second World War.

"Today we have naming of parts. Japonica

Glistens like coral in all of the neighbouring gardens,

And today we have naming of parts."

He hadn't moved, and lay on his back, still as a corpse, eyes closed. There was something odd about his muscle tone. He was not floppy enough. His reflexes were normal. When I used the ophthalmoscope to examine his retina, his pupil accommodation was normal. He breathed normally. I pressed on his sternum to cause a painful stimulus. No response. I pressed harder. He didn't wince. His chest and heart and abdomen were normal. It didn't add up. Maybe he was putting this on, but I daren't suggest a psychogenic cause to Lawrence. He needed a proper diagnosis.

I leant over and whispered in his ear. "Please H. The ward round is this morning. What is wrong?" I asked.

No response.

"H, can you hear me? Do you feel pain?"

Nothing.

After a pause I asked again in desperation.

"H, tell me, please, what is your greatest fear?"

Suddenly, he opened a single left eye and looked straight at me.

"Imminent death," he said. He resumed his coma.

I told Lawrence and the consultant off-stage. The ward round whispered its instructions to the sister for a Vitamin B injection and early discharge. He went home the next day.

At the time none of us knew his story. H was, by repute, a fogey and a BBC literary aristocrat, with a beautiful speaking voice and a talent for mimicry. He was one of the leading poets and radio playwrights of his generation, and a member of the Savile Club. He made frequent trips to Italy, and to Seattle as a visiting professor. In reality, as he grew old, he lived alone and hid his secrets. Though he had studied at Birmingham University, his father had been a builder and he had attended a state school. Like Bacon he was gay when this was taboo, and for most of his life homosexuality had been illegal. His core relationship, at 29, with Michael, had lasted for seven happy years in Dorset, before Michael suffered a nervous breakdown and left him. H returned to London, to a flat in Upper Montagu Street, close to the BBC, where he lived for the rest of his life. He struggled with secret poverty, grew isolated, and remained troubled by his difficult relationship with an illiterate mother, and a hard-drinking, womanising father. He drank alone and, by the time we admitted him, he ate little, apart from Complan. The vitamin complex injection helped, but his reclusiveness and resistance to the comfort of friends meant he was in and out of hospital over the next few years. He died five years later, in 1986. His biographer Jon Stallworthy describes H's diary entry for March 1985:

"After the horrors and the reliefs of the last terrible weeks I have 'resumed' what seemed like a period of hopeful convalescence (though God knows it is very painful to move about and eyesight is at rock-bottom). The Income Tax, and my all but paralysed will about it, stand in the way. Yet prowling round the three or four poems from the '50s I still want to finish, occasional jerks forward do occur."

Unlike M, he had no sympathy group, and hardly any survival clique, apart from his sister and landlady. His diagnosis was loneliness, but we missed it. It wasn't in the textbooks.

LONELINESS EXPERIMENTS

As populations grow wealthier they age rapidly. The US population will rise from 320 million today to 439 million in 2050, when over-65s will number 89 million, more than double the number today. In the UK, 11.1 million (17%) of our population is over 65 and 7.7 million (12%) over

70. But among the elderly loneliness is endemic. More than half of over-75s live alone. In the UK, five million old people say television is their main company. Loneliness has crept up on them, slow or unexpected, caused by the death or divorce of a spouse, a move to a new home, children leaving, the onset of disability or chronic illness, retirement from work, or friends migrating. Loneliness brings stigma, a sense of vulnerability and a big increase in the risk of depression. Many lonely people, at any age, will not admit to being so. Fourteen percent of elderly people meet the criteria for major depression,[254] and clinical depressive symptoms are present in about 20% of over-75s.[255] In Germany, a study of non-dementing people over the age of 75 showed an association between social integration and depression. They concluded that in elderly people increased social networks and enhanced social integration reduce depression.[256] Social integration is also good for physical health and a sense of wellbeing.

The author CS Lewis observed: "As soon as we are fully conscious we discover loneliness. We need others physically, emotionally, intellectually: we need them if we are to know anything, even ourselves." But loneliness is a feeling, whereas social isolation is a remediable state. They're both important risk factors for ill health and death in older people. Health psychologist Andrew Steptoe and colleagues showed that social isolation shortens our lifespan[257] but asked people whether loneliness was the emotional route through which isolation caused ill-health. Surveying 6500 people, they concluded that: "Although both isolation and loneliness impair quality of life and wellbeing, efforts to reduce isolation are likely to be more relevant to mortality." Social isolation is not just a lack of companionship. It deprives people of advice and support and leads to a state of chronic stress, much under-valued as a cause of premature death. And it often ends in the posthumous humiliation of a solitary pauper funeral; UK pauper funerals rose by 11% in the four years up to 2015.[258] Isolation is of great policy significance. For governments, loneliness costs big money. Health conditions in the elderly take up a huge proportion of government time and budget. In the UK, half of local authority spending on adult social care goes on the over-65s. So does two-thirds

of the primary care prescribing budget. Up to 18% of all NHS expenditure on long-term conditions links to poor mental health and wellbeing
– perhaps £13 billion in England each year.[259] A low-cost strategy to
reduce social isolation among older people could save enough money to
abolish tuition fees for all UK students at universities, or pay down a
sizeable chunk of government debt.

So what could we do? Many voluntary organisations focus on old
people to make their lives less isolated.[260] Websites recite well-meaning
but trite advice. Say hello to people. Call the free Silver Line. Smile even
if it feels hard. Start conversations in the street. Invite friends for tea. Join
a club that reflects your interest – art, church, music, yoga, exercise, meditation, political, sports, voluntary organisations. Get online. Learn to enjoy
being alone. Old people, please take responsibility for your loneliness.

But does advice work? Lonely and depressed elderly people, without
confidence, are often the least able to respond. What proportion of poor
elderly people will receive online advice or read a booklet, and how
many will take action? These are testable questions and we need experiments to assess the impact of well-meaning advice. The benefit: cost ratio
to society could be huge if we can prove that elderly people feel better,
and use health services less. My intuition though is that telling people
what to do on a large scale doesn't work well. Let us find out.

What of family and friends though? At 93, my mother Cecilia is
partially sighted, deaf, and with little short-term memory left from multiple
small strokes and 'transient ischaemic attacks'. She can't shop or cook, is
pretty immobile and cannot manage her finances. Yet she has stayed at
home, safe and secure, because my brother and sister have cared for her,
another brother with power of attorney manages her money, and we pay
local women who my mother trusts to give company, lunch and dinner.
But Mum is lucky. Without support she'd have gone to a care home five
years ago. Supportive relationships with close family members keep people
well, but many over-75s lack regular family support.[261]

And should we trust care homes ? Some are great. In 2014, St Leonards
Rest Home in Hayling Island was voted best in the UK. Run by two
inspirational owners, Frank and Mary Bartlett, they accept a perfect

sympathy group of just 15 residents into care and create a homely feel much appreciated by residents and their families. But others are not so lucky. In 2012, a UK government Care Quality Commission survey of 500 care homes found one in six did not always respect the privacy and dignity of residents nor involve them in their own care. More worrying, 20% of homes did not offer residents the support needed to eat and drink enough.

So how to take tens of millions of elderly people out of isolation and loneliness? A 2014 Kings Fund Report[262] accepts the lack of evidence. "Given the complex factors involved in isolation and loneliness, it is perhaps unsurprising that evidence about successful interventions is relatively limited, although group activities tend to have better outcomes than one-to-one interventions."[263] They refer the reader to useful websites and suggest that effective interventions "often combine public services action with volunteering and greater involvement by families and communities". Complacency is palpable. No detail, no trials, no specific policy advice, no indicators of success. Why can't medicine and social science offer rigour in assessing whether millions of valued but unnoticed elderly people, living in isolation and misery, and draining the public purse through depression, deteriorating long-term conditions and premature institutional care, gain from other options tested by experiment? Governments spend billions to unravel the genome and smash atoms in the hunt for theoretical particles. Might a fraction of this money go into the science of sympathy to make sure we end our lives without isolation?

Isolation may have sinister consequences. Witch-hunting remains prevalent in many countries. In 2017 in Tanzania, 479 deaths were reported in the first six months of the year.[264] Lynchings, machete attacks and drownings happen on the lake coast, in the southern highlands and even in the former capital Dar-es-Salaam. In north west Tanzania, for instance, in communities alongside Lake Victoria, accusations of witchcraft against isolated widows are common. Vigilante mobs target women with red eyes, common in the elderly, as a cause of local illness, infertility or failed crops. Witchcraft is often the pretext for a land or property grab. In Tanzania, widows cannot inherit their husband's land but they have residential rights until they die. Male relatives may want an excuse for eviction. So they harass, injure or brutally kill old women as putative witches. Sihaba Nkinga, the permanent secretary in Tanzania's ministry for the elderly, said: "The police . . . haven't got maximum co-operation from members of society where such attacks happen."

In Malawi, a 2017 spate of attacks and killings of blood-suckers led to a national sense of emergency. *Ufiti* or witchcraft has several manifestations. Its roots lie in the breakdown of customary law in rural areas. Growing poverty and the attractions of modern consumables, beyond the reach of poor rural households, creates conflict.[265] Economic pressure builds social tension, encouraging malcontents to seek ancient methods for expulsion or illicit gain. Whatever the cause of elderly loneliness or victimisation, in rich or poor countries, local participatory groups might be very effective. And cheap as chips. We know that the number of groups that a person belongs to predicts the risk of later depression (fewer groups predicts more depression). Depressed people who join social groups benefit more than the non-depressed.[266] In Tanzania, support groups for women defamed as witches has helped them overcome stigma.

Americans have become the loneliest people in the world. Since 1985 the number of US citizens who report they have no one with whom to discuss important matters has tripled.[267] Over the same period, network sizes fell by one third, from a decline in membership of sympathy and neighbourhood groups, rather than severed attachment with family. This social change over a short period has profound implications. In Bowling Alone,[268] social scientist Robert Putnam placed blame squarely on America's declining community ethic. He has since shown that 70% of working class children live in single-parent households, which pre-disposes to social isolation.[269] These US trends have their roots in rising income inequality. Since 1979, market-led economic policies have dominated government policy, and the median real income of middle class Americans has plateaued. For working class Americans it has fallen. Solutions need a fundamental policy shift back to redistribution of wealth, but fiscal policy alone isn't enough. Maybe we must test ways to change our social ecology, and measure the value of this approach through health and wellbeing measures expressed as a return on our investment.

We need experiments. A recent study by Rosebud Roberts of the Mayo Clinic showed that when elderly people get together to do arts and crafts they're protected against intellectual decline and even dementia.[270] She and her team followed 256 people, most in their eighties. Over four years, 121 participants developed mild thinking and memory problems, though not severe enough to affect daily life. Those who painted or drew, both in middle age and when they were 85 and older, were 73% less likely to develop cognitive impairment than those who did not. Doing crafts like woodwork or pottery also protected – of those that did, 45% fewer developed thinking problems. If you don't use it, you lose it. Active use of the brain keeps neurones active and healthy for longer. Other risks for mental deterioration get higher attention – diet, exercise, blood pressure, and cholesterol levels – but social interaction and creativity are as important.

In South Africa, the AgeWell project hired 28 older people, trained them to be peer supporters and to visit 211 older peers.[271] They offered companionship, advice and referral by mobile phone if they suspected a medical problem. Unpublished findings suggest the visits improved wellbeing, self-esteem, decision-making and active contributions by the visited. But we need trials on a very large scale to see if this approach stays effective at scale and over time.

Given the hundreds of large trials on antihypertensives, diuretics, gastric acid blockers and anti-depressants it's strange that no large population experiment has used a sympathy group approach to tackle loneliness. And none at scale to assess the health value of regular meetings of older people in their community. Trials will assess the best coverage of the elderly population, and the nature of self-organised strategies for success. In fact, Australia is ahead of the game. In 1998, the 'Men's Sheds' movement started when Dick McGowan opened a community shed in Tongala, Victoria, to bring isolated 'shedless' older men to meet, chat, share their feelings, work on projects and build friendships. A few months later, the Lane Cove Community Shed in New South Wales opened. Today 900 sheds have thousands of members across Australia and the movement has spread to the UK, Ireland, Greece and Finland. The benefits to lonely older men seem obvious but no randomised trial has assessed impact on quality of life or longevity.[272]

Wendy Holmes, a public health physician from the Burnet Institute in Melbourne, has led a study of the impact of elders' clubs on quality of life in Sri Lanka, one of the fastest ageing countries, with 12% of its population over the age of 60. Her team compare self-reported quality of life measures and care-seeking for better vision services among older people in Nuwara Eliya District in Sri Lanka. An ongoing 40 cluster randomised trial provides money to help set up the elders' clubs, monthly phone calls or visits from programme officers, loan of equipment or musical instruments, health information materials, visits by district medical officers and tea estate medical assistants, and various social and cultural activities. Results are expected in 2018. But we need more studies in Europe, the Americas, Asia, the Middle East and Africa. The demographic transition over the past century, from extended to nuclear families, has created an epidemic of loneliness.

So here is an outline plan for a sympathy group study. Take the United Kingdom. If we assume 12% of the population are over 70, and an average ward population (the smallest geopolitical unit) in England and Wales is 6600, we can expect around 780 over-70 persons* in this catchment. Assuming that only around one quarter will attend groups gives 200 attendees. So offering access to 12 group meetings lasting two hours in the same locality each month can achieve acceptable coverage. We could cap group size at 15-20. Each ward needs three or four trained volunteer facilitators (paid an incentive) to organise the groups. Street volunteers leaflet households on meetings, their aim and availability. Attendees can choose which group to join. Facilitators run a series of structured meetings that encourage members to plan their own strategies and seek their own benefits.

Discussion topics, one for each meeting, might include leisure and exercise, health care, further education, use of IT resources, community resources, cultural events, support for other elderly people, gardening, skill-sharing, monitoring of elderly care, disability, mental health, and long term conditions.

EXPERIMENT 1: Do senior sympathy groups reduce loneliness and depression and improve management of long-term conditions in old age?

Population*	Elderly people (70 plus) in local communities. Ideally include younger elderly people in the groups for more active tasks and to get around to contact isolated and vulnerable older persons.
Intervention	Sympathy groups for elderly people identified in the community by social and care workers. Elderly people invited to a monthly or more frequent group meeting at a venue provided free by local municipal facilities or at a venue paid by them. Transport provided by volunteers, group revolving funds, or the local authority.
	The groups chat and enjoy pastimes but have an action cycle structure for discussion topics (see text). The group will plan their own strategies and benefits.
	Facilitator: local trained volunteer, from retired groups.
	Supervision: local social worker or health visitor or civil society worker.
Comparison	Communities with standard health service and social care
Outcomes Primary Secondary	 Loneliness scores Depression scores Long-term condition scores
Cost and value**	Monitor the costs of incentives for volunteers, the cost of group meeting location hire or use, the cost of user travel or provider transport, the cost of materials and the opportunity costs for participants.
Possible risks	Social exclusion of disadvantaged groups Overload on community health workers Delays in referral for care

* Enrolling from 70 means social capital is built when group members are still relatively young and active.

** Value is the outcomes achieved for patients relative to the money spent.

LONG-TERM CONDITIONS

My second experiment explores a way to improve outcomes for 'long-term conditions'. Seventy per cent of health and social care spend in England is on 15 million people – one third of the population – who have one or more conditions such as diabetes, heart disease, arthritis, asthma, chronic obstructive airways disease, depression or anxiety, psychotic episodes, or long-term infectious or genetic problems like HIV/AIDS, cystic fibrosis, Down's syndrome and sickle cell anaemia. About half of all general practice consultations in the UK, and two thirds of in-patient admissions, relate to these maladies.[273] One long-term problem exacerbates another. Depression is two to three times more common among those with heart attacks, strokes and diabetes.[274] Rates are even higher for arthritis and airways disease sufferers. One third of patients with long-term conditions have a mental health problem.[275]

And mental health works in both directions. Depression predisposes to long-term sickness, which isn't an issue of just clinical interest. The effect on national and state health budgets is huge. A not-for-profit Medicaid health plan in Colorado showed that depression increased annual medical costs for people with diabetes, asthma and congestive heart failure by 103%, 253% and 37%. In insurance claims for over 600,000 Texans and Californians, depression increased costs by between 50% and 190%.

Exacerbating everything is the epidemic of obesity. Two thirds of US adults are overweight or obese (69%) and one in three is obese (36%). Rates doubled between 1990 and 2003, and continue to rise in higher risk groups like non-Hispanic black, Hispanic, and Mexican Americans. One third of children aged two to 19 are overweight or obese, with increased lifelong risks for adult obesity, type 2 diabetes, heart attacks and strokes.[276] As a young paediatrician, 30 years ago, I cannot recall seeing a single juvenile case of type 2 diabetes. Every case was sudden onset insulin-dependent (type 1) cases caused by a viral illness, a genetic predisposition or just bad luck. Now the US SEARCH for Diabetes in Youth Study shows an alarming rise in type 2 diabetes – still only 6% of new diabetes cases in non-Hispanic white children, but an astonishing 22% to 76% in other ethnic groups.[277]

I've read several reports on how society can address long-term conditions. They recommend better community services, more and better trained community providers, multidisciplinary teams, case finding, case co-ordination, in-reach services, packages of care and home visits. It's all about supply, about health worker services, helping out, giving messages. Many diabetic associations promote self-care but organisation of community groups for prevention is not common, apart from a few exceptions. At Stanford University, the department of Family and Community Medicine set up a trial to improve a chronic disease self-management programme, where they ran workshops lasting two to three hours, every week for six weeks, in community centres, churches, libraries and hospitals. The workshop facilitators were non-health professionals who had chronic conditions themselves. Anyone with a long-term health problem could attend. The workshops covered how to deal with problems such as frustration, fatigue, pain and isolation, exercise for strength, flexibility and endurance, appropriate use of medicines, communicating with family, friends, and health professionals, diet and nutrition, decision-making, and how to test new treatments.[278] After six months, the workshop attendees took more exercise, managed anxiety better, communicated better with physicians, and experienced less health distress, fatigue and disability.[279] They had fewer hospital admissions and shorter stays. Two years later, the patients had fewer outpatient visits and less health distress, and 'self-efficacy' improved.[280] Another pilot study, the Health and Recovery Peer Program (HARP), with promising results, used a similar six-session programme to help 90 schizophrenic patients.[281] One wonders if the workshops had lasted longer, the results would be better, and, in the long run, more cost-effective. Both these interventions were relatively short.

Many doctors recognise we need a social rather than a medical approach to chronic problems. James Fleming, a family physician in Lancashire, England, set up the Green Dreams social enterprise project to reach people left behind by the usual agencies.[282] Volunteers run bingo, gardening, art, social and theatre groups. The programme marries health and education. Doctors do a full assessment but then offer patients the chance to 'give something' back and to be part of a sustainable and resilient community. Their evaluation was not randomised but showed benefit. Patients felt healthier, had fewer doctor's appointments, returned earlier to work, and used less medication. Other social prescribing pilots show similar promise.[283] And co-production is catching on – the People Powered Health Project in six UK conurbations,[284] mental health programmes in north west London, and the Nuka programme in Alaska where, for three decades, the South Central Foundation has organised health services for native Alaskan Indians under a self-determination programme. The Nuka system insists that customers drive everything, trust their health care team and face no barriers when seeking care.[285]

As for obesity, the biggest health challenge alongside mental health problems in the wealthy world, almost no population trials of interventions took place before 2016. Paul Aveyard, Susan Jebb and colleagues compared whether primary physicians giving simple advice about losing weight, or inviting obese patients to attend a weight-loss support group, would have a greater impact.[286] The support group received 12 one-hour sessions, once a week. Only one third of patients in the active support group agreed to and attended the weight groups, but overall attendees and non-attendees lost weight by 2.43kg compared with 1.04 kgs in the advice group; but the result didn't quite reach statistical significance.

So my second experiment with sympathy groups aims to test ways to mobilise communities for long-term conditions with greater rigour and at scale. The target is people and their families either at risk or already affected. The aim is to stem the rising tide of diabetes. The World Health Organisation estimates that 422 million people (9%) suffer from diabetes worldwide. One legitimate criticism is that sympathy groups place heavy demands on lay people or lead to withdrawal of responsibility by the state. Neither is true in my experience. Voluntary loads are reasonable, incentives are paid to facilitators for work done, and groups engage the state where service provision is absent or poor. Where government services are reasonable, the groups assess and feed back on the quality and relational component of services. Our proposed trial will assess both overload and benefits to group members.

For groups focused on diabetes prevention and management, self-care topics might include health and hygiene, life skills, nutrition, including healthy drinks, carbohydrate, salt and sodium restriction, maintaining a healthy weight, what to eat and sharing of recipes, physical exercise and general fitness, sleep, stress reduction, anxiety control and use of alcohol.

EXPERIMENT 2: Do groups reduce the rates of pre-diabetes and improve the control and outcomes for diabetics in high-risk populations?

Population	Any rural or urban adult populations where pre-diabetes and diabetes rates are high*
Intervention	Community sympathy groups for diabetics or those with pre-diabetes invited to a monthly group meeting at a venue provided free from local municipal facilities. Transport provided by volunteer diabetics, group revolving fund, or local authority.
	Facilitator: local trained volunteer, perhaps from newly retired groups, who has diabetes which is well controlled.
	Supervision: local social worker or health visitor or civil society worker.
	Action cycle meeting discussion topics: phase 1 meetings where participants themselves identify and prioritise factors that affect their health e.g. lack of awareness of signs and symptoms of diabetes, limited opportunity for physical exercise, weight gain, poor diet, and threats that increase their risk of developing or failing to manage diabetes. Phase 2 where participants design strategies to address the problems identified in phase 1. Phase 3, participants implement these strategies with community support. Phase 4, groups evaluate the strategies implemented.
Coverage or 'dose'	If we assume 35% of the population over 16 are pre-diabetic and 6% diabetic, and an average ward population (the smallest geopolitical unit) in the UK is 6600, with about 5000 over the age of 16, we can expect an average of 300 diabetics and 1750 with pre-diabetes in this catchment. Assuming that 50% of pre-diabetics are screened, and one quarter will actively attend groups when invited, gives potentially around 220 attendees in this area. Groups might be capped at 15-20.

Comparison	Wards or villages without the intervention but which receive standard diabetes prevention and care services
Outcomes	
Primary	Rates of pre-diabetes and levels of blood glucose control.
Secondary	Weight, diet and outcomes among diabetics in the local population.
Cost and value	Monitor the costs of incentives for volunteers, group meeting facility hire or use, of user travel or provider transport, and materials. Possibly the opportunity costs of participants.
Possible risks	Overload on local doctors for screening
	Delays in referral for care

* The prevalence rate of UK pre-diabetes in adults over the age of 16 increased from 11.6% to 35.3% from 2003 to 2011. By 2011, 50.6% of the UK population who were overweight (body mass index (BMI)>25) and ≥40years of age had pre-diabetes.[287]

In fact, this experiment is already being performed in a rural district, Faridpur, in the west of Bangladesh, led by Kishwar Azad, Azad Khan and colleagues in Bangladesh, with Ed Fottrell and the team at UCL.[288] The trial finished in June 2018 and the results will be published by the end of the year. Preliminary analyses show dramatic benefit. But we need studies in several populations to judge the range of impacts.

Prisoners, mothers
and teenagers

PRISONER REHABILITATION

In March 2002 Peter Woolf, a drug addict and career criminal, with a history of offence and incarceration since he was 10-years-old, burgled a house in an exclusive area of west London. While stealing shoes and clothes to replace the stinking ones he was wearing, the homeowner, a much taller businessman called Will Riley, disturbed him.[289] The two struggled and wrestled for some minutes, violently. Will forced Peter down the stairs and outside the house, where he was arrested.

A few months later, after receiving a three-year prison sentence, Peter was invited to meet Will at a restorative justice conference. Peter attended with reluctance, and launched into his routine life story of deprivation, drug addiction and abuse. When he referred to the time he had met Will, Will stopped him in his tracks.

"We didn't meet in a cocktail bar," said Will, "you broke into my house."

He told Peter how the attack had left Will's family feeling anxious, depressed, fearful and even guilty. They were still suffering. For Peter it was a Damascene moment. He realised, with unusual force, that the burglaries he'd done over many years were not anonymous or victim-less. People suffered profound shock. He hadn't ever given much thought

292

to the consequences of his actions. Now he was consumed by sadness. During his servitude he began to grapple with his demons. After leaving prison, Peter became a regular speaker for the Forgiveness Project. He developed a friendship with Will, who had set up a restorative justice organisation, stopped his involvement with drugs and crime, and finally got married. He began to discuss his feelings of hurt and disgust at the physical and sexual abuse he'd suffered as a child, and wrote an autobiography.

Peter is not unique. Many criminals do reform as they get older. They come to appreciate the errors they've made, the hurt they've inflicted on others and the misfortune they suffered themselves. After a Forgiveness Project meeting, I asked Peter about his prison experiences and rehabilitation.

"How many times were you in prison?"

"On and off I spent 18 years inside."

"Do you think probation works?"

"No."

"Why not?"

"Let me tell you. I remember being released once from Wormwood Scrubs. I had nowhere to go and I was picked up by mates in a car outside the prison. At once we did some crack and by the time I got down to Weymouth we was high and needed some money. So we did a burglary. I hadn't been out more than 12 hours."

Woolf saw the probation service as no more than window dressing. He received no preparation for release in prison and no meaningful support outside. I probed further. "Suppose there had been a support group before you were released, led by a few ex-cons who'd gone straight, and who supported you when you left prison. Would that have helped?"

Woolf thought carefully. "Dunno. It might've done. Probably better than anything I ever got. Might have helped me get a roof over my head when I left."

The facts on recidivism – the relapse into criminal behaviour after release from prison – are chilling. Prisons have a revolving door. In the

US, three-quarters of inmates released from state prisons are rearrested within five years; over half return to prison.[290] Prisoners have suffered a high rate of child abuse and delinquency, psychiatric illness and drug addiction. Their psychological problems are not easily solved. Around half the inmates of UK prisons are functionally illiterate. Worse still, sending fathers to prison has serious effects on the next generation. A review by Will Dobbie and colleagues in Sweden showed that in the most disadvantaged families sending a father to prison increased teenage crime by 18%, teen pregnancy by 8%, and employment at age 20 fell by 28 percentage points.[291]

Nonetheless, despite the hostility of right-wing politicians to progressive attempts at rehabilitation, new approaches have been tested – children living in prison with mothers who offend, mediation between victims and offenders, pets in prison, boot camps for minors, education programmes, faith-based interventions, meditation, conjugal partner visits, therapy for drug dependency. Most are focused on individuals.

The Honor Program, conceived by prisoners and staff in California, comes closest to a sympathy group approach. Based in Facility-A (housing 600 men) at the Level IV maximum security California State Prison, Los Angeles County, the programme rewards positive behavior and creates an atmosphere of safety, respect, and co-operation. Prisoners can live in peace while working on specific self-improvement and projects for community improvement. Prisoners must promise to abstain from drugs, gangs and violence, and be willing to live and work with fellow prisoners of any race. In the first year, incidents involving weapons and violence fell by over 85% on A Facility. Whether it will have lasting effects outside prison is yet to be seen.

In Oregon, the Parent Child Study focused on individual behaviour change by prisoners with kids. They did a randomised controlled trial (RCT) of a parenting skills programme[292] called Parenting Inside Out. Trained and supervised coaches delivered Parenting Inside Out to 359 prisoners with young children assessed before, during, and after the skills programme. Prisoners were followed up to one year after release from prison. Data were collected from inmate parents, children, teachers of inmates' children and court records. Participation and parent satisfaction was high. Early results were impressive: fewer crimes in the first year after release, ex-inmates more involved with their children, with lower rates of depression and substance abuse cut by two thirds.

Denis MacShane, a former Labour Member of Parliament who was sent to prison for expenses fraud, spoke perceptively after his release. "Prisoners complain there is no rehabilitation at all . . . and prison officers are stretched to breaking point . . ." Giving up on penal reform makes no social or economic sense. Prisoners will never be a vote-winner, but socially progressive countries generally have enlightened approaches to reintegration of jailbirds. In the UK, the annual probation caseload stood at 241,000 at the end of December 2015, up 11% over the year. The community court order caseload was static but suspended sentence caseload rose by 8% between December 2014 and 2015. The Offender Rehabilitation Act (ORA) 2014 expanded licence supervision so that anyone sentenced to more than a day in prison would receive at least 12 months supervision on release. But 5,800 offenders were recalled to custody in three months at the end 2015, 2,000 of whom were serving a sentence of less than 12 months. Clearly support is inadequate and prison staff are hugely overstretched.

So the next experiment aims to test the power of penal sympathy groups to prepare and support prisoners ready for parole. The hypothesis is that groups will reduce re-offending and hasten a return to employment and self-sufficiency. The benefits and costs to society, at a time when prisons are full to bursting, tinder boxes for unrest and riots, could be enormous. Will groups of former prisoners, and the odd sensitive victim be more supportive than the probation service?

In the UK, 90,000 prisoners in jail need care and support after discharge if they're not to re-offend. And they need help not only between the hours of 9am and 5pm. In the USA, the criminal justice system in 2017 holds more than 2.3 million people in 1,719 state prisons, 102 federal prisons, 901 juvenile correctional facilities, 3,163 local jails, 76 Indian Country jails and military prisons or in US territories.[293] Each year 641,000 walk out of a prison to face an uncertain future. Half a million are locked up for drug offences. The black population makes up 13% of America, but 40% of the prison population.

One approach has already gone national to support sex offenders after discharge.[294] They offer a 'Circle of Support and Accountability' of about six volunteers with a sex offender referred to as the 'Core Member'. They act as a supportive social network, meeting weekly at first, for 12 months in all. The Core Member is 'accountable' for his or her risk management so as to reduce the risk of reoffending. My next experiment aims to set up circles of non-sex offenders to see if recidivism, a major cost to society, can be cut. In 2015, a total of 68,879 offenders were released from determinate sentences.[295]

Experiment 3: Can participatory learning and action groups of offenders before and after release cut re-offending and improve the chances of prisoner rehabilitation?

Population	Prisoners enrolled into study three months prior to release.
Intervention	Sympathy groups of rehabilitated offenders, community representatives and newly released offenders.
	Community action cycle focused on accommodation, support systems and community resources, finance, employment, addiction and medical care, further training, fitness and leisure, creative outlets, relationships, dispute resolution. Phase 1 meetings could focus on problem identification whereby participants themselves identify and prioritise the problems they will face upon release, factors that affect their health, specifically threats that increase their risk of re-offending. Problems might include lack of accommodation, finance, employment, exposure to previous criminal fraternity, drugs and alcohol, physical exercise, eating behaviour, family relationships and stress. Phase 2 could involve the collective design of strategies that participants and their supporting families and peers can implement to address the problems identified in phase 1. During phase 3, the participants (working with appropriate support) will implement these strategies. In phase 4, the participants reflect on and evaluate the success of the strategies they have implemented.
	Facilitator: A trained and incentivised rehabilitated offender who can bring his or her personal experience to the group.
	Supervision: Trained probation and social workers.

Coverage or 'dose'	Criteria would be drawn up by the prison service about eligibility to enter the study. Given the large numbers of prisoners released each year, a random sample of prisoners from selected prisons (at least 12) would be allocated randomly to the group intervention or to standard probationary care.
Comparison	Prisoners released under existing release procedures
Outcomes Primary Secondary	 Re-offending rate over the next 24 months Employment and benefit rates Depression rates Alcohol or drug abuse rates
Cost and value	Monitor the costs of incentives for volunteers, the cost of group meeting facility hire or use, the cost of user travel or provider transport, and the cost of materials. Possibly the opportunity costs of participants.
Possible risks	Recidivism of facilitators Overload on probation officers Political risks in the event of failure

Figure 37. At the municipally-run Addiction Treatment Center in Ciudad
Nezahualcóyotl, Mexico, addicts engage in group therapy

STRESS AND VULNERABLE MOTHERS

In 2015, midwifery and nursing professor Jane Sandall and her team reviewed 15 experimental studies involving 17,674 women. They found that mothers who received midwife-led continuity care were less likely to experience unwarranted procedures and more likely to be satisfied with their care than women who received other kinds of care.[296] A woman with personalised midwife-led care was less likely to experience an epidural anaesthetic, an instrumental vaginal birth, or to face a preterm birth or loss of her baby. She was also less likely to go without pain relief during labour, experience a longer labour, or receive an episiotomy after delivery.

Professor Susan Crowther, another midwife, used a different analytic method, based on Martin Heidegger's philosophy.[297] Using 'a hermeneutic phenomenological approach' she and her colleagues analysed interviews with mothers, birth partners, doctors and midwives. Heidegger saw our 'being in the world' (a phenomenon he called *dasein*) as associated with a mood that arises neither from outside nor inside ourselves. We cannot plan for it, it just happens. And we can replace one mood with another. Birth has a particular mood of joy, which can be easily concealed if disrupted by medical intervention. Crowther's study found that midwives shelter and safeguard 'attunement to mood' and the 'sacred space' at birth, more than simply improving the medical outcome of the birth process.

But midwives aren't always protective. In poor communities, especially in low and middle income countries, facilities are overcrowded and understaffed. Staff who care for increasing numbers of women in childbirth, as a result of large scale cash transfer schemes to incentivise mothers to have their babies in hospital, may become overloaded, stressed and careless. Death rates don't necessarily fall with increased attendance at hospital. Reports multiply on rising rates of abuse, neglect and even extortion, and of poor quality care.[298]

"We haven't figured out how to build an environment that enables people to protect or challenge the system," said Lynn Freedman, director of the Averting Maternal Death and Disability Program at Columbia University. Speaking at a conference in Mexico, Professor Freedman said "the engine of change must always be at the frontline. Only there can we address the hard questions – how to identify and tackle the workings of power that stop us doing a good job. Seventy percent of women experience disrespect and abuse. It's often invisible. And risky for people on the frontline to blow the whistle."

Stress multiplies the risk of complications that women will develop in labour. In 2015, a huge national study in Holland compared death and complications in mothers and babies up to 28 days after birth among 743,070 low-risk planned home and hospital births.[299] No differences in bad outcomes emerged between hospital and home deliveries. Among women who'd already had one baby, the average birth asphyxia score was lower after home delivery. And admissions of babies to a newborn intensive care unit were also 21% lower among planned home births. Michel Odent, a French obstetrician who in the 1970s introduced water births and de-medicalised childbirth to the UK, offers a simple explanation.[300] Oxytocin is the main hormone that controls the progress of labour contractions, the let-down of breastmilk and the protective behavioural changes in newly delivered mothers. "The greatest antagonist of oxytocin is adrenaline," Odent told me. "Anything that stresses the mother will interrupt the smooth progress of labour." In fact, new research suggests far greater impacts of stress and depression on the baby, with genes that regulate stress responses being markedly affected in infancy by a mother's depression during her pregnancy.[301]

Furthermore stress and social position may influence the risk of infection. A 2016 study of macaque moneys published in Science looked at alterations in immune functions, the ability to defend against infection, that occurred when the social status of female monkeys was artificially changed.[302] Social subordination led to antibacterial responses, whereas high social status promoted antiviral responses. In general, bacteria threaten survival more than viruses. So one explanation of the well-known observation that social position affects survival and thrival is that social gradient actually impairs the body's ability to fight infection.

For many women, abuse and stress are part of their everyday lives during pregnancy. Postpartum depression rates average around 10% even in the wealthiest and most well-adjusted women but are more prevalent in poorer countries. A recent randomised experiment in Uganda compared two methods to treat depression in 109 HIV-positive people.[303] Group support psychotherapy, to enhance social support and teach people how to cope and to generate income, was compared with group HIV education. After six months the psychotherapy group had less depression and better daily function scores. Not a big study, and it needs repeating, but interactive groups appeared to bring greater relief than more didactic education. In our own study of women's groups in a population of 230,000 in east India, we found moderate depression rates to be 57% lower among mothers in communities where the social support of a group was present. Since then, a large review of published studies in south Asia showed poor relationships with husbands and parents-in-law are associated with postpartum depression rates.[304]

Pregnant women, under the stress of a violent partnership or neighbourhood, have higher levels of adrenaline and cortisol in their blood stream. Adrenaline will counteract the effects of oxytocin, which controls muscular contractions of the uterus during labour and the release of breastmilk for the baby after birth. Raised cortisol levels lead to constriction of the blood vessels, which impairs muscle contraction by the uterus. And both cortisol and adrenaline conspire as part of the hypothalamic–pituitary–adrenal response to trigger premature birth. Stressed women are therefore more likely to suffer labour complications or problems with breastfeeding. When in 1992 I worked in the Kurdish refugee camps in Piranshahr, Iran, set up for those families escaping from the helicopter gunships of Saddam Hussein, many women saw their breastmilk flow cut, and their babies became sick and dehydrated when given formula milk made with unboiled water. And when I returned to the northern villages of Makwanpur, after the 2015 Nepal earthquake, premature labour rates were said to have increased sharply and midwives described infant deaths from interrupted breastfeeding, while families were unable to get transport for their sick babies to get to hospital.

Sceptics about the generalisability of social interventions for problems such as stress often fall back on the importance of 'context, context, context'. Nonetheless certain generic principles cut across virtually all societies and politics. Solidarity, self-organisation and co-production are foundational tenets in every setting. Geeta Rao Gupta, the former deputy executive director of Unicef, makes this point. "Yes, contexts are always different. But we need a system of feedback loops to deal with context." And it's not just about stress for mothers and their carers during the time of childbirth. Stress during pregnancy and after birth, particularly affecting young teenage mothers and those facing poverty, exclusion or isolation, seriously impairs growth and development in early childhood. The consequence for society and economy is long term and severe.

So what do we know about interventions that work? One important body of work comes from David Olds, a professor of paediatrics and preventive medicine in Denver, Colorado. He realised that women at risk, whether white, black or Hispanic, those who lived in poverty or were homeless or in a violent relationship, needed support at home not just in the clinic. So he designed the Nurse-Family Partnership, and set up randomised trials in three different populations: in 1977 in Elmira, New York; in 1988 in Memphis, Tennessee; and in 1994 in Denver, Colorado.[305] The results were impressive, almost too good to be true. Benefits for the children born included language delay halved at 21 months, a two thirds reduction in behavioural and emotional problems and improved academic achievement at the age of six, a large fall in use of cigarettes, alcohol and marijuana by 12 years of age, and a 59% reduction in the risk of arrest by the time the child was aged 15. As a result, the programme was expanded nationally and serves low-income, first-time mothers and their babies in 43 states, the US Virgin Islands and six tribal communities.

Despite the apparent success of these trials, the numbers of women (around 100) enrolled into each arm were quite small. We cannot be sure that the benefits did not arise by chance or because of some unnoticed differences in the mothers at enrolment. Clearly the nurse family partnership (NFP) approach based on home visits needed replication. In 2008, the UK Department of Health commissioned Cardiff University to provide independent evidence that the NFP approach really did improve outcomes for deprived pregnant women and their babies. The Building Blocks study used a more rigorous design for their randomised trial. In one year they enrolled 1,618 young mums from 18 sites across England, half to receive NFP support and half to receive usual care. Four primary outcomes were measured: mothers smoking, birth weight, hospital accident and emergency attendances and emergency admissions, and whether the mother had another pregnancy within 24 months of birth of the first child.

To everyone's surprise when the trial was published, no differences were found in any of these primary measures.[306] Some secondary benefits were observed – young deprived mothers valued the trust and support from their nurse, and early child development seemed to improve. Mothers also appeared to have better self-esteem, and more desirable relationships and social networks. We can speculate, though, why the Building Blocks study failed to replicate the American studies. They found no impact on smoking, birth weight, use of health care or birth interval. Perhaps the poor British mothers faced different social circumstances, received a less intense nurse home visit, or were better informed from mobile phones and social services. Or maybe home visits really don't have much impact. Maybe the US results arose from chance and small sample sizes.

But both studies generate another hypothesis. Does nurse home visiting have a small impact, which was exaggerated in the US and missed in the UK? And could we amplify this small effect if mothers were empowered by group meetings to boot? Groups might be tricky to arrange, but wouldn't the fun and dynamic of a mothers group boost the confidence of young women who are usually lonely or ignored? In fact, a recent study piloted this exact process.[307] In south London, a group called Citizens UK explored community engagement and co-production to offer social support for new mothers. They planned to tap into the social support of groups to reduce stress and improve wellbeing in mothers who were pregnant or with infants aged nought to two years. And the mothers responded. They asked for rooms and facilities for meetings. They asked health providers for educational classes on parenting, diet and child development, as well as information talks from early years providers. Their preliminary findings strongly support a much larger evaluation.

Other studies show that simply giving advice to mothers in the antenatal clinic doesn't have much impact. The UK Pregnancies Better Eating and Activity Trial (UPBEAT) assessed the impact of an intensive eight-week programme of training to 8820 mothers attending clinics on diet and physical activity. It aimed to cut the numbers of pregnancy-induced diabetes and large-for-gestational-age infants.[308] A rigorous randomised design showed the health education did slightly improve physical activity and cut weight gain in pregnancy but there was no change in the risk of gestational diabetes, or the number of large babies at birth.

Events in pregnancy and infancy have lifelong effects that affect our lives and our economy. A story from south India inspires us.[309] The village of Thennamadevi, mostly low caste Sadhus, has 150 men, most of whom drink themselves senseless every day. Many others have died from alcoholism, leaving widows. So a group of village teenagers, fed up with the sense of hopelessness and the fact that some of their peers had been trafficked, formed a club to run the village in a different way. In six months, they fixed streetlights, did a health audit, organised mobile clinics and built a library. They meet regularly in their 'young girls' club and plan a campaign to get local transport to reach the village. These adolescents have rescued their active network from oblivion. So my fourth experiment derives from this story, and from the strong economic case for a large scale study of sympathy groups for mothers, especially for women who are vulnerable, not only to improve their own health and wellbeing but also the growth and development of their infants.

EXPERIMENT 4: Do sympathy groups of pregnant mothers from vulnerable households (single mothers, socio-economically disadvantaged or with a history of an abusive partner) improve the health and development of mothers and their infants?

Population	Any rural or urban populations where social vulnerability for pregnant mothers is common.
Intervention	Community sympathy groups for pregnant women selected by vulnerability. Transport provided by group revolving fund, or local authority.
	Facilitator: local trained volunteer mothers from similar social backgrounds.
	Supervision: local social worker or health visitor or civil society worker.
	Action cycle meeting discussion topics: Phase 1 meetings will focus on problem identification that increase their risk of pregnancy or, not for mother care problems e.g. access to benefits, infant feeding, support during childbirth, social support once the infant is born, dealing with infant illness, stimulation, maternity leave, baby clothes and equipment, use of health services, infant sleeping and transport. Phase 2 will involve the collective design of strategies that participants and their communities can implement to address the problems identified in phase 1. During phase 3, the participants (working with peers or appropriate community members) enact these strategies. In phase 4, the participants reflect on and evaluate the success of the strategies they have implemented.
Coverage or 'dose'	If we assume the crude birth rate varies from 10-40 babies born annually per 1000 population in wealthy and poor communities (in the US and UK it is around 12 births per 1000 and rural Malawi about 40 per 1000), and an average ward population is 6000 - 8000, we can expect 60-320 pregnant women in a catchment. Let us assume that in poorer catchment areas about 20% are 'vulnerable'. Offering from one to five 15-20 person group meetings lasting two hours in a local space each month would achieve an acceptable coverage of all vulnerable women in a ward. Each ward might need one trained volunteer facilitator (paid an incentive) to organise the groups. They could contact participants by mobile to let them know about the meetings, the aims and appointment times.
Comparison	Wards or villages without the intervention but which receive standard antenatal and postnatal care services

Outcomes		
Primary	Infant weight gain	
	Maternal wellbeing scores	
Secondary	Rates of substance abuse in pregnancy	
	Birth weight	
	Use of emergency as opposed to primary care services during infancy	
Cost and value	Monitor the costs of incentives for volunteers, the cost of group meeting facility hire or use, the cost of user travel or provider transport, and the cost of materials. Possibly the opportunity costs of participants.	
Possible risks	Substance abuse or anti-social behaviour is facilitated by members of the group.	
	Delays in referral for care	
	Overload on local doctors for screening	

THE TEENAGE WINDOW TO IMPROVE HEALTH AND CUT VIOLENCE

Twenty-five years ago, the Iceland government asked their teenage school-children, at 15 and 16, about their habits. The results horrified them. Over 40% had been drunk in the previous month. Nearly one in five smoked cannabis and one quarter smoked cigarettes every day. So they implemented a national plan, Youth in Iceland, based on their analysis of factors that seemed to protect children. "Participation in organised activities – especially sport – three or four times a week, total time spent with parents during the week, feeling cared about at school, and not being outdoors in the late evenings." They prohibited sales of tobacco to under-18s and alcohol to under 20-year-olds. They banned children (13 to 16) from being outside after 10pm in winter and midnight in summer. They encouraged parents to join school councils and spend more time with adolescents. And they recognised that youth sympathy was generative, so they gave teenagers the opportunity to join a group. Groups distracted them from substance abuse. Low-income kids required financial support, so in Reykjavik they provided 35,000 krona ($300) per child every year to join a sympathy group and take part in recreation.

Results were remarkable. Drunkenness fell from 42% in 1998 to 5% in 2016, cannabis use from 17% to 7%, and smoking cigarettes every day from 23% to just 3%.[310] Long-term health benefits will be massive. Cuts in long-term conditions and better life expectancy could make huge savings. Anti-social behaviour and crime will fall. Teenage years are a window of opportunity for lifelong health and citizenship.

One taboo issue, domestic violence, dwarfs others in public health. Could teenage conversations tackle its root cause? Our media focus on rapes by strangers, female genital mutilation, forced marriage and enslavement within violent cult religious or jihadist movements. These brutalities affect millions of women. Up to 140 million women have undergone genital circumcision. Seventy million marry at 17 or younger, many in arranged or forced marriages. Seven per cent of women worldwide experience sexual assault by a stranger or by someone they know who isn't a sexual partner.[311] One third of women worldwide experience physical or sexual violence from their husband or partner. As Ban Ki Moon, former UN Secretary-General, said: "Violence against women is never acceptable, never excusable and never tolerable."[312] Women who suffer physical or sexual abuse by their partners are 16% more likely to have a low-birth-weight baby, twice as likely to seek abortion or experience depression. In some regions, women who face violence are 50% more likely to be HIV positive. Long-term exposure to violence and stress can also change the functions of our brain. Primitive structures such as the hippocampus, amygdala and prefrontal cortex undergo structural changes that have implications for mental health and performance, leading to break-downs and psychosomatic illness. Stress and violence affect our immune system, reducing our protection from infection, cancer, hypertension, ulcers, chronic pain, migraine and other illnesses.

Such a gigantic health, economic and social challenge needs creative and intensive research. Yet despite its immense scale, partner violence receives little attention from science. We need experiments with strategies to reduce violence between partners. Two groups of researchers have assessed mentorship to battered women, showing small cuts in depression scores and future abuse.[313] In an African American population in Washington DC, high-risk women were randomly assigned in their antenatal clinic to either tailored counselling sessions about intimate partner violence (n=521) or usual care (n=523). The counselling dealt with any minor or major violence or actual sexual assault. A theory of 'empowerment training' in pregnancy guided the sessions.[314] The counselling cut repeat episodes of violence by half. For every one woman who benefited, they counselled 20 women. If we were to scale this counselling up during antenatal care, we might just target very high-risk groups.

A much smaller study of 110 abused pregnant women in Hong Kong randomly assigned half to receive either standard antenatal care or the same plus a 30-minute interview with a trained midwife. She or he discussed safety, choice making and problem solving, how to confide in neighbours, and how to avoid husbands after they've lost money when gambling. They found small benefits.

While these studies are welcome they don't tackle the root cause of partner violence. Attitudes of teenage boys towards masculinity and relationships underpin future risk. The Shifting Boundaries study in New York assessed two interventions for school students at sixth and seventh grade to reduce the risks of dating violence and sexual harassment (DV/H). The first classroom intervention was a six-session curriculum that emphasised the law and consequences for perpetrators of DV/H, and healthy gender roles and relationships. A second building-based intervention used restraining orders, higher levels of faculty and security presence in safe or unsafe 'hotspots' mapped by students, and posters to increase DV/H awareness and reporting. The building-only and the combined interventions were effective in reducing sexual violence or victimisation involving either peers or dating partners six months later. Actual sexual violence by peers fell in the building-only intervention.

The Safe Dates study took place in 10 schools in North Carolina, matched by school size. Safe Dates included a theatre production performed by students, a curriculum comprising 10 45-minute sessions taught by health and physical education teachers, and a poster contest. One school of each matched pair was randomly assigned to receive either

Safe Dates or to serve as a control. The programme worked equally for males and females and for whites and non-whites. Compared with controls, adolescents exposed to Safe Dates reported, four years after the programme, between 56% and 92% less dating violence, victimisation and perpetration.

But prevention is better than rehabilitation of already violent men. The root lies in childhood wherein attitudes to masculinity and conflict unfold. As every parent knows, open and confiding 10-year-olds metamorphose into secretive and peer-locked early teens. The peer effect is never stronger in our life course than during adolescence. How you look, the gossip you share, the taboos you break, the substances you abuse, are shared with peers from your neighbourhood, school, club or gang.

And adolescent gang warfare is warfare is nothing new. The violence of Game of Thrones is not imaginary. In the Middle Ages, city guilds and apprenticeships meant that adolescents left the confines of their village homes for towns where they congregated in drunken groups. In 1339, for instance, a series of street fights between fishmongers and goldsmiths spread across London. Another guild, the boys of the bench, apprentice legal clerks, was among the most violent. Throughout the fifteenth and sixteenth centuries, Tudor youth gangs rioted in London, picking on foreigners from Lombardy and the Low Countries. In Germany, Switzerland and France, gangs of youths formed *abbayes de jeunesse* – 'abbeys of misrule', which frequently got out of control. In Avignon, youths at carnivals held the town to ransom, threatening to disrupt celebrations by attacking Jews and prostitutes.

So two experiments come to mind. The first is to facilitate group discussions with teenage boys and girls to discuss their health, relationships, worries, conflicts and attitudes to violence. Whether the groups are mixed or gender separated will depend on local acceptability. The second is to engage with established gangs to see if they can be a force for pro- rather than anti-social behaviour.

EXPERIMENT 5: Do adolescent sympathy groups change a) health outcomes, b) substance abuse and c) gender relations so as to reduce the risk of intimate partner violence?

Given the spectrum and rapid change in adolescence, three different age groups could be studied, 11–13 year olds, 14–15 year olds, and 16–18 year olds.

Population	Teenagers in one of three age categories: 11-13 year olds, 14-15 year olds, and 16-18 year olds.
Intervention	Sympathy groups of teenagers led by young person (under 25). In some settings, groups will have to be single gender only. The action cycle to focus on relationships, concepts of gender and masculinity, reproductive and sexual health, dispute resolution, recreation, parenthood. Ward-based sympathy groups. Where feasible, transport provided by group revolving fund, or local authority. Facilitator: local trained volunteers, under 22 years of age, from similar backgrounds. Supervision: local social worker or health visitor or civil society worker. Action cycle meeting discussion topics: Phase 1 meetings will focus on problem identification whereby participants themselves identify and prioritise factors that affect their health. Issues that might be identified in phase 1 may include: nutrition and diet, weight, personal appearance, physical activity, smoking and drinking, use of cannabis or other drugs, school performance, stress and anxiety, family relationships, peer groups, intimate relationships, hopes for the future*. Phase 2 will involve the collective design of strategies that participants and their communities can implement to address the problems identified in phase 1. During phase 3, the participants (working with peers or appropriate community members) enact these strategies. In phase 4, the participants reflect on and evaluate the success of the strategies they have implemented.
Coverage or 'dose'	If we assume an average ward population (the smallest geopolitical unit) in the UK is 6600, we can expect an average of maybe 500-700 teenagers in the age group 11-18. In countries where secondary school attendance is high, schools will be the best location to identify participants but it might be better to conduct meetings off-site or after school hours. Assuming that half of adolescents invited will actively agree to attend groups means demand will be high. To cover, say, 500 adolescents from a school in groups of 20 meeting monthly would require 25 group meetings per month. Two facilitators running two-hour groups every evening after school might be required
Comparison	Teenagers in similar schools or communities not exposed to the groups.

Outcomes Primary	Life satisfaction scores Physical activity levels Smoking and drunkenness rates Stress scores
Secondary	Relationship violence in the 24 months after exposure (for the 16-18 year old groups only). Relationship satisfaction of partners of boys enrolled in the groups Teenage pregnancy rates in higher risk areas
Cost and value	Monitor the costs of incentives for volunteers, the cost of group meetings, the cost of user travel or provider transport, and the cost of materials. Possibly the opportunity costs of participants.
Possible risks	Substance abuse or anti-social behaviour is facilitated by members of the group Disruption of groups by members Refusal of parents to allow adolescent attendance at groups Confidentiality broken

* The balance of topics discussed will depend on the age group and the cultural acceptability. In traditional societies, adolescents must adhere to the principles of respect for age, to kinship position, and to keeping certain matters strictly within the family or with only key figures in the family. In Gandhi's ashrams, for example, he saw adolescents as a valuable resource whose contribution to local society was sometimes inhibited by fear of family disapproval.

The next experiment aims to reduce delinquency and to change gangs into creative forces through group incentives and meetings. A Campbell Collaboration systematic review of studies to assess ways to reduce youth involvement in gangs and gang crime in low and middle income countries produced no studies. Not one. I was amazed. Given the scale of gang crime, drug trafficking, and sexual violence across the world, scientific experiment appears to offer nothing. Four of the studies did assess reasons for the success or failure of preventive interventions. Success materialised, they reported, if the interventions appealed to youth, built social ties outside of the gang, avoided ongoing gang violence, and engaged with young people actively; findings which are not particularly surprising. A more recent review by Anthony Petrosino and colleagues showed that the system that processes first offenders into a juvenile court does more harm than good.[315] In 2005 there were nearly 1.7 million delinquency cases processed at the intake stage by U.S. juvenile courts. Just under 60% were formally processed, with the rest being diverted or 'kicked out' of the system. Putting first offenders into the juvenile system did not control crime and appeared to actually increase future delinquency.

In 2014, in the International Review of the Red Cross, Doris Schopper reviewed what works to deal with sexual violence during armed conflict.[316] She pointed to the consistent lack of evidence in knowing how to respond and the difficulty in collecting data.

In South Africa, the Sinovuyo Caring Families Programme for Parents and Teens, a parenting skills approach for families who had experienced conflict with their teenage children, was assessed through a trial. They sought pre-teens and teenagers between the ages of 10 and 17, and their caregivers, as part of a multi-country collaboration supported by the WHO.[317] The Parenting for LifeLong Health trial measured the impact of 14 sessions with facilitator, parents and teenagers in a group. Some 270 families in 20 communities received the programme. In a randomised comparison, it reduced measures of violence such as caregiver corporal punishment, improved parenting, relieved parents' stress, and improved family functioning.

So in my next randomised study the challenging question is whether group meetings for gangs will change their behaviour from bad to good. If successfully implemented it will be a world first, so should appeal to any researcher who wants to be a pioneer. I am under no illusion that recruitment of gangs to a study and engaging them in a participatory process will be difficult. But a decision to join a gang is often a combination of fear, neglect and lack of recognition by conventional society. By showing young troubled people respect for their opinions and creativity we might be surprised by the results.

Experiment 6: Do gang sympathy groups affect rates of anti–social behaviour? Can we turn adolescent sympathy groups from bad to good?

Population	Members of teenage gangs
Intervention	Sympathy groups of teenagers led by a young person (under 25), possibly an ex-gang member. In some settings groups will be single gender only. The action cycle will focus on relationships, concepts of gender and masculinity, recreation, community action, respect, dispute resolution, physical violence, substance abuse, hopes and aspirations, discrimination, links with authority and the police.
Comparison	Similar communities where no gang groups are run
Coverage or 'dose'	Formative research will be important – how to identify gangs in the community, who belongs, where they meet, whether they would join the study.
	There are 35,000 gangs in the USA involving 1.5 million participants, over 90% male.[318] In high-risk areas we might find the number of gangs to be up to twenty per 10,000 population.
	Assuming that half the gang members invited will actively agree to attend groups, a skilled full-time facilitator might cover meetings with all gangs in a 10,000 population catchment every month.
Outcomes Primary	Community anti-social behaviour rates (crime rates) in intervention v. comparison population clusters
	Self-esteem of gang members
Secondary	Physical activity, smoking and drunkenness rates
	Perceptions of gang members about violence and intimate partner relations
	Reduced inter-group conflict
Possible risks	Substance abuse or anti-social behaviour is facilitated by members of the group
	Disruption of groups by members
	Poor compliance
	Confidentiality broken over criminal behaviour
	Increased inter-group conflict

Health Care

MENTAL ILLNESS AND PSYCHOSIS

Mental health problems affect more people than all cases of cancer, diabetes, heart attacks and strokes put together. Over a single year, a quarter of us will suffer from a diagnosable mental condition. These conditions may affect the person behind you in the local store, or three children in your kid's class at school, or a dozen on the crowded bus, or as many as a hundred on the commuter train you take to work. In London, for example, 7% of people have an eating disorder, and 1% will have, in the past, suffered from a psychotic illness such as schizophrenia or bipolar disorder. One in 20 adults has a 'personality disorder'. These figures are similar in most cities around the world. And the commonest mental health problem of all, depression and anxiety, affects at least one in six people. Perhaps the most surprising statistic of all is that half of people who suffer a lifelong mental illness will have had their first symptoms by the age of 14, which provides a useful clue to how we might tackle this problem early.

But whereas over 90% of people with cancer, diabetes, heart attacks and strokes will receive treatment, that isn't the case for mental illness. Only one quarter of depression cases get treated. Most people suffer alone, too worried to discuss their symptoms with anybody, even their doctor. As we've seen for elderly people, loneliness is a major cause of anxiety and depression, which increases their risk of medical complications and shortens their lives.

Faced with this tide of suffering, individual care solutions put forward by health planners cannot work on their own. Worthy recommendations in national reports focus on a few areas. Train enough psychiatrists, primary care physicians and social workers; collect information about care provision and health outcomes; distribute budgets with fairness, and invest in real estate for mental health. Fair enough. We need the work-force, the research and evaluation, the cash and the buildings. But mental illness is on such a scale that a social ecological approach, tapping into community self-organisation, must complement the best laid plans of the formal health sector. A focus on individual care alone will never reach out to the most needy, nor be affordable by the state. A reasonable hypothesis is that the secret of prevention and early treatment lies in creating nurturing communities.

This hypothesis is not new. In the Second World War, Edgar Jones found that community cohesion predicted which bombed British communities would fare better in terms of mental health. In Hiroshima, the first response of the maimed and traumatised victims of the nuclear attack was to reconvene small social groups to deal with survival and recovery. And Kate Pickett and Richard Wilkinson in The Spirit Level report that mental illness in developed countries is much higher in unequal countries, where inequality damages the quality of social rela-tionships.[319]

We can think of experiments that could test this hypothesis. What are the benefits, risks and costs of self-organising sympathy groups to get to grips with depression and anxiety? Can groups affect the early rehabili-tation of young people with psychotic symptoms? Do groups help to support families and carers struggling to manage Alzheimer's disease in their loved one? Or to help families cope with a relative addicted to drugs, alcohol or gambling?

We might draw on the experience of group therapy in psychiatry that emerged from the Second World War, inspired by the work of Wilfred Bion, Siegfried Foulkes and Carl Rogers. Foulkes and Bion had observed that tuberculosis patients recovered quicker when they were part of a group. In their Northfield experiments they studied the use of groups to rehabilitate soldiers during the Second World War. They offered men daily exercise, parades and work in groups which focused on specific skills such as handicrafts, map-reading, carpentry and so on. Bion, who was Samuel Beckett's therapist for two years, believed group dynamics and *esprit de corps* was central to recovery. The military authorities closed the experiments after only a few months. But shared decision-making and democracy in psychiatric care, pioneered by Bion and Foulkes, would form the basis for therapeutic communities in the care of schizophrenia and drug addiction.

We can learn more from the success of drinking self-help groups, started in 1937 as Alcoholics Anonymous (AA) by two alcoholics, Bill Wilson and Dr Robert Smith. Both were influenced by the Oxford Group, a non-denominational gathering that drew breath from first century Christian evangelism. Bill Wilson at first put his sobriety down to finding God. But as the historian Ernest Kurtz puts it " . . .more and more, Bill discovered that new adherents could get sober by believing in each other and in the strength of this group. Men [no women were members yet] who had proven over and over again, by painful experience, that they could not get sober on their own had somehow become more powerful when two or three of them worked on their common problem. This, then – whatever it was that occurred among them – was what they could accept as a power greater than themselves. They did not need the Oxford Group."[320]

Wilson called AA 'benign anarchy', but developed a structured 'twelve steps' programme, prayer related, which evolved into a secular process. The American Psychological Association describe these steps as help for sufferers to admit that they cannot control their addiction; prayer to a higher power for strength; examination of past errors with the help of an experienced member; amends made for errors; a new code of behaviour; and help for others who suffer from the same compulsions.[321] Twelve-step recovery programmes offer support for a wide range of addictions and compulsions – for narcotics, cocaine, marijuana, over-eating, sexaholism, self-harm, laziness, hoarding, fear of flying and suicide attempts. Randomised trial evidence testifies to the benefits: for example, twelve-step facilitation outperformed the standard drug treatment, disul-firam, for cocaine addiction,[322] and improved substance use outcomes for women.[323]

Formidable obstacles, though, restrict many patients from joining a group. Attendance at self-help addiction groups does rise in the short term when doctors (or a peer) refer sufferers.[324] When you're feeling down, though, you don't want to socialise. Inviting depressed patients into a sympathy group to share their feelings is probably not the way to go. Instruction and commiseration don't work in changing behaviour and attitudes. Maybe starting much earlier, before severe depression sets in, is more protective.

Most people seek ways to manage stress and protect their sense of wellbeing. Newspapers and TV love the stories of casualties and survivors. The vulnerable jazz singer Amy Winehouse imploded under the pernicious public gaze of an unprotective pop music industry. They neglected to provide professional management of her depressive bulimia, her heroin addiction and the alcoholism that ended her life. Michael Jackson, Philip Seymour Hoffman and Prince each died from intentional or unintentional overdoses, from depression and despair. Robin Williams took his life after suffering terrible stress and anxiety which accompanied rapid onset Lewy body dementia.

Mental illness arises from a mix of personal factors, our brain chem-istry and a family history of illness. Relationship break-ups, substance abuse, bereavement and money worries are common triggers. Social activity is protective as it gives us a sense of identity, purpose and belonging. Joining a group of friends, peers or trusted neighbours can give us the emotional support to buffer our stress. Knowing support is there might help us to cope with the most challenging problem or to seek care earlier. Reassurance can lower stress and its common physical effects such as headaches, fatigue, poor concentration and bowel symp-toms.[325] Feeling abandoned is dangerous.

So what research on Bion and Foulkes' 'social ecology' might help healthy lifestyle groups flourish at scale? Many of us have our networks, clubs and group activities. But many don't. Could local or national government, or health authorities, do more to create opportunities for a 'relational state' to reach out to the most vulnerable? This is a big question so it demands big experiments. The costs are considerable but benefits could repay the investment manyfold.

We need to know what works. How many people would benefit or need such a preventive 'service'? Would they attend? Groups might focus on exercise, healthy diets and simple ways to reduce stress – nothing too threatening, just regular signposted get-togethers, walks, runs, positive things to do, gardening, cycling, half marathons, sharing experiences, joint activities at local events. But the group should also plan to review themselves. Co-production and voluntarism would sustain it in the longer term.

Again, I found no strong evidence for or against the health impact of social ecology for sustaining healthy lifestyles, nor studies to assess the value of a population-based stratagem to tackle depression and anxiety, and almost no experiments on whether a social approach to mental illness works well in the community. Many questions remain unanswered. Would preventive group action reach the right people? Could it go to scale? Is it cost-effective? Several healthy lifestyle randomised trials have been done or are in progress but many are relatively brief and focus on instruction, information, messages or one-to-one counselling on diet or behaviour.[326] The use of Bion and Foulkes' principles or participatory learning and action where groups have time to find their own solutions is limited. Despite billions spent on health services and medical research, the power of self-organising local groups for mental health has had almost no scientific experiments. Odd isn't it.

So here's the outline of a scientific study that is long overdue.

Experiment 7: Do wellbeing groups linked with general practices improve physical health and reduce depression and anxiety?

Target population	All adults in age range 20-70 concerned with their health and fitness and their resilience to stress and depression.
Intervention	Practice-based wellbeing groups for adults in the community linked with local practice nurses or health visitors. Adults invited to a weekly exercise group (run, walk or other activity, graded by age and ability) and monthly group meetings at a venue provided for free from local municipal facilities or health centres. Transport provided by volunteers, a group revolving fund, or local authority.
	Facilitator: local trained volunteer
	Supervision: local health visitor or physical exercise worker
	Action cycle meeting discussion topics: Leisure and exercise, health care, nutrition and diet, dealing with stress, identifying depression and what to do about it, community resources, community wellbeing events, support for other people, gardening, skill-sharing, monitoring progress, disability, mental health, long term conditions.
Coverage or 'dose'	If we assume 60% of the population are 20-70, and an average ward population is 8000, in the US and Europe we will find over 5000 people in this age group in each ward. Assume that doctors identify only one in eight as vulnerable or willing to attend groups if invited. We should then allow for up to 600 attendees. Offering access to older people in this age bracket to attend one of 15 group meetings lasting two hours in a local facility each month would achieve an acceptable coverage of about half the target population. One can cap group attendance at 15-20. Each ward might need two trained volunteer facilitators (paid an incentive per meeting) to organise the right number of meetings per month. Street volunteers could leaflet households to let them know about the meetings, their aim and availability. And facilitators or volunteers could arrange group exercise events for those less fit or vulnerable to depression thrice weekly in the early morning or evening. Local health workers can attend specific meetings when the groups are ready.
Comparison	Communities with standard health and social care provision
Outcomes Primary Secondary	Depression scores
	Physical fitness scores
	Stress and anxiety measures
	Weight loss

Possible risks	Social exclusion of minority groups
	Overload on community health workers
	Delays in referral for care

A similar study design could assess whether groups assist people at high risk of dementia by slowing deterioration and cutting risk factors like high blood pressure, social isolation and poor diets that lead to diabetes and high cholesterol. Families and the public exchequer must deal with soaring numbers of elderly people suffering with dementia. Biomedical research funders pour billions of dollars into a cure for Alzheimer's disease, focused on new drugs to disrupt the formation of plaques, arising from accumulation of an unfriendly mix of proteins which smother brain function. Yet the origins of Alzheimer's precede dementia symptoms by up to 20 years or more. A social strategy might prevent, delay the onset, or modify at least one third of Alzheimer's cases. Prevention research programmes include the Finnish intervention study (Finger) and the French multi-domain trial (MAPT) both of which assess small groups working on nutrition, cognition and physical activity, and the Dutch prevention study through intensive care of the circulation (Prediva).[327]

Might we also address early onset psychosis through experiment? Phil, the eldest son of a family friend, had a brilliant school record, earned Alpha grades in everything, and gained a scholarship to Cambridge University to study natural sciences. In his first year, to everyone's surprise, he received a third class grade. In his second year the College rusticated him for a term, for drug use. At the start of his third year they suspended him for pushing drugs and inappropriate behaviour towards women students. After several months his frantic parents found a diagnosis and care plan. He was eventually sectioned for in-patient psychiatric care after he attacked his father.

Fifteen years later, Phil lives in a hostel. He has never held down a job or a meaningful relationship. He failed to complete his degree. His diagnosis is a schizoaffective disorder; he has hallucinations and sometimes hears voices. He lives on benefits, takes his prescribed medication intermittently, self-medicates with cannabis and amphetamines, and has little insight into his illness. His relationship with his family is sporadic and strained. From 14 years of age Phil smoked cannabis heavily, which, with hindsight, might have triggered his psychotic collapse. When I spoke with his primary school headteacher, she told me Phil was something of a loner before 11. His behaviour was odd despite his brilliance in class and examinations.

Psychosis and severe mental ill-health is not rare. In 2014 in north west London mental health trust, with a population of just 2.1 million, 32,000 people had a severe mental illness and 13,500 people who suffered at least one psychotic episode presented themselves for care. In one year around 2000 patients suffered a psychotic crisis with hallucinations, delusions, or disturbances of thought. They were vulnerable and a risk to others or themselves. For councils and carers, care of psychosis is a massive challenge. Yet early diagnosis and treatment could make all the difference. Many young people experiencing their first psychotic episode will recover fast with early treatment.[328]

The cost of delay is huge. In an average class of thirty, three children will have a diagnosable mental health problem. Youngsters left untreated, or found too late, account for over 80% of later specialist psychiatric contacts, inpatient bed days and total inpatient spend by UK mental health trusts.[329] The UK National Institute for Health Care and Excellence guideline, GC178, recommends that a consultant psychiatrist should see psychotic patients immediately to explore "their psychiatric and medical history, their social, educational, development and work experiences, their use of drugs and quality of life, and (to) start psychological and drug treatment promptly". No health trusts in London meet these national guidelines for psychosis treatment. Similarly, undiagnosed or poorly treated depression remains the commonest risk for suicide, with devastating consequences for family and friends.

In the UK, a staggering two-thirds of people with common mental health conditions receive no care. For those with a physical illness the figure is one quarter. We can redefine Phil's illness. If he'd been identified in primary school as at risk, prevented from early drug use, and rehabilitated as soon as psychotic symptoms appeared, his outcome might have been different. Early signs of odd behaviour in children might alert us to an early intervention programme. The case for routine monitoring of worrying behaviour in a child, and early intervention by joined-up child and adult psychiatric services, appears overwhelming. Almost nowhere in the world does it happen. And even with a quick response, what happens after the psychotic event? A return to college or the workplace after treatment, essential for wellbeing, income and self-respect, is the exception, not the rule.

So let us consider another experiment and another research question of social importance. Would sympathy groups of vulnerable children, identified early in schools, improve mental health outcomes and cut their risk factors for later deterioration?

Experiment 8: Do wellbeing sympathy groups in schools identify and improve relationships among children at risk of mental illness or autistic spectrum disorder?

Target population	All children in the age range 11-14 identified by families, teachers, or health professionals as having difficulties in relationships or challenging behaviour.
Intervention	Practice-based wellbeing groups for children with local practice nurses or health visitors or younger trained volunteers (under 25) so that children might identify with them more. Children would be invited to a weekly exercise group (run, walk or other activity, graded by age and ability) and monthly group meetings at their schools or health centres.
	Facilitator: local trained volunteer
	Supervision: local health visitor or other health professional
	Action cycle meeting discussion topics: Leisure and exercise, health care, nutrition and diet, dealing with stress, identifying anxiety and depression and what to do about it, common adolescent health issues, community resources, coping with family challenges such as divorce, bereavement or separation, skill-sharing, monitoring progress, disability, mental health, long term conditions.

Coverage or 'dose'	If we assume 10% of the school population fall into this category, then a school of 1200 pupils of 11-18 might have 120 children, of which 12 might already have early signs of psychosis. If we focus on the 11-14 age group, we might have half this number. If we had 60 such children we could run four groups of 15 children who meet once every two weeks. That is eight meetings per month. One trained mental health facilitator (paid an incentive) could organise two groups every week in the school. Group exercise events aimed at those less fit or vulnerable to depression could also be offered thrice weekly in the early morning or evening.
Comparison	Schools with no such programme
Outcomes Primary Secondary	 Depression scores Physical fitness scores Referrals and uptake of child psychiatric or educational psychology services
Possible risks	Social exclusion of minority groups Confidentiality within groups Stigmatisation of children

STUNTED BRAINS

Our primary resource is not land or commodities. It's our children. Invest in children, the earlier the better as Nobel Prize winner James Heckman showed, and you solve economic growth and human development. Viewing rising population as relentless and harmful is a mistake made by many clever people since Malthus. What matters to mothers is how many children survive, not the number born. Populations stabilise. The key to a plateauing population is to cut child mortality and invest in education. Then fertility rates fall sharply within a generation or two.

Most improvement in child mortality results from public health measures, a point on which even diehard free market economists and opponents of aid agree. As another Nobel economics laureate, Angus Deaton, puts it: "The improvement of public health required action by public authorities, which required political agitation and consent and could not have been accomplished through the market alone".[330] Once children survive, rising wealth, education and contraception will do the rest. After a population growth surge, when death rates fall faster than birth rates, we move to a stable or even declining population where low birth and death rates equalise.

But strong development and economic progress is retarded if children survive but don't thrive. Poor nutrition in the womb or during the first critical 18 months of infancy makes children's bodies visibly thin and stunted. Stunted height less visibly reflects a stunted brain. Babies don't have fully formed brains. In the first three years of early child development an explosion of 'synaptogenesis', nerve cells making hundreds of millions of connections, computerise the child to see and hear, learn receptive language, develop speech, numeracy and literacy, and form prolific social relationships. This process continues until late adolescence. Early malnutrition and infection interrupt synaptogenesis and also the process of myelination, insulation of nerve fibres to make them secure and effective. Stunted children do less well at school, less well in finding employment, and less well in creating wealth.

Yet high stunting rates bamboozle economists. Why are Indian nutrition rates so poor despite 30 years of continuous economic growth? This is the Asia paradox. Why are most African populations so much taller than in south Asia despite similar poverty? Why do they have fewer babies born small? Overall, average height in China is growing at one centimetre per decade. India has gained only 0.5cm per decade for men, and less for women. At this rate, Indian average height will take hundreds of years to catch up Europeans, whereas Japan and China will do so in a century.

Partly, the economists' and policymakers' mistake is to equate hunger with malnutrition. The two are linked much less than people realise. Malnourished people are usually not hungry. Most suffer anorexia and refuse to eat. You might say malnutrition starts with hunger through lack of food, and they become anorexic only in the late stages of illness. This is true but only in a few cases. The trigger for malnutrition and anorexia is invariably infection. Most children with malnutrition come from households with sufficient food. The filth and miasma theory was true. Every visitor to south Asia knows that tummy upset is common, leading to 'Delhi belly' or tropical sprue. Sprue is where weight loss and diarrhoea result from assault on the gut by aggressive bugs, leaving the digestive and nutrient absorption systems damaged for months.

As a paediatrician, one of my golden rules was 'when in doubt, assume it's because of infection'. I saw many cases of sick babies where well-meaning doctors, me included, had watched and waited before a child 'went off'. So, although economists explain the Asia paradox in other ways – that mortality rates are high and select out weaker and potentially shorter children, or that the African diet includes more meat and is less vegetarian – these explanations are marginal and peripheral to the burden of gastrointestinal infection caused by environmental contamination. The core problem for this contamination is open defecation and the likelihood of ingesting billions of toxic faecal bacteria that it spreads. Data from the latest Indian National Family Health Survey showed that 67% of Hindu households reported open defecation, while only 42% of poorer Muslim households did so. Intriguingly, deaths of Muslim children under the age of five was 18% lower than among Hindus.[331] Muslims are also less stunted by one year of age, although the difference disappears as the child gets older, when other social disadvantages kick in. Further, no Indian city has a comprehensive waste water system so that most rivers are effectively sewers. To tackle stunting we're talking clean water, toilets, drains, water treatment plants and basic hygiene.

In 2017, I was a minor contributor to an Ekjut population trial in Jharkhand, India. We assessed, through another randomised study, the value of women's groups and home visits from a new 'stunting' health worker who helped pregnant mothers to improve the growth of their imminent newborn infants.[332] The study showed benefits of the combined effect of groups and health workers – more dietary diversity when feeding infants, lower rates of them being underweight, more mothers washing their hands before meals – but stunting rates and the frequency of illness and diarrhoea in the children didn't change. At 18 months of age a staggering two thirds of our children were already stunted (using the WHO definition of being less than two standard deviations below the international mean for height-for-age). Other studies in India, Bangladesh and Pakistan have been similarly disappointing.[333] One very striking finding though was the number of households in the study that had no access to a toilet – an almost unbelievable 98.5%. Despite all the initiatives, including the Indian campaign of sanitation for all by 2012, virtually everyone was shitting in the open. As Sunita Narain, a leading campaigner, writes: "Now the government says it will be in March 2022 that we can dream of something that Mahatma Gandhi once said is more important than Independence." Our Jharkhand study concluded: "Achieving the 40% reduction in stunting envisioned by WHO's Global Strategy for Women's, Children's and Adolescents' health will require more substantial investment in nutrition-sensitive interventions, including clean water, sanitation, family planning, girls' education, and social safety nets."

So why have sanitation programmes failed? Every day 620 million Indians deposit 100,000 tons of human waste next to roads, rail tracks, rivers and in fields. That is 180 people per square kilometre. Roughly speaking, a gram of poop has 10 million viruses, one million bacteria, 1,000 parasite cysts and 100 parasite eggs. Multiply these figures by 1000 for a calculation per kilo, times 1000 for a ton, times 100,000 tons per day. Every day. The Indian government frantically tries to build more toilets – 3.5 million per year, or nine per minute – but open defecation for the poorest 40% of people is still the norm. Is it a technical problem? In part, yes. The Bill and Melinda Gates Foundation funded, at a cost of $8000 per loo, new high tech, coin-operated and automatic toilets, which used solar energy and combustion. When installed in Raichur, India, local people didn't use them.[334] Now the Foundation wants to cut the price, and develop a self-sustaining, private sector where companies install and manage the toilets for a fee. It's worth a try. But we assume naievely that toilet use requires only a gadget and strong marketing. Jason Kass of Toilets for People suggests that "complicated imported solutions don't work".[335] We must get the balance right between the social and technical, and understand the complex cultural meaning of pollution. Villagers have varied perspectives on defecation. Many Hindus don't use toilets because they are water conscious, they won't use toilet paper, and don't want to contaminate the soil by burying waste – they prefer a natural process of decomposition.

Toilets illustrate four blind spots in the offices of international and government aid.[336] First, we take complexity of basic interventions for granted without understanding the imperfect relationship of knowledge to behaviour, and the complexity of groupthink and social affairs. Second, we imagine what ought to be the starting point, not what actually is. For example, we should attend more to informal and private providers than government provision of services. Third, we focus too much on supply of units and not the connections. Paying greater attention to the connections of products like toilets to water supply, to sanitation rules, waste disposal, retail corruption, and women's safety in a public urban space is essential. When toilet building programmes suffer scams by officials or contractors, without community understanding or 'connections', people don't protest; or when they're built, toilets aren't used or maintained.

People relate to their environment in intricate ways. Most family units are clean. But often, in traditional societies, a homestead is only clean up to an imaginary line of ritual pollution, beyond which filth and rubbish is accepted. Villagers are reluctant to converse about sanitation. Gram Vikas, a sanitation charity in India, learnt that it takes a year to mobilise villagers before they commit to clean water and toilet improvement. An elected vigilance group then becomes effective and will monitor the use of toilets and drinking water, imposing penalties for misuse. Yet I know of no randomised evaluations of local sympathy groups conversing on WASH (water, sanitation and hygiene). Many studies try 'behaviour change' through hand washing education. Others test 'sanitation committees', occasional bureaucratic gatherings with no deep conversation mandate. So the next experiment tests the power of sympathy groups to converse on how to escape from a societal gridlock of 'toilet torpor'.

Experiment 9: In areas where sanitation rates are low can sanitation sympathy group conversations at scale accelerate safe water and sanitation programmes with rapid falls in diarrhoea and the stunting of growth and brains in children?

Target population	Villages and district where water and sanitation levels are low.
Intervention	Sanitation and water groups in the community linked with local health workers and village leaders. Monthly group meetings at a venue provided for free from local municipal facilities or health centres. Transport provided by volunteers, a group revolving fund or local authority. Facilitator: local trained volunteer Supervision: District sanitation and health offices Action cycle meeting discussion topics to include: The benefits of clean water, germ theory of disease, common infections, the cause of stunting, stunting and education, preventive health care, food hygiene, toilet construction and maintenance, overcoming barriers to toilet use, community resources, protecting water supplies, hand hygiene, skill-sharing, monitoring progress.
Coverage or 'dose'	If we assume we work in areas where toilet access and use is low, more than 80% of the village or peri-urban population may lack access. Groups will cover a small population to ensure adequate coverage and impact. Assuming a village comprises 100 households or 500-600 population, one group capped at 25 persons of would achieve an acceptable coverage of about one quarter of the target population, sufficient to mobilise neighbours and friends towards a 'sanitation shift'. Each ward or cluster of three to five villages might need one trained volunteer facilitator (paid an incentive per meeting) to organise one meeting per month in each of the villages. Street volunteers could leaflet households to let them know about the meetings, their aim and availability.
Comparison	Communities with standard health and sanitation inputs.

Outcomes	
Primary	Access to and use of toilets
	Handwashing practices
	Stunting rates (after three years)
Secondary	Local initiatives to protect water supplies
	Childhood diarrhoea rates
	Composite child development assessment at 24 months of age
Possible risks	Social exclusion of minority groups
	Overload on community health workers
	Delays in access to subsidies and construction materials

Growth is not only about infection prevention and control. Thriving children have household food security and a diverse diet. Many rural areas are vulnerable to climatic shocks. A similar experiment might also examine the role of community sympathy groups which bring together men and women to synergise improvements in infants and child feeding, protection of food production and storage and efforts to diversify and strengthen agriculture and kitchen gardening, and build resilience to climate change.

Experiment 10: Do community groups improve agriculture, food security and child nutrition?

Population	Families in poor rural hamlets and villages most of whom live on subsistence or small scale agriculture.
Intervention	Two intervention arms
	1. Women's groups arm focusing on diet, infant feeding, hygiene and kitchen garden interventions. Men involved in strategy implementation. For landless villagers, sympathy groups will focus on employment and supplementary rights, natural resource management of food products and forage resources in rangeland, livestock management, sustainable use of ecosystem benefits, and management of the village commons.
	2. Intervention 1 plus farmers' groups (mixed gender) focusing on conservation agricultural methods, agricultural production systems and local environmental management.
Comparison	Comparison hamlets and villages without this programme
Outcomes	
Primary	Nutrition in young children measured by moderate and severe stunting rates at 24 months of age.
Secondary	Uptake of benefits, wage rates, crop yields, diversity of family diets, exclusive breastfeeding, start of complementary feeding, indicators of child development

A SOCIAL VACCINE FOR EPIDEMICS
AND DISASTERS

When, in the early 1980s, a wasting disease appeared in gay men in New York, San Francisco and London, the new syndrome mystified doctors. An exploding epidemic of funerals brought fear and prejudice. But the gay community and their networks responded rapidly. As new knowledge emerged about transmission of AIDS through body fluids, and the risks of unprotected sex, health education spread faster than the epidemic. Community groups and networks like the Gay Men's Health Crisis, set up in January 1982, and the Terrence Higgins Trust later the same year, educated, agitated and acted to reach their friends and clients. A year later, in villages around Lake Victoria in Uganda, a similar illness affecting both men and women received the poignant name 'Slim disease'. Again, local communities responded to conversations in families, bars and village sympathy groups. What were the risk factors? What could men and women do? How could communities provide care to growing numbers of orphan children?

By the time health service programmes rolled out at scale in the US, Europe and Uganda, with aggressive treatment for infections in AIDS sufferers, contact tracing, condom distribution, treatment of partners for other sexually transmitted infections and counselling, HIV incidence had already almost halved. Daniel Low-Beer and his World Health Organisation colleagues suggest that "successful HIV prevention occurred where health governance and programmes . . . built on community responses".[337] Before anti-retroviral drugs emerged, randomised controlled trials showed that community groups had more impact than health programmes. Whether communities were trusted and well informed, or dormant and confused, mattered greatly in the spread of the epidemic.

Communities could create a 'social vaccine'. They shared information, identified people at high risk, put pressure on politicians and district leaders for resources and action, encouraged open discussion about social behaviour, addressed stigma and discrimination, supported and comforted patients and their families, and helped with local surveillance and data collection. Networks of sympathy groups don't replace health services, vaccines and drugs, but they enhance them in extraordinary ways. Social capital boosts financial and health capital.

The Ebola crisis in western Africa brought a massive international and media response. TV and newspapers covered personnel in robotic space suits and masks, scare stories of returning sick aid workers, and mobile treatment facilities, which were often unused. They pressed scientists, at the drop of a hat, to develop new vaccines, drugs and diagnostic kits.[338] The technology of infectious epidemics is, of course, important. Vaccines are the holy grail for a long-term solution. But maybe the epidemic would have halted much earlier if planners had listened to Francis Omaswa.[339] In 2000, Omaswa as Director General of Health Services in Uganda, oversaw the previous largest epidemic of Ebola, with 425 cases. "The single most important lesson we learned was that building and holding public trust by the government and health personnel is the foundation for all control efforts. Ebola evokes fear and apprehension . . . which easily results in herd responses, negative or positive. We achieved public trust in Uganda through very intensive communication with the public."

Omaswa recognised two key behaviours to control the epidemic: rapid identification and isolation of new patients, and safe burial of infectious victims. Fatal transmission to grieving relatives who customarily touched and embraced the body was a major risk. Behaviour change required community trust and conversation. He brought together chiefs and government village health teams to "stay very close to all families and households . . ." Omaswa understood that Ebola control rests on strong primary health care principles, "leadership from the top, integrated with routine governance of society and active participation of the people themselves. Once we have controlled this outbreak, let's institutionalise these practices because we need them anyway but also because there will be another Ebola outbreak soon enough."

In the offices of government and international agencies in Sierra Leone, Liberia and Guinea, his wise counsel fell on deaf ears. Cheikh Niang, a Senegalese medical anthropologist, observed that medical experts didn't have the expertise to deal with community resistance.[340] He found buckets of chlorine for hand sanitisation controlled by men not women. And "people fed up with being told about hand sanitisation . . . they knew how Ebola is transmitted but wanted to express themselves, be heard and take charge of their health matters and not be told how to do this in a paternalistic way". Jamie Benson of Restless Development, a small charity, told me the first case in Sierra Leone was reported in May 2014. The first that communities knew was when burial teams, like aliens in white masks and protective clothing, arrived in their village. They were terrified. It took six months before a social mobilisation action consortium got going and much longer to go to scale.

In Sierra Leone, a gang in Freetown called the Tripoli boys, homeless orphans and unemployed adolescents led by a small-time hustler self-styled as 'Gaddafi', survive underneath the smoky, corrugated roof shacks that tumble down to rubbish heaps by the water's edge.[341] Hassled by the army and police, Gaddafi says they are 'soldiers of their terrain' rather than dope pushers or petty criminals. As Ebola took hold and the community descended into fear, the Tripoli boys led house-to-house visits to give simple preventive messages to frightened slum families, and accompanied victims with symptoms to hospital. Their bravery was astonishing. Seven of the boys died. Gaddafi survived his own Ebola infection after a month in hospital. Now they're respected by community leaders. "We did a lot for this country," says Gaddafi, "and we should get something back. The government don't care, but these are the best boys in Sierra Leone."

Social scientist Robert Dingwall reckons that "it was only in December 2014 ... that the first properly designed community campaign was launched, in western Sierra Leone, with ... religious and traditional leaders, and popular entertainers." Once community engagement took hold, infection rates fell rapidly. He concluded that "making friends with social scientists is less glamorous than rubbing shoulders with global political leaders, snuggling up to multinational pharmaceutical companies or helping billionaires tell nice stories about themselves at Davos".

Vaccines and drugs always arrive much later. Creating sympathy groups of scientists and pharmaceutical staff helps to speed things up. The World Health Organisation did, in fact, make up for their slow start, when, under Assistant Director General Marie-Paule Kieny's leadership, they designed, supervised and published a trial of a new Ebola vaccine to protect contacts within 12 months.[342] In 2016 they set up the Research and Development Blueprint for Action to Prevent Epidemics to cut delays and red tape.[343] New vaccines will prevent future outbreaks but a board paper at the World Health Assembly in 2015 was clear. "Community engagement is the one factor that underlies the success of all other control measures."

The Zika virus epidemic is arguably even more devastating than Ebola. Zika destroys the delicate brain tissue of unborn infants, and the hopes and dreams of their young parents. In Recife, Brazil, two paediatric neurologists, mother and daughter Ana and Vanessa van der Linden, identified the new syndrome when they faced a rush of microcephalic babies in their clinic on a single day. They wouldn't normally see more than one case a month. And they found the babies' brain scans unusual and shocking. The brain was horribly deformed, with dilated ventricles and widespread blotches of white where damaged brain was stained with opaque calcium. On examination, they found heaped up rugose scalp skinfolds where the brain had not grown as it should, leaving the soft shrunken skull a deflated balloon. Most affected infants were otherwise healthy. Vanessa knew that they wouldn't die, and that the family would face a lifetime of care for a severely disabled child: unable to chat or go to school, to walk or play, and maybe blind and deaf.

The response of the Brazilian government, health authorities and individuals to the epidemic was rapid and comprehensive. The army mobilised, local groups assisted efforts to spread messages about prevention, and volunteer groups sprayed neighbourhoods to eliminate the *Aedes aegypti* mosquitoes. They removed stagnant pools of water, treated water butts with chemicals to kill eggs and larvae, and helped households to install protective bed and window nets. But they faced a formidable foe. The *Aedes aegypti* mosquito transmits four related viruses, for yellow fever, dengue fever, chikungunya and zikavirus infection. Worse, it bites in the early morning and throughout the day, unlike the *anopheles* mosquito that transmits malaria largely through biting people at night. The mosquito lays its eggs in free-standing water in pools as small as a bottletop or a saucer. This meant that young women in the hot, rainy season living in poor city favelas, accustomed to wearing just shorts and a T-shirt, were especially vulnerable.

I visited Vanessa's rehabilitation centre in Recife in July 2016. I was struck by the way in which affected families had clustered. 'Uma' groups of mothers had come together to share stories and seek safety from public stigma and sympathy for their affected babies. They offered each other comfort and chat on how to cope. Their babies had become media novelties, like Victorian freak shows of dwarves, bearded women and elephant men.

In her developmental follow-up clinic, Vanessa recognised the huge stress on families. Husbands and wives were bereft and helpless, tormented by the unremitting screams and twitches of their damaged babies. She worried that many fathers would abandon the family, unable to cope or to feel involved. She encouraged them to enrol into weekly support groups and to take the Hanen 'It Takes Two' programme.[344] In 1975, Ayala Hanen Manolson, a Canadian speech and language expert, wanted to provide "the important people in a child's life with the knowledge and training they need to help the child develop the best possible language, social and literacy skills". When faced with slow development of their child, parental hope is ever-present. Many mothers and fathers find the groups and programmes a lifeline of comfort and solidarity, even if the prospects for their child's development takes time to assess and is not what they hope for.

Natural disasters provide a different systemic shock to families. In May 2015, three weeks after the earthquakes that destroyed or damaged 900,000 houses in central Nepal, along the faultline where the Indian tectonic plate pushes up the plate of Europe and central Asia, I sat with Kirti Tumbahamphe in a teashop in the village of Simbanjyang. The main road lies along a ridge, tufted with rich, communal forest, above steps of rice terraces that plunge down to the valley of Palung. Half the houses of the village had collapsed. Teenagers stared at their broken homes and kicked footballs around the fields. Local men and women piled stones and sifted grit to prepare for rebuilding. A small guesthouse, its wall blown out as if by a bomb, defiantly flew prayer flags on bamboo poles. It was one of the 18,500 collapsed houses in the 'mildly affected' district of Makwanpur, where 18 of the 33 health and birthing centres were destroyed.

The teashop lady smiled and played with her mobile phone. She gave us a plate of *sel*, rings of greasy doughnut, and small platters of spiced vegetables and curried eggs. Normal service resumed. Sipping milky, sweet spiced tea, Kirti described his plan. We would contact the 200 plus women's groups set up a few years aback to explore their psychological state. Eighty per cent of the groups still met regularly. Disasters of this magnitude, and the shock of sudden destitution, increase the risk of depression and suicide among survivors. We'd also focus on reconstruction in remoter, deprived areas – new builds of birthing centres and hostels for children attending school using ecofriendly, sustainable and earthquake resilient methods.

"Its impressive," I said. "So much activity. But the papers are full of community scepticism about donor relief efforts. Why do they target the aid wallahs?"

Kirti paused and smiled. "I'll tell you a story. A foreign aid expert came to Nepal and advised a farmers' club that their milk output would improve if the native cows cross-bred with a European bull. So the foreign donor despatched a European bull by air cargo to graze the fields in Makwanpur. Villagers brought their cows to the field and waited. Nothing happened. The bull chewed the grass. Then the farmers decided the cows might be too old, so they brought a harem of young heifers. Again the bull showed no interest. The farmers became worried. So they contacted a shaman, who had the power of animal language, and brought him to the field. The holy man strolled over to converse with the foreign bull who gestured and nodded.

When he returned, the farmers gathered around the shaman.

"What did he say?" they asked in chorus.

"He told me 'I'm here for advice. Not for service'."

The Nepal government did bring cash and lorryloads of food and tarpaulins to affected districts. Or rather the army did in the first month because politicians disappeared to argue in smoke-filled rooms about a new constitution. And donors provided helicopters and heavy lifting equipment, tents and water tablets. But for the staggering mass of victims in the hills and mountains, the 900,000 families who'd witnessed their homes and livelihoods destroyed in seismic seconds, most help and support came from neighbours. Many sympathy groups coalesced to help out.

Everywhere, along our seven-hour road trip, communities were coming together, ferrying logs, sawing wood, cooking food, discussing *pujas*, sharing fruits and snacks, shovelling rubble, lifting bamboo. Neighbourliness and trust proliferated. On the edge of the Kathmandu valley, not far from the jungle palace of the ousted King Gyanendra, the Goldhunga community was badly hit. Many houses had collapsed, most were damaged. Soon after the quake, Narayan Acharya, a wiry athlete who twice won the Everest marathon over-40s title and husband of Naomi Saville, our exceptional field researcher, went on a 46 kilometre jog around the valley to see what was happening. He and a friend decided they should help the poorest people and went to meet the club members of the Putuwar Newars in Goldhunga. This indigenous group used to be flower sellers and wood suppliers in the valley. Now they desperately needed shelter, for their elderly to rest and children to study. Narayan is a builder who specialises in rammed earth construction, an ecofriendly and sustainable method that uses bamboo frames and a mix of sand and soil rammed into large blocks to create beautiful and earthquake-resilient homes. His two-storey rammed earth house in Godavari, near the Botanical Gardens, had survived the two quakes unscathed, whereas all around buildings large and small, including the five-storey, four-star Godavari Village Resort, had collapsed.

But rammed earth building takes time, so Narayan and the club chose an earth bag solution for a more rapid response. Plastic bags of a 60/40 soil/sand mix were stacked on a two foot concrete foundation, each layer held together by barbed wire, and the bare walls *lipnued* using traditional clay plaster. The club worked in harmony. Teenagers laughed as they kneaded the clay. Lines of women and men ferried mud, wire and wood to the site. After just two weeks the community centre, gleaming and artistically decorated, was opened. Leading politicians, Marxist, Maoist, Congress and Royalist, rushed to the photo opportunity. In reality their involvement was nil. Resilience in the face of disaster had lain with local people coming together.

Response to an emergency lacks a systematic approach to community mobilisation. Good intentions prevail over evidence-tested care. The next experiment draws on lessons learned from the response to the Nepal earthquake and the aphorism 'never waste a crisis'. Most communities miss their opportunity to rebuild their houses using earthquake-resistant methods or to incorporate other public health benefits into their rebuild. Renewable energy, water and sanitation, and chimneys to cut household air pollution are design options. Instead they'll rebuild as usual and store up a crisis for their children. In most districts of Nepal that is happening. But mobilising sympathy reconstruction groups at scale presents an enormous public health opportunity to reconstruct for a sustainable, better future.

The dominance of men in decision-making during crises or conflict is a striking feature in almost all settings. Women are often better than men when working in small groups, and in finding consensus for conflict resolution.[345] Women's participation and inclusion always makes humanitarian assistance more effective and strengthens the efforts of peacekeepers.

Experiment 11: Do sympathy groups improve the public health benefits of reconstruction following an earthquake?

Population	Villages affected by earthquake damage
Intervention	Sympathy groups of affected families, community representatives and local builders. A community action cycle focused on earthquake-resilient building methods, public health benefits of clean water and sanitation, access to aid handouts and subsidies, community resource and labour mobilisation and sharing, clean energy and available renewable options, protection of clean water supplies, sanitation, finance, involvement of women and adolescents, social inclusion of vulnerable residents, kitchen gardening, environmental protection.
	Facilitator: A trained and incentivised reconstruction volunteer who can bring his or her personal experience to the group
	Supervision: District reconstruction and public health teams
Coverage or 'dose'	One group per thirty affected households.
Comparison	Villages where usual reconstruction methods are employed

Outcomes	
Primary	Number of houses rebuilt using genuine earthquake-resilient building methods
	Number of houses where ventilation, water supply, clean energy and sanitation reconstruction achieves acceptable standards
Secondary	Household and village satisfaction rates
	Environmental protection indicators
Cost and value	Monitor the costs of incentives for volunteers, the cost of group meeting facility hire or use, the cost of user travel or provider transport, and the cost of materials. The opportunity costs of participants.
Possible risks	Lack of access to financial and material support
	Overload on district offices
	Political risks in the event of failure

Figure 38. Community group created earth bag building, Goldhunga, Kathmandu, after 2015 earthquake. Narayan Acharya stands outside the finished community centre. Constructed in two weeks. Photo, the author

CONTINUITY OF MEDICAL CARE

The technology of care has improved through evidence-based medicine. The quality of personal health care has not. We often feel like numbers, not patients, within hospitals. In Britain, the shift system of employment enforced by European Working Time Directives broke continuity of care in hospitals. Working weeks were restricted to a maximum of 48 hours. My long weekend marathons as a junior disappeared. Each time you see a doctor in hospital you see someone new, working the next shift. They come and go, scribble in notes, and hand over. Mixed messages create anxiety. Worse, the staff often remain anonymous. The young doctor and writer Kate Granger, dying of cancer, recorded how few of her doctors would introduce themselves.[346] She launched a successful Twitter campaign, with the hashtag #hellomynameis, which went viral. She reminded us of the most basic salutation in patient communication.

In the US, Planetree, a not-for-profit organisation has worked hard to address the unfriendliness of health organisations.[347] They undertake patient-centred process redesigns where caregivers come together in a group to create a single plan of care for patients. As important, they provide a patient-designed integrated discharge care plan. Other ideas include a patient-to-nurse call system, and a food-is-care plan to ensure that hospital dining gives the right experience and nutrition for the patient. They also focus on creating a better culture through shared governance groups and a family advisory council, where staff and patients interact to discuss sympathetic care.

I trained in an era of excessive working hours, ad hoc attention to supervision, and poor audit of practice. We were often exhausted. But a vocation is a calling not a contract. Despite the stress, I always felt a strong bond to my 'firm'. The medical or surgical firm was sympathy group size – about 15 strong – including senior and junior registrars, house officers, ward sisters, staff nurses, physiotherapists, social workers and medical students. The consultant was the pivot, leader and facilitator, or at least in theory. In his absence, facilitation would fall to the senior registrar and ward sister. The firm built a bond across the team; junior carers and patients were members, with somewhere to go if things weren't working. In good hands the firm provided the bridging capital to others – physicians to surgeons and back, paediatricians to psychiatrists, geriatricians to social workers, orthopaedic firms to physiotherapists. With clear leadership and accountability, communications outside the firm were less likely to go wrong. Firms built a sense of identity and vocation which provided critical reassurance to patients. They knew where they belonged. If one player faltered, others stepped in. Do we know therefore whether the loss of the hospital firm, a proud sympathy group (albeit hierarchical), diminishes the social capital that protected patients? Has the erosion of the firm dissolved the social edge in health care?

As a medical student I spent six weeks at central London's Middlesex Hospital on the paediatric firm led by Roderick Brown. Lean and upright, he wore a thick pinstripe suit, crisp Savile Row shirts and shiny, silk ties – at face value, a consultant who was solid and respectable, but academically limited. He published far fewer papers than his brilliant protégé, the endocrinologist Charles Brook. A colonial son, born in Bengal, India in 1918, Roderick won a blue for Cambridge University against Oxford in the high jump, and played excellent club cricket. He saw active service in India and Burma before training in paediatrics.[348] His uncle, Sir Leonard Parsons, professor of paediatrics at Birmingham Children's Hospital, had, in 1932, been the first doctor to treat scurvy with synthetic Vitamin C.

Brown's lack of academic ambition belied a man of two brilliant insights. He was the first to recognise the profound dangers of low blood sugar levels and dehydration in premature newborns, at a time when paediatricians and midwives denied fluids for 24-48 hours after birth to prevent aspiration of feeds into the lungs.[349] Stopping this mistaken policy was one of the most important advances in the care of the preterm infant, now accepted worldwide. Today, essential preterm care remains poor in emerging economies where hospitals rush to implement new medical technology without attention to basic physiology.

Brown also pioneered our understanding of breastfeeding. One day, on sabbatical to study heart disease at the Hospital for Sick Children, Toronto, he went to the maternity hospital because a mother wanted to breastfeed her preterm baby. The medical and nursing staff were uncertain but Roderick knew the nutritional and emotional value of breastfeeding, which built reciprocity between mother and baby. In the 1960s, paediatricians believed formula-fed babies gained weight faster than breast-fed babies and many pooh-poohed ordinary breastmilk. For pre-term babies, Roderick saw that breastmilk was far superior. He gave larger amounts, expressed by mothers and dripped through continuous stomach tube feeds, started soon after birth and increased in volume over the first week. Blood sugar levels stayed up, dehydration and infections fell, and weight gain improved. Early breastfeeding, using Roderick Brown's methods, even for the tiniest infants, saves the lives of countless newborn infants at zero cost. It's the best way to rehydrate older infants with gastroenteritis.

Neither of these research papers influenced my decision to choose paediatrics. Something else did. Unlike the Sir Lancelot Spratt tendency of many adult surgeons and physicians, Brown didn't announce his presence on the ward with a fanfare. He was quiet, suffusing ward rounds with calm. Children, as sensitive as young foals, are distressed by bleeps, clatter and rush. Crying is epidemic, one child's distress infecting another. Everyone wanted to work for Brown "because he listened attentively to the worries of the children and their families, at a time when good communication was not common".[350] On rounds, he sought the counsel of sisters, nurses, junior doctors, and even medical students, which "allowed staff to develop confidence in their own assessment of problems and to advance their clinical abilities". If he disagreed, he gave his reasons gently. Then he would give his quiet opinion and advice to the mother: sitting next to her, listening, reassuring. The firm ward round gave parents the protection of a social edge, an informed debate, consideration of choices, the wisest decision.

One morning, Brown assessed a thin infant of six months. Why he was failing to thrive was unclear, after a plethora of tests. The parents were frantic about the possibility of cystic fibrosis, a diagnosis mentioned by an indiscreet junior houseman, and which, even pre-internet, instilled terror. The registrar gave the history and Brown invited other opinions. He asked the mother to undress the infant down to his vest and to remove the diaper. The boy was emaciated, with loose folds of buttock skin, his skeletal eyes fixed in the helpless gaze of a concentration camp inmate. Roderick gently held him aloft in the palm of his hand to look for a rash, anaemia or any other tell-tale signs. With a crack of flatus, the boy discharged an explosive watery stool on to Roderick's starched cotton shirt and red silk tie. The firm stood in stifled silence. Mother gasped, the house officer grimaced. Roderick finished his examination as sister handed him a tissue. No fuss. He dabbed at his tie and carried on. After the mother re-clothed her baby he sat with the parents to explain, at length, his diagnosis of cow's milk protein intolerance. The test for cystic fibrosis was negative. He outlined a plan, twice for emphasis, to regrade the baby back on to breastmilk and home within a few days. The parents were in tears of joy. We forgot Roderick's shirt stains. The man had more class than any striding adult physician or surgeon. I wanted to be like him.

The social group of a firm within medicine, critical for good care, was hospital routine in fifteenth century Italy. We gain a glimpse of the social dynamism of hospitals in the late Middle Ages from paintings of the life of the 'ospedale' in Siena. Frescoes by Domenico di Bartolo, painted in 1441-4, displayed in the Sala Pellegrinaio of the Hospital of Santa Maria della Scala, illustrate the crowded social function of the institution. The hospital is a frenetic mêlée of sympathy groups and social support. Three panels – Care of the Sick, The Nurture and Marriage of Foundlings, and the Clothing of Novice and Distribution of Alms – portray the intimate care and feeding of foundlings by groups of Siennese women, the shelter for homeless adolescents, the burial of the dead, protection of the young by the old, the apprenticeship of orphans, end-of-life care by oblate friars, and free bread given to the poorest. As Richard Cork notes, "patients were able to discover, in Domenico's frescoes, consoling evidence of a building dedicated to their wellbeing. A physician and a surgeon with pincers in care of the sick tend to the needs of grievously suffering men with skill, patience and stoical compassion. The paintings were above all a celebration of the hospitals charitable aims".[351] What strikes one most is the vision of a hospital to promote social prosperity, not technical skills of surgery or a physician's prescription. The frescoes emphasise continuity of care and the social determinants of health. Our modern hospitals and health systems have much to ponder.

Figure 39. Care of the Sick, Domenico di Bartolo,
between 1440 and 1447

A further role of the sympathy group of a consultant-led medical firm is to protect the ethical and relational aspects of care because it introduces the element of kinship. The patient joins a group of togetherness, of communion and propinquity. In my experience, the patient and family were proud to be a member of a community of care, the centre of its attention. Most patients also knew and conspired with the subliminal element of care, that decisions are taken in their best interests, out of earshot, informed by discussion and debate beyond the bedside, with family, colleagues and carers. In the confidential safety of firm meetings, ward sisters would share with firm leaders details about patient families, the anxieties expressed by patients in quiet moments, and any concerns about the style and skills of raw juniors. Consultants could see the lab and X-ray results at a glance. They needed the eyes and ears of their caring team to guide relational care and the balance between the medical and the social.

Figure 40. Pellegrinaio di Santa Maria della Scala - The Rearing of Children and The Marriage of Daughter of the Hospital Santa Maria della Scala Hospital (Siena). Domenico di Bartolo

The power of the hospital firm nowadays often appears crushed. Crowded staff rotas, working week directives, medical directors submissive to chief executives, impersonal networks dominant over groups, and the separate lives of doctors and nurses, like estranged parents. Consultants are worn down by paperwork and targets. We could play devil's advocate and argue that the dismantling of medical or surgical firm power may have been beneficial. Not everything about the medical firm was rosy. Before the evidence revolution took hold, membership of medical firms was a junior's source of expert training. In those days we had no plans for 'continuing professional development', and the advice and mentorship received was often incorrect. Your consultant had great power over your career through their technical advice, values, ability to inspire and support for your next move, which wasn't always a good thing. Many doctors and nurses have been entrepreneurial and reorganised into effective teams. The revolution to shift care from hospitals back into communities stimulates new models of team working. The named doctor and nurse in hospital patient care might work.

With arguments on both sides, the value of a firm or its modern equivalent should be assessed. The intervention would be restoration of a ward firm with defined parameters – patients admitted under a named consultant, clear commitments of the consultant team to review the patients at specific times, and assessment of social needs by the same medical team. If so, we need an experiment. The National Institute of for Health Care and Excellence demands evidence for impact on patients' lives, so here goes with a potential protocol.

Experiment 12: Do hospital ward firms improve patient satisfaction, continuity of care and improved case management?

Population	Ward patients, junior nurses and doctors in hospital care
Intervention	Ward firm sympathy groups for patient care. Defined membership of the firm, ward rounds at specified times led by the consultant and senior nurse, and patients assigned to a particular firm with clear labelling of membership and explanation of what that means and what they might expect.
	Facilitator: consultant or next most senior doctor when absent. Joint meetings with the senior nurse.
	Supervision: no need
	The ward firm would comprise three kinds of interaction: I) regular rounds of named patients 2) team discussions of patient care and 3) monthly review of patient-centredness and user-friendliness.
Coverage or 'dose'	Pre-specified by the ward firm workload
Comparison	Wards and medical teams with standard health service care

Outcomes	
Primary	Satisfaction of patients, junior nurses and doctors
Secondary	Measure of continuity of care
	Communication rating by patients
	Time to discharge
Sample size guestimate	Maybe 90 wards, stratified 15 firm v. 15 control wards, across three different specialties e.g. medicine, surgery and paediatrics.
Cost and value	Costs will be minimal. Value will be high if benefits emerge.
Possible risks	Work overload
	Conflict between nurses and doctors over power relations
	Non-compliance due to turnover of junior doctors

Business Performance

SOCIAL ECOLOGY IN COMPANIES

New companies form every day, while old ones get taken over or go bust. The rise and fall of industries, of the corporates that make cars, computers, phones, insurance contracts or credit derivatives, is the daily diet of financial media. Dailies, business analysts, cable channels, traders, MBA courses, management gurus and chief executives pore over industrial evolution. Competitive advantage is the holy grail. How can businesses make new products, build market share, improve productivity, find lower-priced commodities and create a lower share price-to-earnings ratio? Intense competition means the life expectancy of companies has fallen. Only two companies, General Electric and Exxon, remain from the 1929 Dow Jones Industrial Average prior to the Great Depression. With huge variation in the economic performance of companies and nations, we might assume that understanding how small groups bring benefits to management would be a rich area for rigorous research. We would be wrong.

In 1982, two McKinsey consultants, Tom Peters and Bob Waterman, analysed strategy in business in their influential bestseller In Search of Excellence. Their tips targeted individual managers: quick decision making, autonomy and entrepreneurship, nurturing 'champions', hands-on, 'stick to the knitting' – stay with the business you know – and maintain lean staffing at headquarters. The book did tell stories about groups in successful companies – how to build autonomy on the shop-floor, get close to the customer, improve 'productivity through people', and ask rank and file employees to fix quality. But evidence was anecdotal, with no prospective, comparative or intervention studies. Just two years later, Business Week ran an article 'Who's excellent now?' Fourteen of the 43 companies identified had slipped, no longer excellent.[352] Waterman was timid in his response. "Who said excellence was forever?"[353]

Companies now realise group size and teams drive change, innovation and profitability. Google has tens of thousands of employees but Larry Page, its founder, insists that sympathy groups of 10 or so people fix services and products.[354] At Amazon, company chief Jeff Bezos limits the size of his teams to a group size 'fed by two pizzas' so the group maintains focus and accountability. Everyone must know what to do, best communicated in small groups.

Two of the most successful chief executive officers in American corporate history were Steve Jobs of Apple and Jack Welch of GE. Both were irascible, opinionated, towering individuals who, it seemed, brooked no dissent in their passion to be king of the corporate jungle. Steve Jobs had a passion for design so intense that, as he lay on his deathbed, he asked his doctors to provide five different oxygen masks so he could choose the one he liked best. And when Neutron Jack took over as CEO of General Electric he decimated the workforce by 100,000, yet began the company's longest unbroken run of growth, increased market value by $387 billion and created the then most valuable company in the world. He introduced a 20:70:10 value scheme whereby each year the 20% of his top performers received fabulous reward, the 70% were congratulated with bonuses, and 10% of executive staff were sacked, 'pour encourager les autres'.

Jobs and Welch embody the American dream of corporate social Darwinism, individual predators whose metrics of ruthlessness were record product sales, growth and profit. Do they represent the power of individual capitalism? If we fly a little way into the hive to explore their golden honeycombs we find these queen bees less tyrannical than we thought.

The secret of their success lay less in diktat and decree than in communes and groups.

After Apple ousted Jobs from the company he'd founded, its competitive advantage evaporated. Its product line diversified without focus. The competitors caught up. Even Apple aficionados like me considered alternatives. In 1997, the company teetered on the edge of bankruptcy. Survival depended on a cash injection of $150 million from Bill Gates, who didn't want to fall foul of monopoly laws. Microsoft needed a weak competitor to occupy a tiny slice of market share. The Apple board invited Jobs back to advise on product range, but he led a revolution. Incumbent chief executive Gil Amelio was fired. Jobs led a product drive that created the iPod, iPhone and iPad. By 2011, Apple had displaced GE and Exxon as the world's biggest company.

In 1996, before he returned as CEO, Jobs expressed pessimism about groups compared with individuals. "I have a very optimistic view of individuals. As individuals, people are inherently good. I have a somewhat more pessimistic view of people in groups. And I remain extremely concerned when I see what's happening in our country, which is in many ways the luckiest place in the world. We don't seem to be excited about making our country a better place for our kids."[355] He was sceptical of the use of focus groups for market research to help product design. "For something this complicated, it's really hard to design products by focus groups. A lot of times, people don't know what they want until you show it to them."

But Jobs' scepticism about groups didn't align with his practice. Despite his reputation for tyranny, Jobs promoted interaction and creative group networks. The most successful was the small industrial design group of 19 people led by Jonathan Ive. While Jobs acted as devil's advocate in the design process and rejected many prototypes, he saw the design group as the driver behind the company's success and protected its primacy. He joined the secluded design team most days for lunch.

Sir Jony Ive, who designed the iMac, iPod, iPhone and iPad, and, since Jobs' death, the Apple Watch, explained how the group worked. "As we're sitting together to develop a product you would struggle to identify who the electrical engineer was, who's the mechanical engineer, who's the industrial designer ... many of us on the design team have worked together for 15-plus years and there's a wonderful thing about learning as a group. A fundamental part of that is making mistakes together. There's no learning without trying lots of ideas and failing lots of times ... We have become rather addicted to learning as a group of people and trying to solve very difficult problems as a team. And we get enormous satisfaction from doing that. Particularly when you're sat on a plane and it appears that the majority of people are using something that you've collectively agonised over. It's a wonderful reward."[356]

Figure 41: Jony Ive (centre) and his Apple design team 'sympathy group' collect two prestigious awards for British Design and Art Direction, September 2012

Jobs became a groupie to make his focus on simplicity become a reality. "That's been one of my mantras – focus and simplicity. Simple can be harder than complex. You have to work hard to get your thinking clean to make it simple. But it's worth it in the end because once you get there, you can move mountains. But innovation comes from people meeting up in the hallways or calling each other at 10:30 at night with a new idea, or because they realised something that shoots holes in how we've been thinking about a problem."

Welch had a similar social approach at GE. He created a forum at Crotonville, where management executives would come in groups to be grilled and to debate ideas. Welch joined in the mêlée with gusto. "We know where most of the creativity, the innovation, the stuff that drives productivity lies," he said, "in the minds of those closest to the work. Giving people self-confidence is by far the most important thing that I can do. Because then they will act.... Control your own destiny or someone else will."

For management gurus and business schools, GE and Apple superficially provide evidence that an individual CEO is the most important factor in the creation or destruction of a company. Get the right person in charge, give them huge power and they'll knock a company into shape. They will ride roughshod over the Luddites, bureaucrats and indigents who stifle innovation. But we can also think differently. Beneath the rhetoric, the success of Welch and Jobs lay less in their command and more in their talent at creating a social ecology for groups. Yes, they took tough decisions and were ruthless. Welch would sack talented workers who just happened to have a bad year. Jobs did the same. Both would close product lines on a hunch. Both had their idiosyncrasies: Jobs hated market research and inelegant design. Welch hated finance guys and consultants.

But strong CEOs without a culture of sympathy can be disastrous; because 'culture eats strategy for breakfast'. After BP faced near-ruin from the Deepwater Horizon oil leak in 2010, the US Occupational Safety and Health Administration report uncovered a long history of corporate failure under the charming but autocratic leadership of John Browne. For five years, weak company practices had led to gas leaks in Azerbaijan, an oil spill in Alaska, and infringements of the US gas market and Clean Water Act which led to large fines.

The Volkswagen crisis of 2015 also had its roots in an autocratic failure of company governance and an incestuous relationship between VW and the Porsche family. How did Germany's largest company, with a gold carat reputation for reliability, install cheat software in eleven million vehicles to deceive regulators about diesel emissions? It beggars belief. Its share price fell by 40%. Legal challenges for health, safety and loss of vehicle value will continue for years, and the company's reputation is trashed. Governance failure was at many levels. But the root cause was boardroom governance. The Porsche family and company chair, Ferdinand Piech, with over 50% of VW shareholder votes despite only 31% of capital, kept a stranglehold for decades. They protected company leaders and restricted internal scrutiny of a public company. Weak governance leads to sloppy corporate culture whereby sympathy groups stagnate or harness their talents to deception. When CEO Martin Winterkorn resigned, Porsche installed its own insider, Matthias Müller, to limit the damage. Plus ça change.

In the business world many boards realise the importance of creating, managing and giving autonomy to small groups within their organisation. Small companies often give higher returns than large companies. Large beasts risk becoming bureaucratic, blinkered and Byzantine. They resort to financial engineering through share buy-backs, corporate bonds or takeovers to maintain an aura of dynamism and value. In The Future is Small, Gervais Williams argues that in organisations with more than 250 employees productivity falls.[357] Smaller companies are more innovative and generate more jobs. Part of the reason for Tesco's fall from grace was that it simply over-reached itself. The model of huge superstores and competitive pricing was eroded by changing consumer tastes and smaller competitors.

QUALITY COMES FROM THE SYSTEM NOT INDIVIDUALS

Individualism has its place. Some people in any organisation prefer to be alone. Universities are hotbeds of academic seclusion and misanthropy. Slavoj Zizek, the Birkbeck political philosopher, writes: "The . . . problem I have with this grassroots participatory democracy may appear just a personal one. But I think there is a universal truth in it. Can you imagine living in a society where you would have to be engaged all the time in some stupid local problems? Debating this and that, how to organise healthcare, schooling, parks, whatever. It would be hell. I want a certain degree of alienation. I want some nameless agency just to do these relatively efficiently, so that things function, and I can do what I really want to do. Read books, watch good movies, and so on. I don't think that active participation of the majority should be kept as an ideal, it is something that works only in states of emergency[358]."

We might have a sneaking regard for his opinion. But academia, par excellence, has a high proportion of hermetic leopards. Jeremy Farrar, director of the Wellcome Trust and a distinguished medical scientist, puts a different view.[359] We hail individual Nobel Prize winning geniuses like Einstein, Curie and Crick, he argues, and in the twenty-first century Geim, Higgs and O'Keefe. But success in science comes through collaboration, the result of a joint effort in small teams, or large conglomerations of teams like NASA or CERN.

One of the best examples was the Lunar Society of Birmingham, a prestigious sympathy club in which scientists, philosophers and industrialists met monthly for dinner, during a full moon (hence the name), between 1765 and 1813. The 14 core members of the sympathy group were the glitterati of eighteenth century innovation. Matthew Boulton and James Watt created and manufactured steam engines. Erasmus Darwin, a physiologist, and Thomas Day, an educationalist, were slave trade abolitionists. Richard Lovell Edgeworth created a machine to measure land size and built a vehicle with a caterpillar track, the forerunner of the tank. Samuel Galton was both a Quaker and an arms manufacturer. James Keir and Joseph Priestley were chemists: Keir created alloys of copper, zinc and iron and studies of alkalis; Priestley discovered oxygen and wrote clerical and philosophical works that influenced the utilitarian movement. Priestley's religious dissent got him into trouble. In 1791 the 'Priestley riots' were led by conservatives and royalists who burnt down the homes and chapels of dissenters suspected of sympathy with the French Revolution. Priestley and other members of the Lunar Society lost their homes.

William Small was a physician who planned the Birmingham General

Hospital and the Theatre Royal. Jonathan Stokes and William Withering were physician botanists who pioneered and expanded the clinical use of digitalis for heart failure including the use of clinical trials. (Later the two of them and Darwin, like good academics, fell out over issues of poaching of patients and academic plagiarism.) Josiah Wedgwood not only invented the modern ceramics industry but also the principles of modern marketing with innovations like 'buy one get one free', mail shots, catalogues and travelling salespeople. And John Whitehurst was an engineer who made clocks, thermometers, barometers, and hydraulic pumps for water management.

The Lunar group were also brilliant at using their status to attract bridging capital. Visitors and partners included William Herschel, one of the greatest of astronomers, the polymath US physicist and politician Benjamin Franklin, the painter Joseph Wright, and Joseph Black, who discovered carbon dioxide and magnesium, to say nothing of a stream of European scientist visitors of the day.

Figure 42. The Lunar Society

Contemporary research suggests the grand vision of their organisation or company does not drive people at work, but small-scale tasks. The psychologist and author Teresa Amabile emphasises that organisations must nurture helpfulness.[360] She describes work within a design company, Ideo, where trust and accessibility rate higher than competence as factors contributing to success. The company leaders encouraged a culture where 'design community leaders' would facilitate informal meetings with project teams, with more senior design leaders brought in as 'helpers' when required. To encourage a culture of helping within the company means building slack into workers' schedules. If people are too busy and over-loaded they won't have time to help. To do this they build informal meeting places for small groups that encourage interactions across teams and a culture of helping when it's needed.

Figure 43. The attack on Joseph Priestley's home, Fairhill, at Sparkbrook, Birmingham on 14 July, 1791

A social ecological approach might trump one based on efficiency and timelines. Team motivation is about building an ecology favourable to groups and interaction, and the time needed for helpful co-operation. Even small gains on a specific project will energise a team much more than some grandiose mission statement. Mark Zuckerberg of Facebook expresses a similar approach. "When you give everyone a voice and give people power, the system usually ends up in a really good place. So what we view our role as is giving people that power."

The British company Unipart was formed 30 years ago from a management buyout of a division of the car manufacturer British Leyland, notorious for its poor productivity and confrontational industrial relations. Unipart pioneered a new approach to lean thinking, based on best practice from Japan. It shifted from 'command and control' to 'employee engagement'. To engage and motivate employees it uses sympathy groups called 'Our Contribution Counts circles', a six-stage approach to enable teams to solve problems at their own level. It coaches people in small groups to design, test and implement their own solutions, with a deeper sense of ownership and commitment. These methods generated a new consultancy arm, which advises larger organisations like banks, insurance companies, Jaguar, Sky, Homebase, the mobile company 3 and the National Health Service. It claims the methods improve timeliness in response to customers, inventory management and quality of production. For example, at the Countess of Chester Hospital they cut £2 million in operating costs, reduced lengths of patient stay, increased theatre utilisation and lowered spending on medical supplies.[361]

Yet in our enormous industrial landscape, monitored by an army of management consultants and business gurus, experimental evidence is as rare as a winter swallow. Could experiments help chief executives to energise their organisation? Can they test ways to retain the entrepreneurial spirit of the small start-up, help employees spot and respond to emerging crises, and find the sweet spot between competition and co-operation? Many health systems, public and private, have plenty of scope to improve. John Dineen, CEO of GE Healthcare, says a typical hospital has levels of performance and safety that would see most industries go bust: 45% asset utilisation, 65% capacity utilisation, 70% bed occupancy, 18% infusion pump utilisation, 45% hand hygiene compliance. Yet health management is rich in rhetoric and hype, poor in experimental data. At a 2015 workshop on improving quality in health care, I listened to rampant 'jargonism' – 'high growth space', 'changing business model', 'productivity lens', 'precision diagnostics', 'personalised medicine', '100% effective for 50% of the patients', 'prefer precision to personalised', 'the financial crisis was a new market signal', 'technologies doing more with less', and the ubiquitous 'think different'. Data and experiment were missing.

The internet and mobile technology have freed up entrepreneurial ideas. Large political parties, religious organisations, international charities and megalithic unions face smaller, more flexible challengers. In the public sector, the homogeneous big state is fragmented. In the private sector, crony capitalism in dark rooms is exposed to the oxygen of transparency and the energy of the smaller start-up.[362] And the high priests of free market, the University of Chicago department of economics, worry about the growth of megalithic multinationals which, like robber barons, stifle smaller start-ups through predatory takeovers.[363]

One of the most rigorous analysts of how companies improve their performance and quality was William Edwards Deming. Deming was a statistician who, in 1928, completed a PhD in mathematical physics from Yale University. After helping the US war effort he travelled to post-war Japan, where he advised managers on statistical aspects of quality control. For Deming the problem was the upper management systems of organisations, not individual workers. "A manager of people needs to understand that all people are different. This is not ranking people. Everything measured consists of both 'normal' variation due to the flexibility of the system and of 'special causes' that create defects. Quality involves recognising the difference to eliminate 'special causes' while controlling normal variation."

Deming saw that understanding variation includes the mathematical certainty that variation occurs within six standard deviations of the mean. Much later, Motorola introduced six sigma methods, adopted by General Electric, Honeywell, and, later, most Fortune 500 companies. A six sigma process is one in which 99.99966% of the products manufactured are statistically expected to be free of defects, or 3.4 defects per million. One sigma quality would give 69% defects, two sigma, 31%, three sigma 6.7%, four sigma 0.62%, five sigma, 0.023% and six sigma, 0.00034%.

Deming castigated US methods of management in the 1950s. For Deming, none made sense in addressing quality, which depended on the system, not individuals. Only senior and middle management could change the culture of quality, by leadership that emphasised the primary importance of pride in performance, respect for workers, teamwork, and removing any management that introduced competition within teams. He believed in flat company hierarchies and that people from different departments, in research, design, sales, and production must work as a team.

The quality principles that Deming gave to Japanese executives like Akio Morita, the co-founder of Sony Corporation, in the early 1950s, materialised into a 14-point programme. Deming wanted to scrap management by objectives, eliminate absurd and unachievable targets for zero defects, scrap slogans, focus on leadership training, remove barriers to pride of workmanship, abolish annual appraisals, performance incentives, merit rankings, individual bonuses and management by objectives, and institute a strong programme of education and self-improvement. Everyone in the company should learn to use the experimental improvement cycles devised by his mentor Walter Shewhart, called Plan-Do-Study-Act. Managers should break down departmental barriers. Research, design, sales and production could solve production problems only as a team. Above all, managers must drive out fear. Creation of trust between management and workers was central to success.

Deming also taught many intensive short courses on quality management. On one occasion authorities asked him to have his students fill out course evaluation forms. He objected. The students were too inexperienced, he said, to identify what was valuable. He wanted their opinions 10 years later when they had had a chance to mature and to understand the role of 'untamed variation' in causing undesirable results.

Deming died in 1993. Imagine his horror at the management culture of banks that led to the 2008 global financial crisis. Oligarchic leaders and absurd personal incentives rewarded unethical and risky behaviour. Most banks had little culture of quality or risk management. Senior management, by its own admission, had little understanding of the credit derivatives they bought and sold in a market worth a staggering $62 trillion, over five times the size of the entire US economy. The boardroom executives stayed detached from trading floors without understanding what was happening. Individual managers, attracted by bonuses, pursued colossal risky trades that jeopardised the existence of the companies they worked for. Michael Lewis's The Big Short describes the shocking culture of fear and selfishness that pervaded financial institutions. Hundreds of millions of people suffered from these management failings and the world sank into economic stagnation. We still don't know how long the effects will last, nor the political fall-out, such as the rise of 'new nationalism'. Many observers fear another crash around the corner because corporate culture in finance is so little changed. New financial weapons of mass destruction still appear, like so-called 'risk adjusted bonds'. Soaring debt levels in states, companies and households are perilous.

Deming advocated a different organisational culture and management structure. He supported focused groups of workers who understood the values of a company or organisation. Everyone should celebrate group success and maintain an ongoing quest for self-improvement. The team was everything. Can we test this approach through sympathy groups of employees to solve quality of service and productivity within companies? Will a change, from external provider of expertise to recipients using sympathy and self-organisation methods, work better? And change the culture of finance? We might consider experiments to assess Deming's strategies and compare their impact with more traditional solutions like management consultancy.

SMALL GROUP BUSINESS EXPERIMENTS

In 2001, 17 software developers met in Snowbird, Utah, to consider management approaches to software development. They came up with four broad values: a preference for personal interactions over processes and tools, for working software over comprehensive documentation, for customer collaboration over contract negotiation, and for responding to change rather than following a plan. They developed an 'Agile' manifesto to respect these values, which described 12 broad principles.[364] Their approach was social and ecological. For example, business people and developers must work together daily throughout the project, build projects around motivated individuals, give them the environment and support they need, and trust them to get the job done. Information is best given through face-to-face conversations. Self-organising teams reflect on what they're doing and how to adjust plans. In short, they described a sympathy group.

And their influence has spread. 'Scrum values' are promoted in businesses around software, their principles and programmes based on the Agile manifesto. Teams that scrum are pivotal. They "figure out what is to be done, how to do it, and do it . . . teams identify what's getting in their way, and take the responsibility to resolve difficulties . . . (and they) work with other parts of the organisation to resolve the concerns outside their control".[365]

Group membership enhances helping behaviour. In 1964, in the early hours, a 28-year-old woman, Kitty Genovese, was attacked on her way home from work to her apartment in Queens, New York. Newspaper reports said the attack lasted 30 minutes, when she screamed for help, before she was raped and stabbed to death. One report said 38 people had observed the attack (later shown to be exaggerated) but failed to intervene. The public outcry led to analysis of the 'bystander effect' and what encourages people to help others in distress or to stand by. One recent scientific review concluded bystanders were more likely to help when situations were dangerous, perpetrators were present, and the costs of intervention were physical compared with non-physical.[366] In experiments, passers-by were more likely to help an injured person wearing a football jersey from the team they supported compared with those wearing one from the opposition. More interesting, a larger group size encouraged bystanders to intervene in a street violence scenario but only when the bystander group were friends. If the bystanders were strangers they were less likely to intervene.[367] So having a shared identity, best created by a sympathy group, is a strong predictor of empathy and helping, a phenomenon psychologists call 'self-other merging'.

Groups carry their past with them. Once the competition ethic has over-ridden co-operation in business it's difficult to go back. One US study found that "teams that switch from competitive to co-operative reward structures show 'cutthroat co-operation'".[368] On tasks they resembled competitive more than co-operative teams, with quicker but less accurate decisions, and less information sharing.

The Synaptic Leap (TSL) is one example of the growing phenomenon of synaptic learning networks designed to link small groups through a hub and spoke model, using a mix of digital and face-to-face meetings. TSL is a web-based environment designed to generate biomedical research ideas for four important tropical diseases, schistosomiasis, malaria, tuberculosis and toxoplasmosis. Each community has sub-projects involving up to 20 researchers who share a blog for research ideas and results, enhanced by social media and live events. Linking small groups to a broader network of expertise and resources has huge potential for quality improvement and innovation in the private and public realms. We must assess whether TSL leads to greater innovation or success in bringing new products into clinical practice.

Another management approach is Appreciative Inquiry (AI). A friend, Wasu Joshi, an entrepreneurial neonatal paediatrician in Mumbai, introduced me to the method a decade ago. She wanted to inspire and motivate staff working in public health clinics and hospitals serving the slum dwellers of Dharavi, Mumbai. AI motivates by focusing on the strengths within a group. The group moves through a 4D cycle of tasks and plans – they Discover, Dream, Design and Deliver. The word 'problem' is never mentioned. The group celebrate what they're good at, dream about what they'd like to do next, come up with a creative plan of action and build a timeline for delivery. Creative games and trust-building exercises enhance helping and teamwork. Hierarchies, Wasu explained, often use blame and command as their modus operandi, stifling innovation and ideas. Supervision visits by senior doctors or municipal managers were so sporadic or aimless that a self-organising solution had much greater appeal. Her pilot studies with staff elicited a tremendous response. Few workers had experienced respect and conversation from managers. They brought energy and creativity to challenges of patient dignity, hygiene, co-ordination and timeliness of care.

Later I invited Wasu to London to spend a week with my academic team. Her infectious enthusiasm and warm facilitation brought a deeper understanding of team dynamics and how and where we might go. Soon after, I arranged for Kirti and two colleagues in Nepal to attend Wasu's training workshop in Mumbai. Months later in Makwanpur, I joined efforts to mobilise local political leaders and health staff to improve the quality and dignity of maternal health care in the middle hills. Kirti took me to the second day of a training workshop at a health post in the east of the district. Congress, Marxist Leninist, and Maoist local politicians were in the middle of a co-operative marble rolling game. Two years before they had tried to kill one another. Now they laughed and nego-tiated as they tried to solve a puzzle – to find a way to get a rolling marble across three separate metre lengths of wooden grooves. Ideas flowed, they wrote plans on charts, they built friendship.

"This is amazing, Kirti. Imagine if we could scale this up across all 22 health posts."

"We have," he said, with effortless superiority.

"That's ridiculous. Twenty-two workshops like this? I didn't realise."

"We got organised. After Mumbai. It was fun."

"Have you written it up?"

"We shall."

"Of course."

Nepal. They do amazing things at scale, spend days traversing impossible landscapes, wade swollen rivers, reach vertiginous villages, run great work-shops. But to write a one-page report?

If the small team is vital to productivity, we might review social or management experiments to test the value of methods such as scrum values, appreciative inquiry and synaptic learning. Has anyone experimented?

My colleague Dr Abi Merriel reviewed the literature on AI in peer-reviewed journals and grey literature on websites. From 16,289 results in the search, after removing duplicates, she found just 28 studies, with only one randomised controlled trial, six observational studies and four qualitative studies.

The single randomised trial studied quality improvement in 30 primary care practices in north east Ohio using appreciative inquiry.[369] The AI process faced challenges fitting in with the time constraints of hard-pressed practices but observed that teams interacted more respectfully, created a shared vision, their own objectives for change and better motivation. After 18 months they did not observe any differences in preventive service uptake (screening, counselling, immunisation) by patients between the AI and control practices but this may not have been the best choice of outcome indicator.

So let's consider two experiments that might add value and evidence to our impressions and assumptions. The first is a formal randomised trial to measure the impact of sympathy groups to boost productivity in large companies. Another is to evaluate appreciative inquiry as a method to improve quality of health care and to cut case fatality rates in hospitals in low resource settings.

Experiment 13: Do sympathy groups within company departments improve quality of service, productivity and profits?

Population	Departments within a large company or companies
Intervention	Sympathy groups of employees led by a member of similar rank. The action cycle to focus on relationships within the company and between employees and management, productivity, concepts of quality, innovation, trust, community action, respect, dispute resolution.
Comparison	Company departments without sympathy groups. One might also compare with another arm which receives inputs only from management consultants.

Outcomes	
Primary	Profit, turnover, quality indicators
Secondary	Employee satisfaction and wellbeing

Risks	Lack of commitment from senior management
	Lack of access to financial and material support
	Overload on teams in a struggling company
	Organisational risks in the event of failure

Experiment 14: Does Appreciative Inquiry through sympathy groups within hospitals and health centres improve quality of service, dignity and health outcomes?

Population	Hospital or health centre departments or staff in sympathy group sizes
Intervention	Sympathy groups of employees led by a member of similar rank. The action cycle to focus on relationships within the hospital and between employees and management, quality of care, treating patients with respect, communications, hygiene, dealing with emergencies, common conditions, reducing waiting times.
Comparison	Hospital departments or health centres without sympathy groups
Outcomes	
Primary	Case fatality rates, quality and hygiene indicators
Secondary	Patient satisfaction and wellbeing
Risks	Lack of commitment from senior management
	Lack of access to financial and material support; external management fail to support changes recommended by sympathy groups.
	Reputational risks to participants in the event of failure

DOES MANAGEMENT CONSULTANCY WORK?

Rootle around academic libraries to browse the best management journals and you'll find randomised studies are as rare as white truffles. Although word has spread into business schools about evidence-based management, most business academics evangelise about process within their work, based on case studies rather than experiments to see whether their work brings results.[370] This lack of hard evidence on the impact of management methods raises multibillion dollar questions. What does management consultancy really achieve other than income and profit for consultants? In 2016, revenues to global management consulting firms reached a staggering $133 billion.[371] Large accountancy firms have moved back into consulting with a vengeance. Ernst and Young drew 44% of its revenues in 2016 from work giving advice on management to others. In the UK there are now more consultants than bankers – 477,000 compared with 421,000.

But is there evidence that consultant inputs add value to businesses and, if so, under what circumstance? Or is it expensive organisational homeopathy, offering companies unctuous counsel with polished but profitless PowerPoints recycled from over-used templates? One would think company boards sanctioning huge payments to management gurus would seek evidence of effectiveness. We know for sure that company productivity is variable for things like oak flooring, block ice and cement, with more than double the output in the top 10% of companies compared with the bottom 10%.[372] Does management advice shift this productivity curve?

Over the past 20 years, management consultants have invaded large public sector organisations like the UK National Health Service. The NHS spent £640 million on private sector management consultants in 2014, up from £313 million in 2010.[373] Fancy slogans intoxicated the chief executives of NHS trusts. Consultants McKinsey bigged up 'integrated care' in a BMJ article but with no evaluation of what it meant and whether it worked. Now they promote a 'whole systems' approach.[374]

When critics raised their voices, the head of the Management Consultancies Association (MCA), Alan Leaman, said: "The NHS spends 0.3% of its budget on management consultancy and the vast majority of this goes on projects that save the NHS money and improve patient care . . . On average, for every £1 spent on management consultancy, benefits worth the equivalent of £6 are returned to the client." But then he would, wouldn't he. All management consultants claim they add value and save money to justify individual fees of over $6000 per day. But is there any credible evidence to support these claims? Professor David Oliver, former NHS clinical director for elderly services, believes not. "Consultants often sell back the solutions offered to them by the staff they speak to. Or, in glossy reports, they tell service leaders what they want to hear when they haven't the courage to take ownership of their own decisions."

And even if consultants add value to an organisation their roles are blurred. Are they change agents? Purveyors of new management theories and fads? Hired guns for senior management to make organisational changes? Shamans? Or management scientists who assess evidence to advise? And don't they have perverse incentives to ensure that the company does not solve all its problems, so they retain the consultancy company long term? Two management academics suggest "consultants and others who sell ideas and techniques are always rewarded for getting work, only sometimes rewarded for doing good work, and hardly ever rewarded for whether their advice actually enhances performance".[375]

In large companies with many independent units, a randomised evaluation, whereby one compares units that receive consultant inputs with those that don't, is workable and long overdue. The problem is that management scientists don't understand trials, and management consultancy does not want scrutiny.

One group of Stanford economists did a randomised study in India, funded by the World Bank and others, to compare a baseline diagnosis plus one year of intensive management consultant visits provided to 11 textile companies (to promote 38 key management practices), with a control group of six companies that received only the baseline diagnosis.[376] The study used six consultants at a cost of $1.3 million, at a substantial discount they claimed! The intervention companies had 17% greater productivity in the first year after the consultants advised, with improvements in basic management practices, and plants adopting 'lean manufacturing techniques'.

But the study raised as many questions as it answered. Why the small sample size, why the large number of drop-outs of companies invited to join, and what was the validity of a comparison with just a handful of control companies? And why the choice of India in the first place, where family ties are greater predictors of managerial status than any acumen or training? What happened after the consultants left? To be fair, the authors showed great caution and recognised the need for further experiments in other settings.

So another series of experiments could assess management consultancy in various settings using a larger and more balanced design than the Stanford India trial. One option would be to combine this study with our small group study so that the study has three arms – control, small groups and management consultant inputs. The risk of contamination might be high, so one would need a large multinational company with departments enrolled from different locations.

Experiment 15: Which has a more positive impact on company performance and productivity - management consultancy or worker sympathy groups?

Population	Company departments within a large company or companies
Interventions	1. Management consultancy into departments specifically to enhance profit, turnover and quality indicators.
	2. Workers sympathy groups. The action cycle to focus on relationships within the company and between employees and management, productivity, concepts of quality, innovation, trust, community action, respect, dispute resolution.
Comparison	Company departments without sympathy groups.

Outcomes	
Primary	Profit, turnover, quality indicators
Secondary	Employee satisfaction and wellbeing
Risks	Lack of commitment or ownership of results from senior management
	Lack of access to financial and material support
	Management fail to support changes recommended by sympathy groups or management consultants.
	Reputational risks to employees in the event of failure

Climate Change

A SUPER-WICKED PROBLEM

We're told two stories about climate change. One is that we, the human race, are going down the tube unless we get our collective act together as soon as possible. As greenhouse gas emissions pile up in our thin atmosphere, they heat the world. Seventeen of the 18 warmest years in the modern record have now occurred since 2001. Warming has worsening effects on extreme weather, wildlife, food, water, heat and survival. Human population, industrialisation and carbon emissions have made 95% of wetlands disappear. Over three quarters of grasslands suffer from degradation, 20% of drylands risk becoming deserts, and 90% of large fish species have disappeared from the oceans. Tropical forests continue to disappear at 5% per decade, adding 30 billion tons of carbon dioxide to the atmosphere. Greenhouse gas emissions have increased 400% since 1950. So what will happen if we don't take the required action? Over time our prediction models have more data to work with, which makes them more reliable. The latest estimate in Nature gives a 93% chance of a four degree warmer world by 2100.[377] Sir Martin Rees, president of the UK Royal Society, the world's oldest independent scientific academy, believes this gives humanity only a 50-50 chance of surviving the 21st century. We're fast running out of time.

A second, sceptical view is that we've had Armageddon scares before, about over-population, Malthusian food collapse, ozone layers and Silent Spring. Whatever the climate prophets of doom tell us, technology and wealth will save us. Innovation will help us mop up the carbon in the atmosphere and limit climate change. Growing wealth will increase our resilience to the side-effects of global warming. And population growth will end, and the world return to a smaller, more stable population size.

Climate change from human activity is beyond reasonable doubt. Greenhouse gas levels (GHGs) have soared because we devour fossil fuels. Changes in using land through growth in population, urbanisation and agricultural expansion have denuded our planet of forests, key protective carbon sinks that remove carbon dioxide from the atmosphere through photosynthesis. Photographs of our disappearing Arctic ice sheet, thermometer of the planet, are emblematic. The world is heating up. Seasons start earlier, birds migrate to different places, fungus diseases shift northward, and people and crops wilt with more frequent and severe heatwaves. We see visible impacts across the planet with less than one degree of warming.

Comprehensive scientific evidence collated by the Intergovernmental Panel on Climate Change presents an irrefutable scientific case. Their 2014 report showed steady warming of the air and the oceans, sea-level rise speeding up, loss of Arctic and Antarctic ice, ocean acidification and changes in extreme weather events. Atmospheric carbon dioxide monitoring in Hawaii at the Mauna Loa research station shows a relentless climb since 1958 (see figure 44). The sawtooth increase (CO2 levels higher in the winter and lower in the northern latitude summer, when CO2 uptake by vegetation photosynthesis increases) shows an accelerating rise.

After a quarter century of climate negotiations, the rate at which carbon pours into the world's atmosphere has accelerated as emerging nations industrialise, build their economies and increase consumption. Most climate scientists believe we shall head towards a three to four degree warmer world within our children's lifetime, with severe or catastrophic consequences.

Conversations are difficult. Will greenhouse gas levels and warming run in parallel? Might our complex climate system buffer the effects of

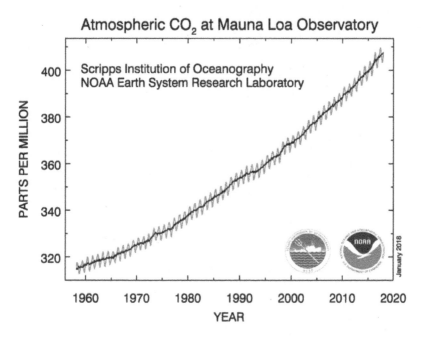

Figure 44. Monthly mean atmospheric carbon dioxide at Mauna Loa Observatory, Hawaii

the GHGs and give us extra decades to respond? Maybe the Pacific Ocean will absorb heat gains in the atmosphere for longer than expected. The upper layers of our oceans have warmed in the past 20 years, and our seas can absorb the heat for only so long. We don't know how long that will be. Or the opposite will happen. Climate change might reach a tipping point sooner than we expect and trigger runaway climate chaos. Ten million carcasses of mammoths and ancient hunted species lie under the Arctic ice. If the permafrost penumbra melts and releases huge amounts of methane, a more powerful GHG than CO2, it could disrupt our ecosystems and lead to the sixth great species extinction of paleohistory. Monumental methane release has happened before. Paleoclimatologists like James Hansen are gloomy. The former NASA climate chief points to rapid climate shifts in the past 65 million years, with sharp lurches in global temperature of several degrees over decades. His colleague Wally Broecker worries that "the palaeoclimate record shouts out to us that, far from being self-stabilising, the Earth's climate system is an ornery beast which overreacts even to small nudges".

What about climate sceptics? Conservative politics throws up most voices among the dwindling band of climate change 'denialists'. In the USA, they have power. Donald Trump wants the US to become the sole country not signed up to the Paris climate agreement. Scott Pruitt, when environment secretary, aimed to scrap Barack Obama's Clean Power Act. In the UK, Nigel Lawson, Chancellor of the Exchequer under Margaret Thatcher, runs the Global Warming Policy Foundation with 'anonymous' donations. His well-written book, A Cool Look at Global Warming, is interesting on how to assess the appropriate rate to discount climate-friendly policies. But his climate science is embarrassing and awry. Lawson's board member Matt Ridley is the scion of a hereditary peer in Mrs Thatcher's cabinet. A popular science writer, and owner of a coalmine, Ridley was chairman of Northern Rock when the bank collapsed in 2007. He drove forward a reckless business model based on leverage, where only a 3% decline in assets led to bankruptcy and the first UK bank run for 150 years. Instead of seclusion or apology, he took up his hereditary peerage in the House of Lords, and published, without irony, a book called The Rational Optimist. The threat of climate change, he argued, was over-hyped.

Another prominent voice is the journalist James Delingpole, a friend of David Cameron and Boris Johnson at Oxford, who writes evidence-free critiques of climate science. When challenged by Sir Paul Nurse, Nobel laureate and a former President of the Royal Society, on why he read no peer-reviewed scientific papers Delingpole said his job was to be "an interpreter of the interpretations".

All good scientists are sceptical about hypotheses and data. But when evidence is overwhelming they don't depart from rationality. So what do we do? Wait and hope that clever scientists will remove carbon from the atmosphere? Wait and hope that politicians, energised by the 2015 Paris agreement, comply with a verifiable protocol to cut emissions? Like an AIDS vaccine, no nearer after 30 years of research, carbon capture is a more intractable challenge than we think. Oil companies and powerful billionaires undermine and oppose global protocols agreed by politicians by foul means and fair. Even if policies are made law, compliance monitoring will be daunting. Can we risk waiting for a top-down magic solution?

Bottom-up action is important. John Maynard Keynes said: "The politicians, who have ears but no eyes, will not attend to the persuasion until it reverberates back to them as an echo from the great public." We must engage with the great public to understand their fears and conflicts about livelihoods and environment. Could sympathy groups play their part in transformational social change? Would they give communities impetus to speed up green growth? Can they promote practical sustainable technologies to millions of people? Or build resilience to climate instability and to slow population growth? The sympathy group has always catalysed technological innovation and diffusion of new ideas. Could it unravel the gridlock of global governance?

As GHGs soar, the question is not whether climate change will happen but how soon. Analysis needs to move away from sterile arguments about the existential threat of climate change and towards practical solutions. One way is to analyse climate change as a 'super-wicked' problem arising from the Kaya identity. In 1993, Japanese energy economist Yoichi Kaya provided a mathematical formula to explain the determinants of global greenhouse gas emissions.[378] Formulae simplify problems and enable policymakers and civil servant sherpas to make measurable inroads to a solution. His equation was simple:

$$F = P * (G / P) * (E / G) * (F / E)$$

or

$$F = P \times g \times e \times f$$

where

F is global CO2 emissions from human sources

P is global population

G is global gross domestic product, GDP ($g = (G/P)$ or global per-capita GDP)

E is global primary energy consumption ($e = (E/G)$ or the energy intensity of world GDP)

$f = (F/E)$ is the carbon intensity of energy.

The equation spells out in stark terms the policy options to reduce carbon dioxide emissions from burning fossil fuel. We can reduce the numbers of people in the world who will use energy. As William Cobbett suggested, "it is not the greatness of a man's means that makes him independent so much as the smallness of his wants".[379] At any wealth level we can reduce our energy consumption. And we can switch from carbon-intense to carbon-zero or carbon-lite sources of energy. In brief, the carbon problem is solved if we stop burning it, if we tax it to shift to renewables, if we lower our consumption of everything, or we remove it.[380]

Climate change is both wicked and super-wicked. Wicked social problems are difficult to resolve because of lack of data, changing politics, interdependencies, absence of stopping rules, and because solutions make things only a little better. In brief, we don't have reliable emission data by country; sceptics may undermine the Paris agreement; we still need fossil fuels for jobs and economic growth; climate change is gradual without an agreed endpoint of failure; and renewable energy will take decades to supplant oil and gas. Super-wickedness adds four additional features:

1. Time is running out.
2. We have no central authority.
3. Those seeking to solve the problem are also causing it.
4. Policies discount the future irrationally.[381]

Emissions are wicked for planners because they arise from several simultaneous and different challenges. They emanate from market failure. Markets do not always price risk correctly. In the global financial crisis, credit derivatives were incorrectly or fraudulently underpriced for their level of risk to bankruptcy and sovereign nation economies. Likewise the true carbon price from greenhouse gas emissions, which reflects future environmental costs and the threat to our common atmosphere, is way too low. Complex economic and global agreements must make the market price equal to the shadow price, which reflects the opportunity cost of carbon emissions to our environment and natural capital.

Climate change also represents political failure. The Paris agreement took 30 years, is not implemented, and with full compliance would leave us up to three degrees warmer. Effective legislation and compliance needs unprecedented inter-governmental co-operation. Worse, climate change is a security failure. It threatens political instability, population migration, worsening weather emergencies, and military threats through competition for scarce resources like water. Preoccupied governments turn a blind eye. In May 2014, the USA Military Advisory Board reported to President Obama that international action on climate change had failed to date, that risks accelerated, would catalyse conflict, and that "we must guard against a failure of imagination". The service chiefs pulled no punches. Climate change within US borders threatened critical national infrastructure, military power and homeland security. They recommended that US Combatant Commanders should factor in the impacts of climate change across their full spectrum of planning and operations. The United States should speed up military operations in the Arctic, and take a global leadership role in preparing for the projected impacts of climate change.

Climate change is also an ethical issue. The poorest billion people, whose carbon footprint is 3% of the total, will bear the brunt of harmful effects. We ignore intergenerational justice at our peril. Our reckless self-interest means our children and grandchildren face profound climate instability. William Cobbett again: "From a very early age I had imbibed the opinion that it was every man's duty to do all that lay in his power to leave his country as good as he had found it."[382]

Climate change damage to ecosystem services is what the economist Sir Partha Dasgupta calls the "unaccounted consequences for others (including future generations) of decisions made by each one of us about reproduction, consumption, and use of the natural environment."[383] Economists the world over undervalue environmental effects. In south Asia, ecosystem damage is already intense from population growth. Ecologists measure the HANPP index, the human appropriation of net primary productivity, to assess how humans dominate vegetation. In most of South America, the west of North America, central Africa and Russia, less than 10% of primary productivity on the land comes from agriculture. In the Indian subcontinent and much of China, HANPP rises to over

60%, in some regions from 80% to 100%. When GDP growth, the usual measure of national economic success, is adjusted for costs arising from environmental damage we get a nasty shock. One study in India, which adjusted for losses in the natural capital component of national wealth, found over five years (1995-2000) that wealth per head increased at less than 0.2% per year, much lower than official GDP growth.[384]

And climate change threatens global health. In 2015, I served as co-chair of an international Lancet Health and Climate Commission, which brought Chinese and European academics together across disciplines. Climate has emerged as a health threat because global heating and loss of biodiversity threatens to undermine the health gains of the past 50 years. Crop yields, food and water insecurity, heatwaves, and geographical shifts in pests and predators and vectors of disease, will cause childhood malnutrition, loss of immunity, infectious disease epidemics, heat stress, allergies, and mental stress from family break-up and migration. Extreme weather disruption in coastal and 'heat-island' city communities is a rising threat. Our message was urgent but optimistic. Climate change is our most serious long-term health threat.

But tackling climate change could be the greatest global health opportunity of the twenty-first century. Cutting greenhouse gas emissions yields big health and economic gains. Active transport, removing air pollution, creating healthier diets, protecting biodiversity and our forests, building green cities, scaling up renewable electricity and cars, insulating homes and conservation agriculture are all good for our health. We can reduce obesity, diabetes, heart attacks, strokes, respiratory disease, stress and depression. Addressing climate change will lead to big savings on health spending and will cut the 'unpaid health bill': the $5.2 trillion the International Monetary Fund calculates as the cost of fossil fuel subsidies and environmental damage.

For once, our report touched a nerve with the world's media. Two million downloads of the report made it among the top 1% of articles ever tracked, and the second highest published in The Lancet. Briefly we trended higher than Taylor Swift on Twitter, and only just below Batman. The report concluded that a decarbonised global economy is no longer a technical or economic question; it's now political. We possess renewable technologies. The finance is there. Financial institutions invest only 0.1%

of 75 trillion dollars in renewable energy. But social and individual behaviour is our biggest challenge. Humans must rediscover a conscious and collective will to seek sustainable modes of consumption. We're the problem.

This touches upon the 'tragedy of the commons', how we use and share common resources, and the tensions between individuals and groups. Proposed by Garrett Hardin in 1968 in Science, the tragedy of the commons deals with the dilemma of managing a common good such as common land or a lake for a village to fish from.[385] People overuse or exploit such a resource. Each individual gains the benefit of grazing and fishing rights whereas loss lies with the community. Those promoting individual freedoms argue that if others exploit the resource so can he or she. In 2011, the then UK Chancellor of the Exchequer, George Osborne, announced that the government would only cut emissions in line with neighbours, to ensure British businesses suffered no disadvantage. "We're not going to save the planet by putting our country out of business," he said. Conversely, if others decide not to abuse the common resource, then it appears to do no harm for an individual to take a little more. The inevitable outcome is the destruction of the resource – unless groups get together to manage their own commons.

Elinor Ostrom, Nobel Laureate in economics, explored how we use common resources such as forests, water systems, fisheries, and the atmosphere. Her review of 47 irrigation systems and 44 fisheries showed that 72% of farmer-managed systems had much higher performance in terms of crops grown and benefit-cost ratio, compared with only 42% improvement among those using governmental irrigation systems with fancy engineering. Small fishery groups gave space, time, and technology to reduce over-harvesting.[386] Groups that did not communicate were more likely to overuse their resource. In Ostrom's earlier study of police practice in Chicago, "not a single instance was found where a large centralised police department outperformed smaller departments serving similar neighbourhoods in regard to multiple indicators". Common resource management improves when small groups take control.

Common wealth creates common health. Public health in our new century is about managing the commons for social benefit, destroying corruption and building community trust. Higher level decisions matter: global leaders, state and city governments, financial regulators, green growth business, scientists, psychologists, engineers, economists and environmentalists will play their part. But could sympathy group experiments add to policy options? Using the Kaya equation, we can explore their role to reduce family size and stabilise population, to reduce overall consumption, to be economical in our energy use and to move towards zero carbon energy sources. All these variables are measurable. But we need social experiments to study impacts. It happens already, slowly, but policymakers need a much larger evidence base to achieve lasting impact at scale, within a timeframe of hope.

SUSTAINABLE SYMPATHY SOLUTIONS

Stories abound of promising conservation initiatives. In North America and Europe, transition groups and farmers markets promote local food produce and new ways to barter and exchange. But they're a middle class phenomenon. Could progressive states create a social ecology where poorer people, whose income and time are restricted, get incentives for these options? Would incentives for sympathy groups at scale increase the uptake of sustainable diets, change dietary diversity and cut malnutrition and obesity rates? These are critical questions.

Sympathy groups for sustainable living are already widespread and diverse. Carbon Rationing Action Groups (CRAGs) agree to reduce their carbon emissions by deciding members' own personal carbon targets and the price of a kilogramme of carbon.[387] Members record their carbon emissions and email their performance to the chair. Each year they meet to share results. People who missed their target pay a penalty. The scheme excludes members who fail to provide CO_2 footprint proof or pay off their CO_2 debt. Members who saved carbon share the fines as agreed. If you opt out of the group for a period you cannot opt back in. Andy Ross set up the first CRAG in 2005 after he read the book High Tide by Mark Lynas and learnt about 'contraction and convergence'. Conceived by the violinist and mathematician

Aubrey Meyer, and developed by Mayer Hillman and Tina Fawcett in *How We Can Save the Planet*, contraction and convergence proposes personal carbon trading accounts as national policy. Global contraction refers to global emissions meeting targets by an agreed year. Convergence refers to equal per capita shares of this contraction phased towards the target by an agreed year. Countries will converge on an agreed and reduced emissions target per person per year.

CRAGs caught on. Twenty-five groups across the UK, from Sevenoaks to Glasgow, gained the attention of the then UK Environment Secretary, David Miliband. But they ran into problems. As writer George Monbiot put it, nobody riots for austerity. Groups had varying structures for governance, carbon targets, emissions accountability and financial penalties. Members argued over whether to include emissions from air travel on business and were reluctant to discuss their personal carbon footprints. Drop-outs were common, even though most members were 'positive greens'. Quick wins in cutting emissions were easy. Longer term cuts depended on outsiders – building regulators, availability of low carbon materials, and local transport options. Few CRAG groups survived. But their innovation inspired others such as Carbon Conversations and Transition Towns. New formats might attract a different clientele, with less onerous targets, and with scalability and sustainability designed from the start. Other low-carbon community groups (LCCGs) have cut consumption or promoted renewable energy. Dr Kersty Hobson at Oxford concluded that scale-up of LCCGs was possible while preserving impact and without losing their grounding in place and community. But "issues of capacity, resources and utility remain paramount". Her group are studying LCCGs in more depth as part of a new trial.

We shouldn't despair if early initiatives founder. At a deep level, we might agree with French philosopher Michel Serres that we must negotiate a new contract with nature, rejecting our mastery "in favour of admiring attention, reciprocity, contemplation, and respect". Our contract implies rights to the natural world but reparations or restrictions on our ability to extract or damage natural resources. In rural India, my colleagues Prasanta, Nirmala and Audrey led a randomised evaluation of women's groups working with nutrition health visitors to tackle malnutrition. Dietary diversity and childhood weight gain and survival improved. Adding environmental management to these group discussions would not be difficult. In the western world, a burning desire for local conservation, urban greening and rebel horticulture links well with plans to cut community carbon emissions.

In Indonesia, Edi Basuno and his team explored participatory groups among poultry farmers.[388] Poultry are climate-friendly meat and a key economic resource. They're also vulnerable to emerging viral infections when they're farmed. Thailand, Indonesia, Vietnam and China recognised the value of creating small groups of local farmers, poultry production clusters (PPCs), to enhance productivity and make farms less vulnerable to bird flu outbreaks. The farmers' groups work away from residential sites, explore economies of scale, and apply biological safety and conservation measures. Assessment was disappointing though. Production did not increase and the numbers of flies, mosquitoes, rats, and smells remained similar to non-PPC farmers, alienating nearby villages. The groups, though, did not structure meetings around production and safety gains, and the evaluation was not randomised. The method has scope for improvement.

Another community randomised trial, ongoing in the eastern Congo, assesses the value of two livestock transfer programmes, Pigs for Peace (PFP) and Rabbits for Resilience (RFR), in building wellbeing and trust within communities.[389] The trials will examine the effectiveness of PFP and RFR to improve economic stability, and also family and community relationships in 10 rural, post-conflict villages. In India, the tradition of community development groups is strong. In Kerala, women from the Muthavan tribe, who live by shifting cultivation and forest produce, are members of Kudumbashree, the state's anti-poverty and gender justice movement.[390] Their group meetings discuss farming, forestry, threats from wild animals, loans and energy. In Edamalakudi, a remote cluster of villages with no electricity, the village council offered money to purchase 100 solar panels, each weighing 10 kilogrammes, so 60 women walked for 12 miles across wild terrain to carry them back on their heads. When asked about which was best – group or individual farming, for *ragi* and paddy, tapioca and plantain – the women agreed they should do both. "In collective functioning, if one person falls behind, the others will help her manage." Another woman said: "Individual farming has its own rewards. But this way helps us feed our families better. As a group, there are effects beyond farming. Members become a source of support and solidarity for each other. This spills over into family life as well. That is very important to us. So why should we not do both?"

In the richest economies, austerity economic policies that cut benefits, real wages and employment protection led to an explosion of food banks. In Canada, Nick Saul and Andrea Curtis set up The Stop, a movement to "increase access to healthy food in a manner that maintains dignity, builds health and community and challenges inequality". They changed a food bank from a last-ditch refuge to one where people could create a community around food security and sharing. They set up kitchen gardens, greenhouses, kitchens, drop-in meals, cooking lessons, education programmes and sustainable food banks for those who need them. The philosophy is to replace handouts with a movement based on dignity and co-operation.[391]

Such non-linear 'solutions' from sympathy groups might contribute to a non-linear problem like climate change. Let us return to the Kaya identity. We wish to reduce population numbers who will use energy, to reduce the wealth that consumes more energy and damages our ecosystems, at any wealth level to reduce our energy consumption, and to switch from carbon-intense to carbon-zero or carbon-lite sources of energy. So how might sympathy groups help to reduce population (p), or gross domestic product (g), while preserving gross domestic happiness, the energy intensity of wealth and happiness (e), and the carbon intensity of energy (f)?

There is no shortage of possibilities. Groups could ensure food and energy security through better land use and conservation agriculture, sustainable intensification of farming, seed selection and breeding, urban horticulture, household energy use and uptake of renewables. They might also advocate for local government action, promotion of family planning methods to cut unintended pregnancy rates, and the scale-up of transition movements for locally sourced food. Groups can help to build our defences for flood protection, for water security (supply, storage and reduced waste), for reduced heat stress among the elderly, and for protection of construction and agricultural workers in hot weather.

So the next two experiments test hypotheses related to this broad agenda. The first is to test group impact on fertility reduction where rates are high. The second is to assess whether community sustainability groups improve the carbon footprint, consumption patterns and health co-benefits of high income communities.

Experiment 16: Do sympathy groups improve rates of family planning uptake and reduce unintended pregnancies in high fertility communities?

If you want to cut birth rates, the key factors are wealth, education, survival of children and access to family planning technology and services. Many countries have cut their fertility rates to replacement level (2.1 births per woman) as the graph below shows.

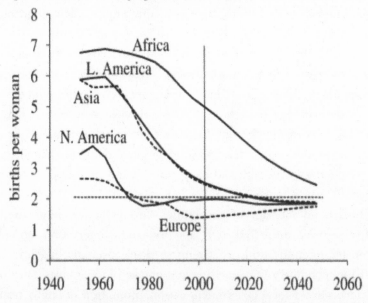

Figure 45: Trends in fertility rate by region[392]

After a mid-century peak, the world's population will stabilise and fall. In China, the current 1.3 billion population could fall by up to half if fertility rates remain at their current rate of around 1.57 births per woman. The only regions that haven't yet seen fertility rates plummet are Africa and the Middle East, but the trend has started. We don't know the speed of decline, nor the peak population, nor to what extent they'll suffer environmental consequences already seen in Asia. But rapid declines in African and Middle Eastern fertility and child death rates will be critical if we're to stabilise world population and cut carbon emissions.

A key issue is to cut unintended pregnancies. Increasing contraceptive use alone is not sufficient. Sporadic use of family planning methods will not protect against an unwanted pregnancy. Women require good information and easy access to appropriate contraception and 'menstrual regulation'. Despite billions of dollars invested in population programmes, I can find no randomised controlled study of interventions to cut unintended pregnancy rates as the primary outcome. And we didn't measure it as an outcome in any of our women's group studies. Yet if we knew how to cut unintended pregnancies in growing populations, we would speed up population stability and slash future carbon emissions by up to one third. Brian O'Neill and his colleagues at the National Centre for Atmospheric Research in Colorado have estimated that slowing population growth could provide us with 16% to 29% of the emissions cuts we need to avoid dangerous climate change by 2050.[393] It's a critical development challenge.

In countries where child deaths are common, women's sympathy groups are among the most effective ways to cut mortality. They also raise women's awareness of family planning services. But men play a key part in family planning decisions. If men disapprove of particular methods of contraception (for example, condom use remains low in Africa) or persist in the desire for a large family, women have little control over their fertility, unless they seek covert, long-acting solutions like injectable hormone injections to prevent conception for several months at a time. Provision of accessible clinical services is a pre-requisite. But community mobilisation might cut numbers of unwanted pregnancies faster.

Population	Couples living in high fertility and mortality areas
Intervention	Groups which bring couples, men and women, together to discuss desired family size, access to reproductive health services, men's health, women's health, child health and development and nutrition. Groups of women to start, joined by men and partners at different stages of the cycle. Led by a member of a nearby community, but not the same, to maintain confidentiality. The action cycle to focus on women's health, men's health, desired family size, gender issues, decision-making, reproductive health, contraception, nutrition, access to care and family planning services, water, sanitation and hygiene. Facilitator: local trained volunteer Supervision: local health visitor or civil society worker
Coverage or 'dose'	In high fertility areas it might be best to target younger couples or newly weds. A population of 10,000 in rural Africa, for example, might have around 400–500 young couples willing to attend groups to discuss not only fertility but also pre-conceptual care, antenatal and infant care, and aspects of women's and men's health.
Comparison	Communities with standard health service and family planning care
Outcomes	
Primary	Rates of unintended pregnancy
Secondary	Contraceptive prevalence rate, newborn deaths, men's and women's utilisation of care
Cost and value**	Monitor the costs of incentives for volunteers, the cost of group meeting facility hire or use, the cost of user travel or provider transport, and the cost of materials. Possibly the opportunity costs of participants.
Possible risks	Social exclusion of disadvantaged groups Overload on community health workers Delays in referral for family planning

Experiment 17: Do community groups improve the carbon footprint, consumption patterns and health co-benefits of high income communities?

A sustainable future means that rich country consumption must fall. We're the problem. We need two to three earths to meet current consumption demands. The burgeoning middle classes of Asian tiger economies will make things worse. The way forward is for families to have fewer children and to cut their consumption. But how? The stability of human civilisation depends on it. At least one or two large scale experiments might be useful.

Population	Local citizens, urban and rural, in high and middle income settings
Intervention	Sympathy groups of cross-political local citizens led by a member of the same community. The action cycle to focus on what sustainability means, waste disposal, local environmental protection, self-sufficiency, transition movements, local biodiversity and horticulture initiatives, farmers' markets, energy conservation, climate change, concepts of climate advocacy, community action, dispute resolution. Facilitator: local trained volunteer Supervision: local health visitor or civil society worker
Coverage or 'dose'	Let us assume we need groups capped at 15-20 household representatives, and that we need at least 25% of households involved to build the social amplification of the initiatives. If household size averages four persons, then a sustainability group of 20 representatives would cover a population of 4 x 20 x 100/25 or 320 people. Volunteers could leaflet or email households to let them know about the meetings, their aim and availability. Attendees would choose groups to join.
Comparison	Communities from similar populations without such clubs
Outcomes	Consumption patterns
Primary	Household carbon footprints
Secondary	Advocacy initiatives for local environmental management, food, climate change and sustainability
Cost and value	Monitor the costs of incentives for volunteers, the cost of group meeting facility hire or use, the cost of user travel or provider transport, and the cost of materials. The opportunity costs of participants.
Possible risks	Social exclusion of disadvantaged groups Overload on volunteers

One depressing thought is that even if our experiment showed positive results, and the method happened on a large scale, would it make a big difference? No, say Paul Wapner and John Willoughby.[394] They suggest that cuts in family members and average consumption will expand household savings. Savings though don't stagnate in banks or pension portfolios. Financial institutions use savings to invest in new projects so "because purchasing power is fungible, it makes little difference ecologically if one saves or invests money rather than spends it". Our individual decisions about family size, car, food preferences and recycling might have no material effect on greenhouse gas emissions, they conclude. It seems illogical that any individual choice about lifestyle, multiplied a hundred million times over, will have no or little impact on our atmosphere but they may be right. Macroeconomics does not behave in the same way as household economics. Nonetheless changing consumption preferences might affect the nature of macroeconomic investments. And cuts in family size in the present generation will have effects on future generations. For example, China found that reversal of its one child policy has led to no rebound in desired family size.

And Wapner and Willoughby acknowledge that investment portfolios are shifting towards companies with sound environment policies. Besides, any efforts to cut poverty and gaps between rich and poor will have environmental benefits. The rich and, to a lesser extent, the poorest families, cause the most environmental damage. "If we had effective public policies that redistributed income, forced polluters to pay for the harm they cause, mandated more environmentally friendly technologies, and reduced the workday in the richer parts of the world, we could change the way we live our material lives."

The hypothesis of our experiment, therefore, is grandiose: groups will promote green positive practices, improve local environmentalism and challenge the 'ecocide' of polluting companies. They will raise their voice for political change, for carbon capture, for wealth redistribution, and start grassroots movements to change the political economy of their country. Is it pie in the sky? In Cambodia, social network analysis of key organisational players engaged in developing health-related climate adaptation activities found that groups within the Ministry of Health, and informal partnerships or 'shadow networks', were far more important than donors, development banks or NGOs.[395] An international movement to reduce emissions from deforestation and forest degradation (REDD+) in Nepal also tested pilot projects of community forest user groups. Groups of *dalits*, indigenous people, women and the poor conversed and tackled social safeguards.[396] But a market approach alone to REDD+ was not attractive to the groups. They needed financial incentives to make any scale-up workable.

We must stay optimistic about building a sustainable future. And apply a scientific lens to whatever we take to scale. Sympathy groups capture the imagination and energy of people: participatory crop breeding, sustainable ecotourism, horticulture groups, group farming, sustainable food and kitchen clubs, and the transition movement. Forest planting groups and biodiversity protection groups celebrate wildlife; not only as a tourist asset, but also for our wellbeing and pride in the beauty of our countryside.

Corruption, Finance and Government Gridlock

QUIET CORRUPTION

When we arrived in Nepal, three decades ago, Colonel Hugh Mackay, inspirational Gurkha officer and head of overseas operations at Save the Children Fund, interrogated me. He was on his annual country visit bearing bottles of Johnnie Walker Black Label and boxes of Benson and Hedges cigarettes. A tall handsome Scotsman, he was pinstripe suited with a handkerchief in his top pocket, a raspy laugh and nicotine-stained forefingers. He was a man for whom I would have gone over the top.

"Let me ask you Tony," he said, smoke clouding his face, "what's the definition of corruption?"

I didn't know.

"Very simple," he said. "Six per cent. Below 6%, commission, above 6%, corruption." He chuckled. I understood the point. Societies vary with definitions of a tip. A 6% service charge to get drugs and vehicles through Kolkata docks is just OK.

Years later I had a white knuckle ride in a jeep of Pakistani medics along a terrifying mountain road in Chitral, North West Frontier Province. The journey took six hours. Conversation took our minds off the fear the driver would fall asleep and plunge over the precipice. Our chat turned to corruption. I happened to mention that Transparency

International, a European advocacy organisation, produced league tables for country corruption based on surveys of businessmen. Immediately I regretted it. The next question from Aisha, a public health doctor, was pointed.

"Where did Pakistan come in the league table?" she asked.

Embarrassed I said, "Er. Well actually you came second."

"Who came first?" asked Khalid.

"Nigeria."

Khalid paused.

"Hmmmm. We must have bribed the Nigerians."

The struggle between individual and group survival is central to the phenomenon of corruption – private gain from a public good. Corruption is a fundamental human trait. Perhaps that's why we don't like to talk about it. The tabooness induces laughter, shame or silence. It's the major obstacle to social development.

More states than ever have the architecture of democracy – elections, presidents, parliaments, judiciaries and a civil service – but spread of democracy worldwide through globalisation and the internet is a comfortable illusion. In 1945, the government in Nepal revolved around a Friday forum on the turfed Tundhikel in the centre of Kathmandu, where the hereditary prime minister stood and answered questions from his subjects. Today Nepal can display the structures of a modern, democratic state – multiparty democracy, a constituent assembly in parliament, an independent judiciary, election commission, army and police force under democratic control, and the paraphernalia of local government. Nepal has done better than other south Asian and African countries in building a democratic house. The rooms open to the public look vibrant and decisive. To donors, the power and decisions live within these rooms, and aid supports their foundations of 'good governance'. But as keen observers know, powerful men and their cronies, in closed, smoke-filled rooms in the west wing, take real decisions about money and patronage. In south Asia, including Nepal, corruption is rife.

In many countries, not just African states, the 'big man' or 'bwana' is king, operating for clan and tribal interests. Personal fortunes and the public exchequer merge. A complex system of patronage ensures loyalty to the big man from obedient, dependent MPs and their voters. The system locks everyone into a prison of corruption. The culture of impunity at the centre creates a thriving market in retail corruption at the periphery. Agricultural officers, utility engineers, health workers and policemen seek unofficial rents for their services. Inflated fertiliser prices, unofficial drug fees and traffic fines add to the cost of living. Public servants, locked into a system that rewards loyalty, where corruption goes unpunished, act in a logical, dysfunctional way to obscure accountability and transparency. When a President or regional chief appeals to crude tribalism and abuses his opponents for foreign travels or outside roots, they don't demur. State media publish deferential reports of presidential meetings and laud party largesse. He harasses independent journalists or closes their newspapers. Big leaders want no loss of control. Civil servants intervene to prevent decentralisation of governance and decision-making. They have little power of patronage, so appointments are not delegated, except for hand-picked district commissioners. Electors are silent when intimidation, assaults, accidents, or disappearances happen to members of the opposition. And the ultimate right of redress, the anti-corruption commission, supported by donors desperate to show 'capacity-building' and 'good governance', is neutered by the savvy appointment of a former cabinet minister or judge, who speaks good English, has gravitas, and kicks any major problems into the long grass. The structures of democracy are anathema to survival of the big man in office. So he bribes the judiciary and places passive judges in senior posts. He rigs elections. His campaigns ignore issues and focus on his personality.

Even opposition politicians are part of the problem. They want power, not to change the system. When they get their 'turn to eat' they gorge themselves and repeat the cycle of corruption and intimidation. For example, Nepal has the highest potential source of hydropower in the world. For 50 years development agencies offered funds and technology to build large megawatt power stations for the growing population and for export to India for valuable foreign exchange. Yet, until recently, Kathmandu has had increasing power cuts and load shedding. Access to electricity for most people is no better. The opposition blocks every attempt by government to start large scale power projects. They protest about environmental damage or tribal rights. They don't want political rivals to enjoy huge kick-backs. In Dhaka, Bangladesh, the same reasoning blocked construction of a new metro or monorail to relieve transport gridlock.

At election time, a country may flash into the international media spotlight. As Diana Cammack, a specialist in southern African politics, observes: "Who to turn to when in need of medicine: the empty shelves and rude staff at the government clinic or the local party boss who can provide a little cash to purchase tablets in town? Staying locked into the patronage system benefits those at the bottom and the top and helps explain why civil society in many countries remains 'weak' and silent, not roused to civic action or demanding of government, even after years of 'strengthening'."[397] We watch "big men and parties calling in their favours, buying more support (handing out food, cash and fertiliser, touring the country making new promises, etc), intimidating those who waver and attacking opponents (with police and youth gangs)". And for voters, their double bind makes them compliant.

The poisonous spread of bwanas and baksheesh induces lethargic fatalism in electorates. Some lament the old days, before democracy, when despots like Barre or Banda or Ershad or Musharraf or Mobutu led a 'disciplined' regime. Others accept that unfair elections, corruption, flashy NGOs with fleets of white 4x4s, and 'our turn to eat' politics are the norm for the foreseeable future. Better to game the system and keep their heads down. When donor governments and pop stars want to double aid, or create a million new fieldworkers, or launch another health campaign, they don't rejoice. They know where the money will go, to prop up a system they detest.

One of the most unaccountable movements of modern times was 'budget support'. In the 1990s, donors decided multiple streams of aid were beyond the 'absorptive capacity' of recipient governments. Much better to place funds into a central government basket to support sectoral programmes for health, education, transport and infrastructure. Donors would scrutinise national plans carefully. In a logical world of strengthened governance and open rooms, budget support has much to commend it. No more pet projects run by Balkanised donors. Except hybrid democracies are not logical. When big men make high-level decisions, donors are not at the table. Budget processes, from ministry of finance to sector ministry to district, are opaque and unmonitored. The opportunity for high-level corruption is irresistible. No one knows how much aid is siphoned off. Maybe billions. Based on newspapers I read in airport lounges, in 2016/17, $50 million went missing from the Kenya Ministry of Health maternity care budget, unknown millions from the Malawi Agriculture Ministry in the 'Maizegate' scandal, and hundreds of millions from malaria and health insurance budgets in the Rwanda Ministry of Health.

Twenty years ago, the World Bank appraised a project in Nepal to strengthen health management and service delivery in the western region. They offered a $100 million loan to the government. I joined the appraisal team as a 'consultant'. The secretary, additional secretaries and section officers at the Ministry of Health greeted us and I chatted in taxi Nepali. The team leader, Jim, was a friendly Canadian World Bank economist. Jim and I were the same age. He wore an open neck shirt, leather jacket and chewed gum. I wore my best black suit, white shirt and college tie. Jim's ruffled hair hung over his collar. My cropped, prematurely grey hair conferred gravitas. He was an economist. I was a doctor sahib. Jim had a chequebook for $100 million. I had a moneybelt. The Nepali officials treated me with great respect and deference, Jim less so.

Early on, Jim told them the money could not go on recurrent costs like salaries or supplies, only on training and refurbishment of hospitals and health posts. The bonhomie of the civil servants evaporated. Capital construction was outside their purview, decided by Finance Ministry officials. They made their commission from staff appointments and procurement of medicines and equipment. Training courses paid per diems, difficult to scam. Over the next year, we found meetings postponed, reports delayed, proposals ignored and files passed from desk to desk. A visit from the vice-president of the Bank raised delays with the King. An edict went out that the Minister must decide on the loan. A Nepali friend, on secondment to the Ministry, told me what happened when the inner cabal of civil servants got together. None was interested in the project. They hadn't read the project appraisal report written by us. The group laughed and discussed local politics. The section officer mentioned that the World Bank had threatened to remove the offer of a loan. As they rose to leave, the Secretary said OK, go ahead.

My consultancy ended but Nepali mates in the Ministry and World Bank kept me informed. Four years later, the final year of the project, they had disbursed just 6% of the loan. Without commission, nothing had happened. The Bank, used to contracting dams and roads, with obedient sub-contractors who knew how to manage commission payments, decided the health sector lacked 'absorptive capacity'.

One might assume that globalisation, the internet, and the spread of hybrid democracies would, through greater transparency, diminish corruption. The opposite is true. In 2017, the Transparency International Corruption Perceptions Index rose in more countries than it fell. Although India was better than its neighbours, the report states "(for) schools, hospitals, ID documents, police, and utility services – more than half the respondents have had to pay a bribe".[398] Corruption in the north also increased. In Russia after 'shock therapy', free market principles promoted by Harvard economists after the collapse of the Soviet Union, state institutions disintegrated. They were replaced by 'Sistema blat', the use of personal contacts to gain scarce resources, and a 'rhizome state', a horizontal network of oligarch mafias and informal networks. In the United States, removal of banking regulation under the Clinton administration, through the 1999 repeal of the US Glass-Steagall Act, had spectacular global ramifications. The largest financial corruption in the history of humanity erupted within a decade. Tentacles of corruption enveloped financial capitals. The reverberations of the collapse of 2008, the 'greatest Ponzi scheme in history', are with us a decade later.

Corruption in the world's finance houses led to central banks, debt and cheap money propping up the world's economy. The crisis isn't over. Capitulation may come in one of three ways. Most probable is a slow and secular stagnation, leading to widespread deflation (already evident in the eurozone and Japan), accumulation of bad loans and debt, and a final flurry of bank failures which sovereign states are incapable or unwilling to bail out. Or inflation from monetary stimulus will surge, leading to a collapse in bond prices and capital flight into the dollar, destabilising emerging economies. A third possibility is regional conflict that, as happened in the 1930s after the last global financial crash, stimulates inflation through military and infrastructure expenditure.

Somehow we need both top-down and bottom-up solutions to the cancer of corruption. Corruption control comes from raising the benefits of honesty and the risks of dishonesty. A first principle, as the British Raj discovered, is to pay your civil servants well. If salaries are too low, employees will seek unofficial 'rent' as a way to supplement meagre incomes. A second principle is to have maximum transparency in government budgets. Published accounts and press freedom will help to scrutinise subsidies, credits, procurement and extra-budgetary funds managed by politicians. In 1994, New Zealand passed the Fiscal Responsibility Act, which gave a legal framework to transparency in public resources. They realised that self-regulation alone wouldn't be enough. As the economist Willem Buiter observed drily, "self regulation is to regulation as self importance is to importance".

Chile, meanwhile, has set up ChileCompra, a business to business internet procurement site which conducts more than $10 billion of government business each year, open to transparent scrutiny. In 2012, the system processed over $9 billion from two million invoices. International frameworks like the OECD's Anti-Bribery Convention, and the UN Convention against Corruption (UNCAC) set up in 2005 and ratified by almost 140 countries, also play their part. Wealthy countries have double standards though, tough on bribery at home but happy to turn a blind eye when their own companies enter foreign emerging markets.

Cutting unnecessary red tape is another wise policy. The more blocks and obstacles, the greater the opportunity for rent-seeking through bribes. Smart technology and online processing of tax and benefits remove the human scams that fuel corruption. The main reason India's Prime Minister Narendra Modi gave for his demonetisation policy in 2016 was to make business and tax more transparent. Online distribution of benefits and poverty subsidies has improved in India, although demonetisation had severe impacts on the poorest people.

Governments put subsidies on food and energy prices to protect the poorest families. Targeted cash transfers might avoid the opportunities for corruption that subsidies create, through shortages, smuggling and black markets. Global energy subsidies amount to over $2 trillion per year, but they don't favour the poorest. One estimate is that 60% of benefits accrue to the richest 20% of households. Replacing generalised subsidies with more poverty-focused transfers, delivered online to beneficiaries, could cut government spending, corruption and opportunity costs in one fell swoop.

These measures – better civil service pay, online technology, international frameworks, transparency and targeted cash transfers – can restrain corruption. But to change the culture and ethical behaviour of organisations, we start at the bottom. Corruption is an imbalance in individual group ecology where corrupt acts go unimpeded. Whether it's health workers who claim for courses they didn't attend, procurement officers who organise fake higher quotes from business cabals to share profits from over-charging, or treasury officials who leak money from the exchequer, the root causes are no transparency and impunity. And there is no Robin Hood effect, where noble health workers exact informal payments from the rich to subsidise the poor. Afrobarometer surveys in 33 African countries show a Sheriff of Nottingham scenario for the poorest patients, who are more likely to face no medicines, absent doctors, long waiting times and 'unofficial fees'.

Could small group experiments help make societies less corrupt? In theory, sympathy groups are both a cause and a solution. In Ghana, Siapha Kamara, director of the Social Enterprise Development Foundation, forms groups of 11 members per district in the 53 poorest regions of Accra to collect data about government spending. Each group monitors local processes to expose corruption by grassroots government officers. This deserves evaluation at scale. That is my next proposal for an experiment.

Community groups may offer the best route to scrutiny. Sympathy groups, chosen by community members on a rotating fixed-term basis, can converse on local government administration and accounts. The groups meet monthly and cover spending across health, education, agriculture and the like. A study would measure 'financial irregularities', completion of planned local investments, drug supplies, and uptake of government cash transfers by marginalised groups and compare results with districts where there are no groups, just standard reporting and procurement processes.

Experiment 18: Do sympathy groups reduce corruption in the public sector?

Target population	All adults living within an authority catchment population
Intervention	Local monitor and benefit sympathy groups drawn from the community to scrutinise and report on local government administration and accountants. Transport provided by volunteers, a group revolving fund, or local authority. Volunteers would serve a three-year term and come from a wide sample of community members
	Facilitator: trained local volunteer
	Supervision: a person with audit and accounts experience from outside the district
	Action cycle meeting discussion topics: procurement procedures, health care and drug availability, education, transport, agriculture, benefits and social safety nets, community mobilisation resources, disability and long term conditions, how to report back to local communities.
Coverage or 'dose'	Cap groups at 15 and elect for three-year terms by the village or other geopolitical unit.
Comparison	Communities with standard district council procedures for procurement and reporting
Outcomes Primary Secondary	Financial irregularities Completion of planned local investments Uptake of cash transfers
Possible risks	Social exclusion of minority groups Infiltration of sympathy groups by corrupt agents. Threats to community participants

THE CULTURE OF FINANCE AND ECONOMICS

When Queen Elizabeth visited the London School of Economics on November 5th, 2008 she described the credit crunch as 'awful'. She asked the director of research, Professor Luis Garicano, "if these things were so large, how come everyone missed them"? He had no ready answer. If economics is a science, why indeed did it not predict such gargantuan global financial problems? Why did macroeconomists and financiers not spot the tipping points from their obsessional analyses of global data? "No science in the world is more elevated, more necessary and more useful than economics," said natural scientist Carl Linnaeus. Yet it failed miserably.

The blinkered culture of academic economics and of financial houses lay at the heart of the crisis. At first sight, world economic instability appears the wickedest of wicked problems. Over-financialisation and the globalisation of capital have created multinational corporations larger than major sovereign states. Companies like Apple (which is larger than the Danish economy), Google, Starbucks, Amazon, and Shell are economic entities almost beyond reach of national laws and taxation regimes. Governments seem powerless to regulate. CEOs demand and receive salaries often 200-300 times the size of their poorest paid workers. Tax evasion is the new normal. The reach of markets has spread from land and commodities to education, health and social relations. Politicians and democratic institutions are being pushed aside. The apogee is now reached in the the corporatisation of American governance, where President Trump chose for his cabinet executives from Goldman Sachs, Exxon, Koch Industries, Amway, hedge funds, corporate raiders and oil-funded climate denial lobbyists. Worse, global and corporate economic giants ignore threats to the local by underestimating the impact of globalisation on economic inequality, social capital and cultural identity. Big banks and multinational monopolies undervalue how small groups make economies more resilient and businesses more sustainable.

Before considering what role experiments with sympathy groups might play in this mess, we should reflect on the cultural problems endemic within economics and finance. In fact, not all economists misread the 2008 global crunch. Ann Pettifor, an economic adviser and co-founder of the Jubilee 2000 campaign, which cut billions of pounds in debt repayments from emerging economies, had argued since 2003 that low savings and rising public and private debt in the US and Europe would lead to a crash.[399] And in 2005, at a Jackson Hole meeting of the world's central bankers and treasury secretaries, IMF chief economist Professor Raghuram Rajan, later Chair of the Federal Reserve Bank of India, presented a perceptive paper showing the dangers of increasing credit risk in global finance.[400] He was publicly ridiculed by Larry Summers and colleagues from the US Treasury. His own organisation's IMF Global Financial Stability Report comically wrote in April 2006, a year before the seismic events:

"There is a growing recognition that the dispersion of credit risk by banks to a broader and more diverse group of investors, rather than warehousing such risk on their balance sheet, has helped make the banking and overall financial system more resilient. The improved resilience may be seen in fewer bank failures and more consistent credit provision. Consequently the commercial banks may be less vulnerable today to credit or economic shocks."

Yet the origins of the global financial crash lay a decade earlier. In the late 1990s, a group of economists and financiers pressured President Clinton to repeal financial regulation laws that restricted bank investment practices. Robert Rubin, the US Treasury Secretary and a former CEO of Goldman Sachs, his deputy Larry Summers from Harvard, the Federal Reserve Chairman Alan Greenspan, a devotee of Ayn Rand, and academics like Glenn Hubbard of Columbia and Martin Feldstein of Harvard, argued strongly the case for deregulation. For 60 years, the Glass-Steagall Act of 1933, introduced after the 1929 Wall Street collapse, severely restricted what banks could do with investment, insurance and commercial activities. Savings banks could not gamble with customers' money. If investment banks did so, they should not expect to be bailed out. The Act brought great financial stability, but was hated by free market thinkers.

In 1999 Rubin and Summers engineered the Gramm-Leach-Bliley Act, which loosened these regulations. Consequences were immediate but took nine years to reach their grisly denouement. Deregulation led to a whole raft of dangerous economic activities: development of securitisation and credit derivatives; expansion of 'leverage' by banks which took greater risks to make money; dangerous credit default swaps as insurance against collateralised debt obligation (CDO) losses; speculation in credit default swaps by traders who did not own the CDOs, thereby multiplying risk; enormous bonuses and fortunes for bankers, middle ranking traders, who gambled the safety of their company for personal gain; blind-eye regulation by rating agencies paid by banks to give favourable credit ratings; and widespread conflicts of interests among economists who did not declare earnings from the financial sector when defending securitisation. After the crash, Ben Bernanke, Federal Reserve Chairman, and Tim Geithner, US Treasury Secretary, insisted that US taxpayers pay out 100% of the losses sustained in AIG by investment banks like Goldman Sachs (which caused the problem in the first place) without any haircut.[401] This was moral hazard at its worst, the privatisation of profit, with banks 'too big to fail' guaranteed bailout by taxpayers.

Eight years on we see only marginal changes in the system. President Obama appointed people who caused the crisis, bank regulation is light, and larger and fewer banks than before the crisis are still 'too big to fail'. And risk has returned, with large trading bonuses and a bubble in stocks caused by central bank largesse through 'quantitative easing'. Working people face prolonged recession and austerity economics, with severe effects on unemployment and health.

When Thomas Carlyle described economics as "the dismal science" in his racist 1849 paper Occasional Discourse on the Negro Question (which argued for the reintroduction of slavery), he meant that economics did not produce "life-enhancing knowledge". It was dismal in the sense of "find[ing] the secret of this Universe in 'supply and demand', and reducing the duty of human governors to that of letting men alone". Linnaeus, by contrast, recognised that economics is profoundly important to our lives, our health and happiness. But modern economics remains a dismal science in a different way — its practice offends the principles and culture of contemporary scientific methods. Science and medicine have fought bitter battles about the meaning of evidence, and the importance of hypothesis, falsifiability and method. Many economists prefer not to accept the criticism. Theirs is not an experimental science, they say. Yet every day they draw causal inference from associations for which scientists would be castigated.

Modern science is also about teamwork, peer review, the critical role of impartiality and declaration of conflicts of interest by authors. Science has a primary need for experiment, repetition and systematic, dispassionate review of data. The average number of authors on scientific papers increased from 3.18 to 4.83 over the past 20 years as collaboration and cross-disciplinary teams came together. On major clinical trials and international physics experiments, hundreds of authors collaborate. Economics is different. Many economists are leopards, working alone or with a single partner. Doctoral students in economics publish alone, without supervisors, expected to do their own thing. The number of articles published in the top five economic journals fell from 400 per year in the 1970s to 300 in the past few years. Acceptance rates have fallen from 15% to 6% (Card et al, 2012). Economic papers are three times longer than in the 1970s and citation counts higher for longer papers. The culture of collaboration in economics has a long way to go. Average authors per paper in 2012 was only 2.3. A recent review reported a lack of credibility in most empirical economic research. A gold standard is that papers report findings only when they have a statistical 'power' of greater than 80%. John Ioannidis and colleagues reviewed 6700 economic studies and found a median statistical power of just 18%.[402] When they examined the studies that did reach the gold standard, they found that nearly 80% of findings were 'exaggerated', one third inflated fourfold or more.

What about peer review? In economics the unreviewed working paper and flamboyant newspaper commentary is more prevalent than peer-reviewed publication. Lack of peer review can have devastating consequences. In 2010, two Harvard economists, Kenneth Rogoff and Carmen Reinhart published a widely cited paper which stated: "Above

90% [debt to GDP ratio], median [economic] growth rates fall by 1%, and average growth falls considerably more." Alongside their best-selling book This Time Is Different, their findings drew from a country database about about debt and growth from across the world. The paper, published by the National Bureau of Economic Research, was not peer reviewed. (Interestingly, the President of the NBER for 30 years was Martin Feldstein, the Harvard professor who designed deregulation policies for Ronald Reagan's administration after administration.) The consequences were far-reaching. Worldwide, politicians and commentators who espoused strict austerity and debt reduction, in the face of Keynesian opposition, quoted Rogoff and Reinhart as their justification for immediate and severe fiscal retrenchment.

In 2013, a PhD student at Massachusetts Amherst College, as part of an exercise, unearthed a crucial spreadsheet error which invalidated the Harvard professors' main conclusion.[403] To their credit, Rogoff and Reinhart immediately acknowledged the error. A good economist peer reviewer would have spotted it. Suddenly their data errors meant that austerity programmes actually had little academic credibility. Ridicule and opprobrium against Rogoff and Reinhart in the world's media followed, unfairly because their book gave many useful insights into debt and growth. Samuel Brittan of the Financial Times reminded us of Aristotle's dictum that each subject has its own degree of precision. It's a mistake to look for a similar degree in all of them. "The general moral is that economic analysis and policy would benefit from a less credulous accept-ance of each purported research finding. It would pay to wait until a number of different studies employing different techniques point in the same direction and have survived professional criticism."[404] Peer review is not perfect but adds value. My name appears on over 295 peer-reviewed papers. Reviewers didn't always show sympathy and often we disagreed with their comments. But every peer review improved our paper or grant proposal in a small way. On occasions review was pivotal, stimulating new data analysis and inquiry.

In academic economics, conflicts of interest are rife. In 2017, a league table of economists constructed by IDEAS, a research group within the

Federal Reserve Bank of St Louis, from 31 ranked indicators, listed Professor Andrei Shleifer of Harvard University as the top economist in the world.[405] His specialist subject is financial economics, behavioural finance and the economics of transition. He's a close friend and protégé of Larry Summers, former President of Harvard University, and a professor of economics. Shleifer's career has been at Harvard and MIT since he moved from Russia as a teenager. In 1994, with two fellow academics, Shleifer founded an investment company called LV Asset Management, which expanded to manage more than $50 billion. In the early 1990s, the US government contracted Harvard University Institute for International Development (HIID) to advise on privatisation in Russia as part of Mikhail Gorbachev's *perestroika*. Shleifer had links with a small group of Russian insiders linked to Anatoly Chubais, an aide to Boris Yeltsin. Under the patronage of Larry Summers, who called the Chubais Clan a "dream team", Shleifer as director of HIID received $40 million for his work setting up a new Russian stock market of privatised companies.[406]

Soon the deals attracted criticism. Shleifer was accused of corruption and insider dealing.[407] Summers, then deputy Secretary at the US Treasury, was accused of helping Harvard and Shleifer win "non-competitive government awards". Stanford University had been offered the contract first, which Chubais had declined because he had a "group of people he was working with". The US General Accountability Office investigated and described the arrangement as "highly unusual". The US government sued Shleifer and Harvard University. In an out-of-court settlement, Harvard, now under Summers' presidency, paid the government $27.5 million. Shleifer himself paid $2 million in damages but retained his academic position. Other Harvard professors accused Summers of nepotism. The case demonstrated an uncomfortable alliance between academia, power and the finance industry.

The problem is still with us. Many academic economists supplement their income from lucrative consultancies to companies and governments. Scientists do the same but on a much smaller scale. Only in the past five years has the American Economic Association adopted conflict of interest rules. Widespread criticism that funding can affect interpretation of evidence, fully understood in other disciplines, pressured them to insist on disclosure of financial information by authors publishing in top economic journals. But working paper disclosures remain voluntary. One academic called for an 'economists' oath' to stop them advising corrupt or dictatorial regimes, and to stand up for the poor. Another complained that economists behave like lawyers, taking a particular view regardless of the evidence.

Documentary maker Charles Ferguson believes that the "convergence of academic economics, Wall Street, and political power" is an extraordinary scandal in American society. Worse, economists maintain a culture of impunity. When they advise politicians with catastrophic consequences, no admission of failure or opprobrium follows. They stay on the A-list. A scientist who retracts a paper is damaged in the eyes of his peers but an economist's mistakes are forgotten quickly. Thirty years ago Jeffrey Sachs, one of Harvard's youngest professors, advised governments in Bolivia, Mongolia and Russia to implement 'shock therapy' through severe austerity programmes.[408] Neoliberal economics held the secret to reanimate dead socialist corpses. Sachs was just 30 at the time with little real world experience. But he carried the lustrous name of Harvard. According to Naomi Klein and others, the consequences of his advice were immediate and lasting.[409] In Russia, an estimated 130 million people fell into poverty, millions of people more lost their jobs or saw their incomes fall.[410] Death rates soared. The political effects remain with us today. Sachs' assumption that fragile Russian institutions would regulate a massive private sector sell-off was a pipe dream. In the chaos, a small group of young oligarchs bought national assets at knockdown prices. KGB officers under Vladimir Putin wrested control from President Boris Yeltsin and his allies. Sachs moved on.

Sachs has defended his role in advising governments at this time.[411] But his belief in shock therapy ended. To his credit, he is now a powerful advocate for development investment in poor countries. But, in both roles, his image, celebrity and media-savviness influenced political decision-making far more than any strong, considered evidence.

In 2018 the resignation of Paul Romer, chief economist at the World Bank, revealed deep concerns about the culture within our most important development agency and lender. Romer accused his Bank colleagues of 'fabricating data', of 'shameless self-promotion' and of using an 'Internal Justice Bureau' that failed to police the Bank's reports for validity. In an email he wrote: "There is no way to bootstrap this field back to a state in which people put effort into maintaining a reputation as someone who is a source of reliable information. Once no one cares about reputation, why should anyone invest in reputation? As a general matter, I'm not sure about how to escape from this kind of equilibrium."[412]

The culture within banks and financial houses is worse. Manipulation of LIBOR and foreign exchange rates, mis-selling of credit derivatives and payment protection insurance, and a succession of corruption scandals have reduced bankers to pariah status. Since the global financial crash, various reviews, select committees, banking standards boards and financial regulation authorities have talked about 'Senior Managers Regimes', making corruption a criminal offence of 'reckless misconduct', and 'certification schemes', where banks review their own staff annually for fitness and propriety. But the culture is little changed. We need a new ecology of banking and finance in which long-term stability takes priority over the quick buck. Bankers must regain professionalism and ethics, where peer pressure winnows out the rogues. Their profession had, and should have, great social value.

A changed economic and financial ecology would promote inclusive growth and evidence-informed policies. Economic and financial small groups might work. Bill Clinton set up a broad-based group of diverse economists and financial leaders to advise him in his first term as President. The UK government has collective Cabinet responsibility, which ties government ministers into group decision-making. Independent monetary policy committees, representatives of workers' groups sitting on company boards, and co-operative-inspired companies like John Lewis bring the energy and benefits of sympathy groups.

The eminent ecologist and physicist Lord Robert May, former President of the UK Royal Society, argues that we should learn lessons from ecosystems and infectious diseases to address instabilities in the financial system. "Implicit assumptions about the ways markets work are fairy tales," he says. He analyses the HIV pandemic to show that 'super-spreaders', highly promiscuous individuals, increased manyfold the spread of infections. He sees those banks 'too large to fail' as 'super spreaders' within overly interconnected markets. Interconnection is highly dangerous for the stability of the global banking system. Ecology depends upon diversity and protected sub-systems for stability. If things get too complex within an interconnected ecology, crashes in animal populations can threaten species survival.

The 2017 UK Inclusive Growth Commission Report, chaired by Stephanie Flanders of JP Morgan, argues that "the system needs to be rewired − structurally and culturally − to support inclusive growth 'on the ground'," which involves "data analysis, public engagement, democratic processes and deliberations with employers, investors, public service professionals and civic institutions".[413] The report is a clarion call for sympathy groups and studies to assess their impact. "The individuals need to know each other, trust each other and be able to work together on an equal basis to find common objectives." The findings echo those of the 1993 Brundtland Commission report Our Common Future, which emphasised that economic growth must be accompanied by social equity and ecological health.

Plenty of stories offer hope. In 1985, in Pittsburgh, a steel city in industrial decline, poor and polluted, a sympathy group got together. Mayor Richard Caliguiri, the presidents of Carnegie Mellon University and the University of Pittsburgh, and the Allegheny County commissioners drew up a Strategy 21 report for a future fit for the twenty-first century. They consulted communities and large and small industries. They brought together advanced technology, modern communications and marketing, university research and development, and natural resources of the region. The plan reached out to the structurally unemployed, to women and ethnic minorities, and emphasised quality of life in the city as a way to attract tourism and immigration. Much of the plan came to fruition.

More recently, the Chicago Arts and Industry Commons used creative ways to link isolated run-down assets. Schools, dilapidated theatres and warehouses can become a thriving community that creates jobs and a healthy environment for people from every background. They've developed a cultural reinvestment model to ensure sustainability. First they renovated an old historic building due for demolition and created an arts centre. The revitalised cultural centre is an engine for non-profit ventures such as education, training, job creation and incubation, and also for commercial ventures in retail, housing, and manufacturing. The virtuous circle is completed by attracting investment to create assets within the neighbourhood. This approach has gone viral, using refurbishment of assets as a catalyst for community education, resources, wellness and mobility.

In London, on a smaller scale, the participatory city movement is typified by the West Norwood community in a poor district, where 1000 people were encouraged to create their own start-ups with orchards, gardens, craft groups and communal kitchens. Sustainability, especially at a time of council budget cuts, is uncertain but a detailed evaluation report, Designed to Scale, suggests many have taken root. The scheme provides a blueprint for other deprived areas to harness community participation into a driving force for regeneration.

So how might sympathy groups change the culture of finance? In the UK, an independent organisation set up by large banks, led by Sir Richard Lambert, former editor of the Financial Times, trains bankers in how to interact with customers and comply with regulatory standards. Groups could help make it happen.[414] Loss of altruism and rampant individualism caused the crash. Tackling culture change at its roots is my choice for the next experiment. If, as is likely, deregulation of banking risks another major crisis, we must design an experiment to test whether bankers in sympathy groups might diminish risky behaviour. Moral hazard results from bankers feeling insured that they'll be bailed out. In large financial houses, we could randomly choose groups of managers and traders to join sympathy groups and converse on subjects such as long-term and short-term company objectives, self-regulation, compliance and incentives, relations with customers, employees and management, trust and respect, productivity, concepts of quality and innovation, dispute resolution and so on. Outcomes would include subsequent risky behaviour scores or the balance between their long and short-term strategies. Comparison would be made with control groups of managers and traders within the same company but based in different locations to avoid contamination.

Experiment 19: Do sympathy groups of financial industry managers improve the culture and safety of banking and credit?

Population	Senior managers of major financial houses
Intervention	Sympathy groups of senior managers within a major financial house facilitated by a trained member (of similar rank) paid for but independent from the Financial Conduct Authority. The action cycle to focus on the nature and culture of credit and finance, how to balance long-term and short-term objectives, self-regulation, compliance and incentives, relations between customers, employees, management, trust and respect, productivity, concepts of quality and innovation, dispute resolution.
Comparison	Financial houses without this initiative
Outcomes	
Primary	Risk behaviour scores
	Short v. long term investment scores
Secondary	Team respect and productivity
	Quality of interactions with customers
	Compliance with regulatory standards
	Ethical investment

As for the culture of economics, I wouldn't dare to risk opprobrium with an experiment. Economists can do four things to restore confidence. *First*, ensure that every financial and economic article has full disclosure of potential conflicts of interests, using detailed checklists sought by medical journals. *Second*, set up an ethics group in every university to ensure that published economic research is peer-reviewed, independent, and ethical. *Third*, make economics, where possible, an experimental discipline. Many younger economists like Imran Rasul, Abhijit Banerjee and Esther Duflo do rigorous experimental trials. Older economists from both left and right regard experiments with haughty disdain – the principles of science cannot apply to them. Experiments take long-term effort and the collection of primary data in real world locations. Much easier to tweet, blog or write a newspaper commentary. Easier to rehash an opinion of Keynes or from the Austrian or Chicago schools. When I studied psychology as an undergraduate, every debate referred to the bitter battles of the psychoanalytic schools of Sigmund Freud, Alfred Adler, Carl Jung and Melanie Klein, based on dreams, fantasies and breastfeeding. A decade later the subject had moved on, scary mid-European tomes removed by the academic refuse collectors.

Microfinance shows the power of experiment over sentimental opinion. Microfinance for poor women in developing countries earned Muhammad Yunus, the Bangladeshi banker, a Nobel Prize. It would lift millions of women out of poverty, he claimed, and demonstrate the power of the free market at the 'bottom of the pyramid'. The director of the huge Bangladesh Rural Advancement Committee (BRAC), Fazle Hasan Abed, had pioneered microfinance and recognised it worked only with support from community workers and groups. The Nobel committee overlooked Abed for his share in the prize. Bankers it seems have more influential friends. When Yunus's Grameen model was scaled up in India, many women and farmers in Andhra Pradesh committed suicide. Unscrupulous microfinance loan sharks coerced poor families into usurious loan contracts. The state government was forced to take action. In 2010 they suspended the whole sordid enterprise.

In the meantime, scientifically minded economists have finally done randomised experiments to test the media hype of the Grameen approach. They studied microcredit through trials and showed no significant improvements in income, consumption, health and education in India, Morocco, Ethiopia, Bosnia-Herzegovina and Mexico. A recent systematic review on women's control of household spending showed that because of a "lack of evidence for an effect of microcredit on women's control over household resources it is ... very unlikely that, overall, microcredit has a meaningful and substantial impact on empowerment processes".[415]

By contrast, Imran Rasul and his team of experimental economists at UCL studied the BRAC graduation model of entrepreneurship. They examined the impact of combined "business asset transfers coupled with complementary and intensive training" in 1409 communities in 40 regions in rural Bangladesh over a four-year period. Their large scale randomised evaluation showed the intervention transformed the lives of some of the world's poorest people with a 38% improvement in income.[416] The same BRAC approach has had even more empowering effects among adolescents in Uganda.[417] Maybe the Nobel Prize committee might reconsider their exclusion of BRAC from its earlier award.

And *fourth*, economists should revisit the courses they provide for undergraduate and postgraduate students. Do their curricula really address Queen Elizabeth's question in 2008, that if economic problems were so large why did everyone miss them? A start might be made by organising some sympathy groups of economics students to appraise their own education.

GOVERNMENT GRIDLOCK AND PATRONISING KINDNESS

Thirty years ago, arterial roads in Asian cities were less thrombosed than today. Most people cycled or took rickshaws. Many families walked to get around. Buses, it is true, belched black, toxic fumes from flailing engines, and the middle classes, in their saris and ties, were ferried by old rust-bucket taxis. But most people took exercise, were fitter, and commuted on time. Today roads are choked with sleek cars, SUVs and colourless pollution. Vehicles have cleaner engines and air-conditioning, their owners hunched over iPads wired to music and vamping emails.

Their drivers stare into the middle distance, alone with their thoughts. But the traffic barely moves. Recently I sat with the Begum in a cool Mitsubishi in Dhaka, travelling eight kilometres from Mirpur to BIRDEM Hospital, a journey that took two and three quarter hours. Dhaka is often gridlocked during commuter hours, as are Delhi, Mumbai, Kathmandu, Bangkok, Jakarta, Beijing and other megalopolises. Millions of safer, cleaner, greener cars stop and start, stuck in stagnant, steamy queues. In cold weather, air pollution soars to 20 times the WHO safety limit. It's a wicked problem.

Traffic gridlock is a metaphor for increasing complexity and paralysis in government. Politicians used to collect taxes, protect the state, build roads, create jobs and provide schools and hospitals. Now they're smothered by a thicket of cross-border complexity, international trade regulations, volatility in capital and credit, the needs and threats of migration, and the challenge of climate change. Every attempt to tackle a problem creates new ones. Politicians and civil servants become depressed through 'learned helplessness' and gridlock.

What creates government gridlock and what can be done? One contributing factor is that powerful people become indifferent. In many countries, elite groups are inured, almost blind, to the poor. The eminent intellectual Noam Chomsky wrote about a phenomenon well known to anyone who travels to India for the first time. "What is really striking to me about India, much more than most other countries I have been to, is the indifference of privileged sectors to the misery of others.[418] You walk through Delhi and cannot miss it, but people just don't seem to see it. Everyone is talking about 'Shining India' and yet people are starving." While driving through the streets he asked the novelist Arundhati Roy why she wasn't looking out of the car. "If you live in India," she said, "you just can't look outside the window. Because if you do, you'd rather commit suicide. It's too horrible. So you just don't look."

A second component of gridlock is the policy fragmentation from ever-increasing initiatives. Civil society and international agencies dream up endless lists of goals, targets, and indicators of accountability. Movements, commissions, panels and working groups spew out action plans, inventing acronyms that confuse even the in-crowd. Task sheets land on the desks of underpaid, bemused bureaucrats.

Another ingredient in gridlock stew is that governance is complex and not helped by well-meaning outsiders or entrepreneurs who over-simplify. A plethora of development reports prescribe innovations of modern science for the survival and health of poor people. Donors, with the best of intentions, provide poor people with vaccines, supplements, drugs, health workers and cash transfers in a blitz of coverage and 'service delivery'. If only we could reach 90% coverage of 150 proven interventions everything would be better.

But charity is not a substitute for justice. Writer Aldous Huxley got it right. "In a poor street, misfortune can't be hidden. Life's too public. People have their neighbourly feeling kept in constant training. But the rich never have a chance of being neighbourly to their equals. The best they can do is to feel mawkish about the sufferings of their inferiors, which they can never begin to understand, and to be patronisingly kind."[419] Charity does not address the slow and painstaking work to build national institutions, for justice, education, public sector regulation and for health and social care.

Donors and politicians find it difficult to absorb a neighbourly approach. Too nebulous, they say. They prefer to distribute charity and to professionalise power. Anything to do with health is targeted through health professionals rather than local politics or community groups. As good entrepreneurs they stay optimistic: 'rational optimists' like Matt Ridley, 'impatient optimists' like Bill Gates, and former World Bank wonks like William Easterly see an array of solutions from the private sector. Everything gets better, democracy multiplies, economic growth abounds and constant innovation brings technology to everyone.

Others see this as hubris. The historian Mark Mazower excoriates billionaires and wealthy celebrities who "apply business methods to social problems, . . . exaggerate what technology can do, ignore the complexities of social and institutional constraints, often waste sums that would have been spent better more carefully, and wreak havoc with the existing fabric of society in places they know very little about."[420] The new world order is, he believes, one of dangerously weakened state institutions. The global financial crisis was a reminder of fragility and vulnerability in banking and credit. Institutions were leveraged with unimaginable debt, run by bankers who had lost any moral purpose or professional integrity. Inequality rises as welfare nets are slashed. Pseudo-democracies, based on rigged elections, or mafia states create disaffected electorates that find less and less accountability in politics.

The writer Evgeny Morozov is more brutal. "That solving any of their favourite global problems would require political solutions – if only to ensure that nobody's rights and interests are violated or overlooked in the process – is not something that the TED elite, with its aversion to conventional instruments of power and its inebriated can-do attitude, likes to hear . . . TED's techno-humanitarians [are another] brigade of what the Nigerian-American writer Teju Cole has dubbed 'The White Savior Industrial Complex'."[421]

In the wealthy west, gridlock accompanies inequality, the eroded working and middle class incomes (average hourly income of production and non-supervisory employees in the US is today what it was in 1970), and what sociologist Saskia Sassen sees as a movement from "exclusion to expulsion".[422] In the USA and UK, the rise of Donald Trump and Nigel Farage on the right, and Bernie Sanders and Jeremy Corbyn on the left, reflects the despair of white and blue collar workers who feel left out. The French philosopher Alain Badiou[423] believes we live under a planetary oligarchy, not unlike the *ancien régime*, where 10% of the population control 86% of the resources, 40% of the world control the remainder as employees and consumers, but almost half the world's population have nothing to contribute to global capitalism. The poor of Asia and Africa are outside global markets. They present a threat to the affluent through migration and terrorism. In many countries, governments pay lip service to education and health for the forgotten, and ignore the retail corruption they face to gain any state benefit.

In poorer countries, government gridlock is also about political rivalry.

In Nepal, a bitter civil war consumed the country for a decade. Since 2007, when the peace agreement led to the monarchy being abolished and a constituent assembly being formed, made up of all major parties including the Maoist Communists, one expected the country to proceed to local government elections. Yet it took 10 years for local elections to be held. Essentially no party wanted another to claim the success for effective constitutional change.

How can we unlock gridlock in government? We can loosen bureaucracy at the top, release voice and energy from below, adopt a behavioural economics strategy to create 'nudges' within the system, or try to improve accountability, especially for spending, through participatory budgeting. Take the first. The assumption that civil service bureaucracy cannot be reformed is false. A recent study of management by bureaucrats and public service delivery in the Nigerian Civil Service by Imran Rasul and Daniel Rogger looked at 4700 projects under civil service control and made assessments of each project's completion rate and delivered quality. When they related performance with management style, they found that autonomy of civil service teams was strongly associated with success, whereas performance-based incentives, or bureaucrats operating under multiple bosses, was strongly associated with project failure.[424] Their findings fit with Deming's emphasis on teamwork and his aversion to individual incentives. They conclude that relatively minor changes in how civil servants are managed could have large gains for public service delivery. They imply that group approaches might also reduce crony capitalism and corruption.

A second strategy to release voices and energy from below is to remove complacency. In the process this will create freedoms. Adam Habib, the South African political scientist, pinpoints the real issue as one of accountability. If there is no accountability of the elites or major corporations, how are people going to feel empowered to make decisions about their lives? For Habib, the fundamental problem of development is how to give power to poor people. Without dismissing the complexities of macroeconomics in an era of secular stagnation, and the terrible confusion of governance and politics after the global financial crisis, a focus on the local and community will bring popularity, comfort and benefit.

Another way, much loved by economists, is to nudge the system and its users. Richard Thaler and Cass Sunstein's best-selling book Nudge (curiously Thaler alone won the 2017 Nobel economics prize) describes ways to change consumer behaviour, with simple ideas taken up by many companies and governments. For example, restaurants learn to place over-priced decoy meal starters to nudge consumers to buy a lower cost pre-main course. Supermarkets place green arrows to shepherd people into the 'healthier' fruit and vegetable sections. Governments and companies use behavioural methods to nudge increases in organ donation rates. Simpler ways are used to nudge employees to make their tax and pension payments automatic rather than by choice. Automation increased company pension payments from 65% to 90%. But nudges may also backfire.[425] Newer studies suggest nudges may be seen as condescending by consumers. They may wear off over time. Some nudges manipulate, creating an imbalance between marketer and consumer.

In the long term, treating customers as equals and giving them the power to make their own choices is more sustainable. Behavioural interventions aim to change consumption whereas social interventions seek to increase power and voice. An excellent example is participatory budgeting.[426] From its origins in Brazilian cities four decades ago, citizens discuss and decide how to spend a budget. In Paris in 2014, Mayor Anne Hidalgo sought a more collaborative style and introduced participatory budgeting. The principle is that local communities understand best their priorities. In the first year, participatory meetings collated many local proposals and put 15 to a referendum vote. In the second year, a website harnessed 5,000 new ideas and 58,000 citizens voted. A year later three times that number voted to decide how to spend over 100 million euros. It sounds easy but required many municipal facilitators. One cannot rely on websites and online voting. Government must help groups to address problems beyond cycle lanes and sports centres, to converse about social exclusion and poverty. But the explosion in Parisian participation and voting shows people crave engagement in sympathy group decision-making. Over time they become more ambitious and creative.

This leaves us with the dilemma of global governance. How can we make co-operative global decisions for all in the face of rising nationalism? We live in a multipolar world. Large states like India, China and Brazil want their voices heard on wicked problems like climate change and nuclear proliferation. There are no simple solutions. United Nations institutions are seen as sclerotic and fragmented, in part because of underfunding and a scornful media. But global governance is a challenge we cannot duck. Mark Mazower is sceptical. In Governing the World, the historian postulates that global governance is an illusion. He believes the age-old desire for a stable global world order draws upon a naive and oft-repeated historical delusion of a global force for good. "The fundamental nineteenth century insight that effective internationalism rests on effective nationalism remains pertinent. Voters around the world still see their primary allegiance to their national state rather than any larger polity." He doubts that everything is getting better, nor that a multipolar world can solve wicked problems. We face financial crises, rising inequality and welfare nets slashed, expansion of black markets, smuggling, and organised crime. Drug violence and endemic rent-seeking blight the lives of millions. Rigged elections and corruption abound, with disaffected electorates unable to hold leaders to account, and no co-ordinated response to climate change. Major conflict is an ever-present threat. Philosopher Jürgen Habermas worries about political and economic decisions "negotiated under asymmetrical relations of power".[427] In Brexit and Trump's America First we see a rebellion against supranational decisions made with little perceived accountability.

Despite the pessimism, we could test alternative strategies to build cross-state sympathy. The United Nations, global and regional fora do exist for large scale meetings and formal interactions. But no evaluation of governance sympathy groups has been done. Maybe global governance is not a pipe dream. Could circles of acquaintanceship of politicians be stimulated to render governance more effective? Politicians are often paralysed by the stress of party loyalties to interest groups and lobbyists. Modern environmental and economic challenges seem intractable. They feel impotent to penetrate cross-boundary problems and to respond to 24-hour media scrutiny, the endless false dichotomies of adversarial politics. Yet most political opponents agree on far more than they dispute. Might sympathy groups of politicians, in confidential arenas, away from the spotlight, find common cause, across political divides? Perhaps redressing gender imbalances is sufficient? Evidence suggests women work better than men in circles and groups, and negotiate and compromise more easily than testosterone-fuelled alpha males, who prefer a hierarchy and pecking order. But maybe experiments can assess different ways to achieve political compromise and decision-making.

My next experiment to tackle gridlock is to use sympathy groups in the promotion and adoption of a specific environmental challenge, enactment of a municipal carbon tax in European cities. Carbon taxes are not easy to implement or sustain. Recently, Republican grandees in the USA, James Baker, Paul Volcker and Hank Paulson, put forward the idea of a carbon tax, where the tax collected was distributed directly to citizens whose carbon usage was less. Citizens, they reasoned as good US Republicans, are more likely to value a carbon tax where they see immediate personal benefit than where taxes collected enter government coffers. So far, their idea has fallen on deaf political ears, even though large oil companies will accept a tax applied across the board.

My experiment could test whether sympathy groups of 'vested interests' and 'honest brokers' e.g. municipal politicians from all parties, sherpas, business leaders, civil rights and union leaders, lawyers, environmental scientists, economists and consumers would thrash out ways to speed up adoption of a carbon tax. Cities interested in exploring the introduction of the tax could be randomised to the sympathy groups or to usual political processes. If the sympathy process works better, control cities could adopt it immediately.

Experiment 20: Do sympathy groups of vested interests increase the speed of adoption of a carbon tax in cities?

Population	Municipal authorities in Europe. Representatives of 'vested interests' and 'honest brokers' e.g. municipal politicians, sherpas, business leaders, civil rights and union leaders, lawyers, environmental scientists and economists.
Intervention	The groups have a community action cycle structure of meetings to discuss whether a successful carbon tax system in the municipality can be successfully introduced. The group will plan strategies and benefits.
	Facilitator: local trained negotiator/facilitator
	Action cycle meeting discussion topics: carbon pollution, impacts of climate change, the pros and cons of a carbon tax, how the pros might exceed the cons, the electoral challenge of a carbon tax, ideas for implementation, compensation for the losers in the short term, how to assess the impact.
Coverage or 'dose'	Groups capped at 15-20 representatives. Several groups convened and their findings shared at a municipal event after a series of meetings.
Comparison	Municipalities across Europe without this sympathy group approach
Outcomes	
Primary	Introduction of a municipal carbon tax
	Popularity among voters
Secondary	Benefits to poorer segments of the population
Cost and value	Monitor the costs of incentives for volunteers, the cost of group meeting facility hire or use, the cost of user travel or provider transport, and the cost of materials. Also the opportunity costs of participants.
Possible risks	Economic slowdown
	Sectoral slowdown e.g. tourism

A second experiment is to repeat the analytic work of Rogger and Rasul's study of civil servant performance in Nigeria in the form of a multi-country trial. We need a large experiment, funded by a major development bank, in which civil servants are randomised to participatory learning and action groups or not.

Experiment 21: Do civil servant sympathy groups improve the perform-ance of government bureaucracy?

Population	Civil servants in, for example, the district education sector
Intervention	The groups have a community action cycle structure of meetings to discuss how their work can be organised better, delivered with better results, and engage their beneficiaries. The groups will plan strategies and benefits.
	Facilitator: local trained negotiator/facilitator
	Action cycle meeting discussion topics (using the example of ministry of education): educational objectives, education workforce, procurement of supplies, school curricula, setting and achieving education targets, children with special needs, motivation and support for teachers, examination efficiency, prevention of cheating, harassment and corruption within schools, participation of parents and teacher-pupil-parent contracts, how to assess the impact.
Comparison	Civil servants in districts or regions where this initiative is not yet started.
Outcomes	
Primary	School attendance
Secondary	Exam performance
	Pupil and parent satisfaction
	Quality of education administration and effectiveness of teacher recruitment
Costs and value	Monitor the costs of incentives for civil servantss, the cost of group meetings, the cost of travel or provider transport, and the cost of materials. The opportunity costs of participants could be significant.
Risks	Positive effects are diluted by civil servant networks causing contamination across intervention and control areas.
	Politicians are not supportive

My final experiment on the gridlock theme is to assess whether a more creative approach to international summits would generate more productive outcomes. Just speaking the same language doesn't mean that international viewpoints and cultures are similar. French historian Alexis de Tocqueville found it remarkable that two nations, America and England, "so recently sprung from the same stock, should be so opposite to one another in their manner of feeling and conversing". He observed that Americans were "impatient of the smallest censure, and insatiable of praise". An Englishman "calmly enjoys the real or imaginary advantages which, in his opinion, his country possesses . . . the censure of foreigners does not affect him and their praise hardly flatters him".

Multiply these cultural misunderstandings tenfold and you have the challenge of global governance at G7, G8, G20, BRICS, ASEAN, Francophonie, Non-Aligned and Regional two-day summits. Leaders are human with their own prejudices, anxieties, personality types and political objectives. In a well-facilitated group, away from the cameras and microphones, with guaranteed privacy and confidentiality, would blockages to reciprocal solutions dissolve as trust and friendship develop?

One way to test this approach is through a quasi-experimental approach, or what psychologist Donald Campbell called a 'queasy' approach. A randomised trial would be difficult but not a multiple time series design. We can analyse perceived quality and outcomes from meetings of global and regional summits over the past three years. We might then choose one or two of the summits, assuming they agree to have a preliminary meeting (before the summit) for two days at which leaders agree to attend a confidential, off the record, preliminary meeting. A distinguished and acceptable negotiator, like Kofi Annan or Stephen Sackur of HARDtalk, will facilitate to build trust and participation. A before-and-after analysis of the global or regional summit(s) will compare outcomes with those where a preliminary social trust meeting was not conducted.

Experiment 22: Do sympathy groups of high level and national leaders improve efforts to cut gridlock in solving global intractable problems?

Population	Leaders and senior sherpas at regional international summits
Intervention	Two-day facilitated and confidential meetings for leaders to build social trust prior to the formal meeting.
Comparison	Before-and-after analysis of outcomes compared with the same from summits not preceded by the social trust intervention.
Outcomes **Primary** **Secondary** **Hypothesis of effect size**	 A score of positive decisions and outputs Rating by senior leaders for success of the summit Rating by sherpas for success of the summit A 25% improvement in summit performance using a time series analysis
Costs and value	Monitor the costs of extended summit and subsistence costs of leadership entourage, the cost of group meeting and high level facilitation, the cost of travel or provider transport, and the cost of materials. The opportunity costs of participants.
Risks	Leaders won't agree to take part Psychopathology in national leaders resists facilitation Negative outcomes will cause geopolitical tension

Part 5

Sympathy Groups Into Policy

The Hearts of Citizens

THE FIVE PROPOSITIONS

Sympathy groups are ubiquitous, powerful and taken for granted. In dictatorships or revolutions their power is harnessed for the purposes of oppression or rebellion. In stable democracies of varied political hue, their power infuses the dark matter of informal civil society, but is untapped by government. Community groups are seen as old-fashioned, part of the social furniture. Some writers are sceptical about the 'self-help myth'. Erica Kohl-Arenas believes too much philanthropy in the USA seeks individual and community solutions to problems which, fundamentally, are structural and require systemic political change to address poverty, mental ill-health and imprisonment.[428] Too often funders avoid solutions that require policy change. I share her concerns about pro-poor policy being avoided, but with the proviso that community groups can have positive benefits even within a negative political environment. Further, investing in an ecology for local action is a pro-poor policy. But politicians will require evidence and persuasion to inform their decisions about investment and legislation at the social edge.

Politicians face complex decisions about wicked problems. Their citizens are wealthier but over-consume; they have greater choice but a sense of anomie; they are more educated but less grateful; they live longer but are lonely and chronically ill as they age. Politicians want to ingratiate themselves with their electorate and cut taxes. But they face the reality of rising bills for social and health care, education and sustainable energy. We should never forget, though, the power of evidence and data. Governments and commentators may choose to denigrate the tyranny and errors of experts.[429] But in the face of mounting evidence, politicians have the knack of bending their ideology to fit new reality. Who would have thought, 15 years ago, that British restaurants and pubs, in light of passive smoking evidence, would be forced to ban smoking from the premises. And within a decade most climate sceptics have changed their tune from denial to an emphasis on the mild consequences of evident global warming. "Without data you're just another person with an opinion," said Deming. With it, you have a powerful advantage.

Further, policymakers are still picking their way through the economic rubble from the aftershocks of the 2008 financial earthquake. Stagnation of the global economy, despite massive injections of money by the world's central banks, has led to deflation, falls in median incomes, loss of manufacturing jobs and rising inequality. Popular discontent with globalisation and tax evasion by multinational companies, 'one law for the rich, one for the poor', has brought rising xenophobia, electoral success for protectionist politicians, and a sense that we need a new economic paradigm.

Neither can we assume that liberal democracies are eternal, promised lands at 'the end of history'. In twentieth century Europe, Greece, Italy, Germany, Spain, Portugal, and Vichy France were democracies that disintegrated through violence and fascism. In the Americas, Argentina, Bolivia, Brazil, Chile, Ecuador, Guatemala, Honduras, Panama, Peru, and Uruguay joined "the roster of democratic reversals . . . de-democratisation remains a possibility everywhere in the world."[430] The late Charles Tilly from Columbia University, a founding father of modern sociology and political science, proposed that democracy is threatened by three key processes – rising inequality between classes or ethnic groups, weakening of trust networks, and declining participation in public politics. These processes are linked. Inequalities damage trust. Trust within small groups is essential to democracy but must also be linked to public politics. Integration of risky long-term commitments such as marriage, long-distance trade, joining a union or profession, or embarking on higher education are assisted by links to government agents who meet their long-term commitments. Citizens expect democracies to give them "binding, protected, relatively equal claims on a government's agents, activities, and resources". They become angry when the system fails. In June 2017 for example, the London Grenfell Tower fire, which killed 71 people, revealed the gross inadequacy of government social housing systems. Residents had expected fire safety standards to protect them.

And connections to government are not necessarily direct; they may run through sympathy groups linked to communities, parties, unions, and other trade or professional organisations "that in turn rely on governmental ratification, toleration, support, or protection".

Our sympathy groups sit below the radar of contrasting national political structures, right, centre and left, and must adapt to all three. Only one country in the world places co-operation and consensus as primary in its national constitution. That country, Switzerland, is the most productive economy on the planet, with three times the productivity per person of the UK; and the nation with the highest confidence of its electorate in government, with 77% satisfaction compared with just 46% in the UK, 35% in the US and 25% in Spain.[431] It's worth a detour to consider why.

The Swiss state is a directorial, or consociational, republic, run at the centre by a committee, or cross-party sympathy group, of seven persons. It is not dissimilar to the original 1776 Pennsylvania Constitution, which had a 12-member Supreme Executive Council chaired by a 'first among equals' President. This, in turn, inspired the Directory of the French Revolution in 1795, a five-member committee that appointed a new President every three months, until the coup by Napoleon Bonaparte in 1799. In fact, a good pub quiz question is to ask someone to name any Swiss federal politician. The central committee is so anonymous, and central elections so much less important than for cantons, that many Swiss don't know the name of their President.

Switzerland practises a decentralised division of taxation and powers between the federal level, 26 cantons and 2600 municipalities. The constitution was built from the bottom up. It is a semi-direct consensus democracy in which representative politics interact with direct decision-making by citizenry. Unlike winner-takes-all party elections in the UK or US, the Swiss system has weak party politics, proportional representation, power sharing, and integration of cultural minorities and of conflicting group interests. They make the most important decisions through referenda and local bodies. The subsidiarity principle is absolutely dominant so that the centre only performs tasks that can't be done more effectively at a lower level. They cannot take on tasks without the express permission of cantons.

In Britain, politics is for the people; in Switzerland, politics is by the people.[432] The Swiss drew upon Republican principles laid out by Enlightenment thinkers like Montesquieu and Rousseau – mixed government, the social contract, civic virtue and the common good. While the country embraces liberal economics, its loyalty to broader republican principles of communitarianism dominates. An intense focus on consensus and co-operation underlies multiple horizontal and vertical methods of communication between centre and periphery. Cantons don't share skills horizontally or push decisions upwards. Every canton wants an excellent hospital, a cultural plan. They prefer operational excellence and control at local level. So they create an optimal ecology for community sympathy groups at the social edge. All manner of groups flourish in every canton, which provide space and support for citizen-led initiatives. They support everything, from the environment to education to theatre, green energy and sport. Four non-binding referenda per year, held on a Sunday, give voice to citizens. Proposals vary from retirement age to motorway speed limits, restrictions on foreigners living abroad owning real estate, dispensing of heroin to drug addicts, maternity allowances, abolition of the army and stem cell research. The results warn politicians against unpopular measures and stimulate modified policy brought back to a later referendum. Switzerland isn't perfect. It sits on a huge throughput of banking money, trillions per year, some from flight capital, to underpin the economy. But Switzerland shows that the narrative of politics as battles between big beasts in capital cities, roared on by competing media, is not the only model for democracies. Co-operative methods promote a more successful economy and contented electorate.

Politicians elsewhere have short attention spans and short-term vision. In the hurly-burly of governance they read little and reflect less. If we asked a focus group of politicians and bureaucrats what would incentivise their use of sympathy groups in governance they might agree on five propositions:

Is the proposed new sympathy group policy ethical?

Can it be applied to the everyday political concerns of people?

Will people become more engaged through a new policy that promotes co-operation?

Is the policy sufficiently beneficial, equitable and evidence-informed to justify the investment or will it preserve unfair power relations and exclude others?

Is the design of the plan sustainable, ecological, and will local relationships improve and be popular?

These 'political principles' define whether decisions are just and good, and will win the hearts of citizens. We shall consider each proposition in turn.

IS A SYMPATHY GROUP POLICY ETHICAL?

Ethics ain't easy. We can ask how democratic governments can consult voters healthily, in proper listening mode, so that competent, moral decisions are taken for their benefit. Philosophers have long debated what affects ethics and morality in human behaviour and relationships. Are there moral absolutes for how we conduct our lives, or is everything determined by culture and contemporary politics? When faced with a decision about what to do, whether to buy a car or to put an elderly relative into residential care or to hunt for food on someone else's land, are there universal laws to guide us with our practical reasoning? It depends, of course, upon the kind of decision we must take. If it's pragmatic, the exercise of individual taste over the colour and make of a car for example, then individual or family preferences alone will guide us. If it's ethical, such as a clinical decision about the removal of a frail grandmother from her home to a place of perceived greater safety, or a moral decision about the choice between infringing another's legal land rights and the need to feed your hungry children, then we must debate and create rules, laws and duties for citizens.

Three broad philosophies of ethics guide us in dilemmas of moral choice. Aristotle created a virtue ethics and believed we should be guided by our concept of *eudaimonia* or 'the good life'. Many contemporary philosophers support Aristotle's morality based on wellbeing. His optimism about a good life born out of human virtue contrasts with the bleaker views of humanity of Thomas Hobbes, Sigmund Freud and Christian Augustinians. Aristotle believed that ethics was a human creation so could not be solid or unchangeable. The society we are born into, and our interactions with others, influences ethical values. Revived in the 1950s by Iris Murdoch, Philippa Foot and GEM Anscombe, and today by Martha Nussbaum and Michael Sandel in America, modern Aristotelian philosophers drive the new politics of wellbeing and happiness.[433] Aristotle's approach is seen as modern, flexible, psychological and able to deal with complexity. In the UK, the economist Richard Layard, policy thinkers like Geoff Mulgan and Jon Cruddas on the centre left, and Anthony Seldon, David Willetts and Steve Hilton on the centre right, believe we should design public policy around whatever it takes to promote, design or nudge people into a life that improves their psychological wellbeing.[434] Unlike neo-cons and Thatcherites, they support the idea of society and are not tied to particular hard-line economic theories. The market place has moral boundaries and must be regulated. Emotions are value judgments about the world, so if we can change the emotional wellbeing of populations their character and values will improve.

A second view of ethics, utilitarianism, proposed by Jeremy Bentham, is more quantitative than Aristotle's. Utilitarians wish to measure the cumulative total of utility or happiness of a population and to design social policy to achieve maximum benefit. Everything is determined by the total of pain or pleasure created, measured using Bentham's dimensions of intensity, duration, certainty, nearness, fecundity (its generative nature, like a domino effect), purity and extent. Utilitarians wish simply to create the most pleasure and the least pain in society, whereas Aristotelians seek a middle way that deals with complexity and uncertainty. Utility influences modern managers in the western world with criteria and targets of utility, and measurement of utilitarian costs and benefits. In the east, the approach of Aristotle to creating what is perceived as a good life is more common.

Immanuel Kant hated both these views of the world. Utilitarians reduced human intention to the mere binary function of seeking pleasure and avoiding pain. Aristotelians denied any universal human rules of morality. Kant believed humans were more than the product of a mechanical brain, and that we had individual duties and rules to follow. Maxims help you to live your everyday life, whereas imperatives are at a higher level: categorical imperatives like the law not to kill, and conditional imperatives like the need to wear a seat belt or not to smoke in a public place. Although individual freedom is the highest goal, and we have a free will to decide our destiny, Kant accepted that governments can make rules and laws to ensure that when different individuals' ideas of freedom come into conflict there is a process of arbitration based on debate and interaction. So although Kant's beliefs were focused on the rules of individual behaviour he conceded the need for social decisions about citizens' rights.

In the twentieth century, Jürgen Habermas attempted to resolve the apparent conflict between Aristotle's belief in the social construction of ethics and Kant's idea of universal rules and laws of moral behaviour. He proposed that communication between free individuals allowed for action based on discourse ethics.

"[In] rational discourse among free and equal participants," he wrote, "everyone is required to take the perspective of everyone else, and thus project herself into the understandings of self and world of all others". In this way, conflicts of interest can be impartially resolved. A universally accepted norm or law will emerge when all people potentially affected by the norm, as long as they are free individuals, subject it to argument and scrutiny. If there is agreement after a process of discourse, then the norm or law can be justified. Without this process of community consultation, philosophy cannot decide or justify in advance what is good or bad. The discourse depends upon "the individual's inalienable right to say 'yes' or 'no'," and second, "his overcoming of his egocentric viewpoint".[435]

Once agreed, the question of how these norms and rules and laws are applied is a separate matter.[436] Habermas suggested that the central process for development and emancipation of people across the world is provided through communication, debate and argument between free and equal citizens. He considered the Marxist view that oppression results from conflict between classes arising from the mode of economic and material production of secondary importance. For Habermas, everyday politics in local communities is central.

Not surprisingly, Marxists find this idea deeply flawed. What guarantees, asks Perry Anderson, do negotiations have for any general normative claim?[437] Habermas argues that majority rule will decide, but majorities change. Habermas also claims that "with moral questions . . . a world republic of citizens constitutes the reference system for justifying regulations that lie in the equal interest of all".[438] Anderson is scornful of legislation arising from the "inhabitants of an unimaginably unequal planet" and also of Habermas's assumptions about a self-steering capitalist economy as fundamental to modernity. Another objection to Habermas comes from non-western writers concerned by his promotion of the primacy of the western view of rational discourse and his relegation of other religious or non-modern approaches to law-making as backwards or false.[439]

Whatever our world view on the morality of rule-making, all philosophies admit to the importance of community involvement in deciding or modifying our laws and imperatives. In pre-literate societies, customary law was the process by which village leaders or elders would implement a moral code or adjudicate on disputes. Customary law still forms the bedrock of decision-making in many states. Law lecturer Sylvie Delacroix describes how in Palestine, in 1988, during the first largely non-violent intifada, 45,000 local committees were the source of most real power in the land. These structures were locally understood. People couldn't cope with the 'tossed legal salad' of British, Jordanian, Egyptian and Israeli pre-1967 laws.[440]

In contrast, customary law in the international arena, for example to penalise cross-border pollution or nuclear threat, is fraught with vagueness. We have no clear path to universally agreed definitions.[441] International courts can declare norms of customary behaviour beyond their usual treaties, but states differ in what is 'customary' in their own behaviour or unacceptable in the behaviour of neighbours. Customary law can reinforce subordination of women and minorities by traditional, chauvinist and sometimes illiterate 'judges'. This is unquestionably true. Fairness is not guaranteed. On the other hand, disputes and contracts may be resolved through sympathy group negotiation rather than from protracted court procedures, or by waiting for central decision-making that may never happen or won't be policed.

Ward level committees can represent everyone – cleaners, servants and the unemployed – not just those with loud voices like powerful union groups. In 1916, the social philosopher Antonio Gramsci wrote: "I'm very much in favour of the factory councils, they are critical political organisations. But they need to be supplemented by the ward committees . . . [which] have a better idea about the condition of the whole working class because the factory council is good at the sector but they don't have a vision of the whole."[442]

Sylvie Delacroix reminds us that Jean-Jacques Rousseau profoundly understood sympathy thinking and its benefits when writing about how to reform Poland. "There will never be a good and solid constitution unless the law reigns over the hearts of the citizens; . . . How then is it possible to move the hearts of men (sic), and to make them love the fatherland and its laws? Dare I say it? Through children's games; through institutions which seem idle and frivolous to superficial men, but which form cherished habits and invincible attachments."[443]

CAN IT BE APPLIED TO EVERYDAY POLITICS?

Politics in its broadest sense is about control of resources, by whom and how and when and where. When science and academia neglect sympathy groups they play down the role that groups play in grass-root decisions that orchestrate people's lives. While we analyse the higher structures of modernity and post-modernity, everyday politics depends upon pre-literate structures of family and community groups. It's a jumble sale hierarchy of decision-making bodies. Our media also focus obsessively on the politics of state and representation, much less on everyday decision-making in local communities.[444] Everyday politics is different from official politics. Official politics is often viewed, negatively, as the province of elites and cronies at the centre, a tiny, privileged fraction of the population. It misses what is politically significant – the allocation of resources on farms, in towns, between and within families, within institutions and factories. It also misses local resistance by underprivileged groups to elite control. We cannot ignore our most basic forms of interaction and decision-making at the social edge. Groups enrich local politics, solve problems, create happiness and entertainment. They provide social support, a defence against bureaucracy, and a celebration of social values, our festivals and culture.

The history given to our children is a story of dates, leaders, monarchs, generals, battles, fealties, treaties and political ideologies. Historians analyse the role of nationhood, religion, class, gender and race, which reflects the ideological bent of the author. David Cannadine argues that history is an undivided past, and that too much attention is given to conflict, which "denies us our just inheritance of what we have always shared, namely a capacity to 'live together in societies sufficiently harmonious and orderly not to be constantly breaking apart'."[445] He reminds us that VS Naipaul pointed to the "missing large idea of human association" in his history of India,[446] a gap addressed by social science and biology but barely by historians. Our history can be divided into Manichean opposites, but, in truth, while Muslim and Christian communities may have "clashed and collided", they also for centuries "co-existed, conversed and collaborated across . . . boundaries of confessional identity".[447] The Peace of Westphalia in 1648 may have imposed secular statehood in defining religiously divided states of modern Europe, but before and since, nations have been what political scientist Benedict Anderson describes as "imagined communities", with shifting boundaries, migrations and identities. In our modern world we see increasing ethnic and linguistic diversity within national boundaries, and the redefinition of states is a constant process, whether in the former Soviet Union, the Balkans, Sudan, many parts of post-colonial Africa, the Middle East, Spain and the United Kingdom.

Most countries deal with the legacy of a range of economic structures, which lie side by side: from newer forms of slavery, through serfdom, rural peasantry and the stratifications of urban classes, from poor to middle to rich, from landless and property-less to landowner and property owner. Over the past 30 years, economic inequality has increased in most countries so the range is now stretched and deformed, with a fat tail of absolute poverty and another of extravagant or super wealth. The nature of hierarchies and stratifications has local flavour, from the British class system, to the French subtleties of 'la petite', 'la moyenne', 'la grande', and 'la haute bourgeoisie'. But elites and the deprived are found everywhere. In the USA, income strata include the super-rich (<1%), the rich (ca 5%), the middle class (ca 45%), working class (ca 40%) and the poor (12%). The Indian caste system is more pernicious because it's heritability excludes the possibility of free social mobility. Babasaheb Ambedkar, leader of India's low-caste Hindus and author of India's constitution, famously warned that "democracy in India is only a top dressing on an Indian soil which is essentially undemocratic".

In the era of the post-modern, the breaking of strict hierarchies and the loosening of separations between capital and labour, we find multiple, almost medieval, identities have re-emerged. Any policy for development must take account of this mêlée. Imagine the challenge facing an Indian politician who must satisfy the demands of pre-literate tribal populations, enslaved and trafficked women and children, bonded labourers, rural peasants, urban industrial classes, an emergent middle class, with several strata within it, and the cronies of big capital. The same policymakers face a cacophony of day and night communications, across communities and borders, with a rowdy younger population, reared with Facebook, Twitter and mobiles, who yearn to break free from traditions of caste and class, conformity and cronyism.

Curiously, in the west, sympathy groups are consonant with both the political left and right. Political opponents sense that something is missing in our lonely and wealthy western lives. When left-wing film-maker Ken Loach laments the absence of the "spirit of '45" we can see it, cynically, as an old-fashioned cry for statism and welfare, rather than his heart pining for communitarianism and a spirit of concern in everyday politics. When politicians of the right wish to roll back the state and create 'tea-party' groups and a 'Big Society' of volunteers, we dismiss it as a cry for the restoration of the selfish free market and the destruction of the mixed economy, rather than a deeper desire for local power to hold in check the centre. Group mobilisation was a key element of leftist movements of the twentieth century, with varying degrees of state control. For socialists, small groups are the building blocks of trades unions, which give workers a voice. Libertarian socialists and anarchic communists believe in a stateless society without coercive structures and see small local groups as a way to monitor common ownership. On the right, the libertarian wing of the US Republican Party, and the short-lived Tory Big Society movement in the UK, ostensibly support measures that take power away from politicians and return it to the people. Mutual societies, co-operatives, charities and social enterprises drive a devolutionary process. Far-right conservatives who aggressively proselytise for naked individualism comprise, without irony, many local groups that determine their own platforms and agendas without central leadership. So sympathy groups can be accommodated across the political spectrum. And across every religion the enormous energy of Muslim, Hindu, Christian, Buddhist and Animist communities depends on sympathy groups for energy, fellowship and recruitment.

At the same time, we must not be naive. History is also a chronicle of sympathy groups in conflict: royal households, feudal landowners, camarillas, militias, cliques, cabals, politburos, factions, gangs, mafias, cartels, pirates, triads, caliphate jihadists, yardies and terrorists or freedom fighters. Groups may control, bully, extort, pillage, rob and murder through pogroms, terror and genocide. Many people still face daily threats from crime and insecurity because groups choose to ignore or confront the rules of civilised culture. Perversely, the long history of abuse by sympathy groups is a testament to their potential power. Sympathy groups can be creative, destructive or simply ineffectual. They can create wealth but also conflict and displacement. They might comfort us in times of distress or expel us from our livelihoods. They are a wellspring of heroism and terrorism, a balm to relieve stress or an irritant to cause distress. They can protect, defend, build and demolish. Understanding how sympathy groups work, and under what conditions they bring the greatest benefits and protection, has enormous potential to improve social and economic policy. We just need more evidence about whether, how, when and why they work.

WILL PEOPLE ENGAGE?

Information technology has transformed the way we communicate, touching our most intimate relationships and daily routines. As consumers, producers, workers, financiers, civil servants, soldiers, renegades, artists and travellers we depend on mobiles, the internet and digital media. Watching commuters or teenagers on their phones, preoccupied, we might ask whether this new network of social communication has made obsolete ancient methods of face-to-face dialogue. Are we Luddites to think that global networks can be managed and regulated by small groups in ways that protect us? Surely mobile technology brings immeasurable individual freedoms and benefits, which supplants our dependence on survival cliques and sympathy groups?

A little critical reflection suggests modern communication networks have made us less free than we think. Go back 40 years. Was it easier or more difficult to get visas for travel across the world? To gain work permits in other continents? To pass through airports unmolested? To walk alone in cities unmonitored by cameras? To be sure your phones were not tapped? To preserve the secrecy of your identity and family details, your sickness record, your credit history? Our mobile freedoms have been constrained by a new imperialism of boundaries, borders, surveillance, restrictions, exclusions, marginalisation, 'fraping', and online abuse. In some ways one might argue the need to confirm our individual identity and voice through face-to-face contact in a small group, living in the moment, as greater than ever before.

For democracy, we need a civic ethos of citizen engagement to challenge the imperialism of security and risk, and to confront concentrations of power and tax immunity within borderless multinationals. The impotence of national parliaments has perverse effects. As miserable MPs watch multinationals and trade blocs emasculate their power, they try to wrest control from local government to the centre. Online petitions to the White House and Downing Street seem a poor and powerless substitute for genuine local accountability.

For those of us who enjoy instantaneous online access to the world's nodal libraries, we experience a compressed world of space and time. James Tully suggests it takes hold of our psyche and "hyperextends" or "glocalizes" (globalizes and localizes). Our online world gives us "not so much ideas as images that structure the form of consciousness of the recipient".[448] Our ideology and world view have been replaced by "a communicative habitus that communicators tend to operate within at work and leisure, on the home computer, the cell phone, the wireless laptop, and the BlackBerry". Sociologist Manuel Castells believes onliners live "a culture of the ephemeral . . . a patchwork of experiences and interests, rather than a charter of rights and obligations".[449]

Communications bypass conventional democratic structures and domestic laws. Saskia Sassen describes our new socio-digital world through two extremes. Global financial markets run by electronic capital elites in major cities practise hypermobility. Globally networked, local social activist movements, traditionally characterised by isolation, dispersal and immobility, do the same.[450] On the one hand, global IT networks led to higher levels of control and wealth concentration in the capital markets; on the other, to greater participation by small local organisations in global debates.

Finance is far ahead. Multi-country networks link financial centres like New York, London, and Beijing as nodes in a global web of instantaneous 24-hour trading. Digitisation, sophisticated financial mathematics, and algorithms have created new financial instruments and liquefied wealth on a grand scale. Internationally traded derivatives rose from $65 trillion in the late 1990s to a cosmic $640 trillion in 2007 before the financial crash. Governments, overtaken by global markets and cities, face a huge challenge to their state powers of regulation. They can fight back by controlling the nodes of these networks with thick legislation. Silicon Valley, Bangalore and Beijing are instantaneously linked but their plans are restricted by territorial 'insertions'. Saskia Sassen observes that "in country after country [financial markets] are not necessarily framed by distinct national or international laws or by visible legal markers".[451] Financial markets regulate themselves and compel governments to adopt measures they prefer and not others. The speed and complexity of transactions make it hard for lawmakers to understand the power and nature of financial markets.

Civil society has many greater obstacles to forming networked platforms, although information exchange about shared interests such as human rights, climate change and development goals creates an 'incipient global commons'. For social scientists, the concept of the local as geographically bounded and trapped by hierarchy and tradition has changed, even if the poorest groups remain immobile.[452] The old Greek idea that citizens should have a basic say and control over the decisions that affect them has been subverted by the glamour of our laptops and smartphones. It's not that technology doesn't offer us the opportunity to create local networks of democratic control, nor to hold the hegemony of taxless, faceless multinational corporate communication to some kind of accountability. It's just that traditional methods of human interaction and democracy have been overwhelmed by the speed and seduction of the mobile revolution.

But maybe a strange synthesis is possible. Into this communication space, linking the internet to the power of sympathy groups could be a game-changer. For billions who live outside the online space, the poorest and most marginalised, the sympathy group remains a traditional way to give voice and method for social justice. It provides a potential nodal point for investment to bring the poorest into the 'oceanic circles' of the online global commons. Despite Gandhi's many flaws, his vision can inspire us. "Independence begins at the bottom . . . a society must be built in which every village has to be self sustained and capable of managing its own affairs . . . there will be ever widening, never ascending circles. Growth will not be a pyramid with the apex sustained by the bottom. But it will be an oceanic circle whose centre will be the individual. Therefore the outermost circumference will not wield power to crush the inner circle but will give strength to all within and derive its own strength from it."[453]

WILL PARTICIPATION EMPOWER OR EXCLUDE?

Power, not behaviour, is central to any analysis of sympathy groups. "The fundamental concept in social science is power, in the same sense in which energy is the fundamental concept in physics," said Bertrand Russell. Which means we can view power with both fear and cheer. The bleak view is about power over people, how one person may affect another in a way that is contrary to the second person's interests. Political theorist Hannah Arendt, though, was more optimistic. She did not see power primarily about conflict, but rather the way in which it can bring strength to groups of people. "Power is never the property of an individual; it belongs to a group and remains in existence only so long as the group keeps together. The moment the group, from which the power originated to begin with (*potestas in populo*, without a people or group there is no power), disappears, power also vanishes."[454] She saw the gathering of people in groups as the essence of power, not what they did. "Power springs from whenever people get together and act in concert, but it derives its legitimacy from the initial getting together rather than from any action that then may follow."

Michel Foucault went further. He saw power everywhere and in everything, diffuse, amorphous, ever changing. It was not just the episodic, sovereign power of states and rulers. Power was in our civil service, our prisons, our hospitals, our sexual relationships. It was above and below politics, immanent in our everyday lives. He recognised that social power is not just coercive or repressive, forcing us to do things against our wishes, but also a necessary, productive and positive force "We must cease once and for all to describe the effects of power in negative terms: it 'excludes', it 'represses', it 'censors', it 'abstracts', it 'masks', it 'conceals'. In fact power produces; it produces reality; it produces domains of objects and rituals of truth. The individual and the knowledge that may be gained of him belong to this production."[455]

Foucault saw the process of discourse, the core of a sympathy group, as a means to change power. "A discourse can be both an instrument and an effect of power, but also a hindrance, a stumbling point of resistance and a starting point for an opposing strategy. Discourse transmits and produces power; it reinforces it, but also undermines and exposes it, renders it fragile and makes it possible to thwart."[456] An African perspective is given by Abdou Maliq Simone. "Power is not the consolidation of ownership and is not within the domain of possession," he suggests. "Rather, it lies in the capacity to generate advantageous relationships with a multiplicity of production forces and flows."[457] Women's, or indeed men's, bargaining power is affected by their personal qualities, their access to support outside the household, and the way the local village perceives them.

At the simplest level, power can be analysed in the way it affects behaviour. For target behaviours, we can measure the way in which decision-making affected them compared with alternative behaviours that were finally adopted. Were decisions open and transparent, were alternatives considered, did participants have a choice? It is a simple, one-dimensional, evidence-based approach, which estimates whether people really shared in decisions that affect their lives. For example, the use of condoms by sexual partners as a method of contraception or to stop transmission of HIV is straightforward to measure through interviews conducted confidentially. One way to observe the impact of participatory groups discussing family planning and HIV would be to measure reported condom use.

But a simplistic approach has limitations. Power may travel through less overt mechanisms than practical decisions. The language of power also involves influence, manipulation, coercion and authority. One can overdo the extent to which people are really involved in specific decisions, or whether they have a power of veto. Much direction of power is behind the scenes. So a proper analysis considers both overt and covert observable conflict. For example, in a Christian community comprising Catholics and Evangelicals, the more devout Catholic members of groups might put pressure on others over condom use because of personal beliefs. Or cash transfers offered during pregnancy might perversely counteract messages about contraception. Even so, this broader, two dimensional view of power is still inadequate.[458]

A three dimensional view of power takes much greater account of the way in which individuals or groups "succeed in excluding potential issues from the political process". Power is not just a series of individual acts and decisions but a "socially structured and culturally patterned behaviour of groups, and practices of institutions". As such, power is not just about conflict, but also about subjective and real interests. "A may exercise power over B by getting him (sic) to do what he does not want to do, but he also exercises power over him by influencing, shaping or determining his very wants." The most insidious use of power is to prevent people from having a sense of grievance in the first place and "to accept their role in the existing order of things, either because they can see or imagine no alternative to it, or because they see it as natural and unchangeable, or because they value it as divinely ordained and beneficial". For example, a local religious leader, aware of group meetings about family planning might prevent the contraceptive agenda from being discussed, and disseminate false information from the pulpit about the risks of HIV transmission. Or politically influenced media might portray clashes between oppressors and oppressed as a clash between two equal viewpoints, as we saw in Charlottesville, where the US President saw "two sides" between white supremacists and anti-racists. The media also portrayed police brutality against Catalan citizens queueing to cast a vote as a clash between two sides. This three dimensional view of power takes an anti-behavioural stance.

At the 2016 World Health Assembly, I witnessed three dimensional power in its diplomatic brutality. A Lancet review reported evidence that

820,000 infants die each year through the effects of mothers not breast-feeding. The inappropriate industrial promotion of formula milk has a fatal impact, especially in poorer countries with wretched hygiene and water quality.[459] Formula milk increases the risk of infants acquiring a gastrointestinal infection and severe dehydration from diarrhoea. In rich countries, breastfeeding also significantly cuts the risk of obesity and diabetes in infants, and of breast and ovarian cancer in mothers.

None of the large formula companies, though, complies fully with the WHO Code on inappropriate promotion of breastmilk substitutes, a Code they all signed up to in 1981. A 2016 WHO report showed that although national legislation on the Code had expanded, very few countries monitor compliance with their legislation, and only a couple took action against companies. Cross-promotion of 'follow-on' formula milks (to be started from six months of age) is a major problem and greatly damages breast-feeding rates in early infancy. Many families don't understand the difference between formula milk fed at any time and 'follow-on' products. The Lancet editorial was explicit. It called for immediate action to stop promotion of follow-on milks, products that the companies claim fall outside the Code. "No Ifs, Buts or Follow-on Milk", went the headline.

So at the World Health Assembly I sat in a meeting of countries as they discussed the resolution on revised WHO technical advice on Code compliance to be placed before the Assembly the next day. Fifteen low and middle income country representatives stood up, unanimously enthu-siastic to endorse the resolution. They saw it as essential to protect their children. Over 2250 deaths occur each day from impeded breastfeeding, while companies rake in over $18 million profit per day on formula milk sales. It's now a $54 billion industry and rising.

A heavy and plethoric man from the European Union stood up. "I represent 28 countries and I have to say that we will not endorse this resolution." He didn't bother to explain and sat down. The New Zealand man backed him up. The US representative stood up and said the same. They were happy to "note" or "welcome" the resolution but not to endorse it, which they feared would open their dairy industry to attack from civil society groups or, worse, lawyers. The G7 countries had been extensively lobbied by dairy advocates and the Obama White House and Brussels were making no concessions. Nothing would shift them. The resolution went to the Assembly but was not endorsed. In 2017 this whole charade was repeated when the WHO child obesity action plan was blocked by the US government in order to protect the food industry from sugar taxes.

Governments do care, though, about trade policing when it suits them. The US government happily imposed a fine of $3 billion on the pharmaceutical company GSK, the largest corporate fine in history, when its sales force bribed doctors to use the company's medicines. China followed up with a $650 million fine because GSK's sales force had used bribes to push its own drugs. Arguably no one died from this illegality; it simply affected the market share of competitors, but that was considered an appalling trade law infringement worthy of fines equal to double the annual budget of the entire World Health Organisation. Yet if infant formula milk companies allow their sales force to distribute free gifts to health workers, advertise inappropriately and infringe the rules they signed up to in the WHO Code, and thousands of children die every day, the companies can do so with impunity. Trade versus health. Trade, as usual, won.

Power might be too hot to handle at times but what about the risks of participation? Whatever definition we use, power is critical to the success or otherwise of sympathy groups. Some social scientists are sceptical about development experts who evangelise for community participation. Can a few meetings with marginalised people really enable them to take key decisions to change their own lives? Are communities always in harmony? Most are divided by age, class, caste, ethnicity, religion, politics and gender. Will all be properly represented? Will chosen facilitators of meetings direct the decision-making and take control? Will they subvert existing decision-making systems? Or will a self-selected group take participatory decisions that buttress vested interests? And will expectations be unrealistic? Perhaps groups will want to do things that challenge the bureaucratic goals of existing health workers, or teachers, or agricultural extension agents. In a clash between top-down orders and bottom-up design who should win?

Psychologists are also cautious about groups exhibiting 'coercive persuasion'. Here members second-guess what everyone else wants to do when the opposite action is actually true (the so-called Abilene paradox). And there is a risk that charismatic leaders of non-government organisations will claim a moral leadership in a community which is neither justified nor sustainable? In Major Barbara, George Bernard Shaw understood the two sides of power. "You cannot have power for good without having power for evil too. Even mother's milk nourishes murderers as well as heroes."[460]

Some observers go further and see participation as a shibboleth of contemporary development.[461] They criticise unwarranted claims made about participation leading to empowerment, failure to observe lasting and meaningful social change, poor engagement with underlying power and politics, and too much emphasis on voluntarism and using 'local' solutions to divert attention from, and protect, disempowering elites. They dislike "a methodological individualism that obscures the analysis of what makes participation difficult for marginal groups in the first place". Non-government organisations come in for particular criticism. Their role is a confusing mishmash of the public, private and civic. Their funds from external donors means their allegiance is divided and they weaken the social contract between state and citizen. NGOs are accused of being neo-imperialist, bringing their own perspective on how the 'third world' should be managed.

These criticisms carry weight, especially if expectations from a participatory approach are set too high in the short term. More recently, analysts have looked favourably once more at participation in development, and the success of many processes, especially those led by political actors from within countries.[462] No one can doubt the value of the anti-dam movement in India, the shift in control from economic elites to political parties in Kerala, democratic decentralisation in many countries, participatory budgeting in Brazil, the rise of local representation for marginalised and tribal groups, the use of social media to protect the forest lands of hunter-gatherers from loggers, the protection of women through pregnancy groups campaigning for birth plans, nor the success of many farmers, forest and credit groups taking control of their resources. Corruption and gender violence in India now receive greater scrutiny and protest from small groups, the Twitterati and journalists, although long-term impact is unclear. In Tamil Nadu, mobilised lower-caste groups came together to gain political power and build schools, health centres, roads, and public transport.[463] The much criticised Public Distribution System of food, previously riddled with scams, is now more effective as small groups hold the system accountable.[464] Participation is not a panacea, but neither is it a placebo. If the principles of a human rights approach to communities are based on non-discrimination, equality, social inclusion and formal legal redress, participatory groups can, by definition, only address the first three. But that is not to be sniffed at.

Formal rules and laws alone cannot deal with informal lives. We cannot just parrot the formal rhetoric and language of human rights and hope it will work, because it doesn't. Real workings of power lie within informal communities. The political scientist Professor Lynn Freedman has spoken about the politics of recognition and the challenge of informality when it comes to access to health resources.[465] For two billion or more people living in poor villages or informal slum settlements, the "conditions of life are not fixed or mapped according to any prescribed set of regulations or the law".[466] Land, housing, labour and wellbeing are insecure. Access is not by rights as a citizen, more by who you know, what influence you have.

A formal district or city cannot survive without its informal dwellers, people who are often invisible, unrecognised by policy and development programmes. The policy challenge is different from just organising a bureaucracy. For the marginalised poor to get access to health services they must navigate a different system of gatekeepers. Life is negotiation with these gatekeepers through informal groups, or mechanisms such as voting for elites in return for payment, or by providing informal services to the gatekeepers – labour, bribes, even sexual favours. "Quiet encroachment of the ordinary" is the way in which families and sympathy groups practise prolonged direct action to achieve the basic necessities of life, in a quiet, unassuming and illegal fashion.[467] It may involve an informal trade-off with the organised encroachment of the powerful. Slum dwellers surrounding wealthy apartment complexes or hotels, many of them employees, may illegally tap electricity lines and water supplies. Cleaners at hospitals hitch rides in ambulances or supply trucks. Tribal people live close to mines on the same land the companies stole from their fore-fathers. The hope is that the marginalised bond together in groups, form bridges of shared interests with other groups, and use combined political strength to agitate for other resources.

Self-enumeration is one key process in becoming recognised. If your birth and death is not registered, the state barely knows if you exist or existed. Childbirth therefore becomes an opportunity to renegotiate the terms of recognition. While millions have benefited from states that register and document their citizens, Saskia Sassen has identified the emerging problem of social expulsion rather than simply exclusion.[468] Exclusion prevents people outside the system from entering it, similar to the problem of the untouchable castes in Nepal and India. Expulsion is the act of ejecting people from within the system, who find themselves on the other side of the line. As a result of industrial developments, from finance to mining, the complex communications, knowledge and technology that determine our modern world "makes it hard to trace lines of responsibility for the displacements, evictions, and eradications it produces". Tribal peoples in India and Nepal, abused by a British civil servant's pen in the nineteenth century, are nowadays expelled from their land and employment rights by impenetrable and misleading words of crony industrialists, backed up by teams of industrial lawyers.

We can see a twenty-first century example of exclusion and expul-sion in Britain with the Grenfell fire disaster. The wealthiest borough in the UK, with a council led by affluent residents, had built no social housing for years. They hoped that the poor would move to other boroughs. And to sanitise the ugly high rise blocks that housed the poor, the council organised cut-price cladding to make the view more attractive to the well-heeled. The shocking fire exposed a dark under-belly of class relations in one of the world's wealthiest cities. The community response to survivors, self-organising and compassionate, stood in stark contrast to that of the authorities. We must wait to see if this leads to lasting change.

So we mustn't be naive. For participation to work, the process must be open-ended, radical and engaged with broader aspects of change than behaviour. Participation does not substitute for citizenship. If participation is an afterthought in an essentially technocratic aid programme it will not be a success. If it's the first and most essential part of an integrated programme to bring benefits of better services and technologies to people, it's much more likely to be embraced. Given the bitter academic disputes over the uses of power and participation, rigorous assessments of interventions through proper evaluation seem all the more important, with hard impact measures analysed alongside social and political context.

CAN WE CREATE AN ECOLOGY FOR A RELATIONAL STATE?

When in March 2001 the Committee on Quality of Health Care in America released its second report, Crossing the Quality Chasm: A New Health System for the 21st Century, two key members were Harvard professor Don Berwick, founder of the Institute for Healthcare Improvement and later director of Obamacare, and Dr Mark Chassin, president of the Joint Commission, a not-for-profit healthcare accreditation organisation. Over the previous decade, Berwick had helped drive forward six aims for health care – that it should be safe, effective, patient-centred, timely, efficient and equitable. And their report judged that the US health system had improved greatly in its use of technology and the process of performance measurement. Chassin felt the first report, a decade earlier, had "helped to change the mindset of those in the healthcare system and put performance improvement high on the priority list".

But in other areas progress was "glacially slow".[469] Systems were far from being 'patient-centred'. Little research was done on user concerns, on impact of 'quality' improvement, or comparative effectiveness of different strategies. Humane care and a lack of harm remained a major challenge. In 1999, the US Institute of Medicine had reported that medical errors caused up to 98,000 deaths and more than one million injuries each year across all States.[470] A decade later, in a study of 10 North Carolina hospitals over six years published in the New England Journal of Medicine in 2010, Dr Christopher Landrigan's team found that "harms remain common, with little evidence of widespread improvement".[471]

A big challenge for government is how to achieve a balance between top-down provision of essentials – democracy, security, infrastructure, justice, education and health – and bottom-up involvement of citizens in a more active way. How can states protect the co-operative element so essential for human relationships? Even political observers of shared persuasion get trapped in arguments about how to achieve this balance. For example, Geoff Mulgan, former head of the Labour government's Downing Street policy unit, and Marc Stears, Oxford professor of political philosophy and policy adviser to the Labour Party, held radically different views. Mulgan believed that governments can use policy, where appropriate, to direct the move from a delivery state to a relational state.[472] Governments stand over their people as warrior, policeman and tax inspector, and extend their reach by delivering, to a passive public, services for education, transport, health and welfare. The UK Labour governments led by Tony Blair and Gordon Brown had become obsessed with performance management of these provider functions. Their language was about reaching targets and managing internal markets. In many ways they were successful, achieving big reductions in waiting times for healthcare, and doubling from 30% to 60% the number of children at 16 years achieving 5 A-star to C grades for their General Certificate of Secondary Education.

Over time, politicians and people in Britain became accustomed to rising statistics through 'new performance management' but craved services that were more caring and respectful of human relationships. Achieving a target for, say, old people treated for high blood pressure says nothing about the manner in which they are treated, how long they waited, or how stressed or relaxed they were when examined. A command and control strategy has inherent limitations. Somehow, our modern state must find solutions which involve agents closer to the action, able to solve the 'relational issues' themselves. We've seen that two thirds of many government health budgets goes on long-term conditions like diabetes, stroke, depression, disability and heart disease. Patients spend 6000 hours awake per year in dealing with their condition and receive at best an hour or two from a paid professional. So a policy question of economic significance is how might social and primary care tap into local resources to prevent deterioration or expensive admissions to hospital?

Mulgan sees many opportunities to create a relational state. Technology and social media allow for user feedback, and 360 degree appraisals of frontline staff, which build in feedback from clients, can improve the relationship skills of carers and civil servants. Targets can include a psychological component in their goals, such as the number of visits made to an elderly person, or the numbers of children at schools receiving careers advice or health education. Many well-intentioned relational solutions exist. In the US a 'peer to patent' scheme was designed to improve patent applications through community feedback online; the UK 'who owns my neighbourhood' scheme used crowdsourcing methods to improve local planning; the US website challenge.gov attempted to mobilise public engagement to solve problems; in New Zealand, the police force briefly put up their legislation as a Wiki to be amended by citizens (this didn't last long); and participatory budgeting is widely used for small scale charitable or local government initiatives. A relational additive to the flavour of essential services is possible but Mulgan is wary that a state must account for public money, and ensure that public servants do a good job. After all, for many other services – public transport, refuse and tax collection – you don't need a personal relationship.

The statecraft needed to create a relational state is complex. Legislation can ensure parental involvement in schools and local scrutiny of health or public park provision. Free speech for non-government organisations in receipt of government grants can also be guaranteed. The purchasing and commissioning of health services can build specifications related to coverage, scale, feedback and rights of patients. Financing models can provide incentives for social outcomes through social impact bonds or the US Pay for Success scheme. And the huge state burden of provision of care for elderly persons can build in social support through housing policy that promotes co-housing for elderly people, home visits from schoolchildren, post-discharge care from hospitals through mobilising friends and neighbours, and by encouraging elderly neighbours to help each other. Legislation to protect employment and building rights are other ways to help the elderly.

For Marc Stears, the notion of relational statecraft through government edict is fundamentally flawed. Two dominant and differing views of what a state should do arose in the twentieth century, he suggests. The tradition of Thomas Hobbes, continued by Max Weber, saw the state as an agency able to dominate its geography by virtue of coercive force. In contrast, Georg Hegel, social democratic thinkers like Émile Durkheim in France, Sidney and Beatrice Webb in the UK, and more recently Amitai Etzioni in the US, viewed the state as a set of interactions between many social actors, just as Durkheim described the state as doctor to the social body. The Yale anthropologist James Scott saw the modern state's duty 'to reduce the chaotic, disorderly, constantly changing social reality beneath it to something more closely resembling the administrative grid of its obser-vation'.[473] The state is an agent of standardisation made up of complex agencies. It can employ coercive force when needed, but also generates diversity of action either through a left government addressing social inequality or of right government on competitive markets and free trade.

Stears proposes that states, in such a messy modern world, cannot themselves determine and drive a relational state. They can only create conditions within which relationships flourish, and avoid doing things that inhibit social support. The analogy with conservation and habitat is clear. Zoos manage the breeding of threatened animal species like gorillas or pandas and return a few to the wild. Ecologists protect the habitat within which threatened species live, and let nature take its course. If we want people to co-operate and to find creative social options for business, health, education and sustainable living, we need to understand the social habitat that will allow it. Stears describes four key determinants of this ecology – power, time, place and organisation – ingredients to create sympathy at the social edge. As we learnt from our experiments with women's groups, the same four principles were primary reasons behind their success.

Power is the most important product of a strong sympathy group. When people come together around a task of mutual interest and benefit they are more likely to form friendships and lasting powerful bonds than when they meet casually for a chat. A sympathy group creates better use of time. Humans need time to solve problems and make friends. Even with our jackdaw nests of time-saving gadgets – dishwashers, microwaves, laptops – most people complain they have too little time for anything. We rush around, clock-watching, making to-do lists, hitting deadlines. Our myriad groups – for sport, choirs, prayer, books, farming, service quality, investment, gardening, yoga, cards, childcare, audit, fraternity and sorority, and recreational drug use like qat-chewing, drinking beer, hookah pipes, and wine-tasting – provide us with time to interact with our friends, neighbours and club members. Time and space away (within reason) from our solitary screens and checklists provides more happiness and a greater sense of being alive.

Groups are sensitive to place. We relate best when we are in familiar or particular identifiable locations. We feel most at home within our neighbourhood or local sports club, our church, mosque or synagogue, our favourite canteen or bar or cafe, our friends' homes or favourite gardens or local park. Where we meet may determine our mood and our performance, how willing we are to open up, how warm or cold we feel. Crucially, we also like to feel part of a shared institution. The ancient schools of England were built around four or five independent 'houses', to one of which every pupil belonged. Houses competed at games, in debates, in singing and plays. Children developed strong affinities to their houses. Many larger state schools have reconstructed to these smaller house identities. Some universities also have collegiate structures for the same reason, and fraternity groups, such as the alpha-beta-kappa groups in the USA become lifelong membership clubs. From the first, often-intimidating initiation rites, through college life, members fashion lifetime friendships through alumni dining clubs and philanthropy groups, still meeting 40 years later.

The vitality of the sympathy group component of a relational state, broadly called social capital, is not easy to predict from the ideology of a nation. There is great heterogeneity within and between nations and localities, between and within different kinds of political systems, whether democracies or continental bureaucratic states. The assumption that modern western economies have fewer sympathy groups than in low income countries is just that, an assumption, often not borne out by experience.

Many states have created such an ecology of sympathy groups for human development. Despite continuing corruption, bureaucracy, conflict, caste and seismic catastrophes, Nepal can claim two towering triumphs over the past 30 years: maternal and child survival gains and the demise of deforestation. When we first arrived in Nepal in 1984, 180 children out of every 1000 born died before the age of five. Lifetime risk of a maternal death for a newly married woman was about one in 20. By 2014, under-five mortality rate was down to 40 per 1000, and the lifetime risk of maternal death was one in 200. Since the 1980s, the country has lost over a quarter of its forest cover, but the rate of loss has fallen by 29%.[474] So what happened? Dr Bihari Krishna Shrestha, former vice-chairman of the National Planning Commission, is in no doubt. In the 1980s, the Ministry of Forests was "corrupt to the core" and refused permission for communities to run their own forests. In 1987, a World Bank mission came to Nepal to decide on a structural adjustment loan of $50 million. Shrestha insisted that user management of forests should be a condition of the loan.[475] "That did the trick. The Finance Ministry forced the Ministry of Forests to amend ground rules so that forestry groups would be allowed to manage community forests. Today there are 18,000 user groups and they are behind the success of Nepal's community forestry programme . . . the Bank supported many projects in Nepal but only one was really successful. And it didn't cost them a cent."

Further, Shrestha, like many others, is convinced the introduction in 1988 of female community health volunteers linked with *Ama Samuha* (mothers' groups) was a primary reason for the survival gains of mothers and children. Most assume the reason was drug and vitamin delivery through hospitals. Our evidence suggests the mobilisation of women's groups and conversations with community leaders around health played a pivotal role. They provided the relational ecology that promoted a shift from traditional to allopathic medicine. For both forests and families, user groups and self-organisation critically let in the light of new skills and practices, hitherto under the stifling canopy of feudal control.

In the service and health sectors of wealthy economies, both providers and users are influenced by peers, sympathy groups and local surroundings. Trish Greenhalgh and her colleagues in Oxford studied the different influences on social practices such as the use of mobiles within health care.[476] Whereas patients and users are more than happy to explore apps and social media, health providers are constrained by legal and regulatory frameworks and professional codes of practice. For doctors and nurses, many studies showed small improvements using audit and feedback to change practice – Noah Ivers and Jeremy Grimshaw and colleagues esti- mated the median impact from many different trials to be small (somewhere between 4% and 16%) improvement.[477] They argue that repetition of similar studies adds little. They call it 'stagnant science'. But studies to measure the impact of provider (doctor or nurse) groups meeting regu- larly to discuss innovations are non-existent. I would hypothesise that getting local groups of doctors or dentists together, e.g. for a monthly lunch and facilitated discussion, would have larger and more sustained impact than an audit nudge.

NINE LESSONS FOR POLICYMAKERS AT THE SOCIAL EDGE

In conclusion, let me distil nine ideas for policymakers to consider for social innovation:

1. Human and economic **development is founded on trust**. How we keep our promises, make our word our bond or honour a contract is fundamental to economic and social progress. No amount of aid

or legislation will help societies that are riddled with corruption, uncertainty and mismanagement. You, as a policymaker, must start at the bottom and build a safe space for community conversations. Sympathy groups at scale can rekindle that trust if you create the conditions for their success.

2. Sympathy groups of around 15 members can scale up explosive and **non-linear solutions to complex and wicked social problems**. In this new science of sympathy groups, policymakers and academics can work together to help communities solve complex human challenges. Groups bring new conversations and ideas to dysfunctional organisations, chronic disease, climate change and unnecessarily lonely and unhealthy lives. You should give it a try. Support for women's groups by you will prove electorally popular.

3. Sympathy groups are powerful but need **political support**. The stories, history and experiments described in this book describe how we might create a space where politics and social evolution meet. The role of the state is not only to legislate what people can or cannot do, nor just to provide essential services. In many countries we face a collective cry for help through an incoherent nationalism, the cry not so much for a voice but rather to be listened to. We have a long way to go to ensure the health of our populations and their right to "the enjoyment of the highest attainable standard of health [as] one of the fundamental human rights of every human being".[478] And the progress we've made in human development is threatened by our changing environment, and the sclerosis of our governance structures. You should ask your team to think carefully about where sympathy group initiatives have the best chance of success.

4. **Analyse your ecology** for sympathy group participation. A group coming together for a conversation to make a plan to solve a problem is simple in theory. But groups are complex in operation, with many components – beneficiaries, enablers, neighbours, focus, interaction, trust and strategies. Once established, groups have an in-built sustainability during their natural life. Such a political ecology should be a major target for science and policymaking. Ask your team to find out

how many communities have active groups. What do they do? Do they meet regularly, at least monthly? Where are they strong and weak? Which factors contribute to success? I'll wager the data will not be available. Ask your district officers to do a rapid appraisal by asking key informants in the community, with support from a social scientist. They can produce a short report to give you a useful overall picture.

5. Sympathy groups demand **a science of their own**. They add value through innovation, ideas, decisions, flexibility, sustainability, self-interest and low cost. But benefits cannot be assumed. If you go to scale without built-in implementation research you could make an expensive mistake. Context matters, coverage matters and, like any powerful treatment, risks and benefits must be measured, ideally through controlled evaluations on a large scale. We also need experiments to assess the power of sympathy groups and how they work in different settings and for different outcomes. We want to find out whether the benefits outweigh the risks and whether the value (benefits over costs) makes it a worthwhile policy. If you want a robust way to assess complex social interventions at scale, use a randomised method that compares outcomes in populations with and without the groups, combined with strong social analysis. The challenge is to:

Document the existing '*epidemiology*' of social groups in different sectors, their utility, popularity and duration of success. Are groups active or inactive?

Use *qualitative methods* to explore the features of success and durability, their contribution to inclusion/exclusion, and ways in which their power is harnessed or abused in different communities. Creating an ecology favourable to their expansion could harness all kinds of social energy to make things happen. We need to understand how social energy works and dissipates, and the diversity of strategies that sympathy groups employ.

Use *quantitative methods* to document coverage, membership and losses, economic conditions, costs and opportunity costs, value and social impact.

Do *experiments* at scale. Don't do extended pilot studies. You'll need some 'formative data' (test a few groups with local experts to see what works best) but then take your group design to relative scale (cover hundreds of thousands in a population, or, within organisations, at least 15 to 20 intervention groups compared with the same number of control groups). Build your evaluation into the scale-up. If you show an impact you will know it can be done at scale.

6.   **Think about promotion and prevention.** The twenty-first century challenge is how you build a system that creates health and wellbeing. Our big industries – big food, alcohol, oil, agriculture, transport, pharma, and tobacco – have 'negative externalities' for health. As a policymaker you face a tidal wave of casualties from too much consumption; obesity, diabetes, stress, cardiovascular disease. Concurrently, economic competition creates not only winners but also many losers. Debt, despair and the emptiness of de-industrialised communities generate an explosion in opiate dependency and substance abuse.[479] A study of trends from 1999 to 2014 investigated the link between drug overdose deaths and social capital. They found "a strong and statistically significant inverse association between county-level social capital and age-adjusted mortality due to drug overdose".[480] It's no different from addictions and compulsions among indigenous peoples, Native Americans, Australian Aborigines, or European travellers, who saw their culture disintegrate.

Preservation of social solidarity and social capital is fundamental to restore resilience and to deal with future economic shocks. In Germany, we see a new economics of durable, sympathy-led social capital in the rapid increase in their club culture. One in two Germans now belongs to at least one club. The number of clubs rose from 417,000 in 1995 to over 603,000 today.[481] These *vereine* create opportunities for millions of Germans to pursue interests in anything from culture, health, handicrafts or animal care to Elvis Presley. One third of Germans report contributing to voluntary social activities compared with only one in 10 in Spain and Italy.

In Italy, though, we also see social co-operatives exploding. They began in the 1970s when state social care collapsed.[482] In Bologna, for example, almost 90% of social services sub-contract to social co-operatives. The co-operatives have formal democratic and legal rights. They provide a genuine sympathy group voice to direction and strategy, and give the co-op power to negotiate contracts. In Quebec, Canada, solidarity co-ops, as in many countries, take an increasing market share of health and home care provision. And in Australia, researcher and nurse Annie Banbury and colleagues are using videoconference groups to bring older people together, especially those living in remote areas, for social support and to help them manage long term conditions.[483] Based on these examples, your own policies can bring the best of state, private and voluntary community provision into a coherent whole.

7. **Create wealth through co-operation.** As a politician you will know deep down that economic growth built solely on competition based on fear and greed, the virtue of selfishness, and behaviour change through nudges, degrades the dignity of human wealth. Economics also depends on culture, trust and groups. Flourishing human capital and individual happiness within a sharing society is your social and political goal. A new economics, which balances competition and co-operation, can bring sustainable prosperity and opportunity for all. Earlier I described the consensual culture of Switzerland with its devolution of power to cantons and communes, high productivity, popularity of devolved government and ecology of support for sympathy groups. And it's happening in many other places.

8. **Sustainable growth is not a pipe dream.** As a politician you must face reality. Economic growth as a panacea is incompatible with a sustainable future. Up to half of our economy is made up of day-to-day services that we call the 'commons' or the 'foundational economy'. It's made up of those boring goods and services we produce, distribute and consume without noticing: water, power, internet, banks, roads, public transport, education, health care, care for our children and older people, affordable housing, food, shops and our local culture and recreation facilities. One third of people in industrialised countries

work in these areas, three or four times the level of manufacturing industry. But most services are run by large monopolies, unconnected with local provision, driven by the principle of maximised profit at the lowest prices.

Progressive economists believe this system should change and reconnect with local communities.[484] One way is to offer social franchises. Under this system, public and private suppliers are compelled to offer social returns. These returns could embrace a living wage, a sustainable and locally sourced supply chain, renewable energy, community action, and support to sympathy groups and small businesses. A group of economists who promote this progressive and sensitive approach to our economy have called it Manchester Capitalism. City planners discuss its value.[485] The slow city movement, workers' ownership, the Q community, participatory boards, disruptive design and many other movements are the cry of the future. The aim is to support thriving towns, linked to their rural neighbours, everywhere, to strengthen local political structures and participatory budgeting, and to harness the boundless energy of sympathy groups.

9. **Sympathy groups fix things quicker than you think.** Everyone wants a magic bullet. One ironic tweet from Gyanu Adhikari in Nepal read: "idevelopment: the idea that the solution to an economic, political, social, or humanitarian problem is to build a website". People see the internet as a short-cut to community action. Without question, mobile messages, websites and advertising campaigns have a part to play. But the modern can work with time-honoured systems. We galvanised large numbers of people through small women's sympathy groups, in multiple experiments, to cut their own maternal and newborn death rates dramatically within two years. Groups, once established, have in-built sustainability. And mobile phones and community radio can support groups in national programmes to tackle issues from credit to agroforestry to social co-operatives, from health services to education, and for all kinds of organisational innovation. You as a politician have the power to create conditions and

incentives to accelerate their expansion. Lead this movement for social change, link it with the power of the internet, and you will achieve your political aims, gain popularity and re-election.

Don't see these arguments as a way to replace *your crucial political work in legislation and taxation to promote a prosperous, sharing and egalitarian state.* State and local government decisions defend our economy, security and welfare. But you have a chance to link this work to the smallest social structures beyond family. Sympathy groups re-engage people, your electors, in ways that are more immediate and compelling than parliaments and councils. The secret of our sustainable future is to harness the power of the law and capital to our ancestral structures of creativity.

Appendix:

Scientific Evidence

EVALUATION PIONEERS

James Lind, one of the first modern clinical investigators, was the father of evidence-based medicine.[486] Born in Edinburgh in 1716, he apprenticed at the age of 15 to George Langlands, a member of the Incorporation of Surgeons. After eight years of training, he travelled south to England to join the Royal Navy as a surgeon's mate. For eight years he sailed the oceans, to West Africa, the West Indies and across the Mediterranean, and by 1747 he was promoted to the role of surgeon on HMS Salisbury. Lind recognised that scurvy was a major threat to the Navy, a sailor's symptoms starting about two to three months into a voyage. Men became listless, red-blue spots appeared on their skin, their gums would bleed, muscles and joints ache, legs and abdomen swell, and their eyes become yellowed by jaundice. A sudden death was from heart failure. In 1740, death rates from scurvy were astronomical. Lord Anson, First Lord of the Admiralty, sailed a convoy of six ships around the world. Of 961 sailors who left England, 626 died of scurvy by the time they reached the Juan Fernández Islands, off the coast of Chile.

So Lind led the first well-described clinical trial to solve this lethal problem.[487] "On the 20th of May 1747, I selected 12 patients in the scurvy, on board the Salisbury at sea," he wrote. "Their cases were as similar as I could have them. They all in general had putrid gums, the spots and lassitude, with weakness of the knees. They lay together in one place, being a proper apartment for the sick in the forehold; and had one diet common to all, viz. water gruel sweetened with sugar in the morning; fresh mutton-broth often times for dinner; at other times light puddings, boiled biscuit with sugar, etc., and for supper, barley and raisins, rice and currants, sago and wine or the like." Lind decided to assign the 12 patients to six different treatments: two drank a quart of cider a day, two took 25 drops of elixir vitriol three times a day, two received two spoonfuls of vinegar three times a day, two had a course of sea-water, two had two oranges and one lemon given daily and the last two received an electary (a drug mixed into a paste with honey and water) recommended by a hospital surgeon.

Lind reported that: "the most sudden and visible good effects were perceived from the use of oranges and lemons; one of those who had taken them, being at the end of six days fit for duty . . . The other was the best recovered of any in his condition; and . . . was appointed to attend the rest of the sick. Next to the oranges, I thought the cyder had the best effects . . ." Lind had no knowledge of vitamins, and the cause of scurvy was not discovered until 1928, when Albert Szent-Györgyi of Hungary isolated l-ascorbic acid (Vitamin C) as the specific vitamin cure for scurvy. But Lind's careful small experiment showed the benefit of citrus fruits compared with other treatments. But it took 200 years before his experimental approach was adopted widely as the best way to assess new treatments for medical progress.

In fact, the Flemish physician JB van Helmont proposed a clinical experiment before Lind.[488] In 1648, he challenged mainstream medics of the day who used purging and blood-letting to treat fever. He suggested using lots cast by him as a method to balance two samples of patients.

"If you speak the truth, you Schoolmen, that you are able to cure any kind of fever without purging but that you are not willing to do so for fear of a worse relapse, come down to a contest, you believers in the Humours. Let us take from the itinerants' hospitals, from the camps or from elsewhere, 200 or 500 poor people with fevers, pleurisy etc and divide them in two: let us cast lots so that one half of them fall to me and the other half to you. I shall cure them without blood-letting or perceptible purging, you will do so according to your knowledge and we shall see how many funerals each of us will have: the outcome of the contest shall be the reward of 300 florins deposited by each of us." No one took him up.

One hundred and seventy years later, in 1816, Dr Lesassier Hamilton in Edinburgh did,[489] with the first study to use alternate allocation of patients to treatment or control. He compared whether blood-letting prior to surgery on 360 wounded soldiers conferred benefit or risk. "It had been so arranged, that this number was admitted, alternately, in such a manner that each of us had one third of the whole. The sick were indiscriminately received, and were attended as nearly as possible with the same care and accommodated with the same comforts. One third of the whole were soldiers of the 61st Regiment, the remainder of my own (the 42nd) Regiment. Neither Mr Anderson nor I ever once employed the lancet. He lost two, I four cases; whilst out of the other third [treated with blood-letting by the third surgeon] 35 patients died."

Despite clear evidence of danger, blood-letting continued. As late as 1892, Canadian physician Sir William Osler wrote that "during the last decades we have certainly bled too little. Pneumonia is one of the diseases in which a timely venesection [bleeding] may save life. To be of service it should be done early. In a full-blooded, healthy man with a high fever and bounding pulse the abstraction of from 20 to 30 ounces of blood is in every way beneficial".[490] Even in the twentieth century physicians in Boston not using blood-letting to treat pneumonia were considered negligent.[491]

The first use of formal randomisation was probably by George Löhner in Nuremberg, Germany.[492] He was the owner and editor of the newspaper Allgemeine Zeitung von und für Bayern. With no medical training, his daily paper carried attacks against homeopathy. In 1835, with Friedrich Wilhelm Von Hoven, a public health physician who had campaigned against homeopathic treatments popular with the aristocracy, he designed a study to compare the effect of homeopathic salt versus snow water in the mitigation of illness. The newspaper published an invitation to anyone interested to attend a local tavern. Löhner designed a protocol in which each patient registered, consented to the trial, the treatment vials were washed with distilled snow-water "before the eyes of those present", and homeopathic potentiation done according to the "strict rules of Dr Reuter", a prominent local homeopath. A grain of salt was dissolved in 100 drops of distilled snow water and the resulting solution was diluted 29 times at a ratio of 1 to 100.

Randomisation was precise: "100 vials, 50 for filling with the potentiation, 50 for filling with pure distilled snow water, are labelled consecutively by Dr Löhner with the numbers 1 to 100, then mixed well among each other and placed, 50 per table, on two tables." Löhner entered the number of each bottle, indicating its contents, on a list, sealed it, and handed it over to the committee. After public assignment of the vials to patients, the committee and patients returned to the Red Rooster Inn a month later "to open the lists which have been handed over to it, in order to compare the effect with the cause". Those who didn't come sent their information, so responses were collected from 50 of the 54 participants. Only eight out of 50 reported anything unusual. Five had received the dilution, three had received water. The rest experienced nothing. They concluded that Reuter's homeopathic water was useless.

The Red Rooster experiment laid down seven principles of modern clinical trials: a careful trial protocol made public; a relatively large sample size; randomised assignment; a control group who received a placebo; a double blind design ("neither the participants nor those who organised the trial, distributed the vials and documented the effects had any idea whether a vial contained the homeopathic high dilution or merely water"); a rough statistical comparison; and irregularities carefully recorded, "such as the failure of four participants to report back, and the fact that several vials were distributed only after the first tavern meeting".[493]

An eccentric and neglected figure in experimental methods and the logic of science was the American philosopher and mathematician, Charles Sanders Peirce, pronounced Purse, born in 1839. The historian Max Fisch described him as "the first modern experimental psychologist in the Americas, the first metrologist to use a wave-length of light as a unit of measure, the inventor of the quincuncial projection of the sphere, the first known conceiver of the design and theory of an electric switching-circuit computer, and the founder of the economy of research."[494] Fisch was not alone in his admiration. Bertrand Russell and Karl Popper both considered Peirce one of the greatest ever thinkers, despite lack of recognition during his lifetime.

Peirce had an undistinguished career at Harvard, where his father had been professor of astronomy and mathematics. His application for a job at the university was vetoed by the President. Peirce had a temper and could be difficult. Seven years after being appointed by Johns Hopkins University as lecturer in logic, they asked him to leave. His wife had left him after his affair with a French woman, Juliette Froissy. Throughout his career, he was also victimised by a leading scientist, Simon Newcomb, who blocked his appointments and applications for grant funding. After leaving Johns Hopkins, Peirce abandoned academia and lived on a farm in Milford, Pennsylvania. Suffering recurrent severe pain from trigeminal neuralgia, he borrowed money to pay debts, went on the run from police after getting into fights, and descended into penury, unable to afford heating. He was fed *gratis* by a local baker. In 1914, he died in obscurity.

But in 1923, John Dewey, an American philosopher and educationalist, a student of Peirce at Hopkins, put him back on a pedestal. Peirce's widow had sold his papers to Harvard, a collection of 100,000 pages and 1650 unpublished manuscripts. Dewey and contemporary historians found an archive of insights into algebra, probability theory, the logic of science, statistics, astronomy, and psychology. Peirce developed a propensity theory of probability, and an analysis of the logic of science. He wrote a paper on the processes of abduction, deduction and hypothesis – abduction, a way to explore data, look for patterns, and suggest hypotheses; deduction, a process to refine a hypothesis based on other literature and premises; and induction, empirical testing of the hypothesis. Peirce believed that science was not based on the French idea of introspection or rationality, but rather on hypothesis and pragmatism. Scientists tested ideas through experiments, criticised findings, and continually tried to correct and improve theories when previous ideas were shown to be false. Peirce described falsifiability and blinded, controlled and randomised experiments in 1884, decades before Karl Popper. He proposed that the scientific method was superior to other methods of reasoning and should be used more widely. Science could never be certain, only deal with probabilities, and probability frequencies analysed only after objective randomisation in experiments. In his development of statistical methods, he was in advance of everyone. He used correlation and smoothing, and introduced 'likelihood' and 'confidence' in statistical analysis.[495]

Experimental methods began to change the practice of medicine.

Harvard physiologist Lawrence Henderson remarked that at some time between 1900 and 1912, a random patient with a random disease, choosing a physician at random, had for the first time in history a better than 50:50 chance of profiting from the encounter.[496] Two twentieth century pioneers of statistical methods to assess evidence are known to undergraduate students by the tests that bear their names. Student, a pen name for William Gosset, invented the 'z test' and the 't test'. Ronald Fisher devised the 'exact test' for considering differences in smaller samples. Gosset trained as a chemist at Oxford, but left academic life and joined the Guinness business, becoming head brewer at factories in Dublin and London's Park Royal.[497] His job was to create new beers and flavours by experimenting with different combinations of barley, hops and malt. He was interested in crop yields on different plots of land and noted there was considerable variation in yield, even across the same plot. In 1911, he wrote: "If we consider the causes of variation in the yield of a crop, it seems that broadly speaking they are divisible into two kinds. The first are random, occurring at haphazard all over the field. Such would be attacks by birds, the incidence of weeds or the presence of lumps of manure. The second occurs with more regularity, increase from point to point or having centres from which they spread outwards; we may take as instances of this kind changes of soil, moist patches over springs or the presence of rabbit holes along a hedge."

He went on: "Now, if we are comparing two varieties, it is clearly of advantage to arrange the plots in such a way that the yields of both varieties shall be affected as far as possible by the same causes to as nearly as possible an equal extent. To do this it is necessary . . . to compare together plots which lie side by side and also to make the [side by side] plots as small as may be practicable and convenient."[498] Gosset recognised he needed balanced comparison groups when measuring crop yields and sufficient statistical power to draw firm conclusions from measured differences, when comparing, for example, different growing conditions. He identified a vital step in experimental methods, developed further by Fisher.

The modern concept of randomisation and selection of control groups really began with Fisher, who, like Gosset, used this approach in agriculture. Fisher was one of the founders of modern statistics, and a pioneer of population genetics. His book, The Genetical Theory of Natural Selection, remains one of the landmark books on evolution and genetics. Richard Dawkins described him as the "greatest biologist since Darwin". Fisher was also passionate about India where, in Calcutta, he helped to develop the Indian Statistical Institute. In his 1938 presidential address to the society he described the tension between academics and policymakers, as true now as then. "The academic mind, as we know, is sometimes capable of assuming an aggressive attitude. The official mind, on the contrary, is and has to be, expert in the art of self-defence."

Fisher was fussy and didn't suffer fools gladly. He was "apt to wash his hands of assistants whom he found muddle-headed or lacking in initiative". He found university administration and red tape intolerable. After moving from University College London to Cambridge during the Second World War he said: "I used to think only University College was difficult, but now I know all officials are obstructive." One of Fisher's students at UCL in 1937 was the American statistician William Edwards Deming. Deming revolutionised the methods of quality improvement in industrial production, mainly in Japan, and his influence on corporate strategy and the assessment of quality in industrial production was pivotal.

Fisher's contribution to the evidence-based movement came in his book The Design of Experiments, published in 1935. He posed a teasing question: "A lady declares that by tasting a cup of tea made with milk she can discriminate whether the milk or the tea infusion was first added to the cup. We will consider the problem of designing an experiment by means of which this assertion can be tested. Every experiment exists only in order to give the facts a chance of disproving the null hypothesis."

The null hypothesis is the scientific status quo, or the default position. In this case, that she can't really tell the order of making the cup of tea through taste. It assumes that a treatment does not work, or a causal relationship does not exist. An experiment must demonstrate that this default position is false (Popper's principle of falsifiability) by providing robust statistical probability estimates that the null hypothesis is disproved.

The null hypothesis can never be proven, only disproved. Conventionally, science and medicine place threshold levels of probability required to show it is disproved, commonly, at least a 95% 'confidence range' and probability that the experiment rejects the null hypothesis. Today, every peer-reviewed scientific publication or international scientific policy report, like the Intergovernmental Panel on Climate Change, uses Fisher's concepts of probability, confidence and levels of certainty.

Fisher courted controversy, which blighted his reputation after retirement. Like several scientists of his generation, he was an ardent eugenicist, and argued that races differed "in their innate capacity for intellectual and emotional development". At the end of his career, in the late 1950s, he raised doubts about the link between smoking and cancer, proposed by Richard Doll and Austin Bradford Hill. They compared causes of death among doctors who smoked and those that didn't. Fisher pointed out, correctly, that a correlation does not necessarily mean causation. He supported his argument by showing that imports of apples correlated with the rise in the number of divorces. His rationale was impeccable, but his motives murky. He was a lifelong, ardent pipe smoker, and a paid consultant to the tobacco industry. Nonetheless, despite his prejudices and mistakes, Fisher built a cornerstone for the foundations of modern evidence assessment.

RANDOMISED EXPERIMENTS

In October 1948, the British Medical Journal published the first large scale medical experiment to use a randomised and controlled design. Dr Geoffrey Marshall led a Medical Research Council Investigation of the value of streptomycin treatment for pulmonary tuberculosis, with statistics and design by Professor Austin Bradford Hill. The paper reported that: "Determination of whether a patient would be treated by streptomycin and bed-rest (S case) or by bed-rest alone (C case) was made by reference to a statistical series based on random sampling numbers drawn up for each sex at each centre by Professor Bradford Hill; the details of the series were unknown to any of the investigators or to the co-ordinator and were contained in a set of sealed envelopes, each bearing on the outside only the name of the hospital and a number."

Results showed that 28/55 (51%) of patients receiving streptomycin injections showed considerable improvement in X-ray at six months (compared with the one taken on admission), whereas only 4/52 (8%) improved in the control group. The probability of a difference occurring by chance was less than one in a million. They explained why a control group was essential. "The need of a control group in trials of a new drug for pulmonary tuberculosis is underlined by the finding that impressive clinical improvement was seen in some of the patients treated by bed-rest alone: 12 gained more than 14lb in weight, and in 13 of 47 (feverish) patients the temperature was within normal limits at the end of six months." In other words, many patients get better without receiving a new treatment, so studies must allow for natural improvement.

This pioneering study contained the elements that 40 years on would underpin a revolution in medical evidence. The study had a comparison group of patients, randomisation of allocation of the drug in order to control for all confounding variables, known and unknown, blinding of the treatment by observers and patients, use of a placebo drug, and a sample size which allowed them to assess effects on the primary outcome. Trials too small to measure statistically significant benefits or risks seriously mislead decision-makers.

Why is randomisation so important? The biggest worry for a scientist when testing interventions like a new drug, a training programme, a social group, or indeed an economic idea like a microfinance group, is that factors other than the intervention being tested may explain differences in outcomes observed between intervention and comparison arms of the trial. For example, our academic team, working in partnership with Dharma Manandhar and his Mother and Infant Research Activities group, conducted a randomised trial of multivitamin supplements for pregnant women in Dhanusha district in southern Nepal. The World Health Organisation and Unicef had developed a new combined vitamin tablet but no one had tested its impact on women and their babies in the developing world. We wanted to know if it increased the birth weight of infants, as a reflection of the mother's own improved nutrition. In Nepal, average birth weight for boys is about 2750 grams (six pounds), compared with 3400 grams (seven and a half pounds) in Europe and America. Nepali babies have shorter, thinner mothers, and are born, on average, about three to four days earlier. We enrolled 1200 women from antenatal clinics, and randomly assigned them to receive one of two identical looking pills, one with the new supplement, the other with just iron and folate, the recommended standard and policy of the Nepal government.

	Control (n=600)	Intervention (n=600)
Residence		
Urban	316 (53%)	314 (52%)
Rural	284 (47%)	286 (48%)
Land owned		
None	39 (7%)	29 (5%)
≤10 kattha*	312 (52%)	337 (56%)
>10 kattha*	247 (41%)	227 (38%)
Husband's occupation		
No work	61 (10%)	69 (12%)
Farming	92 (15%)	89 (15%)
Salaried	252 (42%)	261 (44%)
Small business	114 (19%)	109 (18%)
Waged labour	66 (11%)	53 (9%)
Student	8 (1%)	9 (2%)
Out of country	7 (1%)	10 (2%)
Age		
<20 years	171 (29%)	190 (32%)
20–29 years	398 (66%)	387 (65%)
≥30 years	31 (5%)	23 (4%)
Schooling		
None	271 (45%)	273 (46%)
Primary	67 (11%)	56 (9%)
Lower secondary or higher	262 (44%)	271 (45%)
Parity		
0	266 (44%)	274 (46%)
1–2	261 (44%)	276 (46%)
≥3	73 (12%)	50 (8%)
Enrolment weight (kg)	45·1 (6·0)	45·1 (6·2)
Height (cm)†	151·0 (5·7)	150·5 (5·4)
Enrolment body-mass index (kg/m²)	19·8 (2·4)	19·9 (2·4)
<18·5 kg/m²	170 (28%)	172 (29%)

Data are number of participants (%) or mean (SD). *10 kattha is about 0·3 hectares.
†Control, n=598; intervention n=599.

Table 1: Baseline household and participant characteristics

Figure 46: The beauty of randomisation in achieving balanced groups for variables both known and unknown[499]

From *The Lancet*. 365 (9463): 955-962

We knew that other factors such as household wealth, whether the mother was literate or not, and her pre-existing weight and height, would influence the baby's birth weight. We could, of course, have tried to balance our intervention and control groups by deliberately matching pairs of women who shared similar levels of wealth, education, weight and height. We didn't need to. Randomisation does it for us. Take a look at the levels of these alternative explanatory factors in the two arms of our trial.

They match almost perfectly – a good example of the beauty of random enrolment. With a large enough sample size, random allocation to a drug or placebo produces balanced groups of trial subjects, not only for the alternative explanatory factors that you can think of, but also, and this is critical, for the unknown ones as well. Randomisation is a beautiful and simple way of removing social, economic and other differences between groups in an evaluation study.

As an illustration, one research team compared two methods to assess the impact of the US State Partnership Initiative employment promotion programme: a non-randomised method (propensity-score matching) which attempted to match programme participants to identical non-participants, and a randomised controlled trial with very low vulnerability to selection bias. The matching method suggested large benefits of the employment programme on earnings, the randomised method (the gold standard) showed no impact, with a slight trend towards lower earnings in the promotion group. The results from the non-randomised method would mislead policymakers into investing large sums of money into a job promotion programme that had no real benefit.

Randomisation does have limitations. It's less efficient at balancing out differences when a trial team want to randomise groups, such as villages, school classes or physician practices, rather than individuals. But even in so-called cluster randomised evaluations, alternative explanatory factors (scientists use the term 'confounding variables') can be largely accounted for. And if differences between the study arms are found at baseline they can be adjusted for in the analysis.

And maybe you can't do a trial? In medicine, education and economics a trial may not be feasible. A treatment or intervention might be so obviously effective – like ventilation when a patient collapses, or the introduction of penicillin – that a trial is deemed unnecessary. Or if the benefit is likely to be very small, or take decades to appear – for example assessing whether breastfeeding cuts the risk of diabetes in adulthood – other study types will be sought. Another obstacle to randomisation arises if the intervention is already widely used, or if policymakers have decided to adopt it. For example, we wished to study whether Vitamin A supplements given to mothers at the time of birth would cut deaths of infants in Nepal. During the planning stage we learnt that the Nepal government, despite little solid trial evidence, had chosen to make this national policy. The trial plan was dropped. We couldn't ethically enrol 'control mothers' when national policy dictated they should receive the vitamin.

Last but not least is cost. The assumption that randomised controlled trials are always expensive is misleading. Remember that trials will justify or prevent unnecessary state expenditure for years to come. Well-planned trials are usually extremely cost-effective. But decision-makers are impatient. The idea of spending millions on a trial and delaying a decision for three years or more doesn't appeal. In these circumstances, one option is a kind of randomised assessment called a stepped wedge. For example, we might have provisional evidence of effectiveness of the use of health promotion campaigns to reduce teenage pregnancy in poor UK communities, or to cut HIV infection among teenage girls in southern Africa. The stepped wedge design allows for phased scale-up but also provides a randomised and controlled comparison. The whole population will finally receive the intervention, unlike a standard trial, but in a step-wise manner with clusters or areas or districts enrolled in a randomised process. Population groups act as control populations until the intervention reaches them, when they become intervention groups. This method gives impatient policymakers an option to go to scale but to make a scientific assessment at the same time. It should be used more often.

Observational evidence may be the only option for some policy decisions. Randomised trials are not possible for many aspects of macroeconomic policy such as demand management to stabilise growth and inflation. When private credit and demand plummet, and recession looms, economic history suggests that stimulation of demand through government spending is essential. Or, when growth and demand later accelerate, we know from experience and analysis that increasing interest rates will hold inflation in check. In the financial dailies, economic commentators bitterly disagree about these issues. Supply-siders want governments to not interfere and let the market decide. Keynesians want government to stimulate demand. A trial would be nice, but impossible. Economists use other clever ways to imply causality between economic policy and impact.

When a trial or stepped wedge design isn't possible, Professor Austin Bradford Hill, 60 years ago, gave us beautiful principles by which we might distinguish between associations not causally linked and those that are. Examples include Fisher's observation of the absurd link between apple imports and divorce rates, and those that might be causally linked, such as tobacco use and lung cancer, raised exam performance by boys in mixed vs single sex classrooms, or the economic policy of quantitative easing and future interest rates.[500] Bradford Hill proposed nine criteria to support a causal link: the strength of the association (a strong one is more likely to suggest a cause than a weak one); whether the relationship is consistent (observed repeatedly); specific (a factor influences a specific population or outcome); or linked in time, (the supposed cause precedes the consequence); whether there is a dose-response relationship, with a larger response when the dose of the factor is increased; and whether the association is plausible (in biology or economics does the relationship make sense?); coherent (is it consistent with existing knowledge?); supported by experiment (are there experimental trials to suggest a similar relationship?); and has a similar effect already been shown (for example, thalidomide and rubella cause damage in pregnancy, so another observed drug association in pregnancy might be likely). My colleagues at the WHO successfully used these causality principles to examine the emerging evidence from the Zika virus epidemic about its links to newborn brain damage, faced with competing theories about pesticides or genetically modified mosquitoes as the cause of rising cases of microcephaly.

Figure 47. Sir Austin Bradford Hill

In 1971, the medical evidence movement gained momentum when Archie Cochrane, a clinical epidemiologist in Cardiff, in his classic treatise Effectiveness and Efficiency: Random Reflections on Health Services, called for systematic reviews of trials to build a library of evidence available to all. More than one trial was needed to persuade policymakers and health authorities that an intervention worked. A systematic review trawls the world literature, both published and unpublished, to find all previous trials and studies. The review uses statistical methods to give an overall estimate of benefit (the effect size) and an estimate of certainty such as 'the confidence interval'. For example, a summary of 15 trials of a drug or social intervention might show an overall effect size in cutting population deaths by 18%, with 95% confidence that the true value is somewhere between 11% and 25%. This process is called meta-analysis and distils down a huge amount of scientific work into a summary statistic easily understood by decision-makers. As new evidence emerges, we update the overall estimate through periodic meta-analysis. Despite being called 'mega-silliness' by the psychologist Hans Eysenck, the method has endured the test of time.

From the 1990s, the evidence-based medicine movement spread rapidly across Canada, the USA and the UK aided by public health minded physicians and epidemiologists like Kay Dickersin and the late Anna Donald. They risked their reputations by challenging the privilege and vested interests of consultant wisdom and infallibility. Alarmed fellows of the Royal College of Obstetricians and Gynaecologists wrote in their journal that Iain Chalmers and his Oxford group, who had challenged the evidence for many accepted practices in Effective Care in Pregnancy and Childbirth, were like an "obstetrical Baader-Meinhof gang".[501]

Chalmers and colleagues went on to set up the Cochrane Collaboration, an international group of nearly 30,000 volunteers from over 100 countries, to collate the data from all biomedical trials and to report an unbiased view of the evidence for every conceivable medical treatment. Many routine clinical procedures were found to be ineffective. Tonsillectomy, grommet tubes inserted surgically for middle ear fluid in young children, episiotomy (cutting the vaginal wall just prior to delivery of a baby) and routine bed-rest were gradually withdrawn from routine clinical practice.

Conflicts of interest among scientists and medics also emerged as a threat to unbiased evidence.[502] Gifts from drug and product companies to doctors are ubiquitous. Industry funds most medical research in the US. In every country, drug company reps distribute millions of free gifts or newer, more expensive drugs to physicians to seduce them away from generic, more cost-effective drugs. Some senior physicians accept board positions or consultancies, or speak on behalf of a company, or agree to become 'gift authors' on clinical trial papers long after the data has been collected and analysed. Failure to disclose payments or, worse, to not publish negative results from a drug trial can bias systematic reviews of evidence-based medicine. Failure to publish data on side-effects has had catastrophic consequences: for example, delays in reporting the associations between temazepam and overdose deaths, thalidomide and congenital defects, and the black box US Food and Drug Administration warning given to Prozac, once the most widely prescribed antidepressant, for its effect on suicide risk in adolescents. Some national professional societies or groups that produce clinical guidelines don't report their own corporate funding or conflicts of interest. Lobbying by big tobacco, big alcohol and big food companies is rife.

These practices erode public trust in medicine. Editors of research journals realise now that researchers can be bought. Scientists "who ignore legal requirements to publicly report clinical trial results often have received large payments from drug companies involved in the studies".[503] Most journals have introduced strict rules. Researchers must declare all conflicts of interest at the end of a paper. Readers have the right to know about bias. The sums involved are enormous. In 2013/14 pharmaceutical companies spent $6.5 billion on US doctors for research and for travel, consulting, and speaking fees.[504] That is three times the annual budget of the World Health Organisation.

Other challenges to reliable evidence have surfaced. How can we assess the 'effectiveness' of interventions introduced at scale in the real world compared with 'efficacy' studies in tightly controlled research studies? For instance, suppose we discover a new vaccine cuts transmission of an infection by 85% when we enrol volunteer subjects to receive the vaccine or act as a control, when we protect the stability of the vaccine in a cold chain managed by specially trained research staff, and when we measure side-effects among volunteers. Will the effect be the same when the vaccine is introduced into a real population in a developing country? Maybe their population is less well-nourished than our volunteers, which might impair the immune response to the vaccine. Maybe the cold chain is dodgy and the vaccine subjected to warming and thawing, damaging its biological potency. Maybe the antiseptic skills of vaccinators are shaky, with a greater risk of a vaccine abscess or inflammation. News of unpleasant reactions might deter neighbours from accepting injections. Maybe one or two lazy teams fake their immunisation coverage returns and don't bother to deliver the vaccine to children in remoter villages. In practice, population 'effectiveness' might turn out to be only 10-20%, or even less, in cutting infection rates compared with the 85% 'efficacy' found in the research trial.

Effectiveness studies are as important as efficacy ones. The real world is complex. Some believe complexity is a reason to doubt the importance of evidence from randomised evaluations. These are legitimate concerns. But the randomised approach can be used in both efficacy and effectiveness studies. And resisters to both kinds of experiment risk throwing the evidence baby out with the murky bathwater of the real world.

Image Credits

1. The Dunbar hierarchy of human groups
2. Soccer team of British soldiers with gas masks, World War I. Contributor: GL Archive / Alamy Stock Photo
3. British soldiers at a funeral in France during World War I . Contributor: World History Archive / Alamy Stock Photo
4. A dramatised depiction of a fraternity initiation from the yearbook of Dartmouth College, c. 1896. Dartmouth College Aegis
5. Chester Mystery Plays. Engraving depicting an early Chester Mystery Play. This photographic reproduction is in the public domain in the UK and United States. David Gee Image scanned from first edition of the *Chambers Book of Days* (1864) by Robert Chambers
6. The Tightrope, Peter Brook, Yoshi Oida (gesturing), 2012. Photo: Daniel Bardou ©First Run. Alamy
7. Barnum, a musical. Menier Chocolate Factory theatre, London, 2018. Photo: the author
8. A. With our clinic team in Baglung. B. The day of King Birendra's visit to Baglung. Photos the author
9. Dhamja health post. Dil Bahadur is far right. Photo: the author
10. Duke Ellington and his Orchestra, 1938. Courtesy: CSU Archives/ Everett Collection
11. Sports sympathy groups A. Barcelona football team. Alamy. B. Jardine's cricket team. The author

12. Women's suffrage group, New South Wales, c. 1892. Mitchell Library, State Library of New South Wales

13. President Vladimir Putin, centre, at a cabinet of ministers conference, 2006. Contributor: SPUTNIK / Alamy Stock Photo

14. Interior of a London Coffee House, 17th century. Anonymous. Public domain. Interior of a London Coffee House, 1668. From Pim Reinders, Thera Wijsenbeek et al., *Koffie in Nederland: Viereeuwen culturgeschiendenis,* (Zutphen: Walberg Pers; Deft: Gemeente Musea Delft, 1994)

15. Religious sympathy group appeasing the Gods after the Nepal earthquake, 2015. Photo: the author

16. Namibia, Eastern Bushmanland, Tsumkwe. A band of !Kung hunter-gatherers makes a stealthy approach towards an antelope. Alamy Stock Photo

17. Naro bushman (San) women digging up an edible root, Central Kalahari, Botswana Contributor: Ariadne Van Zandbergen / Alamy Stock Photo

18. The symposium of Plato. Pietro Testa Italy, Lucca 1648. The Los Angeles County Museum of Art

19. Satirical cartoon of the select vestry of St. Paul's, Covent Garden. Thomas Jones, 1828. *Title:* Select vestry comforts *Abstract:* "Eight of the select vestry of St. Paul's, Covent Garden, dine in the Vestry Room, while the beadle blocks the doorway on the extreme right. Forms part of: British Cartoon Prints Collection (US Library of Congress)

20. John Lilburne. Engraver George Glover. Public domain Wikimedia

21. Levellers manifesto. John Lilburne, William Walwyn, Thomas Prince, Richard Overton, 1649. Public domain

22. Alexis de Tocqueville. Photograph of a sketch of the French author and traveller Alexis de Tocqueville. Undated, by an unknown artist. Courtesy of the Beinecke Rare Book & Manuscript Library, Yale University

23. The Boston Tea Party: Colonists dressed as Mohawk Indians dump British imported tea into the Boston Harbor angry at the British

government for taxing the colonies. National Archives and Records Administration. Public domain

24. Figures of Red China theatre on the Long March and a theatrical troupe from the Red Army. People's Literature Publishing House. Public domain

25. Makwanpur, Nepal: A. A women's group in facilitated conversation. Courtesy Thomas Kelly. B. Kirti Tumbahamphe. Photo: the author. C. Women's group receiving revolving fund payments. Photo: the author. D. Women's group members making safe delivery kits. Photo: the author

26. Gathering of two women's groups, Bhimphedi, Nepal. Courtesy, Thomas Kelly

27. A and B. Adivasi women work in groups to create health promotion materials. Orissa State, India. C. Adivasi elder in Jharkhand forest. Photos: the author

28. Azad Khan and Kishwar Azad. Photo: the author

29. Bengali women's group, the Perinatal Care Project, Bangladesh University of Health Sciences. Photo: the author

30. Women's group with community observers, Mchinji, Malawi. Courtesy, Mikey Rosato. B. One thousand villagers attend women's groups' festival watched by local MP, Patience Zulu. Photo: the author

31. A. The Dharavi Biennale Art Exhibition created by community groups, Mumbai. SNEHA, India. B. Women's health leader Nayreen Daruwalla, persuades Mr Sinha, local announcer, singer, mimic and video producer, to support the Biennale. C. Pregnant woman sculpture made from medicine bottles. Photos: the author

32. Nirmala Nair, Dharma Manadhar, Azad Khan, Kishwar Azad, Prasanta Tripathy, Shanthi Pantvaidya and the author. Photo: the author

33. The Santhal Rebellion. Attack by 600 Santhals upon a party of 50 sepoys, 40th regiment native infantry. Illustrated London News – 1856 http://www.columbia.edu/itc/mealac/pritchett/00routes-data/1800_1899/britishrule/northeast/northeast.html

34. Traditional Nepal Caste Hierarchy, courtesy Nepal Federalism Debate blog. https://nepalfederalismdebate.wordpress.com/2015/05/11/

are-newars-aryan-or-mongol-the-great-racialethnic-debate-of-one-
of-nepals-most-important-nationality/?blogsub=confirmed#
blog_subscription

35. Ecole Normale Superieure group photo. 1923. Public domain.
Courtesy http://www.pierrebrossolette.com/ce-quils-disent/pierre-
brossolette-entre-au-pantheon-par-jean-thomas-nordmann-ens/

36. Reginald Gray. Francis Bacon Portrait 1989. Public domain

37. At the municipally-run Addiction Treatment Center in Ciudad
Nezahualcóyotl, Mexico, addicts engage in group therapy. Contributor:
Keith Dannemiller / Alamy Stock Photo

38. Community group made earth bag building, Goldhunga village,
Kathmandu after 2015 earthquake. Narayan Acharya outside finished
community centre. Photo: the author

39. Pellegrinaio di Santa Maria della Scala. Care of the Sick Domenico
di Bartolo, between 1440 and 1447. Wikimedia, Creative Commons.
Domenico di Bartolo, Courtesy Wikimedia Commons

40. Pellegrinaio di Santa Maria della Scala - The Rearing of Children
and The Marriage of Daughter of the Hospital Santa Maria della
Scala Hospital (Siena). Domenico di Bartolo, Courtesy Wikimedia
Commons, Combusken Italy

41. Jony Ive and his Apple design team 'sympathy group' collect two
prestigious awards for British Design and Art Direction, September
2012. Courtesy, Evening Standard

42. The Lunar Society. Alamy

43. The attack on Joseph Priestley's home, Fairhill, at Sparkbrook,
Birmingham on 14 July 1791. By Johann Eckstein - Norton Anthology
of English Literature, public domain, https://commons.wikimedia.
org/w/index.php?curid=6149569

44. Monthly mean atmospheric carbon dioxide at Mauna Loa Observatory,
Hawaii. Courtesy, National Oceanic and Atmospheric Administration.
Earth System Research Laboratory. Global Monitoring Division.
https://www.esrl.noaa.gov/gmd/ccgg/trends/full.html

45. Trends in fertility rates by region. From Bongaerts, John. "Human
population growth and the demographic transition." Philosophical

Translations, Royal Society London B Biological Sciences(2009) 364, 2985–2990

46. The beauty of randomisation in achieving balanced groups for variables both known and unknown. Courtesy, Lancet paper, open access, footnote 498

47. Sir Austin Bradford Hill. Wellcome Collection

Acknowledgments

After years of writing academic papers as part of a team, this perilous solo effort means that any mistake is my sole responsibility. I apologise for errors of fact or interpretation. Over the years many people have influenced and educated me about sympathy groups. In Nepal, massive thanks to Dharma Manandhar, Bhim Shrestha, Kirti Tumbahamphe, Rita Thapa, Ramesh Adhikari, Madan Manandhar, Jyoti Shrestha, Kasturi Malla, Bimala Malla, Buddharaj and the Mother and Infant Research Activities teams in Makwanpur and Janakpur. Huge thanks also to Naomi Saville and Narayan Acharya, Joanna Morrison, Sophia Dulal, Helen Harris-Fry, Delan Devakumar, Kelly Clarke, Basu Dev Pandey and Lu Gram.

In Jharkhand, India, I have learnt so much from Prasanta Tripathy, Nirmala Nair, Suchitra Rath, Shibanand Rath, Rajendra Mahapatra, Rajkumar Gope, Dipnath Mahto, and other members of the Ekjut team. Audrey Prost has supported Ekjut and all of our women's group studies with selfless wisdom. And Arti Ahuja, the former secretary of health in Orissa, after learning of the Ekjut study, created a movement of over 120,000 women's groups across her state, reaching out to 40 million people

In Bangladesh, I've had the opportunity to work with inspiring and dedicated colleagues like Kishwar Azad, Azad Khan, Abdul Kuddus, Sanjit Shaha, Tasmeen Nahar, Sarah Barnett and Ed Fottrell. In Mumbai, Armida Fernandes, Neena Shah More, Nayreen Daruwalla, Wasu Joshi and the whole SNEHA team are wonderfully creative. In Nepal and Mumbai, David Osrin has been a great friend and academic partner, and his wife, Susie Vickery, an inspiration.

In Malawi, Charles Mwansambo and Peter Kazembe are not only brilliant clinicians but have also led large field projects with warmth and humour. Tambosi Phiri, Florida Malamba, Hilda Chapota, Beata Kunyenge, Sonia Lewycka, Mikey Rosato, Stefania Vergnano, Carina King and James Beard were stalwarts of the MaiMwana team. Bejoy Nambiar and Tim Colbourn worked closely with Charles Makwenda and his team in developing the Parent Child Initiative, in partnership with the Ministry of Health. Address Malata taught me much about leadership in nursing and midwifery, and Mahima Nambiar about friendship, conversation and nurturing.

In WHO Geneva, Annie Portela's work brought community empowerment through women's groups into global policy. Many great WHO colleagues built highly effective sympathy teams for research, programmes and monitoring of mother and child health, under the direction of Rajiv Bahl, Bernadette Daelmans and Theresa Diaz respectively.

And the ideas of others influenced this book - Lisa Howard Grabman, Hilary Standing, Jerome Lewis, Harry Rutter, Tanja Houweling, Nadine Seward, Melissa Neumann, Jolene Skordis, Christina Pagel, Marina Cantacuzino and Dan Levy. The team at Women and Children First, especially Ros Davies, Ruth Duebbert, Dorothy Flatman and Mikey Rosato, have taken women's health groups to scale in many resource-poor countries

In the UK, members of my sympathy book group Paul VerBruggen, William Field, Simon O'Hagan, Antony Randle, Peter Williamson and Richard Smith have argued and disagreed about almost 200 books, and taught me that literature is in the eyes of the beholder. My Jardine sympathy group cricket team were sadly never able to achieve their dream of being humourless and ruthless. Joining the eleven piece Blue Frogs soul band was a deep, though unmerited, pleasure for me, especially because Gilles Guilbert was such a fine saxophonist and teacher

Throughout my pinball career I have learnt much from leaders who inspired groups through passion, ideas and a sense of fun. They included Leonard Strang, Os Reynolds, David Nabarro, John Stanford and Graham Rook, Andrew Tomkins, Malcolm Grant, Anne Johnson, David Price and Graham Hart. And of course Flavia Bustreo, who gave me the opportunity to work with passionate and committed people at WHO, and who campaigned for rights-based approaches to health.

Lindsay O'Hagan, Helen Bilton and Matt Young supported the production of the book magnificently, and Linda Olson at Thornwick Press offered great advice

Most of all, my thanks go to my wonderful survival clique – to Helen, my muse, partner and best friend, and to my children Harry, Freya and Ned, and my daughter-in-law, Masara, whose daily affection and gentle scorn put me in my place.

References

PART 1. SYMPATHY GROUPS

An Ecology for Social Action

1　Ridley, Matt. *The Rational Optimist: How Prosperity Evolves*. New York; Toronto, Ontario. Harper Perennial, 2011.

2　McKibben, Bill. "Global Warming's Terrifying New Math. Three Simple Numbers That Add up to Global Catastrophe." Rolling Stone, http://www.rollingstone.com/politics/news/global-warmings-terrifying-new-math-20120719
　　Kolbert, Elizabeth. *The Sixth Extinction: An Unnatural History*. London: Bloomsbury, 2015.

3　Dunbar, Robin. *Human Evolution*. London: Pelican, 2014.

4　ibid

5　Williams, Michael. "Rise of Isis Forms Part of a Pattern." *Financial Times*, July 7th 2014.

6　Holt-Lunstad, Julianne, Smith, Timothy B., and Layton, J. Bradley. 2010. *"Social Relationships and Mortality Risk: A Meta-analytic Review."* Public Library of Science. http://www.ncbi.nlm.nih.gov/pmc/articles/PMC2910600.

7　Brook, Peter. *The Empty Space*. London. Penguin Books, 2008.

8　Okun, Arthur M., and Lawrence Summers. *Equality and Efficiency, the Big Tradeoff*. Washington, District of Columbia: Brookings Institution Press, 2015.

9　Fanon, Frantz, and Mary Turner. *Black Skin, White Masks*. New York: Grove Press, 1967.

10　Anderson, Roy and Alison Bettis. *Lancet Global Health Blog* http://globalhealth.thelancet.com/2017/04/19/top-five-investments-we-should-be-making-tackle-ntds

11　Bookchin, Murray. *The Ecology of Freedom: The Emergence and Dissolution of Hierarchy*, AK Press, 2005.

12　Murray Bookchin, interview by David Vanek (October 1, 2001) Harbinger, *Journal of Social Ecology*, Vol. 2 No. 1. Institute for Social Ecology.

13 Macfarlane, Alan. *The Origins of English Individualism: The Family, Property and Social Transition*. Oxford: Blackwell, 1979.

14 Sassen, Saskia. *Expulsions: Brutality and Complexity in the Global Economy*. Belknap, Harvard, 2018.

15 Juvenal, and Richard George. *The Satires of Juvenal* [Translated from the Latin]. St. Albans: Baikal, 2012.

16 Naipaul, V.S. *India: A Million Mutinies Now*. London: Mandarin Paperbacks, 1993.

17 Srimati Totchaire was the common newsreader pronunciation of the British Prime Minister Mrs Thatcher.

18 Costello, A.M. de L, and G. Tudor-Williams. "Nepal Improvement of Rural Health Services." *The Lancet* 327, no. 8495, 1986:1433-34.

Ancestral Benefits

19 Bill Clinton. Speaking at the EAT forum, Stockholm, May 27th 2014.

20 Dunbar, Robin. *Human Evolution*. London: Pelican, 2014.

21 Smith, Adam. *The Wealth of Nations. Books 1-3*, Seven Treasures Publications, 2009.

22 Wolfe, Tom. "The Me Decade and the Third Great Awakening." *New York Magazine*, August 23rd 1976, 26-40.

23 Andersen, Kurt. "The Downside of Liberty." *The New York Times*, July 4th 2012.

24 Anderson, Benedict R.O'G. *Imagined Communities: Reflections on the Origin and Spread of Nationalism*. Verso, 2016.

25 Ledeneva, Alena V. *Can Russia Modernise? Sistema, Power Networks and Informal Governance*. Cambridge: Cambridge University Press, 2014.

26 Spykman, Nicholas John, and Richard Edes Harrison. *America's Strategy in World Politics*. New York: Harcourt, Brace & Co., 1942.
Anderson, Perry. *American Foreign Policy and its Thinkers*. London; New York: Verso, 2017.

27 Mead, Walter Russell. *Power, Terror, Peace, and War: America's Grand Strategy in a World at Risk*. New York: Knopf, 2005.

28 Johnson, Steven. *Where Good Ideas Come From: The Natural History of Innovation*. New York: Riverhead Books, 2011.

29 Hale, Deborah. "The London Coffee House: A Social Institution" http://nomu-personal.blogspot.ch/2010/10/london-coffee-house-social-institution.html

30 "The Women's Petition against Coffee 1674." https://www.gopetition.com/famous-petitions-in-history/232/the-women-s-petition-against-coffee-1674.html

31 Ackroyd, Peter. *The History of England. Volume IV*. Chapter 10. London: Macmillan, 2016.

32 Matthew 5:13. The New Testament.

33 Rodwell, J M 1808-1900. *The Koran*. 2: 177. Palala Press, 2016.

34 Darwin, Charles. *The Descent of Man*. New York: American Home Library, 1902.

35 Blackburn, Simon. *The Oxford Dictionary of Philosophy*. Oxford University Press, 2016.

36 Rosato, Mikey, Charles W. Mwansambo, Peter N. Kazembe, Tambosi Phiri, Queen S. Soko, Sonia Lewycka, Beata E. Kunyenge, *et al.* "Women's Groups' Perceptions of Maternal Health Issues in Rural Malawi." *The Lancet* 368, no. 9542 (2006): 1180-88.

37 Blackburn, Simon. *The Oxford Dictionary of Philosophy.* Oxford University Press, 2016.

38 Anglemyer, Horvath, and Rutherford. "The Accessibility of Firearms and Risk for Suicide and Homicide Victimization among Household Members. A Systematic Review and Meta-Analysis." *Annals of Internal Medicine* 160, no. 2 (2014): 101-10.

39 Christakis, Nicholas, and James Fowler. *Connected: the Amazing Power of Social Networks and How They Shape Our Lives.* London: Harper Press, 2011.

40 Kim, D. A., A. R. Hwong, D. Stafford, D. A. Hughes, A. J. O'Malley, J. H. Fowler, and N. A. Christakis. "Social Network Targeting to Maximise Population Behaviour Change: A Cluster Randomised Controlled Trial." *Lancet (London, England)* 386, no. 9989 (2015): 145-53.

41 Dalal, Farhad. *Taking the Group Seriously: Towards a Post-Foulkesian Group Analytic Theory.* London: Jessica Kingsley, 2000.

42 Allport, Gordon Willard. *The Nature of Prejudice. Abridged.* Albany, N.Y.: Doubleday, 1964.

43 Nitsun, Morris. *The Anti-Group: Destructive Forces in the Group and Their Creative Potential.* Hove; New York: Routledge. 2015.

44 Phillips, Katherine, and Evan Apfelbaum. *"Delusions of Homogeneity? Reinterpreting the Effects of Group Diversity."* In: *Looking Back, Moving Forward: A Review of Group and Team-Based Research.* Edited by Elizabeth A. Mannix and Margaret Ann Neale Bingley, UK: Emerald Group Pub, 2012.

45 Forget, Evelyn. Evocations of Sympathy: Sympathetic Imagery in Eighteenth-Century Social Theory and Physiology. *History of Political Economy.* Volume 35, Annual Supplement, 2003 pp. 282-308

46 Gregory, John. "A Comparative View of the State and Faculties of Man with Those of the Animal World by John Gregory, MD. FRS. Late Professor of Medicine in the University of Edinburgh, and First Physician to His Majesty in Scotland." (1788).

47 Evelyn Forget. She reports that Lord Kames used this phrase in 1751.

48 ibid

49 ibid

50 ibid

51 ibid

52 Hunter, John, James F. Palmer, and Drewry Ottley. *The Works of John Hunter, FRS. With Notes.* London: Longman, 1837.

53 Hume, David. *Treatise of Human Nature : Being an Attempt to Introduce the Experimental Method of Reasoning into Moral Subjects.* The Floating Press, 2009.

54 Hamilton, W. D. "The Genetical Evolution of Social Behaviour. I." *Journal of Theoretical Biology* 7, no. 1 (1964): 1-16.

55 Hamilton, W. D. "The Genetical Evolution of Social Behaviour. II." *Journal of Theoretical Biology* 7, no. 1 (1964): 17-52.

56 Kenny, Charles. *Getting Better: Why Global Development Is Succeeding: And How We Can Improve the World Even More.* New York: Basic Books, 2012.
Impatient Optimist: Bill Gates in His Own Words. Chicago: Agate Publishing, 2012.

57 Toynbee, Arnold. *A Study of History.* Beijing: China Social Sciences Publishing House, 1999.

58 Kirchhoff, Michael, Thomas Parr, Ensor Palacios, Karl Friston, and Julian Kiverstein. 2018. "The Markov blankets of life: autonomy, active inference and the free energy principle". *Journal of The Royal Society Interface.* 15 (138): 20170792.

59 Adams RA, KE Stephan, HR Brown, CD Frith, and KJ Friston. 2013. "The computational anatomy of psychosis." *Frontiers in Psychiatry.* 4.

60 Kirchhoff M.D., and Froese T. 2017. "Where there is life there is mind: In support of a strong life-mind continuity thesis". *Entropy.* 19 (4).

61 Ostrom, Elinor. *The Drama of the Commons.* Washington, DC: National Academy Press, 2003.

62 Housden, L., S. T. Wong, and M. Dawes. "Effectiveness of Group Medical Visits for Improving Diabetes Care: A Systematic Review and Meta-Analysis. Wider Implementation of Group Medical Visits for Patients with Diabetes May Have a Positive Effect on Patient Outcomes." *Canadian Medical Association Journal* 185, no. 13 (2013): 1137.

63 Batalden, M., P. Batalden, P. Margolis, M. Seid, G. Armstrong, L. Opipari-Arrigan, and H. Hartung. "Coproduction of Healthcare Service." *BMJ Quality & Safety,* 25, no. 7 (2016): 509-17.

64 Williamson, Oliver E. "The New Institutional Economics: Taking Stock, Looking Ahead." *Journal of Economic Literature.* 383 (2000): 595-613.

Immediate Return Societies

65 Service, Elman R. *Primitive Social Organization: An Evolutionary Perspective.* New York: Random House, 1976.

66 Choi, C. Q. "Humans Did Not Wipe out the Neanderthals, New Research Suggests." Live Science, http://www.livescience.com/47460-neanderthal-extinction-revealed.html

67 Oppenheimer, Stephen. "A Single Southern Exit of Modern Humans from Africa: Before or after Toba?" *Quaternary International* 258, no. 21 (2012): 88-99.

68 Lahr, Marta Mirazon, and Robert Foley. "Multiple Dispersals and Modern Human Origins." *Evolutionary Anthropology: Issues, News, and Reviews* 3, no. 2 (2005): 48-60.

69 McBrearty, S., and A. S. Brooks. "The Revolution That Wasn't: A New Interpretation of the Origin of Modern Human Behavior." *Journal of Human Evolution* 39, no. 5 (2000): 453-563.

70 Wilson, Edward O. *The Social Conquest of Earth.* New York: Liveright, 2013.

71 Proctor, D., R. A. Williamson, F. B. de Waal, and S. F. Brosnan. "Chimpanzees Play

the Ultimatum Game." *Proceedings of the National Academy of Sciences of the United States of America* 110, no. 6 (2013): 2070-5.

72 O'Shea, John M., Guy A. Meadows, and Bruce D. Smith. "Evidence for Early Hunters beneath the Great Lakes." *Proceedings of the National Academy of Sciences of the United States of America* 106, no. 25 (2009): 10120-23.

73 Dunbar, Robin. *Human Evolution*. London: Pelican, 2014.

74 Deacon, Terrence William, *The Symbolic Species: The Co-Evolution of Language and the Brain*. Cambridge: International Society for Science and Religion, 2007.

75 Miller, G. Sexual selection for cultural displays. In: *The Evolution of Culture an Interdisciplinary View*. New Brunswick, NJ: Rutgers University Press, 2003.

76 Redhead, G., and R. I. Dunbar. "The Functions of Language: An Experimental Study." *Evolutionary psychology: An International Journal of Evolutionary Approaches to Psychology and Behavior* 11, no. 4 (2013): 845-54.

77 Lanning, Tess, Laura Bradley, Richard Darlington, Glenn Gottfried, and Research Institute for Public Policy. *Great Expectations: Exploring the Promises of Gender Equality*. London: Institute for Public Policy Research, 2013.

78 Iredale, Wendy, Mark Van Vugt, and Robin Dunbar. "Showing Off in Humans: Male Generosity as a Mating Signal." *Evolutionary Psychology* 6, no. 3 (2008).

79 Tognetti, A., D. Dubois, C. Faurie, and M. Willinger. "Men Increase Contributions to a Public Good When under Sexual Competition." *Scientific Reports,* 6 (2016).

80 Woodburn, James, and British Museum. *Hunters and Gatherers: The Material Culture of the Nomadic Hadza*. London: British Museum, 1970.

81 Sahlins, Marshall David. *Stone Age Economics*. London: Routledge, 2004.

82 Panter-Brick, Catherine. "Motherhood and Subsistence Work: The Tamang of Rural Nepal." *Human Ecology* 17, no. 2 (1989): 205-28.

83 Wells, Jonathan C. K. "Maternal Capital and the Metabolic Ghetto: An Evolutionary Perspective on the Transgenerational Basis of Health Inequalities." *AJHB American Journal of Human Biology* 22, no. 1 (2010): 1-17.

84 Calvin, William H. *A Brief History of the Mind: From Apes to Intellect and Beyond*. New York: Oxford University Press, 2005.

85 Baka women from Gbiné singing their traditional "Yelli" songs using polyphony
    http://www.youtube.com/watch?v=cATZe_jlc9ghttp://www.youtube.com/watch?v=cATZe_jlc9g
    Aka pygmy polyphony
    https://www.youtube.com/watch?v=yKLxFmnYO_I&feature=related

86 Grauer, Victor A. "Echoes of Our Forgotten Ancestors." *The World of Music* 48, no. 2 (2006): 5-58.

87 Eliade, Mircea. *Shamanism: Archaic Techniques of Ecstasy*. Princeton, NJ: Princeton University Press, 2004

88 "Time and a Place: A Luni-Solar 'Time-Reckoner' from 8th Millennium BC Scotland." *Internet Archaeology*, no. 34 (2013).

89 Power, C. and L. C. Aiello, 1997. "Female proto-symbolic strategies." In L. D. Hager (ed.), *Women in Human Evolution*. New York and London: Routledge, pp. 153-171.

90 Power, C., C. Arthur, and L. C. Aiello. "On Seasonal Reproductive Synchrony as an Evolutionarily Stable Strategy in Human Evolution." *Current Anthropology* 38, no. 1 (1997): 88-90.

91 Provine, Robert R., and Kenneth R. Fischer. "Laughing, Smiling, and Talking: Relation to Sleeping and Social Context in Humans." *Ethology* 83, no. 4 (2010): 295-305.

92 Shalvi, S., and de C. K. W. Dreu. "Oxytocin Promotes Group-Serving Dishonesty." *Proceedings of the National Academy of Sciences of the United States of America* 111, no. 15 (2014): 5503-07.

93 De Dreu, C. K., L. L. Greer, G. A. Van Kleef, S. Shalvi, and M. J. Handgraaf. "Oxytocin Promotes Human Ethnocentrism." *Proceedings of the National Academy of Sciences of the United States of America* 108, no. 4 (2011): 1262-6.

94 Hrdy, Sarah Blaffer. *Mothers and Others: The Evolutionary Origins of Mutual Understanding.* Cambridge, Mass: Belknap Press of Harvard University Press, 2011.

95 Burkart, J. M., E. Fehr, C. Efferson, and C. P. van Schaik. "Other-Regarding Preferences in a Non-Human Primate: Common Marmosets Provision Food Altruistically." *Proceedings of the National Academy of Sciences* 104, no. 50 (2007): 19762-66.
Hauser, M. D., M. K. Chen, F. Chen, and E. Chuang. "Give Unto Others: Genetically Unrelated Cotton-Top Tamarin Monkeys Preferentially Give Food to Those Who Altruistically Give Food Back." *Proceedings of the Royal Society B: Biological Sciences* 270, no. 1531 (2003): 2363-70.

96 Silk, J. B., S. F. Brosnan, J. Vonk, J. Henrich, D. J. Povinelli, A. S. Richardson, S. P. Lambeth, J. Mascaro, and S. J. Schapiro. "Chimpanzees Are Indifferent to the Welfare of Unrelated Group Members." *Nature*, no. 7063 (2005): 1357-59.

97 Tronick, Edward Z., Gilda Morelli, and Steve Winn. "Multiple Caretaking of Efe (Pygmy) Infants." *American Anthropologist* 89 (1987): 96-106.

98 Ivey, Paula K. "Cooperative Reproduction in Ituri Forest Huntergatherers: Who Cares for Efe Infants?" *Current Anthropology* 41, no. 5 (2000): 856-66.

99 Sear, R., R. Mace, and I. A. McGregor. "Maternal Grandmothers Improve Nutritional Status and Survival of Children in Rural Gambia." *Proceedings of the Royal Society of London B*, no. 1453 (2000): 1641-47.

100 Sear, R. "Kin and Child Survival in Rural Malawi: Are Matrilineal Kin Always Beneficial in a Matrilineal Society?" *Human Nature* 19, no. 3 (2008): 277-93.

101 Hawkes, K., J. F. O'Connell and N. G. Blurton Jones. 1989. Hardworking Hadza Grandmothers. In *Comparative Socioecology: The Behavioural Ecology of Humans and Other Mammals*, edited by V. Standen & R.A. Foley, pp. 341-366. London: Basil Blackwell. Published, 6/1989.
      http://content.csbs.utah.edu/~hawkes/Hawkes_al89ha . . . .

102 Hawkes, Kristen. "Human Longevity: The Grandmother Effect." *Nature* 428, no. 6979 (2004): 128-29.

103 Spieker, Susan J., and Lillian Bensley. "Roles of Living Arrangements and Grandmother Social Support in Adolescent Mothering and Infant Attachment." *Developmental Psychology* 30, no. 1 (1994): 102-11.

104 Furstenberg, Frank F. *Destinies of the Disadvantaged: The Politics of Teenage Childbearing.* New York: Russell Sage Foundation, 2010.

105 Mauss, Marcel. *The Gift: Forms and Functions of Exchange in Archaic Societies.* Miami: HardPress Publishing, 2014.

106 Herrmann, E., J. Call, M.V. Hernández-Lloreda, B. Hare, and M. Tomasello. "Humans Have Evolved Specialized Skills of Social Cognition: The Cultural Intelligence Hypothesis." *Science (New York.)* 317, no. 5843 (2007): 1360-6.

107 Perner, J., T. Ruffman, and S. R. Leekam. *Theory of Mind Is Contagious – You Catch It from Your Sibs.* Chicago: University of Chicago Press, 1994.

The Other Side of Silence

108 Westermann, William Linn. *The Slave Systems of Greek and Roman Antiquity.* Whitefish: 2012.

109 Plato, and Robin Waterfield. *Symposium* [Translated from the Ancient Greek.]. Oxford; New York: Oxford University Press, 2008.

110 Johri, Mira. *"On the Universality of Habermas's Discourse Ethics."* National Library of Canada.

111 Phillips, Adam, and Barbara Taylor. *On Kindness.* London: Hamish Hamilton, 2010.

112 Granovetter, Mark. "The Strength of Weak Ties: A Network Theory Revisited." *Sociological Theory* 1 (1983): 201-33.

113 Greif, Avner. *On the Social Foundations and Historical Development of Institutions that Facilitate Impersonal Exchange: From the Community Responsibility System to Individual Legal Responsibility in Pre-Modern Europe.* Stanford, CA: John M. Olin Program in Law and Economics, Stanford Law School, 1997.

114 Kleinschmidt, Harald. *Perception and Action in Medieval Europe* [in Italian]. Woodbridge: Boydell, 2005.

115 ibid p.98.

116 Hobsbawm, E. J. "Peasants and Politics." London, 1972.

117 Weber, Eugen. 2007. *Peasants into Frenchmen: the modernization of rural France; 1870-1914.* Stanford, CA: Stanford University Press.

118 Perkin, H. J. "The Social Causes of the British Industrial Revolution." *Transactions of the Royal Historical Society* 18 (1968): 123.

119 Macfarlane, Alan. *The Origins of English Individualism: The Family, Property and Social Transition.* Oxford: B. Blackwell, 1979.

120 Trevisano, Andrea, Charlotte Augusta Sneyd, Camden Society, and England. *A Relation, or Rather a True Account of the Island of England; with Sundry Particulars of the Customs of These People, and of the Royal Revenues under King Henry the Seventh, About the Year*

1500. [by Andrea Trevisano.] Translated from the Italian, [with the Original Text] with Notes, by *Charlotte Augusta Sneyd.* London 1847.

121 Green, Ron. *A View from the Headland.* Flamborough: Fleyn Publications, 2006.

122 *Feoffments* mean (in feudal law) a grant of ownership of freehold property to someone.

123 Pollock, Frederick, and Frederic William Maitland. *The History of English Law before the Time of Edward I.* Birmingham, AL: Legal Classics Library, 1982.

124 Macfarlane, Alan. *The Origins of English Individualism: The Family, Property and Social Transition.* Oxford: Basil Blackwell, 1979.

125 Waterlow, Lucy. Mail Online. September 2016. http://www.dailymail.co.uk/femail/article-3767087/Meet-Britain-s-gypsy-kids-s-REALLY-like-growing-traveller.html

126 Tocqueville, Alexis de, and Isaac Kramnick. *Democracy in America.* New York: W.W. Norton, 2008.

127 Blair, Karen J. *Joining in: exploring the history of voluntary organizations.* Malabar, Florida: Krieger Pub. Co, 2006.

128 ibid

129 Snow, Edgar. *Red Star over China: The Classic Account of the Birth of Chinese Communism:* Grove Press Atlantic Monthly, 2018.

130 ibid.

131 ibid.

132 Dikotter, Frank. *Mao's Great Famine: The History of China's Most Devastating Catastrophe, 1958-62.* Bloomsbury, 2017.

133 ibid.

PART 2. TRIALS OF WICKED WOMEN

Makwanpur

134 Loevinsohn, Benjamin P. "Health Education Interventions in Developing Countries: A Methodological Review of Published Articles." *International Journal of Epidemiology* 19, no. 4 (1990): 788-94.

135 Hancock, Graham. *Lords of Poverty: The Freewheeling Lifestyles, Power, Prestige, and Corruption of the Multibillion Dollar Aid Business.* New York: Atlantic Monthly Press, 2001.

136 Easterly, William Russell. *The Tyranny of Experts: Economists, Dictators, and the Forgotten Rights of the Poor.* New York: Basic Books, 2015.

137 Hutt, Michael, and David N. Gellner. *Nepal: A Guide to the Art and Architecture of the Kathmandu Valley.* New Delhi: Adroit Publishers, in association with Vajra Publications, Kathmandu, Nepal: Distributors, Akhil Book Distributors, 2010.

138 Kiyoshi Saijo, Kazuo Kimura. Expansion of an ancient lake in the Kathmandu basin of Nepal during the Late Pleistocene evidenced by lacustrine sediment underlying piedmont slope. *Himalayan Journal of Sciences* Vol.4(6) 2007 p.41-48.

139 Lévi, Sylvain. *Le Népal, étude historique d'un royaume Hindou*. Paris: E. Leroux, 1905.

140 Shresthas are also Newar business people who have become Hinduised and usually speak Nepali. Many of them, unlike the Buddhist arm of the Newar caste hierarchy, do not speak Newari.

141 Chambers, Robert. *Rural Development: Putting the Last First*. Routledge, 2014.

142 Rittel, Horst W. J., and Melvin M. Webber. *Dilemmas in a General Theory of Planning*. Berkeley, Univ. of California, IURD, 1973.

143 Freire, Paulo, and Myra Bergman Ramos. *Pedagogy of the Oppressed*. London Penguin Books, 2017.

Replicants

144 Rath, Suchitra, Nirmala Nair, Prasanta K. Tripathy, Sarah Barnett, Shibanand Rath, Rajendra Mahapatra, Rajkumar Gope, *et al*. "Explaining the Impact of a Women's Group Led Community Mobilisation Intervention on Maternal and Newborn Health Outcomes: The Ekjut Trial Process Evaluation." *BMC International Health and Human Rights* 10, no. 1 (October 22, 2010): 25.

145 ibid

146 Tripathy, Prasanta, Nirmala Nair, Sarah Barnett, Rajendra Mahapatra, Josephine Borghi, Shibanand Rath, Suchitra Rath, *et al*. "Effect of a Participatory Intervention with Women's Groups on Birth Outcomes and Maternal Depression in Jharkhand and Orissa, India: A Cluster-Randomised Controlled Trial." *The Lancet* 375, no. 9721 (2010): 1182-92.

147 Azad, K., B. Banerjee, S. Shaha, K. Khan, A. R. Rego, S. Barua, S. Barnett, *et al*. "Effect of Scaling up Women's Groups on Birth Outcomes in Three Rural Districts in Bangladesh: A Cluster-Randomised Controlled Trial." *The Lancet* 375, no. 9721 (2010): 1193-202.

148 Tripathy, Prasanta, Nirmala Nair, Rajesh Sinha, Shibanand Rath, Raj Kumar Gope, Suchitra Rath, Swati Sarbani Roy, *et al*. "Effect of Participatory Women's Groups Facilitated by Accredited Social Health Activists on Birth Outcomes in Rural Eastern India: A Cluster-Randomised Controlled Trial." *Lancet Global Health* 4, no. 2 (2016): e119-e28.

149 Sinha, R. K., H. Haghparast-Bidgoli, P. K. Tripathy, N. Nair, R. Gope, S. Rath, and A. Prost. "Economic Evaluation of Participatory Learning and Action with Women's Groups Facilitated by Accredited Social Health Activists to Improve Birth Outcomes in Rural Eastern India." *Cost Effectiveness and Resource Allocation*: 15 (2017).

150 Fernando, Benita. The Dharavi Biennale, Mumbai's new arts and science festival - in pictures. Feb 16, 2015.

https://www.theguardian.com/cities/gallery/2015/feb/16/dharavi-biennale-mumbai-new-arts-science-festival-in-pictures

The Power of Conversation

151 Gordon, Paul. *The Hope of Therapy*. Ross-on-Wye: PCCS, 2010.

152 Jaspers, Karl, Edith Ehrlich, Leonard H. Ehrlich, and George B. Pepper. *Karl Jaspers: Basic Philosophical Writings: Selections*. Amherst, New York: Humanity Books, 2000.

153 Salaman, Kurt. "Death, Deathlessness and Existenz in Karl Jaspers." *Philosophy Now* 72 (2009): 35-36.

154 Cobbett, William. *Advice to Young Men and (Incidentally) to Young Women, in the Middle and Higher Ranks of Life: In a Series of Letters, Addressed to a Youth, a Bachelor, a Lover, a Husband, a Father, a Citizen or a Subject*. London: The Author, 1829.

155 Barnabas, Ruanne V., Heidi van Rooyen, Elioda Tumwesigye, Justin Brantley, Jared M. Baeten, Alastair van Heerden, Bosco Turyamureeba, *et al*. "Uptake of Antiretroviral Therapy and Male Circumcision after Community-Based HiV Testing and Strategies for Linkage to Care Versus Standard Clinic Referral: A Multisite, Open-Label, Randomised Controlled Trial in South Africa and Uganda." *The Lancet HIV* 3, no. 5 (2016): e212-e20.

156 Edwards, Phil, Caroline Free, Judy Gold, Kazuyo Machiyama, Ona McCarthy, Thoai D. Ngo, Emma Slaymaker, *et al*. "Effect of a Mobile Phone-Based Intervention on Post-Abortion Contraception: A Randomized Controlled Trial in Cambodia." *Bulletin of the World Health Organization* 93, no. 12 (2015): 842-50A.

157 Freire, Paulo, and Myra Bergman Ramos. *Pedagogy of the Oppressed*. London: Penguin Books, 2017.

158 Davis, Elizabeth and Carol Leonard. *The Circle of Life: Thirteen Archetypes for Every Woman*. Berkeley, California. Celestial Arts, 2002.

159 Mace, Barbara J. "Full Insurance in the Presence of Aggregate Uncertainty." *Journal of Political Economy* 99, no. 5 (1991): 928.
Townsend, Robert M. "Risk and Insurance in Village India." *Econometrica (New Haven)* 62, no. 03 (1994): 539-91.

160 May, Robert M. "Will a Large Complex System Be Stable?" *Nature* 238, no. 5364 (1972): 413-14.

161 Houweling, Tanja A. J., Prasanta Tripathy, Nirmala Nair, Shibanand Rath, Suchitra Rath, Rajkumar Gope, Rajesh Sinha, *et al*. "The Equity Impact of Participatory Women's Groups to Reduce Neonatal Mortality in India: Secondary Analysis of a Cluster-Randomised Trial." *International Journal of Epidemiology* 42, no. 2 (2013): 520-32.

162 Hart, Julian Tudor. *The Inverse Care Law*. The Lancet, 1971.

163 Akerlof, G. "The Market for Lemons: Qualitative Uncertainty and the Market Mechanism." *Uncertainty in economics: readings and exercises*. Edited by Peter Diamond and Michael Rothschild, 1970.

164 Gaynor, M., C. Propper, and S. Seiler. "Free to Choose? Reform, Choice, and Consideration Sets in the English National Health Service." *American Economic Review* 106, no. 11 (2016): 3521-57.

165 Marx, Karl. *[Letters]*. Moscow: Progress, 1970.
http://is.gd/SFijGp Marx to Kugelmann In Hanover 1868.

166 Zakaria, Rafia. "The Myth of Empowerment." *New York Times*, Oct 5 2017. https://www.ccny.cuny.edu/sites/default/files/Emissaries%20of%20Empowerment%202017.pdf

167 Prost, Audrey, Tim Colbourn, Nadine Seward, Kishwar Azad, Arri Coomarasamy, Andrew Copas, Tanja A. J. Houweling, *et al.* "Women's Groups Practising Participatory Learning and Action to Improve Maternal and Newborn Health in Low-Resource Settings: A Systematic Review and Meta-Analysis." *The Lancet* 381, no. 9879 (2013): 1736-46.

168 Victora, Cesar G., and Fernando C. Barros. "Participatory Women's Groups: Ready for Prime Time?" *The Lancet* 381, no. 9879 (2013): 1693-94.

169 Berger, Shelley L, Tony Kouzarides, Ramin Shiekhattar, and Ali Shilatifard. "An operational definition of epigenetics." 2009. *Genes & Development*. 23 (7): 781.

170 Bourdieu, Pierre. *Systems Of Education And Systems Of Thought*
(In Hopper E. (1971) ed. Readings in the Theory of Educational Systems. London: Hutchinson.

171 Grenfell, Michael. *Pierre Bourdieu: Agent Provocateur*. London: Continuum, 2007.

172 Bourdieu, Pierre, and Richard Nice. *Outline of a Theory of Practice*. Cambridge; New York: Cambridge University Press, 2015.

173 Bhaskar, Roy. *Plato Etc.: The Problems of Philosophy and Their Resolution*. London; New York: Verso, 1994.

174 Tripathy, Prasanta, Nirmala Nair, Rajesh Sinha, Shibanand Rath, Raj Kumar Gope, Suchitra Rath, Swati Sarbani Roy, *et al.* "Effect of Participatory Women's Groups Facilitated by Accredited Social Health Activists on Birth Outcomes in Rural Eastern India: A Cluster-Randomised Controlled Trial." *Lancet Global Health* 4, no. 2 (2016): e119-e28.

175 Nair, N., P. Tripathy, H. S. Sachdev, H. Pradhan, S. Bhattacharyya, R. Gope, S. Santhal, *et al.* "Effect of Participatory Women's Groups and Counselling through Home Visits on Children's Linear Growth in Rural Eastern India (Caring Trial): A Cluster-Randomised Controlled Trial." *Lancet Global Health* 5, no. 10 (2017): 1004.

PART 3. DEVELOPMENT AS TRUST

Keeping Promises

176 Dasgupta, Partha. "A Matter of Trust: Social Capital and Economic Development." In *Prepared for presentation at the Annual Bank Conference on Development Economics (ABCDE), Seoul, June 2009*.

177 Narayan, Deepa, and Lant Pritchett. "Cents and Sociability: Household Income and Social Capital in Rural Tanzania." *Economic Development and Cultural Change* 47, no. 4 (1999): 871-97.

178 ibid Dasgupta

179 ibid

180 Ganghadar, V. "Roots of Corruption." *The Hindu*, 2004.
http://www.thehindu.com/thehindu/mag/2004/06/06/stories/2004060600250400.
htm

181 Doshi, Vidhi. "Gurgaon: What Life Is Like in the Indian City Built by Private
Companies" https://www.theguardian.com/sustainable-business/2016/jul/04/
gurgaon-life-city-built-private-companies-india-intel-google?CMP=twt_a-glob-
al-development_b-gdndevelopment.

182 Sen, Amartya. *Development as Freedom*. Oxford; New York: Oxford University Press,
2001.

183 Marshall, Monty G. "Polity IV Project: Political Regime Characteristics and Transitions,
1800-2013." http://www.systemicpeace.org/polity/polity4.htm.

184 MacFarquhar, Roderick. "China: The Superpower of Mr. Xi". *The New York Review
of Books*, no. August 13, 2015.

Social Capital

185 Hanifan, Lyda Judson. 1916. *The Rural School Community Center*. Philadelphia.

186 Bourdieu, Pierre, and Richard Nice. *Outline of a Theory of Practice*. Cambridge; New
York: Cambridge University Press, 2015.

187 Szreter, Simon. "The State of Social Capital: Bringing Back in Power, Politics, and
History." *Theory and Society* 31, no. 5 (2002): 573-621.

188 Dunbar, R. I. M. "Do Online Social Media Cut through the Constraints that Limit
the Size of Offline Social Networks?" *Royal Society Open Science* 3, no. 1 (2016):
150292.

189 Bickart, K. C., C. I. Wright, R. J. Dautoff, B. C. Dickerson, and L. F. Barrett. "Amygdala
Volume and Social Network Size in Humans." *Nature Neuroscience* 14, no. 2 (2011):
163-4.

   Powell, J., N. Roberts, M. Garcia-Finana, P. A. Lewis, and R. I. M. Dunbar. "Orbital
   Prefrontal Cortex Volume Predicts Social Network Size: An Imaging Study of
   Individual Differences in Humans." *Proceedings of the Royal Society B: Biological
   Sciences* 279, no. 1736 (2012): 2157-62.

   Kanai, R., B. Bahrami, R. Roylance, and G. Rees. "Online Social Network Size Is
   Reflected in Human Brain Structure." *Proceedings of the Royal Society B: Biological
   Sciences* 279, no. 1732 (2012): 1327-34.

   Sallet, J., R. B. Mars, M. P. Noonan, J. L. Andersson, J. X. O'Reilly, S. Jbabdi, P. L.
   Croxson, et al. "Social Network Size Affects Neural Circuits in Macaques." *Science*
   334, no. 6056 (2011): 697-700.

190 Fukuyama, Francis. "Social Capital, Civil Society and Development." *Third World
Quarterly* 22, no. 1 (2001): 7-20.

Colonialism, Caste and Class

191 Harvey, David. *The Enigma of Capital and the Crisis of Capitalism*. Oxford University Press, 2011.

192 Eliot, George, Viola Huggins, and Scoular Anderson. *Middlemarch*. Glasgow: Collins, 1989.

193 Bayly, Christopher Alan. *The Birth of the Modern World: 1780 - 1914; Global Connections and Comparisons*. Malden, Mass: Blackwell, 2012.

194 Willes, Margaret. *The Gardens of the British Working Class*. 2015 New Haven: Yale University Press.

195 Wheen, Francis. 2008. *Marx's Das Kapital: a biography*. New York: Grove Press.

196 Bayly, Christopher Alan. *The Birth of the Modern World: 1780 - 1914; Global Connections and Comparisons*. Malden, Mass: Blackwell, 2012.

197 Mamuna, Munatasira, Mahbubar Rahman, and International Centre for Bengal Studies. *Material Conditions of the Subalterns: Nineteenth Century East Bengal*. Dhaka: International Centre for Bengal Studies, 2009.

198 ibid

199 Costello, Edward. *The Adventures of a Soldier, Or: Memoirs . . . Comprising Narratives of the Campaigns in the Peninsular [Sic] under the Duke of Wellington, and the Recent Civil Wars in Spain*. Nabu Press, 2011.

200 Adivasi Arts Trust. *Tribal Art, Culture and Storytelling*. http://adivasiartstrust.org/

201 Maddison, Angus. *Monitoring the World Economy: 1820-1992*. Paris: Development Centre of the Organisation for Economic Co-operation and Development, 2000.

202 Davis, Mike. *Late Victorian Holocausts: El Nìòo Famines and the Making of the Third World*. 2017.

203 Ferguson, Niall. *Empire. The Rise and Demise of the British World Order and the Lessons for Global Power*. New York: Basic Books, 2004.

204 Foucault, Michel, and Colin Gordon. *Power/Knowledge : Selected Interviews and Other Writings, 1972-1977*. New York: Vintage Books, a division of Random House, Inc., 1980. p82.

205 Morris, Rosalind C., and Gayatri Chakravorty Spivak. *Can the Subaltern Speak? Reflections on the History of an Idea*. New York: Columbia University Press, 2010.

206 Said, Edward W. *The World, the Text, and the Critic*. Harvard University Press, 2010.

207 Foucault, Michel. *Discipline and Punish: The Birth of the Prison*. Harmondsworth: Penguin Books, 1991.

208 Foucault, Michel, and Robert Hurley. *The Will to Knowledge*. London: Penguin Books, 1998.

209 Gandhi, M. K., L. N. Tolstoj, and B. Srinivasa Murthy. *Mahatma Gandhi and Leo Tolstoy Letters*. Long Beach, CA: Long Beach Publications, 1987.

210 Dixit, Kanak Mani. *The South Asian Sensibility: A Himal Reader*. New Delhi: Sage, 2012.

211 Anderson, Perry. *The Indian Ideology*. London: Verso, 2013.

212 Chisti, Seema. "Biggest Caste Survey: One in Four Indians Admit to Practising Untouchability. Going by Respondents' Admissions, Untouchability Is the Most Widespread among Brahmins, Followed by Other Backward Castes." *Indian Express*, 2014. http://indianexpress.com/article/india/india-others/one-in-four-indians-admit-to-practising-untouchability-biggest-caste-survey/#.VHr0pijrohI.email

213 Satwik, Ambarish. "Scrambled Eggs. Third-Party Reproduction, as It Plays Itself out in the Market, Is a Violation of the Fundamental Premise of Caste – Endogamy." *Blink. The Hindu Business Line.* March 13, 2015.

214 Anderson, Perry. *The Indian Ideology*. London: Verso, 2013.

215 Anklesaria Aiyar and S. Swaminathan. "Policy Analysis No. 776. Capitalism's Assault on the Indian Caste System: How Economic Liberalization Spawned Low-Caste Dalit Millionaires." https://www.cato.org/publications/policy-analysis/capitalisms-assault-on-the-indian-caste-system

216 Swathi, V. "Hyderabad. Untouchability Creeps into Mid-Day Meals: Report." *The Hindu*, July 25, 2015. http://www.thehindu.com/news/cities/Hyderabad/untouchability-creeps-into-midday-meals-report/article7462905.ece

217 Bosher, Lee, Edmund Penning-Rowsell, and Sue Tapsell. "Resource Accessibility and Vulnerability in Andhra Pradesh: Caste and Non-Caste Influences." *Development and Change* 38, no. 4 (2007): 615-40.

218 Dominiczak, Peter. "Shaun Bailey, the Prime Minister's Only Black Aide, was 'Frozen out by David Cameron's Clique'." *The Telegraph*, May 10 2013. http://www.telegraph.co.uk/news/politics/david-cameron/10050502/Shaun-Bailey-the-Prime-Ministers-only-black-aide-was-frozen-out-by-David-Camerons-clique.html

219 St. Aubyn, Edward. *Never Mind*. London: Picador, 2012.

220 Donhorf, G. William. "Power in America. The Class-Domination Theory of Power." http://whorulesamerica.net/power/class_domination.html

221 Mentan, Tatah. *Democracy for Breakfast: Unveiling Mirage Democracy in Contemporary Africa*. Cameroon: Langaa RPCIG, 2013.

222 Gumbel, P. *France's Got Talent. The Woeful Consequences of French Elitism.* Amazon Kindle, 2013. https://www.amazon.co.uk/gp/product/B00CMMF0S6/ref=x_gr_w_bb?ie=UTF8&tag=x_gr_w_bb_uk-21&linkCode=as2&camp=1634&creative=6738

223 Kuper, Simon. "The French Elite: Where It Went Wrong. France's 'Énarques' Weren't Trained to Succeed in the World but in Central Paris." *Financial Times*, 2013.

224 Anderson, Perry. *The Origins of Postmodernity*. London: Verso, 2014.

225 Ibid

226 Weeks, John. "By the Numbers: Barack Obama's Contribution to the Decline of US Democracy." https://www.opendemocracy.net/john-weeks/by-numbers-barack-obama-s-contribution-to-decline-of-us-democracy

PART 4. TWENTY TWO EXPERIMENTS
AT THE SOCIAL EDGE

Why experiment?

227 Lee, Roger Irving, Lewis Webster Jones, and Barbara Jones. *The Fundamentals of Good Medical Care: An Outline of the Fundamentals of Good Medical Care and an Estimate of the Service Required to Supply the Medical Needs of the United States.* Hamden, Ct.: Archon, 1962.

228 Jiang, H., X. Qian, G. Carroli, and P. Garner. "Selective Versus Routine Use of Episiotomy for Vaginal Birth." Cochrane Reviews, http://www.cochrane.org/CD000081/PREG_selective-versus-routine-use-episiotomy-vaginal-birth

229 Dwyer, T., A. L. Ponsonby, L. Blizzard, and N. M. Newman. "The Contribution of Changes in the Prevalence of Prone Sleeping Position to the Decline in Sudden Infant Death Syndrome in Tasmania." *Obstetrical & Gynecological Survey.* 50, no. 10 (1995): 704.

Mitchell, E. A., B. J. Taylor, R. P. K. Ford, A. W. Stewart, D. M. O. Becroft, J. M. D. Thompson, R. Scragg, *et al.* "Four Modifiable and Other Major Risk Factors for Cot Death: The New Zealand Study." *Journal of Paediatrics and Child Health* 28 (1992): S3-S8.

Mitchell, E. A., P. G. Tuohy, J. M. Brunt, J. M. D Thompson, M. S. Clements, A. W. Stewart, R. P. K Ford, and B. J. Taylor. "Risk Factors for Sudden Infant Death Syndrome Following the Prevention Campaign in New Zealand: A Prospective Study." *Pediatrics* 100, no. 5 (1997): 835-40.

230 Willinger, M., H. J. Hoffman, and R. B. Hartford. "Infant Sleep Position and Risk for Sudden Infant Death Syndrome: Report of Meeting Held January 13 and 14, 1994, National Institutes of Health, Bethesda." *Pediatrics* 93, no. 5 (1994): 814-9.

231 Save the Children. "State of the World's Mothers 2014: Saving Mothers and Children in Humanitarian Crises". (2014).

232 Azad, Kishwar, and Anthony Costello. "Extreme Caution Is Needed before Scale-up of Antenatal Corticosteroids to Reduce Preterm Deaths in Low-Income Settings." *The Lancet Global Health* 2, no. 4 (2014): e191-e92.

233 Althabe, Fernando, Jose M. Belizan, Elizabeth M. McClure, Jennifer Hemingway-Foday, Mabel Berrueta, Agustina Mazzoni, Alvaro Ciganda, *et al.* "A Population-Based, Multifaceted Strategy to Implement Antenatal Corticosteroid Treatment Versus Standard Care for the Reduction of Neonatal Mortality Due to Preterm Birth in Low-Income and Middle-Income Countries: The Act Cluster-Randomised Trial." *The Lancet* 385, no. 9968 (2015): 629-39.

234 Chantler, Cyril. "The Role and Education of Doctors in the Delivery of Health Care." *The Lancet* 353, no. 9159 (1999): 1178-81.

235 Dunn, William N. ed. "The Experimenting Society: Essays in Honor of Donald T. Campbell." *Journal of Planning Literature* 13, no. 3 (1999).

236 Colquhoun, David. "Diet and Health. What Can You Believe: Or Does Bacon Kill You?" http://www.dcscience.net/2009/05/03/diet-and-health-what-can-you-believe-or-does-bacon-kill-you/

237 Ioannidis, J. P. A. "Implausible Results in Human Nutrition Research." *BMJ* 2013;347:f6698

238 White, Howard. "Using Global Evidence for Local Policy: The Third Wave of the Evidence Revolution." https://campbellcollaboration.org/blog/using-global-evidence-for-local-policy-the-third-wave-of-the-evidence-revolution.html

239 Bharadwaj, Preeti, Jennifer C. Saxton, Susan N. Mann, Eva M. A. Jungmann, and Judith M. Stephenson. "What Influences Young Women to Choose between the Emergency Contraceptive Pill and an Intrauterine Device? A Qualitative Study." *The European Journal of Contraception & Reproductive Health Care* 16, no. 3 (2011): 201-09.

240 Institute of Medicine, US Military Malaria Vaccine Research Committee on, Patricia M. Graves, and Myron M. Levine. *Battling Malaria: Strengthening the US Military Malaria Vaccine Program.* Washington, DC: National Academies Press, 2006.

241 Tu, Y. "The Discovery of Artemisinin (Qinghaosu) and Gifts from Chinese Medicine." *Nature Medicine* 17, no. 10 (2011): 1217-20.

242 Pawson, Ray. *The Science of Evaluation: A Realist Manifesto.* London: Sage, 2013.

243 ibid.

244 ibid.

245 Hadley, Alison. *Teenage Pregnancy and Young Parenthood: Effective Practice and Policy.* Routledge, 2017.

246 Pawson, Ray, and Nick Tilley. "Realist Evaluation." 2004 http://www.community-matters.com.au/RE_chapter.pdf

247 Oakley, Ann, and Manchester Statistical Society. *Evidence-Informed Policy and Practice: Challenges for Social Science.* Manchester Statistical Society, 2001.

248 Archer, Margaret Scotford. *Critical Realism: Essential Readings.* London; New York: Routledge, 2009.

249 Meadows, Donella H., and Club of Rome. *The Limits to Growth: A Report for the Club of Rome's Project on the Predicament of Mankind.* New York: Universe Books, 1982.

250 Rose, G. "Strategy of Prevention: Lessons from Cardiovascular Disease." *BMJ* 282, no. 6279 (1981): 1847-51.

251 Singla, D. R., B. A. Kohrt, L. K. Murray, A. Anand, B. F. Chorpita, and V. Patel. "Psychological Treatments for the World: Lessons from Low- and Middle-Income Countries." *Annual Review of Clinical Psychology* 13 (2017): 149-81.

252 Hitchens, Christopher. 2011. *Hitch-22: a memoir.* London: Atlantic Books.

253 Zeki, S., and T. Ishizu. "The 'Visual Shock' of Francis Bacon: An Essay in Neuroesthetics." *Frontiers in Human Neuroscience* 7 (2013).

Loneliness and long-term conditions

254 Licht-Strunk, E., H. W. J. Van Marwijk, T. Hoekstra, J. W. R. Twisk, M. De Haan, and A. T. F. Beekman. "Outcome of Depression in Later Life in Primary Care: Longitudinal Cohort Study with Three Years' Follow-Up." *BMJ*, no. 7692 (2009): 463-66.

255 Luppa, Melanie, Tobias Luck, Hans-Helmut Konig, Matthias C. Angermeyer, and Steffi G. Riedel-Heller. "Natural Course of Depressive Symptoms in Late Life. An 8-Year Population-Based Prospective Study." *Journal of Affective Disorders* 142, no. 1-3 (2012): 166-71

256 Schwarzbach, Michaela, Melanie Luppa, Claudia Sikorski, Angela Fuchs, Wolfgang Maier, Hendrik van den Bussche, Michael Pentzek, and Steffi G. Riedel-Heller. "The Relationship between Social Integration and Depression in Non-Demented Primary Care Patients Aged 75 Years and Older." *Journal of Affective Disorders* 145, no. 2 (2013): 172-78.

257 Steptoe, Andrew, Aparna Shankar, Panayotes Demakakos, and Jane Wardle. "Social Isolation, Loneliness, and All-Cause Mortality in Older Men and Women." *Proceedings of the National Academy of Sciences of the United States of America* 110, no. 15 (2013): 5797-801.

258 Fraser, Giles. "Lest We Forget: The Growing Numbers of Our Outcast Dead, Destroyed by Poverty." *The Guardian*, Dec 3, 2015.

259 Naylor, Chris, King's Fund, and Centre for Mental Health. *Long-Term Conditions and Mental Health: The Cost of Co-Morbidities.* London: King's Fund, 2012.

260 Mind. "*How to Cope with Loneliness.*" https://www.mind.org.uk/information-support/tips-for-everyday-living/loneliness/loneliness/#

261 Hoban, M, V James, P Beresford, and J Fleming. "Involving Older Age: The Route to Twenty-First Century Well-Being. Shaping Our Age." Cardiff: Royal Voluntary Service, 2013.

262 Patterson, L. "Making Our Health and Care Systems Fit for an Ageing Population: David Oliver, Catherine Foot, Richard Humphries. King's Fund, March 2014." *Age and Ageing* 43, no. 5 (2014).

263 Frost, Helen, Sally Haw, John Frank, and Scottish Collaboration for Public Health Research. "Promoting Health and Wellbeing in Later Life: Interventions in Primary Care and Community Settings." (2010).

264 Migiro, Katy. "Despite Murderous Attacks, Tanzania's 'Witches' Fight for Land." Reuters, https://www.reuters.com/article/us-tanzania-women-landrights/despite-murderous-attacks-tanzanias-witches-fight-for-land-idUSKBN16S2HU

265 Lwanda, John. "John Lwanda Take on Malawi Vampires, Victims and National Hysteria." *Nyasa Times*, 2017. https://www.nyasatimes.com/john-lwanda-take-on-malawi-vampires-victims-national-hysteria/

266 Perry, B. L., and B. A. Pescosolido. "Social Network Activation: The Role of Health Discussion Partners in Recovery from Mental Illness." *Social Science & Medicine (1982)* 125 (2015): 116-28.

267 McPherson, Miller, Lynn Smith-Lovin, and Matthew E. Brashears. *Social Isolation in America: Changes in Core Discussion Networks over Two Decades.* American Sociological Association, 2006. http://www.asanet.org/galleries/default-file/June06ASRFeature.pdf

268 Putnam, Robert D. *Bowling Alone: The Collapse and Revival of American Community.* New York, Simon & Schuster, 2007.

269 Putnam, Robert D. *Our Kids: The American Dream in Crisis.* New York: Simon & Schuster, 2016.

270 Roberts, R. O., R. H. Cha, M. M. Mielke, Y. E. Geda, B. F. Boeve, M. M. Machulda, D. S. Knopman, and R. C. Petersen. 2015. "Risk and protective factors for cognitive impairment in persons aged 85 years and older." *Neurology.* 84 (18): 1854-1861.

271 World Health Organization. *World Report on Ageing and Health.* Geneva, Switzerland: World Health Organization, 2015. M Besser and S Rohde; World Health Organization, Kobe Centre; Case study in South Africa: AgeWell, a peer-support service in a community setting to improve well-being and health among older persons living in a peri-urban township of Cape Town; 2015; unpublished data.

272 Golding, Barry. *The Men's Shed Movement: The Company of Men.* Champaign, Illinois: Common Ground Publishing, 2016.

273 Naylor, Chris, King's Fund, and Centre for Mental Health. *Long-Term Conditions and Mental Health: The Cost of Co-Morbidities.* London: King's Fund, 2012.

274 Fenton WS, and ES Stover. 2006. "Mood disorders: cardiovascular and diabetes comorbidity." *Current Opinion in Psychiatry.* 19 (4): 421-7.

275 Cimpean D, and RE Drake. 2011. "Treating co-morbid chronic medical conditions and anxiety/depression." *Epidemiology and Psychiatric Sciences.* 20 (2): 141-50.

276 Flegal, Katherine M., Margaret D. Carroll, Brian K. Kit, and Cynthia L. Ogden. "Prevalence of Obesity and Trends in the Distribution of Body Mass Index among US Adults, 1999-2010." *JAMA* 307, no. 5 (2012): 491.
Ogden, C. L., M. D. Carroll, B. K. Kit, and K. M. Flegal. "Prevalence of Obesity and Trends in Body Mass Index among US Children and Adolescents, 1999-2010." *JAMA* 307, no. 5 (2012): 483-90.
Singh, A. S., C. Mulder, W. Van Mechelen, M. J. M. Chinapaw, and J. W. R. Twisk. "Tracking of Childhood Overweight into Adulthood: A Systematic Review of the Literature." *Obesity Reviews* 9, no. 5 (2008): 474-88.
Baker, J. L., L. W. Olsen, and T. I. A. Sorensen. "Childhood Body-Mass Index and the Risk of Coronary Heart Disease in Adulthood." *YMVA Journal of Vascular Surgery* 47, no. 4 (2008): 893-94.
Dietz, W. H. "Childhood Weight Affects Adult Morbidity and Mortality." *The Journal of Nutrition* 128, no. 2 (1998).

277 Liese, A. D., R. B. D'Agostino, Jr., R. F. Hamman, P. D. Kilgo, J. M. Lawrence, L. L. Liu, B. Loots, *et al.* "The Burden of Diabetes Mellitus among US Youth: Prevalence Estimates from the Search for Diabetes in Youth Study." *Pediatrics* 118, no. 4 (2006): 1510-8.

278 Self Management Resource Center. "Help Your Community Take Charge of Its Health." SMRC, 711 Colorado Avenue, Palo Alto CA 94303, http://patienteducation. stanford.edu/programs/cdsmp.html.

279 Lorig, K. R., D. S. Sobel, A. L. Stewart, B. W. Brown, A. Bandura, P. Ritter, V. M. Gonzalez, D. D. Laurent, and H. R. Holman. "Evidence Suggesting That a Chronic Disease Self-Management Program Can Improve Health Status While Reducing Hospitalization: A Randomized Trial." *Medical Care* 37, no. 1 (1999): 5-14.

280 Lorig, Kate R., Philip Ritter, Anita L. Stewart, David S. Sobel, Byron William Brown, Albert Bandura, Virginia M. Gonzalez, Diana D. Laurent, and Halsted R. Holman. "Chronic Disease Self-Management Program: 2-Year Health Status and Health Care Utilization Outcomes. *Medical Care* 39, no. 11 (2001): 1217-23.

281 Druss, B. G., L. Zhao, S. A. von Esenwein, R. DiClemente, J. R. Bona, L. Fricks, S. Jenkins-Tucker, E. Sterling, and K. Lorig. "The Health and Recovery Peer (Harp) Program: A Peer-Led Intervention to Improve Medical Self-Management for Persons with Serious Mental Illness." *Schizophrenia Research* 118, no. 1-3 (2010): 264-70.

282 CIC, The Green Dreams Project. "*History and What We Do.*" (2017). http://www.greendreamsproject.co.uk/aboutus/index.html

283 Dixon, Michael. "How Social Prescribing Is Cutting the National Health Service Drugs Bill." *The Guardian Healthcare Network*, 2014. http://www.theguardian.com/healthcare-network/2014/sep/17/social-prescribing-cutting-nhs-drugs-bill

284 People Powered Health Projects. https://www.nesta.org.uk/sites/default/files/the_business_case_for_people_powered_health.pdf

285 Gottlieb, Katherine. "The Nuka System of Care: Improving Health through Ownership and Relationships." *International Journal of Circumpolar Health* 72, no. 1 (2013): 21118.

286 Aveyard, P., A. Lewis, S. Tearne, K. Hood, A. Christian-Brown, P. Adab, R. Begh, *et al.* "Screening and Brief Intervention for Obesity in Primary Care: A Parallel, Two-Arm, Randomised Trial." *Lancet* 388, no. 10059 (2016): 2492-500.

287 Mainous, A. G., R. J. Tanner, R. Baker, C. E. Zayas, and C. A. Harle. "Prevalence of Prediabetes in England from 2003 to 2011: Population-Based, Cross-Sectional Study." *BMJ Open* 4, no. 6 (2014): e005002.

288 Fottrell, E., H. Jennings, A. Kuddus, N. Ahmed, J. Morrison, K. Akter, S. K. Shaha, *et al.* "The Effect of Community Groups and Mobile Phone Messages on the Prevention and Control of Diabetes in Rural Bangladesh: Study Protocol for a Three-Arm Cluster Randomised Controlled Trial." *Trials* 17, no. 1 (2016).

Prisoners, mothers and teenagers

289 The Forgiveness Project. "*Peter Woolf and Will Riley* (England)." http://theforgivenessproject.com/stories/peter-woolf-will-riley-england/

290 Goldstein, Dana. "*The Misleading Math of Recidivism.*" The Marshall Project, https://www.themarshallproject.org/2014/12/04/the-misleading-math-of-recidivism

291 Dobbie, Will, Hans Grönqvist, Susan Niknami, Mårten Palme, and Mikael Priks. "*The Intergenerational Effects of Parental Incarceration.*" NBER working paper series, 24186. Cambridge, Mass: National Bureau of Economic Research 2018.

292 Parenting Inside Out. "*Prioritizing, Parenting, and Protecting Our Children.*" http://www.parentinginsideout.org/

293 Wagner, Peter, and Bernadette Rabuy. "*Mass Incarceration: The Whole Pie 2017.*" https://www.prisonpolicy.org/reports/pie2017.html

294 Circles of Support and Accountability. http://www.circles-uk.org.uk/

295 UK Ministry of Justice. "Offender Management Statistics Quarterly, England and Wales: (with Prison Population as at 31 December 2015)." https://www.gov.uk/government/uploads/system/uploads/attachment_data/file/519437/offender-management-statistics-quarterly-bulletin-oct-dec-2015.pdf

296 Sandall, Jane, Hora Soltani, Simon Gates, Andrew Shennan, and Declan Devane. 2015. "Midwife-led continuity models versus other models of care for childbearing women." *Cochrane Database of Systematic Reviews.* (9).

297 Crowther, Susan, Liz Smythe, and Deb Spence. "Mood and Birth Experience." *Women and Birth* 27, no. 1 (2014): 21-25.

298 International Federation of Gynecology and Obstetrics. "Mother-Baby Friendly Birthing Facilities." *International Journal of Gynecology & Obstetrics* 128, no. 2 (2015): 95-99.

299 De Jonge, A., C. C. Geerts, B. Y. van der Goes, B. W. Mol, S. E. Buitendijk, and J. G. Nijhuis. "Perinatal Mortality and Morbidity up to 28 Days after Birth among 743,070 Low-Risk Planned Home and Hospital Births: A Cohort Study Based on Three Merged National Perinatal Databases." *International Journal of Obstetrics & Gynaecology* 122, no. 5 (2015): 720-28.

300 Odent, Michel. *Entering the World: The De-Medicalization of Childbirth.* London: Marion Boyars: Distributed by Scribner, 2009.

301 Oberlander, Tim F., Joanne Weinberg, Michael Papsdorf, Ruth Grunau, Shaila Misri, and Angela M. Devlin. "Prenatal Exposure to Maternal Depression, Neonatal Methylation of Human Glucocorticoid Receptor Gene (Nr3c1) and Infant Cortisol Stress Responses." *Epigenetics* 3, no. 2 (2014): 97-106.

302 Snyder-Mackler, N., J. Sanz, J. N. Kohn, J. F. Brinkworth, S. Morrow, A. O. Shaver, J. C. Grenier, *et al.* "Social Status Alters Immune Regulation and Response to Infection in Macaques." *Science* 354, no. 6315 (2016): 1041-45.

303 Nakimuli-Mpungu, Etheldreda, Kizito Wamala, James Okello, Stephen Alderman, Raymond Odokonyero, Ramin Mojtabai, Edward J. Mills, *et al.* "Group Support Psychotherapy for Depression Treatment in People with HIV/Aids in Northern Uganda: A Single-Centre Randomised Controlled Trial." *The Lancet HIV* 2, no. 5 (2015): e190-e99.

304 Jones, E., and E. Coast. "Social Relationships and Postpartum Depression in South Asia: A Systematic Review." *International Journal of Social Psychiatry* 59, no. 7 (2013): 690-700.

305 Olds, David, Peggy L. Hill, Elissa Ramsey, United States Office of Juvenile Justice and Delinquency Prevention. *Prenatal and Early Childhood Nurse Home Visitation.* Washington, DC: US Dept. of Justice, Office of Justice Programs, Office of Juvenile Justice and Delinquency Prevention, 1998.

Olds, David L., Peggy L. Hill, Sharon F. Mihalic, Ruth A. O'Brien, Center for the Study and Prevention of Violence, Boulder University of Colorado. *Nurse-Family Partnership.* BoulderCenter for the Study and Prevention of Violence, Institute of Behavioral Science, University of Colorado at Boulder, 2001.

Olds, David L., Peggy L. Hill, Ruth O'Brien, David Racine, and Pat Moritz. "Taking Preventive Intervention to Scale: The Nurse-Family Partnership." *Cognitive and Behavioral Practice* 10, no. 4 (2003): 278-90.

306 Robling, M., M. J. Bekkers, K. Bell, C. C. Butler, R. Cannings-John, S. Channon, B. C. Martin, *et al.* "Effectiveness of a Nurse-Led Intensive Home-Visitation Programme for First-Time Teenage Mothers (Building Blocks): A Pragmatic Randomised Controlled Trial." *Lancet* 387, no. 10014 (2016): 146-55.

307 Bolton, M., I. Moore, A. Ferreira, C. Day, and D. Bolton. "Community Organizing and Community Health: Piloting an Innovative Approach to Community Engagement Applied to an Early Intervention Project in South London." *Journal of Public Health (Oxford, England)* 38, no. 1 (2016): 115-21.

308 Poston, L., D. Pasupathy, N. Patel, J. Sandall, P. T. Seed, A. L. Briley, The Upbeat Trial Consortium, *et al.* "Effect of a Behavioural Intervention in Obese Pregnant Women (the Upbeat Study): A Multicentre, Randomised Controlled Trial." *The Lancet Diabetes and Endocrinology* 3, no. 10 (2015): 767-77.

309 Townsend, Mark. "Indian Village Run by Teenage Girls Offers Hope for a Life Free from Abuse." *The Guardian,* 2017, https://www.theguardian.com/global-development/2017/oct/21/india-villagers-child-abuse-trafficking-alcoholism

310 Young, Emma. "Iceland Knows How to Stop Teen Substance Abuse but the Rest of the World Isn't Listening." *Wellcome Trust,* https://mosaicscience.com/story/iceland-prevent-teen-substance-abuse

311 Ellsberg, Mary, Diana J. Arango, Matthew Morton, Floriza Gennari, Sveinung Kiplesund, Manuel Contreras, and Charlotte Watts. "Prevention of Violence against Women and Girls: What Does the Evidence Say?" *The Lancet* 385, no. 9977 (2015): 1555-66.

312 United Nations. Ban Ki Moon Press Release. https://www.un.org/press/en/2008/wom1664.doc.htm

313 Sullivan, Cris M., and Deborah I. Bybee. "Reducing Violence Using Community-Based Advocacy for Women with Abusive Partners." *Journal of Consulting and Clinical Psychology* 67, no. 1 (1999): 43-53.

Taft, A. J., R. Small, L. F. Watson, J. A. Lumley, K. L. Hegarty, and L. Gold. "Mothers' Advocates in the Community (Mosaic) – Non-Professional Mentor Support to Reduce Intimate Partner Violence and Depression in Mothers: A Cluster Randomised Trial in Primary Care." *BMC Public Health* 11 (2011).

314 Parker, B., J. McFarlane, K. Soeken, C. Silva, and S. Reel. "Testing an Intervention to Prevent Further Abuse to Pregnant Women." *Research In Nursing And Health* 22, no. 1 (1999): 59-66.

315 Petrosino, Anthony, Carolyn Turpin-Petrosino, Meghan E Hollis-Peel, and Julia G Lavenberg. 2013. "'Scared Straight' and other juvenile awareness programs for preventing juvenile delinquency". *Cochrane Database of Systematic Reviews.* (2).

316 Schopper, D. Sexual Violence in Armed Conflict. Geneva: Cambridge Univ. Press, International Review of the Red Cross, 2014(96), 894.

317 World Health Organisation, Parenting for Lifelong Health. 2017. http://www.who.int/violence_injury_prevention/violence/child/plh/en/

318 Isaac, Lauren. "Gang Activity: Prevalence and Prevention." http://www.socialjustices-olutions.org/2015/10/12/gang-activity-prevalence-prevention/

Health Care

319 Wilkinson, Richard G., and Kate Pickett. *The Spirit Level: Why Greater Equality Makes Societies Stronger.* New York; London: Bloomsbury, 2011.

320 Kurtz, Ernest. *Not God: A History of Alcoholics Anonymous.* Minneapolis: Hazelden Publishing, 2010.

321 Vanden Bos, Gary R. *APA Dictionary of Psychology.* Washington D.C.: American Psychological Association, 2015.

322 Carroll, K. M., C. Nich, J. M. Shi, D. Eagan, and S. A. Ball. "Efficacy of Disulfiram and Twelve Step Facilitation in Cocaine-Dependent Individuals Maintained on Methadone: A Randomized Placebo-Controlled Trial." *Drug and Alcohol Dependence* 126, no. 1-2 (2012): 224-31.

323 Morgan-Lopez, A. A., L. M. Saavedra, D. A. Hien, L. Ruglass, A. N. Campbell, and E. Wu. "Synergy between Seeking Safety and Twelve-Step Affiliation on Substance Use Outcomes for Women." *Journal of Substance Abuse Treatment* 45, no. 2 (2013): 179-89.

324 Manning, Victoria, David Best, Nathan Faulkner, Emily Titherington, Alun Morinan, Francis Keaney, Michael Gossop, and John Strang. "Does Active Referral by a Doctor or 12-Step Peer Improve 12-Step Meeting Attendance? Results from a Pilot Randomised Control Trial." *Drug and Alcohol Dependence* 126, no. 1-2 (2012): 131-37.

325 Holton-Burke, R. Conor, and David S. Buck. "Social Interventions Can Lower Costs and Improve Outcomes." In *Patient Engagement: New England Journal of Medicine Catalyst,* 2017.

326 Shrewsbury V. A., J. O'Connor, K. S. Steinbeck, K. Stevenson, A. Lee, A. J. Hill, MR Kohn, S. Shah, S. Torvaldsen, and L. A. Baur. 2009. "A randomised controlled trial of a community-based healthy lifestyle program for overweight and obese adolescents: the Loozit study protocol." *BMC Public Health.* 9.

327 Molinuevo, José Luis. "Early Intervention is Key to Tackling Alzheimer's." *Financial Times,* December 13th 2016.

328 Birchwood, Max. "Lost Generation. Why Young People with Psychosis Are Being Left Behind, and What Needs to Change." In *Rethink Mental Illness*, edited by The IRIS Network, 2013.

329 NHS England. 2015. *Future in mind: promoting, protecting and improving our children and young people's health and wellbeing.* http://dera.ioe.ac.uk/22591/2/Childrens_Mental_Health_Redacted.pdf

330 Deaton, Angus. *The Great Escape: Health, Wealth, and the Origins of Inequality.* Princeton University Press, 2015.

331 Geruso, Michael. "Muslim Mortality Paradox and the Importance of Sanitation for Children." http://www.livemint.com/Opinion/vkvuknMxLInXEs3lXN1LDM/Muslim-mortality-paradox-and-the-importance-of-sanitation-fo.html

332 Nair, N., P. Tripathy, H. S. Sachdev, H. Pradhan, S. Bhattacharyya, R. Gope, S. Gagrai, et al. "Effect of Participatory Women's Groups and Counselling through Home Visits on Children's Linear Growth in Rural Eastern India (Caring Trial): A Cluster-Randomised Controlled Trial." *The Lancet Global Health* 5, no. 10 (2017): 1004.

333 Bhandari, N., S. Mazumder, R. Bahl, J. Martines, R. E. Black, M. K. Bhan, and other members of the Infant Feeding Study Group. "An Educational Intervention to Promote Appropriate Complementary Feeding Practices and Physical Growth in Infants and Young Children in Rural Haryana, India." *Journal Of Nutrition* 134 (2004): 2342-48.

Menon, Purnima; Nguyen, Phuong Hong; Saha, Kuntal K.; Khaled, Adiba; Sanghvi, Tina; Baker, Jean; Afsana, Kaosar; Haque, Raisul; Frongillo, Edward A.; Ruel, Marie T.; Rawat, Rahul. "Combining intensive counseling by frontline workers with a nationwide mass media campaign has large differential impacts on complementary feeding practices but not on child growth." *Journal of Nutrition.* October 1, 2016 vol. 146 no. 10 2075-2084.

334 Staff Correspondent. "Raichur City Fails to Wake up to E-Toilets." *The Hindu*, 2013. http://www.thehindu.com/todays-paper/tp-national/tp-karnataka/raichur-city-fails-to-wake-up-to-etoilets/article4764796.ece

335 Kass, Jason. "Bill Gates Can't Build a Toilet." *New York Times*, 2013. http://www.nytimes.com/2013/11/19/opinion/bill-gates-cant-build-a-toilet.html?_r=1&

336 Ugwumadu, Judith. "Sierra Leone: ODI Urges Health Sector Reform Following Ebola Outbreak." http://www.publicfinanceinternational.org/news/2015/07/sierra-leone-odi-urges-health-sector-reform-following-ebola-outbreak

337 Low-Beer, Daniel, and Musoke Sempala. "Social Capital and Effective HIV Prevention: Community Responses." *Global Health Governance* IV, no. 1 (2010): 1-18.

338 Dingwall, Robert. "Ebola – WHO (Still) Don't Get It: Social Science Saves Lives." https://www.socialsciencespace.com/?s=Social+science+saves+lives

339 Omaswa, Francis. "Regaining Trust: An Essential Prerequisite for Controlling the Ebola Outbreak." *Lancet Global Health Blog*, 2014. http://globalhealth.thelancet.com/2014/08/11/regaining-trust-essential-prerequisite-controlling-ebola-outbreak

340 Fleck, F. "The human factor." *Bulletin of the World Health Organization* 93: 72-73.

341 Kamara, M. and A. Bayoh (2013). "Love, loss and reconnection: Stories of life in Sierra Leone after Ebola". Chapter 7: Gaddafi and the Tripoli Boys. Back in Touch. From https://backintouch.org/

342 Henao-Restrepo, A. M., et al. (2017). "Efficacy and effectiveness of an rVSV-vectored vaccine in preventing Ebola virus disease: final results from the Guinea ring vaccination, open-label, cluster-randomised trial." *The Lancet* 389 (10068): 505-518.

343 Hombach, Joachim, Martin Friede, Vasee Moorthy, Anthony Costello, Marie Paule Kieny. Developing a vaccine against Zika, *BMJ* 2016; 355:i5923. http://www.bmj.com/content/355/bmj.i5923

344 Manolson, H. Ayala, and Hanen Centre Early Language Resource. *It Takes Two to Talk: A Hanen Early Language Parent Guide Book.* Toronto: Hanen Early Language Resource Centre, 1985.

345 United Nations. "15th Anniversary of Security Council Resolution 1325 (2000), on Women, Peace and Security." https://www.youtube.com/watch?v=BfS2R8mATaU&feature=youtu.be

346 Granger, Kate. "Hello My Name Is." https://hellomynameis.org.uk/ 2016.

347 Frampton, Susan B., and Patrick A. Charmel. *Putting Patients First: Best Practices in Patient-Centered Care.* San Francisco: Jossey-Bass, 2009.

348 Strallen, C. "Roderick John Kilner Brown." *BMJ* 2008;337:a2071.

349 Valman, H, C. D. Heath, R. J. K. Brown. Continuous Intragastric Milk Feeds in Infants of Low Birth Weight Br Med J 1972;3:547.

350 Valman, Bernard. "Lives of the Fellows. Roderick John Kilner Brown." http://munksroll.rcplondon.ac.uk/Biography/Details/6054

351 Cork, Richard. *The Healing Presence of Art: A History of Western Art in Hospitals.* New Haven; London: Yale University Press, 2012.

Business Performance 345-368

352 "Oops! Who's Excellent Now?" *Business Week,* November 5th[th] 1984.

353 Waterman, Robert. "Who Says Excellence Is Forever?" *Business Week* November 26th 1984.

354 Hill, Andrew. "Tiny Bursts of Joy Pave the Way to Big Hairy Audacious Goals. Motivating Staff Is Often About Small Victories." *Financial Times*, September 12th 2011.

355 Wolf, Gary. "Steve Jobs: The Next Insanely Great Thing." *Wired*, January 2nd 1996.

356 Richmond, Shane. "Jonathan Ive Interview: Simplicity Isn't Simple." *The Telegraph*, May 23rd 2012.

357 Williams, Gervais. *The Future Is Small: Why AIM Will Be the World's Best Market Beyond the Credit Boom.* Petersfield: Harriman House, 2014.

358 Žižek , Slavoj. "Slavoj Žižek Webchat – as It Happened." *The Guardian*, October 8th

2014. http://www.theguardian.com/books/live/2014/oct/06/slavoj-zizek-webchat-absolute-recoil

359 Farrar, Jeremy. "We Hail Individual Geniuses, but Success in Science Comes through Collaboration." *The Guardian*, October 1st 2017. https://www.theguardian.com/commentisfree/2017/sep/30/we-hail-individual-geniuses-success-in-science-collaboration-nobel-prize

360 Amabile, T., C. M. Fisher, and J. Pillemer. "Ideo's Culture of Helping." *Harvard Business Review*, Jan-Feb 2014.

361 Unipart Expert Practices. "A Trust-Wide Transformation at Countess of Chester Hospital." Unipart Group, https://www.unipartconsulting.com/insights/case-studies/healthcare/nhs-trust-wide-transformation

362 Lent, Adam. *Small Is Powerful: Why the Era of Big Government, Big Business and Big Culture Is Over*. Unbound, 2016.

363 Rajan, Raghuram G. "Has Financial Development Made the World Riskier?" National Bureau of Economic Research, Cambridge, MA (2005).

364 Poth, Alexander, Susumu Sasabe, and AntÚnia Mas. "Lean and Agile Software Process Improvement - an Overview and Outlook." (2017).

365 Alliance, Scrum. "Scrum Values. The Agile Manifesto." https://www.scrumalliance.org/why-scrum/core-scrum-values-roles

366 Fischer, P., J. I. Krueger, T. Greitemeyer, C. Vogrincic, M. Heene, M. Wicher, M. Kainbacher, A. Kastenmuller, and D. Frey. "The Bystander-Effect: A Meta-Analytic Review on Bystander Intervention in Dangerous and Non-Dangerous Emergencies." *Psychological Bulletin* 137, no. 4 (2011): 517-37.

367 Levine, Mark, and Simon Crowther. "The Responsive Bystander: How Social Group Membership and Group Size Can Encourage as Well as Inhibit Bystander Intervention." *Journal of Personality and Social Psychology* 95, no. 6 (2008): 1429-39.

368 Johnson, Michael D., John R. Hollenbeck, Stephen E. Humphrey, Daniel R. Ilgen, Dustin Jundt, and Christopher J. Meyer. "Cutthroat Cooperation: Asymmetrical Adaptation to Changes in Team Reward Structures." *The Academy of Management Journal* 49, no. 1 (2006): 103-19.

369 Ruhe, M. C., L. Wu, S. J. Zyzanski, J. J. Werner, K. C. Stange, D. Litaker, C. Schroeder, et al. "Appreciative Inquiry for Quality Improvement in Primary Care Practices." *Quality Management in Health Care* 20, no. 1 (2011): 37-48.

370 Barends, Eric. "A Reader's Guide to Evidence-Based Management." *Controlling & Management Review* 60, no. 1 (2016): 36-40.

371 Gapper, John. "The Curse of the Consultants Is Spreading Fast." *Financial Times* May 10th 2017. https://www.ft.com/content/ecfcaf46-34bc-11e7-99bd-13beb0903fa3

372 Foster, Lucia, John Haltiwanger, and Chad Syverson. "Reallocation, Firm Turnover, and Efficiency: Selection on Productivity or Profitability?" *The American Economic Review*. 98, no. 1 (2008): 394.

373 Consultancy.UK. "NHS Spends 640 Million on Management Consultants." https://www.consultancy.uk/news/1240/nhs-spends-640-million-on-management-consultants

374 Vize, R. "Integrated Care: A Story of Hard Won Success." *BMJ* 344, no. May 31 1 (2012): e3529. http://www.bmj.com/content/344/bmj.e3529 http://www.bmj.com/content/344/bmj.e3529/rapid-responses http://www.bmj.com/content/344/bmj.e3529/related North West London Whole Systems Integrated Care. "'Toolbox' – Additional Integrated Care Tools Launched 2015." http://integration.healthiernorthwestlondon. nhs.uk/chapters

375 Pfeffer, Jeffrey, and Robert I. Sutton. *Hard Facts, Dangerous Half-Truths, and Total Nonsense: Profiting from evidence-based management.* Boston: Harvard Business School Press, 2006.

376 Bloom, Nicholas, Benn Eifert, Aprajit Mahajan, David McKenzie, and John Roberts. 2012. *Does Management Matter? Evidence from India.* World Bank Policy Research working paper; no. WPS 5573 http://hdl.handle.net/10986/3340

Climate Change

377 Brown, P. T., and K. Caldeira. 2017. "Greater future global warming inferred from Earth's recent energy budget." *Nature London.* 552 (7683): 45-50.

378 Kaya, Yoichi, Kenji Yamaji, and Keigo Akimoto. *Climate Change and Energy: Japanese perspectives on climate change mitigation strategy.* London: Imperial College Press, 2015.

379 Cobbett, William. (1830). Rural Rides in the Counties. Cambridge University Press, 2009; ISBN 978-1-108-00408-4

380 Berners-Lee, Mike and Duncan Clark. 2013. The *Burning Question: We can't burn half the world's oil, coal and gas. So how do we quit?* London: Profile.

381 Levin, Kelly, Benjamin Cashore, Steven Bernstein, and Graeme Auld. 2012. "Overcoming the tragedy of super wicked problems: constraining our future selves to ameliorate global climate change." *Policy Sciences.* 45 (2): 123-152.

382 Cobbett, William. *Advice to Young Men and (Incidentally) to Young Women, in the Middle and Higher Ranks of Life: In a Series of Letters, Addressed to a Youth, a Bachelor, a Lover, a Husband, a Father, a Citizen or a Subject.* London: The Author, 1829.

383 Dasgupta, Partha, and Economics Faculty of Cambridge University. *The Nature of Economic Development and the Economic Development of Nature,* 2013.

384 Arrow, Kenneth J., Partha Dasgupta, Lawrence H. Goulder, Kevin J. Mumford, and Kirsten Oleson. 2012. "Sustainability and the measurement of wealth." *Environment and Development Economics.* 17 (03): 317-353.

385 Hardin, Garrett. "The Tragedy of the Commons." *Science* 162, no. 3859 (1968): 1243-48.

386 Ostrom, Elinor. *The Drama of the Commons.* Washington, DC: National Academy Press, 2003.

387 Hielscher, Sabine. "Carbon Rationing Action Groups: An Innovation History." https://grassrootsinnovations.org/2013/02/01/carbon-rationing-action-groups-an-innovation-history/ (2013).

388 Ilham, Nyak, Worapol Aengwanich, Libin Wang, Tuan Nguyen, Xiaoyun Li, and Edi Basuno. "An Ecohealth Assessment of Poultry Production Clusters (Ppcs) for the Livelihood and Biosecurity Improvement of Small Poultry Producers in Asia." *Infectious Diseases of Poverty* 4, no. 1 (2015): 1-9.

389 Kohli, Anjalee, Nancy A. Perrin, Mitima Mpanano Remy, Mirindi Bacikenge Alfred, Kajabika Binkurhorhwa Arsene, Mwinja Bufole Nadine, Banyewesize Jean Heri, Mitima Murhula Clovis, and Nancy Glass. "Adult and Adolescent Livestock Productive Asset Transfer Programmes to Improve Mental Health, Economic Stability and Family and Community Relationships in Rural South Kivu Province, Democratic Republic of Congo: A Protocol of a Randomised Controlled Trial." *BMJ Open* 7, no. 3 (2017).

390 Sainath, P. "Empowering India's Women through Community Groups." http://www.bbc.co.uk/news/world-asia-india-27615599

391 Saul, Nick, and Andrea Curtis. *The Stop: How the Fight for Good Food Transformed a Community and Inspired a Movement.* Toronto: Vintage Canada, 2014.

392 Bongaerts, John. "Human population growth and the demographic transition." Philosophical Translations, Royal Society London B Biological Sciences(2009) 364, 2985–2990.

393 O'Neill, Brian C., Michael Dalton, Regina Fuchs, Leiwen Jiang, Shonali Pachauri and Katarina Zigova. "Global demographic trends and future carbon emissions". PNAS October 12th 2010, vol. 107 no. 41 17521-17526.

394 Wapner, Paul, and John Willoughby. "The Irony of Environmentalism: The Ecological Futility but Political Necessity of Lifestyle Change." *Ethics & International Affairs* 19, no. 3 (2005): 77-89.

395 Bowen, Kathryn J., Damon Alexander, Fiona Miller, and Va Dany. 2014. "Using Social Network Analysis to Evaluate Health-Related Adaptation Decision-Making in Cambodia." *International Journal of Environmental Research and Public Health.* 11 (2): 1605-1625.

396 Maraseni, T. N., P. R. Neupane, F. Lopez-Casero, and T. Cadman. "An Assessment of the Impacts of the Redd+ Pilot Project on Community Forests User Groups (Cfugs) and Their Community Forests in Nepal." *Journal Of Environmental Management* 136 (2014): 37-46.

Corruption, Finance and Government Gridlock

397 Booth, David, and Diana Cammack. "Governance for Development in Africa: Solving Collective Action Problems." Zed Books, 2013.

398 Barrington, Robert. "Corruption in 2017." http://www.transparency.org.uk/corruption-in-2017/#.WisXm0trx0c

399 Pettifor, Ann. *Real World Economic Outlook: The Legacy of Globalization: Debt and Deflation.* Basingstoke: Palgrave Macmillan, 2004.

400 Rajan, Raghuram G. "Has Financial Development Made the World Riskier?" NBER

Working Paper No. 11728 (2005). http://www.nber.org/papers/w11728

401 Lewis, Michael. *The Big Short: Inside the Doomsday Machine*. London: Penguin, 2011.

402 Ioannidis, John P. A., Tom D. Stanley, and Chris Doucouliagos. "The Power of Bias in Economics Research." *The Economic Journal*. 127. F236 - F265 2017.

403 Herndon, Thomas, Michael Ash, Robert Pollin, University of Massachusetts at Amherst, and Institute Political Economy Research. "Does High Public Debt Consistently Stifle Economic Growth? A Critique of Reinhart and Rogoff." Cambridge Journal of Economics, Volume 38, Issue 2, 1 March 2014, Pages 257–279, https://doi.org/10.1093/cje/bet075

404 Brittan, Samuel. "Kenneth Rogoff, Carmen Reinhart and the Spell of Magic Numbers." *Financial Times*, May 2nd 2013.

405 IDEAS. Top 10% Authors, as of November 2017. https://ideas.repec.org/top/top.person.all.html

406 Janine R. Wedel. "How the Chubais Clan, Harvard Fed Corruption." http://articles.latimes.com/1999/sep/12/opinion/op-9170

407 Wedel, Janine R. 2001. *Collision and Collusion: the Strange Case of Western Aid to Eastern Europe*. New York: St. Martin's Press.

408 Passell, Peter. "Dr Jeffrey Sachs, Shock Therapist." *New York Times*, June 27th 1993. http://www.nytimes.com/1993/06/27/magazine/dr-jeffrey-sachs-shock-therapist.html?pagewanted=all

409 Klein, Naomi. *The Shock Doctrine: the rise of disaster capitalism*. London: Penguin, 2008. Goldman, Marshall I. *Lost Opportunity: why economic reforms in Russia have not worked*. New York: W.W. Norton & Co, 1994.

410 Milne, Seumas. *The Revenge of History: the battle for the twenty-first century*. London: Verso, 2013.

411 http://jeffsachs.org/2012/03/what-i-did-in-russia/

412 Donnan, Shawn. "Paul Romer's comments on World Bank economists." Financial Times. Jan 25th, 2018. https://www.ft.com/content/be72f8e2-0144-11e8-9650-9c0ad2d7c5b5

413 Flanders, Stephanie. *Inclusive Growth Commission: Making our economy work for everyone*. Royal Society for the encouragement of Arts, Manufactures and Commerce. March 7th 2017. https://www.thersa.org/discover/publications-and-articles/reports/final-report-of-the-inclusive-growth-commission

414 Goff, Sharlene. "Sir Richard Lambert launches UK banking standards council." *Financial Times*, May 19th 2014. https://www.ft.com/content/40acded2-df38-11e3-a4cf-00144feabdc0

415 Vaessen, J., A. Rivas, M. Duvendack, R. Palmer-Jones, F. Leeuw, G. Van Gils, R. Lukach, et al. 2014. *The effects of microcredit on women's control over household spending in developing countries*. The Campbell Collaboration.

416 Bandiera, Oriana, Robin Burgess, Narayan Das, Selim Gulesci, and Imran Rasul. 2013. *Can basic entrepreneurship transform the economic lives of the poor?* London: STICERD, LSE. http://sticerd.lse.ac.uk/dps/eopp/eopp43.pdf

417 Bandiera, Oriana, Niklas Buehren, Robin Burgess, Markus Goldstein, Selim Gulesci, Imran Rasul, and Munshi Sulaiman. 2015. *Women's empowerment in action: evidence from a randomized control trial in Africa*. http://www.ucl.ac.uk/~uctpimr/research/ELA.pdf

418 Borpujari, Priyanka. "What Is Striking in India Is the Indifference of the Privileged: Chomsky." *Tehelka*, 2013. http://bit.ly/120uEbb

419 Huxley, Aldous. *Point Counter Point*. Dalkey Archive Press, 2009.

420 Mazower, Mark. 2012. *Governing the world: the rise and fall of an idea*. London: Allen Lane.

421 Morozov E. 2012. "The Naked and the TED." *New Republic*. 243 (13): 30-35.

422 Sassen, Saskia. *Expulsions: Brutality and Complexity in the Global Economy*. Cambridge, MA: Belknap Press, Harvard, 2018.

423 Badiou, Alain. *Our Wound Is Not So Recent: Thinking the Paris Killings of 13 November*. Malden, MA: Polity Press, 2016.

424 Rasul, Imran, and Daniel Rogger. 2015. "The Impact of Ethnic Diversity in Bureaucracies: Evidence from the Nigerian Civil Service." *American Economic Review*. 105 (5): 457-461.

425 Agrawal, Amol. "Why Nudging Your Customers Can Backfire." *Mostly Economics, Harvard Business Review*, 2016. https://hbr.org/2016/04/why-nudging-your-customers-can-backfire

426 Boelman, Victoria "Félicitations Madame Mayor: Participatory Budgeting in Paris Hits New Highs." In *Nesta*, 2016. https://www.nesta.org.uk/blog/felicitations-madame-mayor-participatory-budgeting-paris-hits-new-highs

427 Habermas, Jürgen, and Max Pensky. *The Postnational Constellation: Political Essays*. Cambridge, UK: Polity Press, 2007.

428 Kohl-Arenas, Erica. *The self-help myth: how philanthropy fails to alleviate poverty*. Oakland, California. University of California Press, 2016.

PART 5. SYMPATHY GROUPS INTO POLICY

The Hearts of Citizens

429 Mance, Henry. "Britain Has Had Enough of Experts." *Financial Times*, June 3rd 2016. https://www.ft.com/content/3be49734-29cb-11e6-83e4-abc22d5d108c
Easterly, William Russell. *The Tyranny of Experts: Economists, Dictators, and the Forgotten Rights of the Poor*. New York: Basic Books, 2015.

430 Tilly, Charles. "Inequality, Democratization, and De-Democratization." *Sociological Theory* 21, no. 1 (2016): 37-43.

431 OECD. "Trust in Government." (2017). http://www.oecd.org/gov/trust-in-government.htm

432 Linder, Wolf. *Swiss Democracy: Possible Solutions to Conflict in Multicultural Societies* [in English]. Basingstoke; New York: Palgrave Macmillan, 2010.

433 Sandel, Michael J. *What Money Can't Buy: The Moral Limits of Markets*. London: Penguin Books, 2013.
Nussbaum, Martha C. *Creating Capabilities: The Human Development Approach*. Cambridge, MA; London: The Belknap Press of Harvard University Press, 2013.

434 Evans, Jules. *Philosophy for Life and Other Dangerous Situations: Ancient Philosophy for Modern Problems*. London: Rider, 2013.

435 Habermas, Jürgen. *Moral Consciousness and Communicative Action*. Cambridge: Polity, 2007.

436 Johri, Mira. "*On the Universality of Habermas's Discourse Ethics*." National Library of Canada, 1999.

437 Anderson, Perry. *Spectrum: From left to right in the world of ideas*. London: Verso, 2007.

438 Habermas, Jürgen. *Between Facts and Norms: A Conversation About Questions of Political Theory*. Cambridge MA: MIT Press, 1997.

439 Johri, Mira. "*On the Universality of Habermas's Discourse Ethics*." National Library of Canada, 1999

440 Delacroix, Sylvie. "Drafting a Constitution for a Country of Words". *Middle East Law and Governance* 4, no. 2-3 (2012): 306-25.

441 Bodansky, Daniel. "Does Custom Have a Source?" In *AJIL Unbound,* American Society of International Law, 2014.

442 Burtenshaw, Ronan, and Audrey Robinson. "Interview with Prof. David Harvey." http://www.irishleftreview.org/2013/11/04/interview-prof-david-harvey/

443 Rousseau, Jean-Jacques. "Considerations on the Government of Poland and on Its Proposed Reformation", [Completed but Not Published] (April 1772). http://www.constitution.org/jjr/ poland.htm

444 Tria Kerkvliet, Benedict J. "Everyday Politics in Peasant Societies (and Ours)." *The Journal of Peasant Studies* 36, no. 1 (2009): 227-43.

445 Cannadine, David. *The Undivided Past: Humanity Beyond Our Differences*. New York: Vintage Books, 2014.

446 Naipaul, V. S. *India: A Million Mutinies Now*. London: Mandarin Paperbacks, 1993.

447 Cannadine, David. *The Undivided Past: Humanity Beyond Our Differences*. New York: Vintage Books, 2014.

448 Tully, James. Communication and Imperialism. In Kroker, Arthur, and Marilouise Kroker. *Critical digital studies: a reader*. Toronto: University of Toronto Press, 2013.

449 Castells, Manuel. *The Information Age: Economy, Society and Culture*. Oxford: Wiley-Blackwell, 2010.

450 Sassen, S. "Interactions of the Technical and the Social Digital Formations of the Powerful and the Powerless." *Information Communication And Society* 15, no. 4 (2012): 455-78.

451 Sassen, Saskia. 2017. "Embedded borderings: making new geographies of centrality." *Territory, Politics, Governance*. (4): 1-11.

452 ibid.

453 Gandhi, M. K., L. N. Tolstoj, and B. Srinivasa Murthy. *Mahatma Gandhi and Leo Tolstoy Letters*. Long Beach, CA: Long Beach Publications, 1987.

454 Arendt, Hannah. *On Violence*. 2014. Stellar Classics.

455 Foucault, Michel. *Discipline and Punish: The Birth of the Prison*. Harmondsworth: Penguin Books, 1991.

456 Foucault, Michel, and Robert Hurley. 1998. *The Will to Knowledge*. London: Penguin Books.

457 Simone, AbdouMaliq. "Urban Social Fields in Africa." *Social Text*. 16, no. 3 (1998): 71.

458 Lukes, Steven. *Power: A Radical View*. New York: Palgrave Macmillan, 2009.

459 Victora, Cesar G., Rajiv Bahl, Aluísio J. D. Barros, Giovanny V. A. França, Susan Horton, Julia Krasevec, Simon Murch, *et al*. "Breastfeeding in the 21st Century: Epidemiology, Mechanisms, and Lifelong Effect." *The Lancet* 387, no. 10017 (2016): 475-90.

460 Shaw, Bernard. *Major Barbara*. Charleston: CreateSpace, 2015.

461 Cooke, Bill, and Uma Kothari. *Participation: The New Tyranny?* New York, NY: Zed Books, 2007.

462 Hickey, Samuel, and Giles Mohan. *Participation: From Tyranny to Transformation: Exploring New Approaches to Participation in Development*. Development In Practice Oxford. 15, no. 5, (2005): 717. Kindle edition 2013.

463 Mishra, Pankaj. "Which India Matters?" *The New York Review of Books* 60, no. 18, November 21st 2013.

464 Dreze, Jean, and Amartya Sen. *An Uncertain Glory: India and Its Contradictions*. Princeton, New Jersey: Princeton University Press, 2015.

465 Freedman, Lynn, and Shanon McNab. "Maternal Newborn Health and the Urban Poor: A Global Scoping." 2017. https://www.wilsoncenter.org/sites/default/files/lynn_freedman_and_shannon_mcnab_mnh_and_the_urban_poor.pdf

466 Roy, A. "Why India Cannot Plan Its Cities: Informality, Insurgence and the Idiom of Urbanization." *Planning Theory* 8, no. 1 (2009): 76-87.

467 Bayat, Assef. *Life as Politics: How Ordinary People Change the Middle East*. Cairo: The American University in Cairo Press, 2013.

468 Sassen, Saskia. *Expulsions: Brutality and Complexity in the Global Economy*. Cambridge, MA: Belknap Harvard, 2018.

469 McKinney, M. "About That Quality Chasm. 10 Years after Institute of Medicine Report, Authors See Progress, But . . ." *Modern Healthcare* 41, no. 8 (2011): 38-9. http://www.modernhealthcare.com/article/20110221/MAGAZINE/110219950

470 Kohn, Linda T., Institute of Medicine, and Committee on Quality of Health Care in America. *To Err Is Human: Building a Safer Health System*. Washington, DC: National Academy Press, 2009.

471 Landrigan, Christopher P., Gareth J. Parry, Catherine B. Bones, Andrew D. Hackbarth, Donald A. Goldmann, and Paul J. Sharek. "Temporal Trends in Rates of Patient Harm Resulting from Medical Care." *New England Journal of Medicine* 363, no. 22 (2010): 2124-34.

472 Cooke, Graeme, Rick Muir, Geoff Mulgan, Marc Stears, and Institute for Public Policy Research. *The Relational State: How Recognising the Importance of Human Relationships Could Revolutionise the Role of the State*. London: IPPR, 2012.

473 Scott, James C. *Seeing Like a State. How Certain Schemes to Improve the Human Condition Have Failed.* New Haven, Yale University Press, 2008.

474 Statistics, Nepal. *Change in forest cover.* http://rainforests.mongabay.com/deforestation/archive/Nepal.htm

475 Shrestha, Bihari Krishna. "Follow the People." *Nepali Times* June 5th-11th 2015, p5.

476 Shaw, James, Sara Shaw, Joseph Wherton, Gemma Hughes, and Trisha Greenhalgh. "Studying Scale-up and Spread as Social Practice: Theoretical Introduction and Empirical Case Study." *Journal of Medical Internet Research* 19, no. 7 (2017): e244.

477 Ivers, Noah, Gro Jamtvedt, Signe Flottorp, Jane M. Young, Jan Odgaard-Jensen, Simon D. French, Mary Ann O'Brien, *et al.* "Audit and Feedback: Effects on Professional Practice and Healthcare Outcomes." *Cochrane Database of Systematic Reviews*, no. 6 (2012).

478 World Health Organization. *Basic Documents.* Geneva: World Health Organization, 2009.

479 McLean, Katherine. "There's Nothing Here: Deindustrialization as Risk Environment for Overdose." *International Journal of Drug Policy* 29 (2016): 19-26.

480 Zoorob, Michael J., and Jason L. Salemi. "Bowling Alone, Dying Together: The Role of Social Capital in Mitigating the Drug Overdose Epidemic in the United States." *Drug and Alcohol Dependence* 173 (2017): 1-9.

481 Buck, Tobias. Germany's club culture offers clue to political consensus. Up to 600,000 clubs and volunteer groups function as 'schools of democracy'. *Financial Times.* September 8th 2017.
https://www.ft.com/content/660651ee-931d-11e7-a9e6-
11d2f0ebb7f0?segmentid=acee4131-99c2-09d3-a635 873e61754ec6

482 Restakis, John. "John Restakis on the Emergence of Social Care Coops." In *P2P Foundation*, edited by Stacco Troncoso, 2017. ://blog.p2pfoundation.net/john-restakis-emergence-social-care-coops/2017/09/18

483 Banbury, Annie, Daniel Chamberlain, Susan Nancarrow, Jared Dart, Len Gray, and Lynne Parkinson. 2017. "Can videoconferencing affect older people's engagement and perception of their social support in long-term conditions management: a social network analysis from the Telehealth Literacy Project". *Health & Social Care in the Community.* 25 (3): 938-950.
Banbury A, S Nancarrow, J Dart, L Gray, L Parkinson. Telehealth Interventions Delivering Home-based Support Group Videoconferencing: Systematic Review. *J Med Internet Res* 2018;20(2):e25.

484 Leaver, Adam, and Karel Williams. "After the 30-Year Experiment: The Future of the Foundational Economy." *Juncture* 21, no. 3 (2014): 215-21.

485 Brett, Will, Adrian Bua, and Rachel Laurence. "Cities and Towns: The 2017 General Election and the Social Divisions of Place. Towns and Cities Are Divided. Here's What to Do About It." *New Economics Foundation*, 2017. *http://neweconomics. org/2017/10/cities-and-towns-2017-election/*

APPENDIX: SCIENTIFIC EVIDENCE

486 Lind, James, Andrew Millar, A. Murray, W. Sands, and J. Cochran. *A Treatise of the Scurvy: In Three Parts: Containing an Inquiry into the Nature, Causes, and Cure of That Disease: Together with a Critical and Chronological View of What Has Been Published on the Subject*. 1753.

487 Dunn, Peter M. "James Lind (1716-94) of Edinburgh and the Treatment of Scurvy." *Archives of Disease in Childhood* 76, no. 1 (1997): F64-F65.

488 Helmont, Jan Baptista van, and Francisco Mercurio Helmont. *Ortus Medicinae, Id Est, Initia Physicae Inaudita. [The dawn of medicine: That is, the beginning of a new Physic. A new advance in medicine, a victory over disease, to (promote) a long life]*. 1648. Bruxelles: Culture et Civilisation, 1966.

489 Hamilton, Alexander, and Georgii Baird. *Dissertatio Medica Inauguralis De Synocho Castrensi* [in Latin] *[Inaugural medical dissertation on camp fever]*. Edinburgh: J Ballantyne, 1816.

490 Osler, William. "The Principles and Practice of Medicine: Designed for the Use of Practitioners and Students of Medicine." New York: D. Appleton and Company, 1901.

491 Silverman W. In Royal College of Obstetricians and Gynaecologists, (eds) Iain Chalmers, and Gillian McIlwaine. "Perinatal Audit and Surveillance: Proceedings of the Eighth Study Group of the Royal College of Obstetricians and Gynaecologists, 14-16 April 1980." (1981).

492 Löhner, G. "Löhner G, on Behalf of a Society of Truth-Loving Men (1835). Die Homoöopathischen Kochsalzversuche Zu Nürnberg [the Homeopathic Salt Trials in Nurnberg]. Nürnberg in März." In *The James Lind Library. Illustrating the development of fair tests of treatments in health care*. 1835.

493 Stolberg, M. "Inventing the Randomized Double-Blind Trial: The Nuremberg Salt Test of 1835." *Journal of the Royal Society of Medicine*. 99, no. 12 (2006): 642-43.

494 Sebeok, Thomas A. *The Play of Musement*. Bloomington: Indiana University Press, 1981.

495 Hacking, Ian. *The Taming of Chance*. Cambridge: Cambridge University Press, 2010.
    Sigler, Stephen M. "Mathematical Statistics in the Early States." (1978). *Annals of Statistics*, v. 6, March, pp. 239-265, see p. 248.

496 Henderson, Lawrence J. Henderson quoted in Prioreschi P. A. *History of Medicine — Volume I: Primitive and Ancient Medicine*; p. xviii. 11. Omaha, Nebraska: Horatius Press, 1995.

497 Levitt, Steven D., and John A. List. "Field Experiments in Economics the Past, the Present, and the Future." (2008).
    Ziliak, Stephen T. "Field Experiments in Economics: Comment on an Article by Levitt and List." (2011). http://sites.roosevelt.edu/sziliak

498 Student, W. S. Gosset, E. S. Pearson, and J. Wishart. *'Student's' Collected Papers* [in English]. London: University College, 1947. Appendix to Mercer and Hall's paper on "The experimental error of field trials." *Journal of Agricultural Science* 4, 128-131.

499 Osrin, David, Anjana Vaidya, Yagya Shrestha, Ram Bahadur Baniya, Dharma S Manandhar, Ramesh K Adhikari, Suzanne Filteau, Andrew Tomkins, and Anthony M de L Costello. 2005. "Effects of antenatal multiple micronutrient supplementation on birthweight and gestational duration in Nepal: double-blind, randomised controlled trial". *The Lancet*. 365 (9463): 955-962.

500 Hill, Austin Bradford. 2005. "The environment and disease: association or causation?" *Bulletin of the World Health Organization*. 83 (10): 796-798.

501 Mann, C. 1990. "Meta-analysis in the breech." *Science*. 249 (4968): 476-480.

502 Lo, Bernard, and Marilyn Jane Field. *Conflict of Interest in Medical Research, Education, and Practice*. Washington, DC: National Academies Press, 2009.

503 Piller, Charles. "Do drug firm ties affect researchers reporting of study results?" *STAT*. December 18th 2015. http://www.statnews.com/2015/12/18/researchers-drug-firm-ties/

504 Centers for Medicare and Medicaid Services. https://www.cms.gov/

Index

Page numbers in *italics* indicate an illustration